Praise for Wesley J. Smith's

Forced Exit

"This important book puts forth an argument that is less and less acceptable in America . . . against the quick fix. In this compassionate, courageous work, Wesley Smith proposes turning toward our dying, making the hard choice of staying in connection to the end."

BOSTON GLOBE

—

"Smith's evidence . . . is outstanding. After *Forced Exit*, dismissing the slippery slope argument will be impossible."

DETROIT NEWS

—

"*Forced Exit* argues against legally assisted suicide in so many compelling ways. It should drive the terms of the debate on this highly charged controversy."

RALPH NADER

—

"A lucid, comprehensive, and absorbing account of the dangerous movement that will eventually affect us all if assisted suicide is legalized, for it will inexorably lead to lawful euthanasia."

NAT HENTOFF

"A wakeup call . . . [Smith] succeeds in warning that . . . America has given little thought to what must be done to make sure that assisted suicide remains an option of last, not first, resort."

—

"Powerful arguments from a passionate, articulate, sometimes strident spokesman."

—

"*Forced Exit* shows why the public should reject Kevorkianism in all its forms. Laying out his case with clarity and restraint, Smith blends reasoned argument with blood-curdling anecdotes, proving beyond a reasonable doubt that legalizing assisted suicide would be a sure step toward bureaucratized euthanasia."

—

"Society will rue the day it permits doctors to be killers as well as healers. Wesley J. Smith offers a compelling argument against legalizing assisted suicide and clearly explains the devastating effects it would have on an unwary public. Smith has done us all a great service with this important primer."

FORCED EXIT

FORCED EXIT

The Slippery Slope from
Assisted Suicide to Legalized Murder

WESLEY J. SMITH

SPENCE PUBLISHING COMPANY • DALLAS
2003

Published in the United States by
Spence Publishing Company
111 Cole Street
Dallas, Texas 75207

Library of Congress Control Number: 2003105590

ISBN 1-890626-48-1

Printed in the United States of America

To my father, Wesley L. Smith,

who faced his own death with such courage,

and to my mother, Leona Smith,

who loved him, and loves me, so well.

Contents

Introduction to the
Revised Edition

I N THE SIX YEARS since this book was first published, much has happened in the international cultural struggle over euthanasia. In the original edition, I worried deeply about cases in the Ninth and Second United States Circuit Courts of Appeals that had declared a constitutional right to assisted suicide. Happily, the Supreme Court of the United States disagreed. Its 1997 unanimous ruling that assisted suicide is not a constitutional right prevented the euthanasia death agenda from being imposed upon the nation through judicial fiat. The supreme courts of two states separated by thousands of miles—Florida and Alaska—have ruled in subsequent decisions (1997 and 2001, respectively) that nothing in their state constitutions requires the legalization of assisted suicide.

In Europe, litigation to permit assisted suicide also failed. In 2001, Diane Pretty, a woman from Britain, sued in an English court for a ruling preventing her husband from being prosecuted for assisting her suicide. Pretty, who was terminally ill with ALS (Lou Gehrig's disease)—called motor neurone disease in England—achieved much public sympathy and became the talk of Great Britain. When she lost in the trial court, she took her case to the House of Lords. After the British high court also turned her down, she appealed to the European Union Court on Human Rights, claiming among other allegations, that the British law against assisted suicide violated her EU right to be treated with dignity. The EU court, however, rightly noted that the law was not the cause of Pretty's difficulties, her disease was. The case was the equivalent in Europe of the United States Supreme Court's ruling against a constitutional right to assisted suicide. (Diane Pretty died naturally of her disease in May 2002.)

The one exception to this record of judicial restraint occurred in Colombia, where the courts imposed euthanasia on Colombians. That ruling is not yet in effect, awaiting the promulgation of death regulations to govern how and when doctors will be allowed to kill patients.

With courts internationally refusing to impose assisted suicide upon free people—and it is debatable whether Colombians are free—the issue is now, quite literally, up to us. If the door is going to be opened wide to the death culture, in a free country *we* will be the ones doing it. And if we do invite the wolf inside, we will only have ourselves to blame when we suffer the consequences of our own foolishness.

When this book first came out, many worried that the euthanasia movement's success in passing Oregon's Measure 16 would be repeated throughout the nation, indeed, that the death culture would sweep the country. Although the threat still remains, it hasn't happened yet— though not for lack of effort by euthanasia advocates.

There have been two state assisted-suicide-legalization initiatives on state ballots since the original publication of *Forced Exit* in 1997. In 1998, voters in Michigan, who had the most intimate knowledge of the death agenda, thanks to Jack Kevorkian, rejected legalization by a whopping 71 to 29 percent. In 2000, Maine also refused to approve assisted suicide, albeit by a narrow 51 to 49 percent margin. As I write these words in March 2003, there appears to be no state whose voters will, in the immediate future, be asked via initiative to legalize assisted suicide.

Stymied by voters, assisted suicide advocates have introduced legalization legislation in several state legislatures each year. So far, these efforts have been for naught. But in May 2002, out of the blue, Hawaii came within a whisker of legalizing assisted suicide—nearly passing legislation patterned on Oregon's law. Strongly pushed by assisted suicide enthusiast Governor Benjamin Cayetano, the legislation passed the Hawaii House of Representatives 30 to 20 and then passed a preliminary state senate vote 13 to 12. Thankfully, after much pressure was brought to bear on state senators by Hawaiian voters in a very short time, two days later the senate ultimately refused to legalize assisted suicide by a too narrow 14 to 11 vote.

Still, proponents of assisted suicide had much to cheer. For the first time in history one house of a state legislature had voted to legalize medicalized killing. With Hawaii proving itself to be a "weak link" in defense of the equality-of-human-life ethic, we can expect that beautiful state to become the front line of the international euthanasia debate for many years to come.

When *Forced Exit* was first published, Jack Kevorkian seemed unstoppable. Juries had refused repeatedly to convict him of assisted suicide, and he seemed able to prey upon disabled and dying people at will. Then, Kevorkian videotaped himself lethally injecting ALS patient Thomas Youk. Kevorkian promptly took the tape to euthanasia proponent Mike Wallace for airing on *60 Minutes*. Finally Kevorkian had gone too far. The public ruckus that resulted from a televised murder literally forced the Oakland County, Michigan, prosecutor—who had won his elective office on a plank of leaving Kevorkian alone—to prosecute him. A jury convicted Kevorkian of second-degree murder, the judge told Kevorkian to "consider yourself stopped," and he is now in prison, a virtually forgotten man.

Meanwhile, the sparsely populated Northern Territory of Australia legalized euthanasia, albeit briefly. This did not sit well with the Australian Parliament, which acted quickly to overturn the territorial law. Tragically, before parliament could act, four people had been poisoned to death using a computer program designed by the "Australian Kevorkian," Philip Nitschke.

Still, despite their many defeats, proponents of euthanasia and assisted suicide have achieved more than perhaps even they would have imagined was possible only ten years ago. Oregon's assisted suicide law has gone into effect and more than 129 people (that we know of) have had their lives extinguished by poison that was legally prescribed by doctors. Former attorney general Janet Reno granted Oregon doctors a waiver to the usual requirement of the Controlled Substances Act that federally controlled drugs not be used to kill. When Attorney General John Ashcroft sought to undo Reno's waiver, he was enjoined from doing so by an Oregon-based federal judge determined to protect that state's assisted suicide law. Advocates for euthanasia applauded the decision enthusiastically as a matter of upholding "states' rights." Yet, a great irony went unnoted in media reports about the court's ruling: some of these very same euthanasia advocates who now waxed so enthusiastically about states' rights had, only a few years previously, sought to destroy the states' very ability to legislate against assisted suicide by pushing or supporting the case to create a constitutional right to assisted suicide. But then consistency is not the point of the euthanasia movement; legalizing mercy killing is. (As these words are written, the case is being appealed by the United States Government.)

Despite the ongoing horrors associated with euthanasia in the Netherlands, which have only accelerated in the years since this book's first printing, that country has now formally legalized the practice, in the process doing away with the one remaining impediment to euthanasia: the technical illegality of mercy killing. Demonstrating that emotionalism rather than fact too often matters more, the well-documented horrors in the Netherlands did nothing to dissuade lawmakers in Belgium from legalizing Dutch-style euthanasia in May 2002. There are also strong and ongoing attempts to legalize euthanasia in France, South

Africa, Australia, and Switzerland (where informal assisted suicide is already tolerated).

Meanwhile, the problem of futile-care theory has grown more dangerous than when described in the first edition of this book. Futile-care theory holds that when a doctor believes that the quality of a patient's life is not worth living (or spending the resources upon), the doctor can unilaterally refuse *wanted* medical treatment. When I first warned about the subject in *Forced Exit*, futile-care impositions tended to be ad hoc and hence easier to thwart in court—as the parents of Baby Ryan did in Spokane. Today, there is a systematic, nationwide attempt by many in the bioethics movement to impose futile care upon the populace through formal hospital protocols that give anonymous ethics committees the power to turn thumbs up or thumbs down to wanted medical treatment deemed "inappropriate." Indeed, as the expanded discussion of the topic of futile care in this edition of *Forced Exit* will demonstrate, these protocols are designed explicitly—at least in part—to stack the legal deck *against* the patient and family seeking treatment that the doctor or hospital wishes to refuse. Will these protocols work, opening the door to explicit health-care rationing? Only time will tell, but there can be little doubt that futile-care theory presents an acute and rising threat to the equality-of-human-life ethic.

The attempt by the bioethics movement to permit the dehydration of conscious, cognitively disabled people requiring feeding tubes to stay alive, such as people discussed in the first edition of this book like Robert Wendland, Michael Martin, and Ronald Comeau, has not yet succeeded. Indeed, so long as family members disagree, the courts still protect conscious patients by requiring a high level of proof before allowing feeding tubes to be removed. That is the good news. The bad news is that those deemed permanently unconscious have fewer protections despite that diagnosis often being wrong. Indeed, in the Robert Wendland case, the California Supreme Court seemed to state that unconscious people do not have the same constitutional rights as the conscious. If my reading of that decision is correct, it marks a terrible precedent, creating a dual system of rights that could strip the weakest and most vulnerable among us of their legal personhood.

The euthanasia struggle is one that is eminently winnable. But if victory is to be won, it won't be easy or quick. Indeed, the struggle to maintain morality in medicine and protect the inherent equality of sick and disabled people is the challenge of our times. It is my hope that this revised edition of *Forced Exit* will help its readers pierce through the emotionalism, fear mongering, and euphemisms that are the standard fare of the euthanasia movement toward a greater understanding of the issue and the importance of the stakes involved. Since the more people learn about euthanasia the less they tend like it, such education is vital if we are to maintain a moral health-care delivery system.

Finally, it is important to reemphasize that we must do much more than merely say no to killing. Our ill, elderly, disabled, and despairing brothers and sisters deserve to have their suffering taken seriously and addressed. We must commit ourselves to the task of resolving the problems that may give rise to a desire to commit suicide: the under-treatment of pain and depression, isolation and marginalization, worries about being a burden on loved ones and society. These are tasks that require our time, attention, and above all, love. If we truly want to be compassionate—which, after all, means to suffer with—we will reject euthanasia and assisted suicide and do our part as individuals and as a society to ensure that each of us, regardless of our age, state of health, or physical or mental abilities, has access to life with dignity. If we succeed in doing that, the battle will be won and the euthanasia movement will simply fade away.

Introduction

THE SEEDS FOR THIS BOOK, and my efforts as an anti-euthanasia activist, were sown on November 1, 1992. On that day, a Sunday, my friend Frances went to a hotel, checked in, got into bed, took some sleeping pills, pulled a plastic bag over her head, and died.

Frances's suicide was not an act born of impulse or momentary despair. She had been planning it for years. Indeed, almost from the moment I met her in Los Angeles in 1988, she had spoken enthusiastically about how empowering and ennobling it would be for her to take her own life. In her mind's eye, she saw herself beginning to experience the debilitations of age. Rather than endure a slow decline and become a "burden" to her friends, Frances would say, "I'm going to hold a going away party," where she hoped her many friends would surround her as she lay on a couch, tell her how much she meant to them, hold her hands and stroke her brow as she swallowed the drugs from her "hoard of pills," and where she would slowly and quietly transform from living friend to deeply treasured memory.

Most of us who were among Frances's closest friends were appalled by her suicide fixation, and each in our own way tried to convince her not to do it. We told her repeatedly that we valued her presence among us. We tried to assure her that growing old did not make one less valuable as a human being and that illness or disability did not make one a burden. We urged her to seek counseling, hoping that if she put as much effort into living as she seemed to be putting into plans for dying, she could find renewed meaning and joy from a life that clearly did not satisfy her. We worried about her continually and wondered where on earth she had picked up all the euphemisms for self-destruction that sprinkled her vocabulary, such as "deliverance" and "final passage"?

It is important to note that in the first two years of our friendship, as Frances fantasized about her future death, she was not ill. She was, however, very unhappy. She had divorced years before, and her husband had remarried a younger woman, a fact of Frances's life that deeply humiliated and embittered her. The divorce had also hit her hard in the pocketbook, removing her from a thoroughly enjoyed life of upper-middle-class ease and gentility and forcing her to count pennies from her rent-controlled one-bedroom apartment. Meanwhile, the fact that her successor and her ex (who was ill with Alzheimer's) continued to live well was a constant wound that ate at Frances with every meager alimony check she cashed, money she genuinely needed and at the same time deeply resented.

Frances had other emotional burdens. She said that one of her two sons was cognitively and emotionally disabled from injuries sustained in an auto accident. The accident had come just as the young man was making a big breakthrough in the screenwriting trade and had cut him off from a dream come true. Frances never stopped worrying about him, and she despaired about his future once she was gone. Even more painful, Frances was so estranged from her other son that it would be an exaggeration to call their interaction a relationship.

Frances's talk about her future suicide would wax during her more unhappy times and wane during the times she felt productive and useful—surely no coincidence. She was very active in local community clubs and was always thinking about how she could help her friends with business ideas, introducing them to others in her stable of associates and acquaintances who, she felt, could provide sage advice, opportunity, or help with ideas. Her female friends told me that hers was a great shoulder to cry on, especially for pals who had relationship difficulties. She definitely helped me, and she knew it. She took great pride in being the inspiration for my book *The Senior Citizen's Handbook: A Nuts and Bolts Guide to More Comfortable Living.*

Unfortunately, Frances's happy times were generally short-lived, and thoughts about suicide would again tug at her as relentlessly as gravity. It was like some perverse dance. She would plan the thing, we would change her mind, and then, for no apparent reason, she would announce she was planning it again.

At one point we all became convinced that Frances wasn't just talking anymore, that she was about to do it. Interventions were held. We pleaded, cajoled, doing everything we could think of to help her keep a firm grip on life—all to no avail. It would take a miracle, it seemed, to dissuade her.

Then, a miracle of sorts did happen. But it was nothing supernatural: her alimony was cut off. Suddenly, Frances had a cause. The suicide was forgotten as Frances headed for court on a full head of steam, acting as her own attorney to force resumption of her payments, and she succeeded. Clearly, here was a woman who, despite all her romanticized talk of her warm and fuzzy "deliverance," desperately needed a reason to live. But her triumph did not satisfy her for long. As the glow of her court victory wore off, Frances again spoke of suicide. At about this time she was diagnosed with lymphatic leukemia, which was treatable but certainly upsetting. She developed a neuropathy (a degeneration of the nervous system), from which she experienced a distressing burning sensation on her skin. (Frances would complain bitterly that her HMO doctors did not take her pain seriously, but she also refused to take the pain medication prescribed for her.) Though she had no visible limp, she was also a candidate for a hip replacement. And underneath it all was the abiding sadness about her many disappointments.

By this time, I had moved to San Francisco, so I had less personal contact with Frances than in previous years, although we kept up a lively interaction over the phone. Then, one day, one of her friends called, very upset, telling me, "Frances is planning to die next week, on her birthday." I called Frances immediately. I implored her at least to see a psychiatrist before doing it. She refused, saying, "He might give me a pill that would make me not want to kill myself."

I was later told that she invited her friends in Los Angeles to her long-planned going-away party. All of her friends refused to attend. They loved her. They did not want her to kill herself. They would not support this chosen action. Frances then told everyone the suicide was off. She even called my mother, who had also become her friend, and said that a "divine intervention" had saved her life. We all breathed a sigh of relief.

Frances was lying. Secretly, she paid a distant cousin five thousand dollars to go with her to a hotel, where her only luggage was a stash of pills and a plastic bag. Two days afterward, I and her other friends received her photocopied suicide note (the return address was simply "Frances"); in it she spoke of herself as being "in control" and stated that the "act is not one of 'suicide'—I consider that [it] is my final passage."

Frances's death was not noble and uplifting, as she had fantasized. We miss Frances and mourn her loss, but she has not left behind the sweet garden of memory she fervently believed her death would create. None of us appreciated the morbid experience of receiving photocopies of her suicide letter in the mail after she was gone, and most of us felt angry, betrayed, and empty in the wake of her self-destruction.

With her death, Frances took her place among suicide statistics. More than thirty thousand people die by their own hand each year in the United States, more than are murdered and only about ten thou-

sand fewer than are killed in auto accidents. Suicide is the second leading cause of death among college students and the third leading cause
of death among young people ages 15 to 24. The suicide rate for children ages 10 to 14 has more than doubled in the last ten years. The elderly, like Frances, are particularly susceptible to self-destruction: rates
among that group rose 9 percent between 1980 and 1992.

Usually after a suicide, those who were close to the deceased person wonder why, grieve, and finally go on with their lives. But I had a
queasy feeling that there was more to Frances's death than appeared on
the surface. It was as if she had somehow been *encouraged* to pursue
death. Yet, I knew her friends had all tried to persuade her to embrace
life. I tried to set this feeling aside, but it would not go away. My unease was abstract; yet it was very real. I reminded myself of a character
in a Stephen King novel who can sense, yet cannot see, the darkness
that lurks behind a façade of normalcy.

I decided to investigate. Frances was one of the most organized
women I have ever met. She kept a file on everything. I called the ex-
ecutrix of her will and asked her to look through Frances's papers to see
whether she had kept a suicide file and, if so, to send it to me.

A week later, the file arrived. It wasn't very thick. There were some
news clippings that put a positive spin on suicide and a smattering of
poetry. But most of the material was from an organization I had paid
scant attention to before: the Hemlock Society. Specifically, Frances had
collected several issues of the organization's newsletter, the *Hemlock
Quarterly*. That these writings had a major influence on Frances there
can be little doubt. She had highlighted much of the text with a yellow
marking pen. Several issues were dog-eared from frequent reading.

As I read the material, my jaw literally dropped. I could not believe
my eyes. The documents seemed scurrilous to me—nothing less than
pro-suicide propaganda extolling self-destruction as a morally correct
and an empowering experience. Most of the newsletters had stories in
them—allegedly letters from satisfied readers—of warm and successful

suicides, or advocacy pieces by euthanasia proponents. The articles had an almost religious tone to them that made me feel as if I were reading tracts from some bizarre death cult.

The January 1988 issue of the *Hemlock Quarterly* caught my eye because it was especially worn from frequent reading.[1] One of the stories inside, entitled "A Peaceful Passing," signed by "A New Member in California" (supposedly a grief counselor), told in glowing terms of the suicide of Sam, allegedly a terminal cancer patient. Frances had underscored these words from the story: "Believe it or not, we laughed and giggled and [Sam] seemed to relish the experience. I think for Sam it was finally taking control again after ten years of being at the mercy of a disease and medical protocols demanded by that disease."

Suicide promoted as uplifting, enjoyable fun sickened me.

This wasn't the only disturbing passage. Sam's suicide was described as peaceful and calm, and the reader was assured that "all went smoothly" through the suicide, funeral, and burial. The writer even extolled the act of assisting the death as "very profound in my life," one that "has changed me and grown me."[2] In other words, the author depicted suicide as empowering and beneficial, not only for the deceased, but for the "helper."

Another story, called "Planning Made Death Peaceful," written by a "loving family member," described the author's "instant" agreement to assist the "self-deliverance" of a relative with an "uncurable [sic], debilitating and hideous illness." (We should remember, by the way, that "incurable" isn't a synonym for "terminal." Arthritis is incurable.) The story described how the author collected the drugs to be used over time, just as Frances had done, and how the relative died "in complete peace within 15 or 20 minutes at most." The last paragraph had caught Frances's attention, as evidenced by the yellow highlighting: "It was indeed a good deliverance; much of it was due to foresight and planning. We had the necessary medications and the necessary knowledge. But I will always believe that most of it was due to the steadfast will and soul of my family member, who made a decision for self-deliverance and fully accepted it."[3] In other words, this "good deliverance" occurred because the ill person had the moral fortitude to go through with it, seeming to imply that those who don't have such courage are somehow not "steadfast" or lack "soul."

Other articles in the issue explained how to commit suicide. One provided a listing of the drugs that were good for suicide, describing the relative toxicity and the amount of each drug required to constitute a lethal dose ("Drug Dosage Table").[4] Frances had underscored the names of the drugs with the highest toxicity levels.

In "Self-Deliverance with Certainty," the reader was instructed on the proper use of a plastic bag, described as a death method that is "less than perfect but . . . not very much less than perfect."[5] Chills ran up my spine. It was as if I were reading an exact description of Frances's death, so closely had she followed these instructions.

There was a disclaimer of sorts in the article on drug dosages that read, "Only for information of members of the National Hemlock Society for possible self-deliverance from a future terminal illness and used in conjunction with material found in the book, *Let Me Die Before I Wake*."[6] That was just not credible to me. The entire message of the newsletter was so positive and supportive of suicide as an answer to life's difficulties that this caveat seemed to be less than veneer, in the end meaning absolutely nothing. Frances, who was *not* terminally ill, had not underscored the warning passage.

The more I thought about the Hemlock Society propaganda and its direct connection with Frances's death, the angrier I grew. Who were these people to push a pro-suicide message on the depressed and vulnerable, people looking desperately for some way to be in control of their unhappy lives? They didn't even know Frances. Yet they had given her the moral support to kill herself and had taught her how to do it. Although Frances was without question responsible for her own self-destruction, I felt that the Hemlock Society had fostered in her romanticism about suicide that helped her move to consummation. As I saw it, morally they had much to answer for.

I am not alone in believing that the euthanasia movement, in which the Hemlock Society plays an active part, has influenced the rise in our country of suicide rates, at least among the elderly. For example, Barbara Haight, who directs a program at the University of South Carolina College of Nursing to prevent suicide among the elderly, believes that the rise in euthanasia advocacy over the last ten years, the publicity surrounding Jack Kevorkian, and other related events have "made suicide more acceptable to people who once would not have considered it because of religious and family concerns. They see it as a solution to their problems."[7] Frances is a case in point.

One of the benefits of being a writer is that the word processor provides a productive outlet for painful feelings. In my anger, I wrote an article for the "My Turn" section of *Newsweek* called "The Whispers of Strangers," which was meant as a wake-up call about the dangers of the euthanasia movement and the message it sends to weak and vulnerable people.[8] My article touched people emotionally, but not in the way I had expected. I received about 150 letters. A few were supportive, thanking me for warning about the euthanasia movement and commiserating about the pain that suicide causes survivors. But the vast majority of my correspondents were outraged that I had criticized euthanasia. They did not believe it can destroy moral concepts, that "the preservation of human life is our highest moral ideal," that "a principal purpose of government" is to protect human life, that "those who fight to stay alive in the face of terminal illness," such as actor Michael Landon, are "powerful uplifters of the human experience."[9]

These sentiments enraged my detractors. I was lectured that the idea of human life as "sacred . . . is no longer tenable."[10] I was accused of wanting "the pleasure of seeing her [Frances] as an incontinent living corpse ravaged by pain and drugs."[11] My thoughts about protecting life were seen as proof that "Wesley Smith lacks genuine compassion."[12] Another writer accused me of "self-righteous arrogance" because I disapproved of Frances's act to "advance slightly the date on which . . . she must inevitably shuffle off this mortal coil."[13] An especially harsh critic compared me to "Torquiemada [sic] of the Spanish Inquisition who devised fiendish tortures because our highest moral ideal was to get infidels to adapt [sic] Christianity."[14] And more than one correspondent echoed the hope expressed by 'M.B.' that "you live a long and suffering life."[15] Many correspondents expressed views that can only be described as pro-suicide. "This is the 90s, and suicide IS an alternative to life," one letter writer advised me.[16] "I congratulate Frances," another reader wrote," on her decision to end her life when and how she wanted."[17] R.K. thought that "we as a society will come to see the day we view suicide (and euthanasia) as acceptable and even good."[18] L.M.S. was moved to proclaim that "suicide, as the act is called—for a person without responsibilities, or with a chronic disease—*is* a noble act."[19]

I was genuinely surprised. Were my correspondents outside the cultural mainstream, I wondered, or was I? If I was, when had the values that not so long ago were deemed self-evident truths by most of society change so dramatically? And where was I when this changed occurred?

The next paragraph in my article also attracted attention and criticism. I wrote: "Of greater concern to me is the moral trickle-down effect that could result should society ever come to agree with Frances. Life is action and reaction, the proverbial pebble thrown into the pond. We don't get to Brave New World in one giant leap. Rather, the descent to depravity is reached by small steps. First, suicide is promoted as a virtue. Vulnerable people like Frances become early casualties. Then follows mercy killing of the terminally ill. From there, it is a hop, skip, and a jump to killing people who don't have a good 'quality' of life, perhaps with the prospect of organ harvesting thrown in as a plum to society."[20]

Every reader who commented on this passage, both supporters and detractors of my point of view, was convinced I was overreacting. Each believed that such a progression was unthinkable in the United States, that as a humane people we would never allow ourselves to engage in such inhumane conduct. I was advised earnestly to have a bit more faith in people.

Would that my correspondents had been correct. Unfortunately, I wasn't paranoid or alarmist; I was prescient. As this book will detail, my fears about "moral trickle-down" (more commonly known as the "slippery slope," to which I will refer frequently)—and more—are justified either by events already happening or by proposals put forward seriously by mainstream opinion setters, by the medical intelligentsia, and by public-policy makers. For example:

- In the United States, several courts have ruled that laws prohibiting assisted suicide are unconstitutional. One state, Oregon, has passed a law (Measure 16) that would specifically permit doctors to prescribe lethal drugs to patients diagnosed as having six months or less to live.

- Advocacy in favor of assisted suicide "only" for the terminally ill is already passé among euthanasia advocates. Legalizing hastened death is now promoted for the "hopelessly ill" or "desperately ill," as well as the dying. The "hopelessly ill" are disabled people, those with chronic illnesses, the frail elderly. Some "rational suicide" proponents advocate including those with severe mental or emotional problems who have no physical illness.

- Ann Landers endorsed the establishment of death clinics where the elderly could go to be put to death rather than receive long-term care, calling the notion "a sane, sensible, civilized alternative to existing in a nursing home, draining family resources, and hoping the end will come soon. To bad it's against the law."[21]

- Some people are already being killed on the basis of quality-of-life considerations, specifically the cognitively disabled, both unconscious and conscious, by having their feeding tubes removed in order to cause their deaths. Tube feeding has in fact been classified as a medical procedure, to permit the process of withholding it in such cases.

- The American Medical Council on Ethics and Judicial Affairs for a short period of time advocated that vital organs be harvested from anencephalic babies (babies born with parts of the brains missing) while they are still alive. The council was forced by AMA opposition to retract this opinion, pending further study. But it is highly likely that the issue will return in the near future. If ever implemented, this would mark the first time in the United States since the end of slavery that the bodies of living human beings could be legally exploited as a natural resource without their explicit consent.

And these items represent just the tip of the iceberg.

As the great Supreme Court justice Benjamin Cardozo once wrote about an earlier drive to legalize euthanasia, "Just as a life may not be shortened, so its value must be held as equal to that of any other, the mightiest and the lowliest."[22] Cardozo's point was that legalized euthanasia, which would permit the killing of certain categories of people by doctors (and perhaps others), is fundamentally incompatible with the traditional Western ethic, which I call the *equality-of-human-life ethic*.

The equality-of-human-life ethic requires that each of us be considered of equal inherent moral worth, and it makes the preservation and protection of human life society's first priority. Accepting euthanasia would replace the equality-of-human-life ethic with a utilitarian and nihilistic "death culture" that views the intentional ending of certain human lives as an appropriate and necessary answer to life's most difficult challenges. As I hope to demonstrate, the dire consequences that would flow from such a radical shift in morality are profound and disturbing.

Frances always used to say that her forte was helping people find their proper place in life. Ironically, her suicide has done that for me. Since her death—largely because of the way she died—I have immersed myself in the euthanasia issue, reading volumes of material pro and con, writing and speaking out about the issue in the print and electronic media and in public speeches, as often as I can. I have worked in close association with the International Task Force on Euthanasia and Assisted Suicide, an organization dedicated to raising awareness of the dangers inherent in legitimizing and legalizing euthanasia and assisted suicide. I have become acquainted with an international network of concerned people who share my views and who help me in my work as I help them. In short, I have become an activist. It is not an overstatement to say that I consider this the most profound endeavor in which I have ever engaged.

During these last few years, as I have immersed myself in euthanasia and related health-care issues, I have pondered, explored, and learned. It has not been easy. Euthanasia is an emotional and controversial subject, one that has confronted me with my fears about my own mortality, about growing old or becoming disabled. It has torn at my heart as I have been moved to tears in compassion for the ill, the dying, the discouraged, those in unrelieved pain, and the abandoned among us.

I have not come to my conclusions easily or glibly. I worry about whether my views are correct, my concern justified, my insights valid. But the more I think it through—the more I observe the trends, the more I learn, the more I ponder, the more I understand context—the more convinced I become that euthanasia is unwise, unethical, and just plain wrong, a social experiment that if implemented will lead to cultural and ethical catastrophe.

In this book I share what I have learned and trace how I have come to my conclusions. Or, as one of my friends described this project, I hope the book will help readers "connect the dots" about what the euthanasia path will do to our culture, our health-care system, our morality, and the way we view and treat ill and vulnerable people.

Finally, it is not enough to be a naysayer. The euthanasia issue did not arise in a vacuum. In my view, it has been driven by the despair caused by too many people watching helplessly as their loved ones writhe in pain because they receive inadequate medical care. It has been fueled by the very reasonable fear of being victimized by our money-driven, dehumanizing, and increasing impersonal health-care system. It is also a symptom of malaise, caused by the unraveling of community ties and the breakdown of families. But the death culture is not the answer to these abiding problems. Rather, it is a surrender to them.

There is another way. Humane and effective alternatives to euthanasia exist, alternatives that receive far too little attention. I will close this book by exploring some of these options in the firm belief that we can effectively meet the challenges of death, dying, and human suffering without losing our humanity.

We know the way. The only question is, can we find the will?

A NOTE ON TERMINOLOGY

Many different terms are used by different sources for the acts of killing that I will discuss: *Active voluntary euthanasia, non-voluntary euthanasia, involuntary euthanasia, passive euthanasia, good death, death with dignity, planned death, assisted death, aid in dying,* etc. These terms and phrases, which may have great meaning in the ivory tower of academia or among assisted-suicide ideologues, are of little use in a book designed for a general audience; in this context, they would only be confusing (as sometimes they are meant to be).

I will generally use the terms *kill, euthanasia,* or *assisted suicide.* I use the word *kill* because it is accurate and descriptive of what euthanasia and assisted suicide are about: "to deprive of . . . or put an end to life." Some may object to this word because it elicits a strong emotional reaction—and well it should. But killing is precisely what we are discussing. The subject is too serious, in my view, to accept the fuzzy words and euphemisms preferred by euthanasia advocates as the spoonful of sugar that helps the hemlock go down.

By *euthanasia* I mean the killing of one person by another (usually, but not always, a doctor) because the person killed has a serious disease or injury, is disabled, is emotionally or mentally disturbed, is anguished, or is elderly. *Euthanasia* means, literally, "good death." While it was not coined originally to describe mercy killing, by now it is so much a part of the language that no usable alternative exists. *Assisted suicide*, for my purposes, means self-killing for the same reasons that euthanasia is undertaken. It differs from suicide in that it is not a solitary action but rather a joint effort. Another person actively participates, assists in, and/or facilitates the termination of life. Thus, if a doctor injects a patient with a sedative followed by curare (a lethal poison)—the usual practice in the Netherlands—that is euthanasia. A doctor knowingly prescribing drugs for use in a suicide or someone mixing a lethal dose of drugs in liquid form for another knowingly to drink are examples of assisted suicide. In my view, the distinction between euthanasia and assisted suicide is about as substantial as the differences between the actions of the left and right leg while walking: one naturally follows the other.

ACKNOWLEDGMENTS

The creation of this book would literally have been impossible without the active assistance of so many people who freely shared their feelings, knowledge, attitudes, and opinions with me, including: Peter Admiraal, MD; Dr. William S. Andereck; Dan Avila; Robin Bernhoft, MD; James

Bopp; William Burke, MD; Ira R. Byock, MD; Dana Cody; Diane Coleman; Matthew E. Conolly, MD; Yeates Cornwell, MD; Paul Corrao, MD; E. J. Dionne; Richard Doerflinger; Ljubisa J. Dragovic, MD; Beth Roney Drennan; Vincent Fortanasce, MD; Michael J. Franzblau, MD; Cheryl Eckstein, MD; Carol Gill; K.F. Gunning, MD; Jacqulyn Hall; Herbert Hendin, MD; Nat Hentoff; Professor Dianne Irving; Larry Johnson; Melanie Zdan and Cara Elrod; Professor Yale Kamisar; Evan J. Kemp Jr.; W.C.M. Klijn; Dr. Gerald (Chip) Klooster and Mary Klooster; Charles Krauthammer; Madelaine Lawrence; Gary Lee, MD; Paul Longmore; Tom Lorentzen; Tom Marzen; Ginny McKibben; Steven H. Miles, MD; Donald Murphy, MD; Fr. Richard Neuhaus; Mark O'Brien; Timothy Quill, MD; Harvey Rosenfield; Matthew Rothschild; Daniel P. Sulmasy, MD; Dame Cicly Saunders, MD; Randolph Schiffer, MD; Janie Hickock Siess; Lonny Shavelson, MD; Elizabeth Skoglund; Beverly Sloane; William Stothers; Eugene Sutorius; W. Russell Van Camp; Teri Van Camp; Terry Stimpson; William F. Stone; I van der Sluis, MD; Dr. Maurice Victor; Nancy Valco; Richard Vigilante; Rebekah Vinson; Kathy Weaver; Jos. V. M. Wellie; James Wirth; Kathy Wolfe; and Jessica Yu.

Special thanks to special friends and colleagues who do such good and important work with the International Task Force on Euthanasia and Assisted Suicide: Rita Marker, Mike Marker, Kathi Hamlon, John Hamlon, Robert Hiltner, and Nancy Minto.

I want to thank everyone at Times Books, the original publisher of this book, especially my editors Peter Smith and Betsy Rapoport. Much appreciation to my new publisher, Spence Publishing, particularly Thomas Spence, Mitchell Muncy, and William Tierney.

Finally, my deep appreciation to, and love for, all of my friends and family who have put up with me lo these many years of my activism in equality-of-human-life issues, with such patience, good cheer, encouragement, and affection, especially Ralph Nader; Mark Pickup; my brotherman, Arthur Cribbs; Pastor Ross Merkel; Bradford William Short; pal Steve and Allison Hayward; John Russo and Chris Lavin; Peter B. Collins and Kathy Shatter, Peter and Lexie Demeralie, Glenn Davis; and Michael Green. My special thanks to the Saunders family, Florida, Connecticut, and Rhode Island branches: Jerry, Barbara, Jim, Vickie, Jennifer, Jeremiah, Stephen, Leslie, Rebecca, Eric, and Joshua, to my dear mother; and, most of all, to Debra J., wife and total sweetheart.

FORCED EXIT

Death Fundamentalism

O N OCTOBER 23, 1991, fifty-eight-year-old Marjorie Wantz and
forty-three-year-old Sherry Miller kept their appointment at
a cabin in a park near Detroit with an unemployed pathologist named Jack Kevorkian, who was then still relatively unknown. Over
a year before he had made headlines after hooking up Janet Adkins,
who had early-stage Alzheimer's disease, to a suicide machine of his
own design that killed by intravenously administering barbiturates and
poison when the patient flipped a switch. Adkins died well before her
disease became debilitating, a good ten years before it could have been
expected to end her life. Now Wantz and Miller wanted to die.

Neither woman was terminally ill. According to later court testimony, both were suffering from depression. Miller was disabled by
multiple sclerosis. A few years earlier, just when Miller's disease had
begun to worsen and restrict her activities, her husband had left her,
taking custody of their children. Miller was forced to live with her elderly parents, and she worried about being a burden to them.[1] She
claimed that disgust with her disabilities was her reason for wanting to
die. Yet at her age Miller might eventually have adapted to her disability—as so many people disabled later in life do—as well as to the loss
of her family, and might have created a new life for herself.

3

After benign growths had been removed from Wantz's vagina, she began to complain bitterly of severe pelvic pain. Many doctors tried to discover the cause through various means, including surgery. None was found. Indeed, her autopsy would show that she had no organic disease whatsoever. Not coincidentally, Wantz suffered from a depressive disorder, had been treated in mental hospitals, and according to an article in the *Detroit News*, had been using a sleep aid called Halcion in higher-than-recommended doses.[2] Halcion, if abused, has the side effect of suicidal impulses.

Entering the cabin, the women lay down on cots. Kevorkian hooked up Wantz to his suicide machine, and soon she was no more. But he couldn't find a vein in Miller's emaciated arms. Always a tinkerer, he improvised. He rushed out, obtained a canister of carbon monoxide and a facemask, and rigged another suicide machine. Soon Miller was dead too. Their bodies would later be found amid dozens of burning candles.

On May 10, 1996, a jury acquitted Kevorkian of the common law crime of assisting the suicides of Wantz and Miller, despite there being no dispute that he had done just that.[3] (He was never charged in the Adkins case.) Much ado was made in the media about the jury's swallowing Kevorkian's specious claim that he did not intend for the women to die and merely wanted to alleviate suffering. In all of the commentary, perhaps the most important point was missed: the statement by some jurors that it did not matter to them that Miller and Wantz were not terminally ill. That incontrovertible fact simply was not significant to them. (Of the 130 or so people Kevorkian helped kill, approximately 70 percent were not terminally ill. Five had no diagnosable illness upon autopsy.)[4]

Although he would be imprisoned for murder in 1999, Kevorkian's acquittal in the deaths of Wantz and Miller was a watershed in the history of euthanasia in the United States. The proposal to give doctors the legal right to kill certain patients was no longer unthinkable but, rather, distinctly possible.

The acquittals also exposed the often avoided truth about the so-called "right to die" movement. The jury's shrug of the shoulders over the tragic deaths of Wantz and Miller—one disabled, the other deeply emotionally disturbed—demonstrates that euthanasia is not about allowing the "terminally ill" who are in "unrelievable pain" and on the brink of death to "die with dignity," as the issue is usually described in the media. Rather, as the more candid proponents of euthanasia acknowledge, it is about creating a culture and medical system that accepts assisted suicide, not only for the terminally ill, but for anyone suffering a "hopeless illness" (a term I will define in a few pages), a beneficence for suffering individuals and a good for society as a whole that will reduce healthcare costs and the burdens of care on society and families.

This is a truly radical idea. If we accept it, we will have become a society that accepts killing as compassionate, where we once promoted improved medical care and emotional support as the humane response to a patient's desire to die. If euthanasia is legalized, doctors will be given a license to kill some of their patients, and these patients will be given a legally enforceable right to be killed.

What makes this proposition so extraordinary is that protecting human life is the central purpose of organized society. Intentional killing by private persons is profoundly disfavored and severely restricted, legally allowed only in exceptional circumstances. Killing by the state, too, is severely restricted. Police may kill only when necessary to protect themselves, other officers, or the public. A soldier may kill if following legal orders in combat. The death penalty is permitted only after the condemned is accorded a fair trial and multiple appeals often taking many years.

Legalized euthanasia would dismantle this venerable tradition. To permit killing in the commonplace circumstances of terminal illness, chronic illness and pain, disability, and prolonged mental illness, including depression—as is currently advocated by many in the euthanasia movement—would corrode the ethical, moral, and legal foundations of society. Legalization would shake the relationship of physician and patient to its core. For one thing, the essential bond of trust between doctor and patient would likely be torn asunder. A recent survey of cancer patients found that if their doctor were to raise the issue of assisted suicide with them, they would lose trust in their physician. Moreover, the cancer patients stated they would change doctors if they discovered that their physician had helped kill another patient.[5] Add the changing economics of healthcare to the equation, in which doctors actually lose money if they provide patients with "too much" care (in chapter six, I discuss doctors' conflicts of interest), and the potential for the estrangement of patient and doctor is undeniable.

LOSING OUR WAY

What is driving people to abandon traditional moral standards and embrace the death culture? The Canadian newspaper columnist Andrew Coyne, reacting to the widespread public support of Robert Latimer, who murdered his twelve-year-old daughter because she was disabled by cerebral palsy (which I discuss further in chapter seven), said it most eloquently: "A society that believes in nothing can offer no argument even against death. A culture that has lost its faith in life cannot comprehend why it should be endured."[6]

Seen in this light, support for euthanasia is not a cause, but rather a symptom, of the broad breakdown of community. The consequences of this moral balkanization can be seen all around us: in the disintegration of the family; in the growing nihilism among young people, leading to a rise in suicides, drug use, and other destructive behavior; in the belief that the lives of the sick, disabled, and dying are so meaningless, unimportant, and without value that killing them—or helping them kill themselves—can be countenanced and even encouraged.

But there is more to this story than passive cultural decay. There are several related cultural phenomena that have combined to produce the euthanasia juggernaut. The most visible is a radical notion of individualism that elevates personal autonomy above all other values. Though there is nothing wrong with a healthy respect for the rights of the individual, unbridled, near-absolute individualism leads to social anarchy and asphyxiates true freedom. That is why self-determination, while very important, is but one of several equally important and sometimes conflicting values that add up to the dynamic concept the Founders called "ordered liberty." One such competing value—let's call it "community"—promotes mutual care, concern, and support between persons. The government and society promote community when they prevent harm to the weak and vulnerable—for example, by stopping suicides—not out of paternalism, but as a fulfillment of our obligation to protect, care for, and love one another.

Ordered liberty protects and defends the forest and the trees, the society as well as the individual. Individual freedom is certainly valued and encouraged, but in order to protect the greater good, it is not absolute: it is properly limited when individual acts are unduly harmful to self, others, or to the whole, even if the harm is indirect. The community therefore prevents individuals from injecting heroin because drug addiction harms both the person who is abusing the drug and the overall society. To prevent individual harm and to ensure that the poor will not be exploited, people are not allowed to sell their vital organs, even if they want to. Likewise, the law absolutely prohibits adult siblings from marrying, even if they are deeply in love, because of the adverse social consequences that would follow from allowing open sexuality between close blood relatives. In these and many other such cases, individual self-expression and fulfillment are subordinated to other vital community concerns.

This mix of competing and complementary values has created a nuanced public policy around issues of death, dying, and suicide. There are laws against euthanasia and assisted suicide to reduce the danger that the dying or chronically ill will be exploited or coerced into an early death. Such laws also protect society from the moral harm that would result should the killing of the dying, the sick, and the disabled become routine.[7] At the same time, the law properly allows people to refuse unwanted medical treatment, even if that choice might lead to death. (I discuss in later chapters the vital distinctions between being killed and refusing medical treatment.) Suicide, in and of itself, however, is not considered a crime in any state, being viewed as a cry for help rather than a violation of law. But even though suicide itself is not a crime, there has heretofore never been a "right" to self-destruction. Police generally are empowered to use non-deadly force to prevent a suicide and are authorized, if necessary, to bring the self-destructive person to a psychiatric facility for observation. Moreover, if the patient is found beyond a reasonable doubt to present a danger to himself, he can be hospitalized for treatment until the threat passes. A multitude of once suicidal people are happily alive today, who would have been dead had "society" not cared enough to protect them from themselves during their time of despair.

Euthanasia proponents deem such laws paternalistic, at least as they relate to the sick, disabled, and chronically mentally distraught. These proponents urge us to accept a relatively new concept known as "rational suicide," which views self-destruction as the result of a rational decision and hence appropriate when one's circumstances become particularly difficult. According to proponents of this view, if suicide is a rational choice, as opposed to an irrational urge, then it should not only be accepted but also facilitated upon request. To these advocates, committing physician-facilitated suicide is, in the words of the Hemlock Society's cofounder, Derek Humphry, the "ultimate civil liberty."[8]

Who should have the right to a hastened death? Early on, euthanasia proponents swore that it was to be reserved only for those who were terminally ill, when nothing else could be done to relieve their pain and suffering. But once entered upon, the slippery slope grows progressively steep. Now, even before euthanasia has been legalized widely, many advocates have broadened their criteria, arguing that it should be available for those suffering from "desperate," "incurable," or "hopeless" illness.

These terms are cleverly designed to fool the listener into believing that the reference is still to terminal disease. In reality, advocates of rational suicide are opening the door to physician-assisted suicide for almost anyone who has a sustained desire to die. For example, "hopeless illness," the preferred term of the moment, is generally defined in psychiatric literature as including, but not limited to, "terminal illnesses, [maladies causing] severe physical and/or psychological pain, physically or mentally debilitating and/or deteriorating conditions, and circumstances where [the] quality of life [is] no longer acceptable to the individual."[9]

This definition is wide enough to drive a hearse through. Virtually any illness, injury, or emotional malady could cause severe physical or psychological pain. By definition, a person only wants to commit suicide because, at the time, he believes that "life is no longer acceptable." Thus, the concept of "hopeless illness" is a prescription for abandoning depressed and suffering people to a policy of death on demand.

This kind of thinking has advanced so far that proposed guidelines have been published under which mental health professionals could participate in their patients' decision to "suicide." (Some advocates of "rational suicide" now use the word as a verb). Among these guidelines, a mental-health counselor could "validate the client's decision to commit suicide," should become "knowledgeable about the various methods of self-administration, including types of drugs, lethality of dosages, and efficacy of methods," and, if objecting to rational suicide, would be required to refer "the client to a qualified counselor who does not have any conscientious objection" to suicide.[10]

Legalized euthanasia would not occur in a vacuum. The anti-community values it represents would undoubtedly ripple throughout our culture. Our duties and responsibilities to the community and to each other would be eclipsed, sacrificed on the altar of individual fulfillment. We would become so many islands, interacting but isolated individuals placed side by side with few mutual commitments. As for the unfortunates who "can't keep up," they can do with their bodies what they want; we will shrug, as an increasing number of despairing individuals "choose" to end their lives.

The bioethicist Arthur Caplan writes of the sad case of Thomas W. Passmore, a man with a history of mental illness, who, thinking he saw the sign of the devil on his right hand, cut it off with a circular saw. He was taken to a hospital, where, according to Caplan, things took a "crazy turn." Upon being told by the surgeon that his hand could be saved, Passmore refused treatment, still believing that his hand carried the sign of evil. A psychiatrist interviewed Passmore; lawyers were consulted; a judge refused to intervene. In the end, no one would decide that Passmore was incompetent to make his own medical decisions, and his hand was permanently lost.

This was a profound abandonment of a mentally ill, self-destructive man in desperate need of help from his community. Thanks to our extreme view of self-determination, those who should have assisted Passmore were instead morally paralyzed. So distorted were their perceptions of their responsibility to Passmore, so stunted was their thinking, that they allowed a hallucinating man to dismember himself. As Caplan so aptly put it, "a nation that has created a healthcare system in which doctors, nurses and administrators are not sure whether it is the right thing to do to sew a mentally ill man's severed hand back onto his arm is a society gone over the edge regarding autonomy."[11]

What happened to Passmore's hand will happen to people's lives if this trend continues. Euthanasia and assisted suicide represent the ultimate abandonment of people made vulnerable by physical or mental illness, inadequate medical care, and depression. Legalization would lead to a moral and ethical catastrophe in which those least able to defend themselves would be victimized.

It is interesting to observe that the most vocal people pushing the death agenda seem to be those least likely to be victimized by it. Jack Kevorkian aside, most leaders of the euthanasia movement, such as the author Betty Rollin, the head of the Compassion in Dying Federation, Barbara Coombs Lee, the former president of the Hemlock Society,

Faye Girsh, and the euthanasia advocate, physician Dr. Timothy Quill, are people of the "overclass": well-off whites with a strong and support-ive family or social structure, who never believe they could be victim-ized or pressured into an early death. They want what they want (to be able to die) when and how they want it. They downplay the harm that will follow for the poor, the uneducated, those without access to medi-cal care, or the disabled, many of whom view themselves as being in the crosshairs on this issue. Not to worry, these death culture leaders breezily assert, "protective guidelines" will fix everything.

Euthanasia is being promoted by its advocates through a very so-phisticated political campaign. Proponents use all the tools of the po-litical trade. Focus groups and polls have told them that people respond negatively to words such as "euthanasia," and so they resort to euphe-misms to describe killing such as "aid in dying," "deliverance," and "gentle landing." Their research also shows that people respond best to argu-ments that appeal to traditional notions of freedom. Hence, they pep-per their advocacy with the rhetoric of freedom and elicit an emotional response in the listener, especially with that sound bite of all sound bites, "choice." They argue that legalizing physician-assisted suicide is about personal autonomy, the right to be left alone. Appealing to our traditional distrust of government, advocates self-righteously assert that legalization of physician-hastened death would deny the state "any right to compel innocent, competent adults to needlessly suffer," as if laws prohibiting killing authorize torture.[12] Some even compare the cam-paign to create a "right to die" with the civil rights movement. Martin Luther King Jr. must be turning over in his grave.

Claiming the civil-liberties high ground for the idea of "choosing the manner and timing of one's death" serves another polemical pur-pose. It keeps the discussion on a theoretical level and allows suicide proponents to avoid an analysis of the dysfunctional context in which the "choices to die" would be exercised. As Matthew Rothschild, the editor of *Progressive* magazine and a strong civil libertarian, puts it, "I think a lot of people are persuaded by the civil-liberties cloak that has falsely been placed around this issue. But the reality is quite the opposite. Euthanasia is not a 'choice' issue at all. Rather, choices to die would be made by others for people who are powerless and who are weak, whose right to live would be taken out of their own hands."[13]

Another driving force behind the euthanasia movement is the issue of "control." At the same time that they hoist high the banner of hastened death as a liberty, proponents exploit people's fear of death and the suffering that can precede death, promising that choosing the time and manner of death will somehow tame the Grim Reaper. In this atmosphere, dying is increasingly promoted as "bad death" if it involves extended discomfort, and hastened death is presented as empowering, courageous, and somehow noble. For some suicide advocates, controlling death has become a fixation. One cannot seriously engage the issue for long without hearing certain terms: good death, planned death, assisted death, death with dignity, rational death, deliverance, gentle landing, soft landing—the list goes on and on.

The Dutch physician Dr. I. van der Sluis, who has opposed his country's slide down euthanasia's slippery slope for more than twenty years, has observed the same phenomenon in the Netherlands. "I have studied [euthanasia proponents'] mentality," he told me. "They are like a little church, a cult of death. The subject fascinates them. They are always obsessing on dying and the suffering that may be a part of dying."[14] The disability-rights activist and professor Paul Longmore, who resists legalized euthanasia as a form of bigotry against the disabled, agrees. "Some of these people can only be described as 'death fundamentalists,'" he says. "They are so fixated on death and their ideology, that the facts of the debate have little meaning for them."

Death fundamentalism, an apt description, may be contagious. My friend Frances was a death fundamentalist; so fixated was she on her own self-destruction, even before she became ill, that no appeal could convince her to search for a different answer to her problems. When the suicide guru Derek Humphry published his how-to-commit-suicide book, *Final Exit*, in August 1991, it made the *New York Times* bestseller list. A few years ago, 175 people attended a "self-deliverance" course taught by Humphry, in which people were instructed on how to commit suicide by using a plastic bag. He has since run "how to commit suicide" television shows on cable-access television. For those who missed the course, Humphry's current organization, ERGO (Euthanasia Research and Guidance Organization), sells illustrated instructions (ingredients: a plastic bag, two elastic bands, a paper painter's mask, and an ice bag).

Suicide has become something of a cottage industry. Conventions are held in which manufacturers of suicide contraptions display their wares. One such device is the "debreather," a mask through which air is recycled and oxygen is removed.[15] Another popular item is the "Exit Bag," which the Right to Die Network of Canada advertises in the following breathless terms: "The customized EXIT BAG is made of **clear** strong industrial plastic. It has an adjustable collar (with elastic sewn in back and a six-inch Velcro strip in front) for snug but *comfortable* fit. It is extra large (22x36 inches) to reduce heat build-up. It comes with flannelette lining inside the collar so that the plastic won't irritate sensitive skin. AND it comes with an optional separate *terry-cloth neckband* to create a 'turtleneck' for added comfort and snugness of fit."[16]

I was able to purchase an Exit Bag with instructions for suicide for forty-four dollars, no questions asked.

Meanwhile, in Australia, Philip Nitchske, an Australian pro-euthanasia physician topped Jack Kevorkian's suicide machine by creating a computer program to allow people to commit assisted suicide at the push of a button; the program has been posted on the Internet. (The first PC-facilitated death occurred on September 26, 1996.) He has since received a grant from the Hemlock Society to develop a suicide formula made up of everyday household items, the so-called "peaceful pill." Nitchske caused a furor in Australia when he stated in an online magazine interview that he intended his research to be made available to "the troubled teen."[17] He later justified his assertion on the basis that "we seem to think eighteen-year-olds are old enough to go and kill people in war."[18]

Jack Kevorkian is a high priest of death fundamentalism. According to *Newsweek*, Kevorkian, while in medical school in the 1950s, "made regular visits to terminally ill patients and peered deeply into their eyes. His objective was to pinpoint when the precise moment of death occurred."[19] Kevorkian is a ghoulish artist who paints grotesque pictures, such as one "of a child eating the flesh off a decomposing corpse."[20] He has long been fascinated with the mechanics of capital punishment.[21] He even transfused blood from corpses into living human beings without testing the procedure on animals to make sure it was safe.[22]

Kevorkian is so death obsessed that he proposed the nauseating prospect of performing live human experiments on people being killed in order to learn more about human death, a procedure he named "obitiatry." He used to call assisted suicide "medicide," but changed it to "patholysis." In his own words, from his book *Prescription Medicide*: "If we are ever to penetrate the mystery of death—even superficially— it will have to be through obitiatry. Research using cultured cells and tissues and live animals may yield objective biological data . . . but knowledge about the essence of human death will of necessity require insight into the nature of the unique awareness or consciousness that characterizes human *life*. That is possible only through obiatric [sic], research on living human bodies."[23]

Indeed, the primary motivation behind Kevorkian's death crusade was to pave the way for live human experiments on those being killed, not to ease suffering. As he admits candidly, again in *Prescription Medicide*, "[Assisted suicide] is not simply to help doomed persons kill themselves—that is merely the first step, an early distasteful professional obligation . . . . [W]hat I find most satisfying is the prospect of making possible the performance of invaluable experiments or other beneficial medical acts under conditions that this first unpleasant step can help establish."[24]

The increase in the popularity of legalized euthanasia is also a vote of no confidence in the medical profession. Many supporters are afraid—nay, terrified—at the prospect of being victimized by doctors who will hook them up to machines and force them to linger in an agonizing limbo until they die or their health insurance runs out—whichever comes first. Thus, euthanasia is sold as a guarantee of sorts against both suffering and financial difficulty.

While the ongoing changes in healthcare financing make it more likely that patients will receive too little care rather than too much, fear of a lingering death is not irrational. Too many people have seen their loved ones writhing in pain that could have been relieved, too many have had their own suffering ignored, too many have been treated impersonally and dismissively by healthcare professionals. As one study put it, "Public perceptions about . . . assisted suicide and euthanasia are determined by many issues, including fears of intolerable suffering at the end of life, and a perception that the healing professions have paid inadequate attention to relieving suffering when a cure is not possible. This perception may well be right."[25]

Paradoxically, the very people who support euthanasia because they don't trust the medical profession, who fear they will be victimized by unwanted care or medical neglect of their suffering, accept the idea that doctors should be relied on to engage in medicalized killing. Yet these same doctors, it is widely recognized, are generally poorly trained in treating pain and do a terrible job of diagnosing clinical depression in their chronically ill and dying patients.

Then there is the issue of compassion, which euthanasia advocates claim as their primary motivation. Some speak as if they have a monopoly on the virtue, while casting euthanasia opponents as people who care more about legalism than about relieving suffering. It's not true, of course. Dignified, compassionate, and effective means exist today to reduce or eliminate pain and suffering without eliminating the patient. Unfortunately, these measures receive only a fraction of the publicity of the drive to legalize killing. For example, most people don't even know what hospice care is, much less how to obtain it. This is tragic, because these underutilized and underfunded programs can make all the difference in the lives of people who are suffering and often can change a desire to die into a drive to live, or, perhaps, a decision to let nature decided the time of passing.

Euthanasia advocates' compassion argument also overlooks the prospect that legalizing euthanasia would lead to more suffering rather than less. Think about what could happen to funding for AIDS research and efforts to improve the care and long-term prospects for people suffering from that horrible disease. Some with little sympathy for AIDS victims might say that with a quick and painless death available, money now spent on curative research could be better invested elsewhere. And what about improving pain-control education and increasing access to hospice care? Chances are both would wither on the vine. And what about the desperate need to improve access to medical care? Dr. Joanne Lynn, professor of medicine at Dartmouth Medical School, has said, "If we choose to kill [those] with limited life prospects [rather than] trying to serve them, we will have foreclosed the possibility of reforming our dysfunctional care systems," which cause feelings of "isolation, meaninglessness, and abandonment," emotions that often lead the ill to want to kill themselves.[26]

Finally, there is a less visible, but perhaps the most influential and dangerous, force driving the euthanasia juggernaut: money. Our healthcare system is quickly being transformed from a fee-for-service system, where medical professionals earn money by treating people, to a system dominated by for-profit health maintenance organizations (HMOs), in which health insurance companies make money primarily by reducing costs. In an HMO, a penny saved is literally a penny earned. That is why legalized euthanasia would be especially profitable for HMOs. Just imagine the money that could be saved—and thus earned—by not treating those with AIDS, cancer, or physical disabilities, because their lives were ended by euthanasia. When doctors may legally kill patients, investors in for-profit HMOs will be dancing in the streets.

Derek Humphry, the co-founder of the Hemlock Society, made this point explicitly in his book *Freedom to Die: People, Politics and the Right to Die Movement*:"Elders or otherwise incurable people are often aware of the burdens—financial and otherwise—of their care." Humphry and his co-author, Mary Clement, go on to observe:

> A rational argument can be made for allowing PAS [physician-assisted suicide] in order to offset the amount society and family spend on the ill, as long as it is the voluntary wish of the mentally competent terminally ill and incurable adult. There will likely come a time when PAS becomes a commonplace occurrence for individuals who want to die and feel it is the right thing to do by their loved ones. There is no contradicting the fact that since the largest medical expenses are incurred in the final days and weeks of life, the hastened demise of people with only a short time left would free resources for others. Hundreds of billions of dollars could benefit those patients who not only can be cured but who also want to live.[27]

Money imperatives often help shape our values and ethics. If promoting certain behavior can make fortunes, rationalizations to justify the conduct will soon be found, even if it is inherently immoral. One reason that slavery became so entrenched in the Old South was that the peculiarities of the Southern economy at the time made human bondage profitable for those in power. Similarly, the genocide of Native Americans was often stimulated by the expectation that there was money to be made from taking their lands. For a modern equivalent of putting dollars ahead of the lives of people, just look at the activities of the tobacco industry, which has been accused, among other moral wrongs, of promoting tobacco use by the young despite knowing tobacco's profound health dangers.

It may not be a coincidence, then, that the ethics of end-of-life medical care are changing just as financial imperatives in medical practice have reversed themselves. When the system was primarily fee-for-service, the prevailing medical ethic was to keep patients alive at all

costs, or at least until the health insurance ran out. But now that managed care is supplanting fee-for-service, we hear much talk about "good
death" and "death with dignity," about how patients should be more
willing to give up the ghost and refuse end-of-life medical treatment.
Then there is the worrying prospect that doctors may soon be empowered to refuse *wanted* life-sustaining medical treatment in order to save
medical resources. (I will discuss this new threat to vulnerable patients,
known as "Futile Care Theory," in detail in chapter six.)

EUTHANASIA CONSCIOUSNESS

Most people are not activists either for or against euthanasia, paying
little attention to the issue except in passing. Consequently, what many
think they know and what they believe about the issue is often the
result of attitudes seeping unnoticed into their consciousness from the
society around them. It is here, among the uninvolved, that organs of
popular culture have for years been quietly altering public perceptions
about death and dying.

People with certain mindsets dominate the popular culture. These
attitudes are reflected in our entertainment, particularly in Hollywood
movies, where euthanasia is thoroughly accepted. Television shows often deal with the issue, almost always presenting hastened deaths in a
sympathetic light as the "only" choice available to alleviate a desperate
patient's suffering. Popular television series such as *ER*, *Homicide*, *Chicago Hope*, *Star Trek—Deep Space Nine*, *Star Trek Voyager* (in which we
learn that Vulcans like Mr. Spock practice ritual suicide in old age),
and *Law and Order*, just to name a few, have all aired episodes dealing
positively with the theme of hastened death. At the same time, magazines we subscribe to or pick up in a doctor's waiting room present the
same message, typified by an article in the *New Yorker* in which the
writer extols his mother's assisted suicide. He concludes, "having seen
the simple logic of euthanasia in action and witnessed the comfort of
that control, what astonishes me is how many people die by other

means."[28] Similarly, the January 1997 *Ladies' Home Journal* had a "special report" on assisted suicide consisting of a "round table" discussion. Amazingly, there were no opponents of legalization presented in the entire article.

This is powerful stuff. When a popular television program depicts a courageous and handsome doctor killing a patient as the "only way" to relieve unremitting suffering, or the sympathetic and beautiful homicide inspector winks at a mercy killing because she would have done the same thing in the suspect's place, the audience gives no thought to the false premises that underlie the drama or to the systemic consequences of making such acts routine. When famous talk-show hosts bring families on television to justify the hastened deaths of their loved ones, it is difficult to see past our sympathy for the plight of the deceased or the grief of his or her family to the broader issues. Consequently, viewers tend to come away from these programs and reports thinking favorably of "the right to die." When popular magazines and newspaper stories deal with the issue, they invariably concentrate with laser-like intensity on a suffering individual who "just wants to die," while failing to train an equally penetrating light on the many ways of relieving suffering without killing or on the potential for coercion or abuse inherent in legitimized euthanasia. Thus, it is not surprising that viewers and readers develop pro-euthanasia attitudes.

The news media, driven by ratings and circulation concerns, cannot be relied upon to plumb the depths of the issue: A "good story" is often short on thought and long on emotion. If a doctor or family member assists an ill person in suicide, "news" coverage focuses intently on the reasons the person wanted to die. Friends speak of his or her great suffering. With few exceptions, little investigation, if any, is undertaken to discover whether the deceased was receiving adequate medical care, proper pain control, or treatment for depression. Even if doubts are raised about the propriety of the hastened death, right-to-die advocates will be brought in to assure us that abuses wouldn't happen if assisted death were legalized.

Most of the stories written about Kevorkian's reign of assisted killings are cases in point. The reporting about the September 3, 1996,
death of Jack Leatherman, seventy-three, who had pancreatic cancer, is
just one example. The story carried in the *Boston Globe* is typical. It told
about the man's death and the nature of his illness and reported the
allegation by one of Kevorkian's representatives that "no amount of pain
relief could control the pain that he was suffering." That assertion was
not questioned or investigated. Had it been, reporters would have discovered that morphine pills are very effective in controlling the pain
associated with pancreatic cancer. Moreover, according to the board-
certified oncologist and pain-control specialist Dr. Eric Chevlen, in
the rare event that opioids are insufficient to adequately control pancreatic cancer pain, a medical procedure can be performed to numb the
nerve that transmits pain stimuli from the abdomen to the spinal cord
and the brain, thereby eliminating all pain caused by the cancer.[29] Yet
that story, which would have given cancer victims and their families so
much hope, was never reported.

With a few exceptions, stories that highlight the reasons to oppose
legalization of euthanasia do not receive equivalent coverage. If reported
at all, these stories are not presented with the same level of emotional
intensity. A story of hospice care helping someone die a natural death
in comfort, surrounded by a loving family, doesn't make the news unless the person is famous. It is no big deal if a cancer patient is no
longer suicidal because he received effective pain control, and when a
patient is somehow coerced into early death, it rarely becomes a public
matter, since the abuser will not be anxious for exposure.

This is not to assert that the media have joined in some vast conspiracy to legalize euthanasia: their treatment of the subject follows
from the nature of our popular culture. Entertainment and the news
both require conflict to grab the audience and hold its interest. Euthanasia fits the bill. What could be more dramatic than the television
doctor risking his license and a jail sentence to "selflessly" help end the
life of an irremediably suffering patient on the brink of death? With

the media and the various organs of popular culture playing the same tune, and with opposition voices generally muted, the power of repetition, like ocean waves breaking against a rock, contributes individually and collectively to the gradual erosion of the equality-of-life ethic.

Also contributing mightily to the growing acceptance of euthanasia is a form of pervasive cultural decay that I call "terminal nonjudgmentalism" (TNJ). Our society has become so steeped in relativism, so unable to distinguish right from wrong, that it fails to react to, or to criticize, truly reprehensible ideas or conduct. When destructive ideas and practices are not condemned, it is a form of praise: that which is not seen as wrong must be right. As the winds of the death culture blow with increasing velocity, the vitality of the equality-of-life ethic recedes like a green valley slowly turning into desert. Where one year there was life, in the next there is only sand. Soon, the lushness that once was is forgotten and the barren landscape seems the norm.

A good example of TNJ in action—or better, inaction—can be seen in the book *A Chosen Death*, by Lonny Shavelson, and the reaction of critics to it.[30] Shavelson, described on the book jacket as an emergency-room physician and a photojournalist, writes about five assisted suicides he observed, or participated in, during the book's preparation. One case, that of "Gene," stands out for its heartlessness and brutality.

As depicted by Shavelson, Gene is a depressed, lonely widower with a pronounced alcohol problem. Twice previously he has tried to commit suicide. The first attempt occurred before he had two strokes that left him moderately impaired—but definitely not terminally ill.

Gene wants to end it all. He contacts an undisclosed chapter of the Hemlock Society and asks its head, a woman given the pseudonym "Sarah," to assist in his death. According to Shavelson, Sarah has experience in this dark business, having previously assisted the suicide of a close friend. Sarah found her first killing experience tremendously satisfying and powerful, "the most intimate experience you can share with a person. . . . More than sex. More than birth . . . more than anything," including being present for "the deliveries of my four grandchildren."[31]

A committed death fundamentalist, Sarah wants again to enjoy the intense rush she experienced facilitating her friend's death, and so she jumps at the chance to help kill Gene.

Gene hems and haws, avoiding suicide and seemingly relishing the newfound companionship of Sarah and Shavelson that his suicide wish has provided him. Then, one night, he decides the time has come to die. He calls Shavelson and Sarah to his home. Shavelson watches as Sarah mixes Gene a poisonous brew and gives it to him, saying, "O.K., toots, here you go," as if she were handing him a beer.[32]

Gene drinks the liquid and begins to fall asleep, with Sarah holding his head on her lap. As he begins to snore, Sarah places a plastic bag over his head and begins to croon, "See the light. Go to the light."[33] (Sarah apparently had seen the movie *Poltergeist* once too often.)

But then, suddenly, faced with the prospect of immediate death, Gene changes his mind. He screams out "I'm cold!" and tries to rip the bag off his face. But Sarah won't allow it. From Shavelson's account: "His good hand flew up to tear off the plastic bag. Sarah's hand caught Gene's wrist and held it. His body thrust upwards. She pulled his arm away and lay across Gene's shoulders. Sarah rocked back and forth, pinning him down, her fingers twisting the bag to seal it tight at his neck as she repeated, 'the light, Gene, go toward the light.' Gene's body pushed against Sarah's. Then he stopped moving."[34]

If Shavelson's depiction of the event is accurate, the word that describes what happened to Gene is *murder*.

The right, proper, ethical, and humane thing for Shavelson to do as he watched Sarah asphyxiate Gene would have been to knock Sarah off the helpless man and then quickly call for an ambulance and the police. But Shavelson did not do anything, so paralyzed was he by his own self-described TNJ as he watched the Sarah-Gene tableau, just before the old man tried to rip the bag off his face: "'Stop, Sarah' raced through my mind. For whose sake, I thought—Gene's, so intent on killing himself? The weight of unanswered questions kept me glued to my corner. Was this a suicide, Gene's right finally to succeed and die?

Or was this a needless death encouraged by Sarah's desire to act? Had Gene's decision to have me there, to tell me his story, given me the right to stop what was happening—or, equally powerful, the responsibility not to interfere? Or was I obliged by my very presence as a fellow human being, to jump up and stop the craziness? Was it craziness?"[35]

Suddenly, Sarah is holding Gene down, preventing him from tearing off the plastic bag. But Shavelson's TNJ continues. Unable to distinguish right from wrong, he is paralyzed and merely watches the struggle that culminates in Gene's death.

I interviewed Shavelson about all this. When asked whether he agreed that Gene's death was a murder, Shavelson said that his answer was too complex for a "sound bite response."[36] How could he watch a woman snuff the life out of a man clearly struggling to stay alive? I asked. I reminded Shavelson that when he and I had met previously, in a radio-station greenroom before a debate, I had asked him why he hadn't tried to stop Sarah. His response at the time was "I am a journalist."[37] Shavelson now acknowledged saying this, but he correctly noted that our conversation about the issue at that time was brief and not conducive to a more detailed response. (Nor, in fairness to Shavelson, was it a conversation geared toward inclusion in a book, although I did mention I would want to interview him about the issue for this book.) So I asked him to clarify. Shavelson demurred, citing the "complexity" of his answer and worries about the "sound bite" nature of any quotation that I might use. He did, however, point to the section in his book where he describes Gene's asphyxiation: "Events suddenly moved faster than my thoughts."[38] In other words, Shavelson is claiming that it all happened too fast. Yet Shavelson is an emergency room physician. Surely he should be equipped to deal with fast-moving events.

I then asked Shavelson whether he thought Gene's death fell within the guidelines that are being proposed to regulate legalized assisted suicide. He said that he believed Gene's condition to be "outside" the acceptable reasons for assisted suicide of any guidelines he knew of or supported, and added that regulating assisted suicide would mean that such deaths as Gene's could be prevented because legalization would "clarify what is and is not acceptable."[39] However, he agreed that nothing in any guidelines would prevent a death cultist like Sarah from acting outside the guidelines, just as her killing Gene was clearly outside the law as it exists today. (On the contrary, I contend that Gene could easily have been labeled "hopelessly ill" and thus would have fallen within some proposed "guidelines.")

The point that Shavelson and other death fundamentalists miss is that so-called protective guidelines are meaningless; they provide only a veneer of respectability. They don't close the door to deaths outside their parameters. Rather, they break the doors of hastened death wide open by destroying the existing locks. Once killing is deemed an appropriate response to suffering, the threshold dividing "acceptable" killing from "unacceptable" killing will be continually under siege. But the fiction of control, essential to the public's acceptance of euthanasia, will have to be maintained, so the definition of what will be seen as "legitimate" killing will be expanded continually, as has occurred in the Netherlands (see chapter four).

What about the reviewers of Shavelson's book? Surely they shared my horror at Gene's murder and Shavelson's passivity. Not a chance. None I read materially criticized Gene's killing. The *San Francisco Chronicle* review is typical. The reviewer, Steve Heilig, a bioethicist and coeditor of the *Cambridge Quarterly of Healthcare Ethics*, didn't condemn Shavelson for allowing a murder to take place, unimpeded, under his very nose. Nor did he demand that Shavelson reveal the identity of Sarah and Gene so that the death could be appropriately subjected to a criminal inquiry. Rather, the review merely recounts that Shavelson is "appalled" at Sarah's "unregulated secretive approach" (not appalled enough to protect Gene, however) and opines that "the book superbly tackles this most difficult of ethical issues." What we don't condemn, we allow.

Another recent pro-euthanasia book that has been praised with faint condemnation is *Rethinking Life and Death: The Collapse of Our*

Traditional Ethics by Peter Singer.[40] *Rethinking Life and Death* can fairly be called the *Mein Kampf* of the euthanasia movement in that it drops many of the euphemisms common to pro-euthanasia writing and acknowledges euthanasia for what it is: killing. Indeed, Singer is straightforward about how pervasive these death practices have become in our society and, unlike his fellow death fundamentalists, is quite candid about their destructiveness to the concept that all human life is inherently equal, a degeneration he celebrates. Indeed, what makes Singer's book noteworthy is that he takes the step that most euthanasia proponents avoid for tactical reasons: he specifically advocates the outright destruction of the equality-of-human-life ethic that has undergirded Western civilization for two thousand years.

Singer advocates what he calls a "quality-of-life ethic." Under the quality-of-life ethic, being a human being is not a crucial determinant of one's inherent rights, since, Singer believes, all human lives do not have an inherently equal moral value. Rather, being a "person" is what counts to Singer, and only persons enjoy the right to life.

Most of us think "person" and "human" are synonymous. Not Singer. He elevates some "nonhuman animals" (such as dogs, elephants, and pigs) to the status of persons, on the basis of his contention that they are self-aware. At the same time, he strips some human beings of personhood, specifically those with cognitive disabilities and all newborn infants, because of their lack of the "relevant characteristics" of self-awareness over time and the ability to reason. (Singer is far from alone in this advocacy. The odious notion of the born-human non-person pervades current bioethics thinking.[41])

The practical application of these theories? Singer specifically embraces infanticide. Since, according to the author, an infant has no inherent right to life, a baby can be killed ethically if parents and doctors decide this is for the best. Speaking specifically of Down's syndrome babies, Singer writes: "We may not want a child to start on life's uncertain voyage if the prospects are clouded. When this can be known at a very early stage in the voyage, we may still have a chance to make a fresh start. This means detaching ourselves from the infant who bas been born, cutting ourselves free before the ties that have already begun to bind us to our child have become irresistible. Instead of going forward and putting all our efforts into making the best of the situation, we can still say no, and start again from the beginning."[42] In other words, according to Singer an acceptable answer to the difficulties of having a baby with Down's syndrome or another birth defect is to kill the child, an option that Singer muses should be available to parents for the first twenty-eight days of an infant's life.

Singer has been making such proposals for years. That he is nevertheless *respected* internationally as a "philosopher" and "bioethicist" is proof enough of rampant TNJ. Further proof is the book review in the *New York Times*, May 7, 1995, by Daniel J. Kevles of the California Institute of Technology. The closest Kevles comes to criticizing Singer's thesis is to suggest that some of his opinions are "highly debatable." Indeed, the review states that *Rethinking Life and Death* "is analytically rich on the moral rights of newborns compared with those of unborn fetuses, and how we treat anyone who is so physically or cerebrally degraded that they have no chance of a life of reasonable fulfillment."[43] In other words, that the right to live often depends on the values and attitudes of those with the power to kill is of no serious concern.

The death fundamentalist community expressed nothing but admiration for the book. A book review in *Hemlock TimeLines*, the successor to the *Hemlock Quarterly* as the official newsletter of the Hemlock Society, applauds: "The true message of this book is one of reason and responsibility."[44] The comments of Ralph Mero, former director of Compassion in Dying, an offshoot of Hemlock created to actively assist the suicides of the terminally ill, reveals a similar death-cult mindset: "*Rethinking Life and Death* . . . should be required reading for physicians, legislators, and judges. The new medical ethics being forged today will revolutionize our attitudes toward everything from fertilized zygotes to comatose bodies. Out of it should come a heightened respect for *persons and personhood* and just in time."[45] Derek Humphry, cofounder of the Hemlock Society, donated a book jacket blurb that states in part, "Brilliantly debunks old concepts and introduces honesty to modern medical ethics."

It is a sad and frightening day when a noted author writes a book advocating infanticide and involuntary euthanasia of the cognitively disabled, when a major New York publishing company publishes it, and when it is generally well received. (Singer has, however, been severely criticized and demonstrated against in Germany, a country with an acute memory of the horrors that can result from adopting such values as his. See chapter three.)

When pondering these matters, it is important to consider that Singer is far from being a fringe character. Indeed, he may be the most famous philosopher in the world today, a man who enjoys an international following not only for his advocacy of infanticide but as the inspiration for the "animal rights" movement. Incredibly, despite his advocacy of the right of parents and doctors to kill unwanted babies, in 1999 Singer received the ultimate symbol of respect when Princeton University named him the first Ira W. De Camp Professor in Bioethics at its Center for Human Values.

EXPLORING HIDDEN PREMISES

"There's No Such Thing as a Simple Suicide"

The abuse and exploitation inherent in the euthanasia consciousness are rarely discussed explicitly but are often readily apparent, even in pieces that promote the practice. A prominent article published in a major magazine typifies the kind of euthanasia promotion that is so depressingly common throughout the media.

On November 14, 1993, the cover story of the *New York Times Magazine* was "There's No Such Thing as a Simple Suicide."[46] It is the sad saga of a dying woman, "Louise," who killed herself with the active assistance and moral support of Ralph Mero, a Unitarian minister and the cofounder of the pro-euthanasia group Compassion in Dying.

An offshoot of the Hemlock Society at the time, Compassion in Dying actively counselled dying people who expressed a desire to commit suicide and assisted in their self-killing. Its founder and former director, Mero insisted that he eschewed publicity and acted only out of selfless compassion. Yet he and his "work" somehow managed to be featured in an Ann Landers advice column, complete with mailing address, in the major article in the *New York Times Magazine*, and in many national print and television newsmagazine pieces and documentaries.[47]

Lisa Belkin, a former *New York Times* reporter and author of the book *First Do No Harm*, about medicine and ethics, wrote the "No Simple Suicide" story. This excellently written piece presents Louise's story as melodrama, taking the reader on an emotionally wrenching roller-coaster ride of her assisted suicide, complete with a cast of heroes and villains and a gripping life-and-death plot. To make matters more compelling, we are told that the tale is true, with only the dying woman's name changed to protect her family's privacy.

The Story

"No Simple Suicide" chronicles the last few months of Louise's life. We learn early on that Louise suffers from an unidentified degenerative brain condition. Her doctor, described as "a warm, down-to-earth woman," informs Louise that she has only months, perhaps weeks, to live. Louise is afraid of dying in a hospital, hospice, or other "facility," a scenario her doctor bluntly tells her is quite likely to occur. Louise tells her doctor that rather than die in a cold, impersonal facility, she would rather kill herself. The doctor almost leaps at the chance to prescribe the drugs for Louise to take.

We are told that the doctor had previously "cooperated" with another patient's suicide, but that there had been difficulties, so she contacts Ralph Mero at Compassion in Dying to solicit his help and active assistance in facilitating Louise's death. The doctor later tells Belkin, "I was ecstatic to find someone who's doing what [Mero is] doing. I loved the fact that there were guidelines. It made so much sense. This was a human being who could help, not some book."[48]

A few days later Mero visits Louise, who lives with her mother. He tells Belkin that Louise appeared relieved when he didn't flinch or judge her desire to kill herself and that she asked Mero to be with her when she died. He agreed, stating that the decision was hers.

Louise has asked her friends to attend her suicide, but none will. When a medical assistant of one of her doctors hears that Louise's "trusted friends" have refused to sanction her suicide, she befriends the ill woman and supports her in her self-destruction.

Mero, the medical assistant, Louise, and Louise's mother become a cohesive group with one firm goal: Louise's assisted suicide. They meet to discuss how the self-termination will be performed. The deadly drugs will be mixed with a small amount of food and anti-nausea medication so that they can be kept down. Louise is to be monitored as she dies, and the assistant is to administer anti-pain medication if Louise seems to be suffering. After the death, the doctor will report to the authorities that the deceased was terminally ill and that the death was from natural causes after a prolonged illness, so no autopsy will be conducted. The doctor is also to falsify the death certificate as to the actual cause of death.

Weeks pass. Louise grows ever weaker. Yet the frail woman does not kill herself. Mero becomes alarmed. He calls Belkin to inform her that he and the group have been told by the doctor that Louise is running out of time to kill herself. It is feared that the disease may soon render Louise mentally incompetent. Mero worries that Louise's "window of opportunity will slam shut" because Compassion in Dying will assist suicides only for persons who are mentally competent. He also worries that if Louise waits much longer she will be unable to self-administer the deadly drugs.

Lisa Belkin drops everything and flies to Seattle to speak with Louise, who tells the reporter that she wishes to conclude some business and spend some more time with her mother before killing herself. This upsets Belkin, who blurts out the doctor's prognosis: Louise does not have much time within which she will be capable of killing herself.

Yet, for all of her stated desire to commit assisted suicide, Louise still does not act. Some time later, the medical assistant-turned-friend tells the group she will talk to Louise to see if she can get the suicide back on track. She asks the dying woman, "I kind of want to get an idea of what your time line is. Where do we stand?" Louise's eyes brim with tears, and she tells the medical assistant that she does not want to talk about it. The woman apologizes. Louise justifies her delay by saying that she wants to wait until Mero returns from out of town to get his opinion of her condition. The medical assistant replies that is a "bad idea" because Mero might not notice subtle changes in her condition.

Still Louise does not kill herself. Mero withdraws, checking in by phone but keeping the conversations short. He tells Belkin that he wants to remain in the background so as not to influence the outcome.

Then Mero gets a message: Louise is finally ready. The group assembles. Louise eats poisoned ice cream and applesauce that has been prepared according to Mero's instructions and immediately falls asleep on the couch clutching a teddy bear. Hours pass as Louise sleeps. The group waits for her to die. She does not. Mero worries that he might have to accelerate the process with a plastic bag. Finally, Louise's breathing slows, and she expires. Mero contacts the funeral director and leaves.

As the article concludes, we are informed that Louise's death was not listed as a suicide and that her friends and relatives were told that she "died in her sleep with her mother at her side, as she had wanted."

The Propaganda

Every drama is supposed to elicit a response from the audience. "No Simple Suicide" is no exception. On its face, the article appears to be an objective piece of journalism: Belkin does not praise or criticize the people involved or the events, nor does she give her personal opinion on the merits of Mero's cause. Scratch the surface, however, and the piece can be seen as an advertisement for legalizing and legitimizing assisted suicide and euthanasia.

What leads to this conclusion? First is the manner in which the article came to be written. Belkin didn't find the story; the story found her. As Belkin appropriately reveals, the board of directors of Compassion in Dying, who invited her to observe their usually secret suicide assistance activities, contacted her.

There is nothing illegal, immoral, or unusual about a reporter being contacted about a story. Stories are often found in this manner. It is safe to assume that nevertheless Mero and the board had more in mind than merely illustrating the emotional difficulties surrounding terminal illness. Surely they hoped to further their cause through the article. That being so, it is likely they would carefully choose a writer in the hope of finding one who could be expected to take a positive view of their work. In fact, in her story Belkin exhibits an uncritical acceptance of the methods and motives of Mero, the doctor, and the friend.

Whether Belkin approached her work with a pro-assisted suicide bias, a more important matter is the powerful message communicated by "No Simple Suicide." Bluntly stated, whether Belkin intended it, the article promotes euthanasia by seeking to persuade the reader that assisted suicide is acceptable. Proponents of legalizing assisted suicide and euthanasia are ever about the task of proselytizing. The more we are exposed to depictions of assisted suicide, the more commonplace it will seem and, then, the more acceptable. Through this process we become desensitized. Practices that we once found abhorrent begin to seem like a normal part of life—or, more precisely, death. "No Simple Suicide" serves this purpose in several ways.

1. *"No Simple Suicide" presents a false dilemma.* One of the tools used by pro-euthanasia advocates when arguing for legalization is to create a

false premise: Either we provide "deliverance" to suffering people, or they will be forced into cruel and unnecessary anguish. Either they die peacefully and painlessly now, or in agony later.

"No Simple Suicide" similarly casts Louise's plight as a forced choice between two horrible options: assisted suicide or an out-of-control death at a "facility." Not once is the reader (or Louise, as far as we know) informed that hospice and palliative care could probably have mitigated most, if not all, of her pain and discomfort. As reported, not once is the reader told that the hospice experience is designed to provide love, comfort, and support for the patient and the family, supplied by medical and mental-health professionals and volunteers. Not once is the reader told that hospice care can be supplied *in the home*—clearly a major issue for the dying woman. Not once is the reader told that the very purpose of hospice care is to facilitate a gentle and peaceful transition from life to whatever comes next. The fact that the truly compassionate option, from what is reported, was virtually unexplored speaks volumes about the doctor's agenda, and that of Mero and perhaps the friend.

It is also notable that Louise's doctor treats her patient's suicidal desire as expected, rather than as a cry for help. Yet studies prove that the vast majority of dying people do not exhibit suicidal tendencies. When dying patients do ask for suicide, they are almost always clinically depressed, just as are suicidal people who are not terminally ill. Depression is a treatable condition. Unfortunately, most doctors are not adept at recognizing depression in their dying patients. Thus, whether through ignorance or arrogance, Louise's doctor probably abandoned her patient to the throes of depression which could well have been overcome.

It is also assumed by all involved in the young woman's assisted suicide that she will not change her mind. Yet medical studies have shown that this is often not true. Indeed, the "will to live" among terminally ill people "shows substantial fluctuation."[49] In other words, one day a patient may request suicide but the next week be very glad they are still alive. And that seems to have been the case here. Louise did not have an unremitting desire to self-destruct. The only people with that unyielding death agenda were those who surrounded her.

2. *"No Simple Suicide" creates the impression that euthanasia is a loving rather than a violent act.* The suspicion that there was an unspoken agenda behind "No Simple Suicide" is supported by the striking art-work that illustrates many of the scenes described in the text. While Belkin undoubtedly had little or nothing to do with their creation, the pictures, which appear to be oil or watercolor paintings, are powerful and moving. The article doesn't tell us Louise's actual age or what she looked like, but the pictures depict Louise as a woman in her late twen-ties, her youth and delicate beauty adding to the tragedy of her condi-tion. In one picture, Louise is curled up peacefully asleep on a couch after eating the poisoned ice cream. She is holding a teddy bear as her gray-haired mother sits beside her, the older woman's hand resting lightly upon her dying daughter's leg. In another picture, we see Louise and Mero in a counseling session. He is a strong presence, solid and dependable with his white beard and black suit, a striking contrast to the frail Louise, who has a blanket wrapped around her shoulders. In another picture, Louise's mother is pictured leaning over her daughter, who is so weak the older woman can barely hear her speak.

The paintings have been created in the warm colors of autumn to invite us in, to linger as if we were standing in front of a crackling fire, indeed, to enter and become intimate participants in the unfolding drama. The paintings grab our hearts and rivet our attention solely on the suffering of the dying woman. In that way we are less likely to think critically, to look beyond Louise's personal tragedy to the broader im-plications of what is being done to her. Also, by making the scenes seem gentle and warm, we are far less likely to recoil in horror at the actual events.

3. *"No Simple Suicide" creates the impression that Louise's assisted suicide
was a necessary choice.* The article supports the merit of Louise's assisted
suicide on several levels. Belkin's prose creates the impression that Mero
and the others are compassionate pioneers leading the country toward
an enlightened view of facing and overcoming the ravages of terminal
illness. In fact, according to Belkin, that is how the group viewed themselves, writing that each saw Louise's pending assisted suicide as a "po-
etic expression of control, a triumph over the indignities of disease."
That is a typical view held by death fundamentalists and no doubt is
the view Mero hoped Belkin's readers would accept.

Belkin came to a less romantic but equally erroneous conclusion
about the affair. The only time she expresses a personal opinion in the
article, she describes Louise's assisted suicide as a "second choice" to
not being sick, and as the "most acceptable" of the dying woman's "unacceptable options." But that is a distinction without a difference.
Whether euthanasia is pushed as a heroic statement of control or a
rational choice between the lesser of two evils, the result is the same:
legitimization of that which is ultimately profoundly destructive to
individuals, the healthcare system, and society.

Whether motivated by the death-fundamentalist notions of Mero,
the "pragmatic choice" view of Belkin, the participants' genuine desire
to serve Louise, or a combination of these factors, Louise was pushed
by those around her into suicide because that was the death they wanted
her to have. As the psychiatrist Dr. Herbert Hendin, former director of
the American Foundation for Suicide Prevention, has written about
the case, "Like many people in extreme situations, Louise . . . expressed
two conflicting wishes—to live and to die—and found support only for
the latter."[50] One wonders what the outcome would have been had someone—*anyone*—supported Louise's often expressed desire to live and
had stayed with her to the natural end of her life. Perhaps, then, her
friends would have surrounded her in her final days. Perhaps Louise
and her mother would have had a more meaningful time together, spared

the undignified and excruciating dilemma over when and whether Louise would kill herself. Perhaps Louise could have truly died in peace.

4. *"No Simple Suicide" suggests that it should be easier to help people die.* Louise's assisted suicide took place in the underground, amid people who lied and broke the law in order to facilitate her so-called death with dignity. The attitude of the article is implicitly critical of the fact that this subterfuge was necessary. The reader is given a subliminal message, often voiced out loud by assisted-suicide advocates, that goes something like this: Unreasonable people who refuse to allow others to control their own destiny are insensitive, thoughtless, and cruel. They force dying people to endure unnecessary suffering. Such judgmental attitudes caused Louise's friends to abandon her when all she wanted to do was control the time and place of her own death. Her caring doctor was prevented from actively participating in her patient's final "treatment" because euthanasia by lethal injection is forbidden. Mero, a compassionate clergyman, was forced to risk imprisonment in his pursuit of providing care and comfort to the suffering.

THE OTHER SIDE OF THE STORY

The irony is that the members of the little group surrounding Louise were the ones who were thoughtless, insensitive, and cruel, for they took from Louise, in Dr. Hendin's words, "her own death."[51]

1. *Louise was unable to give informed consent to her suicide because she was denied information about hospice care.* The story indicates that both the doctor and Mero allowed Louise to believe that she would have to either die in a "facility" or kill herself at home. Apparently, neither discussed hospice care with Louise or described the palliative care that could have reduced her discomfort. It appears they presented Louise with a false dilemma.

2. *The medical assistant pushed Louise into going forward with the assisted suicide.* The medical assistant who suddenly embraced Louise as a friend is suspect. Was she part of a pro-euthanasia group? Did she have an agenda? We are not told. Was not Belkin even a little curious about this? Regardless of her motives, the assistant is a powerful actor throughout the drama, urging Louise on to self-destruction. Recall that when it became clear that Louise was delaying her self-destruction and appeared not to want to go forward, the medical assistant grew impatient and confronted the ill woman, saying, "I kind of want to get an idea of what your time line is. Where do we stand?"[52] When Louise says she doesn't want to talk about it but would rather wait for Mero to return to give his opinion of her medical condition, the friend tells her it is a "bad idea" and urges her not to wait because Mero may not be able to notice "subtle changes in Louise's temperament and thus might give the wrong advice."[53] That is pressure disguised as advice.

3. *Ralph Mero's "compassion" was available to Louise only if she carried out her designated role.* This is the most insidious part of the story. It is important to remember how emotionally vulnerable most terminally ill people are as the end of life approaches. Louise was certainly no exception. Then, along comes "compassionate" Ralph Mero—a minister, no less—who tells Louise, "I'll be with you and I'll support you." From that point on it is quite clear that Louise has become dependent on the moral judgment and emotional support of Mero, to the extent that she even wanted to rely on him for medical advice as to how far her decline had progressed.

Note that throughout the early part of the process, Mero was there for Louise. He held her hand. He patiently and gently went over the guidelines for the assisted suicide. He presented himself as a source of strength, a nonjudgmental rock to lean on in this difficult time. But when Louise hesitated and refused to be pressured into suicide, what did this altruistic man of compassion do? Did he hold her hand and discuss alternatives to killing, such as hospice care? Did he pray with

Louise so that together they could seek God's guidance? (He is a minister, after all.) Did he assure her that whatever her choice might be, he was her friend and would be there to the end? No. He withdrew: "Over the next few days, Mero checked in with Louise and her mother by telephone, but kept the conversation short. 'I was measuring my phone calls,' he says. He wanted to remain in the background and allow Louise to control the timing and pace. Her growing dependence on him was making him uncomfortable, and he needed to keep it clear in her mind, and his, that she was the driver and he was just along for the ride."[54] But when she seemed to be choosing a different course, his absence made it clear that Louise was on her own if she chose a natural death.

Imagine how painful it must have been for Louise when her minister, the man she was leaning on for strength and guidance, was suddenly holding her at arm's length, especially after being so intensely a part of her life over the previous weeks. This certainly looks like emotional manipulation on Mero's part, communicating a harsh and powerful message to the dying woman: kill yourself and I am your man; stick it out to the end and I am out of here. That is not compassion. That is cruel abandonment.

4. *The reporter also pushed Louise toward killing herself.* As if all of that isn't disturbing enough, what are we to make of the reporter, Lisa Belkin, and her participation in these sad events? Recall when the doctor informed Mero and the reporter that Louise was likely to slip quickly and become mentally incompetent and therefore become unable to kill herself or receive Mero's assistance, Belkin immediately flew to Seattle, unaware that Louise has not been told of this prognosis. During an interview on that occasion, Louise tells Belkin that she wants to wait a week or so before killing herself. Belkin is appalled:

> I was surprised, confused and extremely uncomfortable. . . . Without thinking, I blurted out a question: "Your doctor feels that if you don't act by this weekend, you may not be able to . . ."

My words were met with a wrenching silence. Louise blanched, her pale skin turned even paler. I was horrified with myself . . .

"She didn't . . . she never . . . I didn't know that," Louise said, sharply looking at her mother.

"That's what she told me," her mother offered gently.

Louise became silent. . . .

"It's O.K. to be afraid," her mother said.

"I'm not afraid. I just feel as if everyone is ganging up on me, pressuring me," Louise said. "I just want some time."[55]

Indeed, Louise was being pressured, now even by the reporter who at that point crossed the line from an observer and chronicler of events to a participant in them.

5. *There is no compassionate voice of opposition.* "No Simple Suicide" presents a one-sided version of assisted suicide. Except for one brief passage, people who resist legalizing euthanasia are not heard from, nor are the many reasons given why opponents of the death culture are so devoted in their resistance. Notice also that the one quotation selected for use in the article by Belkin, presumably from a longer interview, describes opponents to euthanasia as "harsh," reinforces the false stereotype that opposition is based primarily on religion, and does not express any concern for the well-being of Louise.

Such short shrift was not accorded proponents of assisted suicide. At one point in the article, Mero describes his work for Compassion in Dying as an experiment to "show, demonstrate, prove, that when people make a claim for humane treatment, it can be provided in a way that does not jeopardize vulnerable people or pose a threat to the social fabric."[56] Leaving aside the perversion of the word "treatment" in that sentence, we can assume that Mero hoped that by inviting Belkin to observe his work, his vision of a world where the ill can be routinely euthanized would be accepted by readers.

But as this analysis of "No Simple Suicide"—an article typical of this genre—demonstrates, what actually happened to Louise was just the opposite of the impression the story sought to convey. Instead of receiving compassion (literally, "suffering with") from those she trusted, a sick and vulnerable woman *was pushed* by them into suicide. In Dr. Hendin's words, Louise's "death was virtually clocked by their [Mero's, the doctor's, her mother's, the medical assistant's, Belkin's] anxiety that she might want to live. Mero and the doctor influence the feelings of the mother and the friend so that the issue is not their warm leave-taking . . . but whether they can get her to die according to the time requirements of Mero, the doctor, the reporter, and the disease. . . . Individually and collectively, those involved in [Louise's assisted suicide] engender a terror in Louise with which she must struggle alone, while they reassure each other that they are gratifying her last wishes."[57] Ralph Mero was unavailable for comment about my criticisms.[58]

THE STORY CONTINUES

A tragedy similar to Louise's took place in Australia in 2002. Nancy Crick had once believed she had terminal cancer. Urged on by euthanasia advocates who wished to use her assisted suicide as a bludgeon against anti-assisted suicide laws in that country, Crick created a website to publicize her planned self-destruction.

Crick's case and her decision to allow her suicide to be used as a political wedge led to planned suicide becoming a political and media sensation. Euthanasia advocates vocally urged her on, assuring Nancy and the country that her self-destruction would be a blow for self-determination and modernity. Some media outlets requested to be present to video tape her death. Instead of supporting her life, most of the public clamor urged Crick toward suicide. When Crick temporarily wavered, opting for palliative care, the disappointment of euthanasia advocates was obvious. One advocate complained that one of Crick's few remaining pleasures was smoking and she wouldn't be able to smoke in a hospital. Crick even received notes from assisted suicide advocates criticizing her for wavering in her desire to self-destruct.[59]

When Crick finally decided to take her poison, twenty-one "friends" and family joined her, adding further social pressure to the decision to die and making it difficult to change her mind. Demonstrating the mindset of many in the assisted suicide movement, they *applauded* when she swallowed the poison.[60]

Crick's death elated euthanasia advocates, especially her doctor, Dr. Philip Nitschke. Nitcshke was labeled with the moniker "Dr. Death" in Australia after his participation in assisted suicides (when the act was briefly legal in the Northern Territory) and because of his advocacy for buying a ship to commit mass euthanasia in international waters. For months he had orchestrated the publicity surrounding Crick's promised assisted suicide, but in the end did not even have the courage to be with her when she died. Yet despite his absence, Nitschke claimed triumphantly that with Crick's death "mass civil disobedience" had begun in the euthanasia movement.[61]

But then something happened that the euthanasia campaigners had not anticipated as they planned a public relations campaign around the Crick death. Crick's autopsy revealed that she was *not dying of cancer*. In fact, she wasn't dying at all. Rather, a twisted intestine had caused her difficulties. Her pain was apparently caused by a hernia and bowel adhesions, conditions that might have been correctable by surgery.[62]

After Crick died, the media reported that she actually knew beforehand that she was not dying of cancer—as did the primary booster of her suicide, her adviser Philip Nitschke. He and Crick had been told weeks before her suicide that Crick did not have terminal cancer. Proving that those in the right-to-die movement believe that their advocacy of assisted suicide means never having to say they are sorry, Nitschke brushed aside the news. Claiming to be "annoyed" that people were making an issue of Crick's non-cancer, Nitschke admitted that deceiving the media about her condition beforehand was "a mistake," but he called the matter "irrelevant" because Crick had thought that "death was preferable" to living with her ailment.[63, 64]

Still, there was little doubt that the news of Crick's non-cancer was a blow to the euthanasia cause. Dr. David Van Gend, a spokesman for TRUST, an Australian anti-euthanasia organization, reacting to the macabre circus-like atmosphere euthanasia advocates and the media had made of a desperate woman's suicidal state, said, "An atmosphere of pressure and expectation was put on this lady from which she could not retreat without extreme loss of face," a circumstance that he criticized as "akin to the psychological and emotional entanglement of a cult. She was a vulnerable lady."[65]

Dr. Hendin's point about the travesty of "No Simple Suicide" and Dr. Van Gend's observation about the appalling events leading to Crick's death are exactly right. What happened to Louise, Nancy Crick—and would happen to others if the euthanasia movement continues to metastasize—is not merely a "threat to the social fabric." It is, in fact, a rending of it.

2

Disposable People

ALMOST TWENTY YEARS AGO, I was an attorney working for a firm
that represented a sixteen-year-old girl, whom I will call Sally.[1]
Several years earlier Sally had undergone surgery to correct
progressive scoliosis, commonly known as curvature of the spine. At
the time of her operation, Sally was a bright, happy, alert twelve-year-
old with long blond hair. Her mother said she had a ready laugh, and
photographs showed a smile to knock your socks off.

As Sally was wheeled out of her room on a gurney for her surgery,
she turned to wave to her parents, a half-fearful smile on her face, and
her parents snapped a picture. This would be the last smiling picture
that would ever be taken of Sally.

Less than an hour later, Sally's heart stopped, a result of the negligence of her anesthesiologist. CPR was successful within a minute.
Inexplicably, surgery continued, and Sally had a second cardiac arrest.
This time her heart was still for twelve minutes before resuscitation
succeeded in saving her life.

Sally's brain, starved of oxygen, was severely injured. She was now
a quadriplegic and had a profound cognitive disability. She could not
feed herself, speak, or, some said, interact meaningfully with others.

The hospital doctors did what they could for her; then Sally was transferred to a state hospital where she lived in what used to be pejoratively called "the basket ward."

This was as difficult and tragic a case as I had ever seen in my legal career. A young girl's life was ruined, her family destroyed by grief and self-recriminations, which contributed mightily to her parents' subsequent divorce. Four years after her injury, Sally's father rarely spoke her name, and her mother had put her own life on hold so that she could devote herself almost entirely to her disabled daughter's care. The point of the lawsuit was to obtain enough money from the negligent doctor's malpractice insurance company to ensure that Sally would be cared for properly for the rest of her life.

Early on I decided that it was my professional duty to visit with my client, even though she would not know who I was or why I was there. But month after month I found excuse after excuse to put it off. I was busy, after all. Many clients required my attention. Besides, I worked hard. I deserved that fishing trip.

These were all rationalizations, of course. I was not so busy and in demand that I couldn't spare a few hours for the drive to the hospital and back. And even if the hectic pace of an active civil litigation practice kept me tied to my desk or in courtrooms, there were always the weekends. Finally I faced the hard fact: the real reason I hadn't visited Sally was that I was afraid.

It isn't easy seeing the Sallys of this world. They remind us too much of our own mortality, of life's caprice, of the possibility that we or a loved one could, like Sally, lose the ability to control our body, the ability to communicate, perhaps even to perceive. Is it any wonder, then, that many of us ignore such people and, when confronted with the reality of the severely disabled (and sometimes even the not-so-severely disabled), wish they would just go away?

As time passed and the case moved closer to trial, my shame at my cowardice finally overcame my fear. One day the unexpected settlement of a case opened up a block of free time. I found myself phoning

Sally's mother to arrange the visit. Twenty-four hours later I pulled into the parking lot next to the state hospital building in which Sally now resided.

I sighed nervously as I got out of the car. I did not want to do this! I still remember my heart pounding as I opened the door, walked to the elevator, and pushed the up button. My hands were sweating. Please, God, I thought as I entered the elevator, don't let it happen to me.

The elevator door opened. I breathed a deep sigh, walked down a hall, and entered Sally's ward. On my right was a long, narrow room filled with profoundly disabled people: dwarfs with heads enlarged by hydrocephaly; people of all ages apparently in comas; one unconscious or sleeping young woman, her face half-covered with small tumors while the other half was as clear as the skin of a magazine cover girl. A nurse later told me that she had one of the most rare conditions known to medical science.

Then, quietly, almost imperceptibly, my fear evaporated and was replaced by feelings of comfort, then warmth, and then, much to my amazement, joy. Here was a very human place. Curtains were hung, and bright colors were painted throughout. There were plants around. Window shades were open to admit sunlight. The place smelled clean, fresh—not antiseptic. The nurses were deeply caring toward, indeed loving to, their patients. The mood in the ward was relaxed and gentle. I realized this was a home in the truest sense.

Then the nurses wheeled Sally to me. I would not have recognized her. She was lying in a bed, her eyes open but seemingly unaware and unable to focus on her surroundings. The pretty, optimistic face I knew from her pre-surgery photographs was gone, obliterated and distorted by her anti-seizure medication. Many of her teeth were now missing. Her hair was short and stringy.

Yet none of that mattered. Sally was profoundly disabled, but that did not prevent her humanity from shining brightly through the veneer of difference. I experienced her as a sublime, even beautiful, presence. My heart opened like a blossom unfolding.

I held her hand and began to sing to her. For some reason, I chose Dean Martin's theme song: "Everybody loves somebody sometime. Everybody loves someone somehow." As I sang, Sally's eyes focused, and she looked up at me. She smiled and lifted her head. She liked my singing. The nurses gathered around. Sally began to "sing" too, although it sounded more like a moan because she could not form words. Still, there was no doubting the happiness in her eyes and the smile on her face. Tears were in all our eyes (except Sally's) as we all joined in singing together. It was a precious moment that will remain with me for the rest of my life. I spent an hour with Sally, holding her hand, singing to her. She was no longer an abstraction but a client and, I felt, a friend.

I came away from that experience a better man, unalterably convinced of two things: Sally had bad taste in music, and she was fully and completely a human being, worthy of the same love, care, and respect as all of us. Sally's case ultimately was settled for a very large sum, enough to assure her the best of medical care for the rest of her life.

A CHANGED WORLD

Before the euthanasia consciousness seeped into America's culture, society expected the Sallys among us to receive proper and humane care. The equality-of-human-life ethic demanded it. They, like those who were not cognitively disabled, were human beings, equally endowed with the inherent human right to live.

The actual practice of caring for disabled people did not always rise to the ideal, of course. Some of our most vulnerable citizens were subjected to horrible conditions and truly terrible abuse. That did not mean, however, that the equality-of-human-life ethic itself was compromised. Quite the opposite. It was the belief that each of us has inherent equal worth that caused us to demand reform and improved care whenever gross misconduct was exposed.

Times change, and not always for the better. People like Sally are for the most part viewed quite differently today. "In a short time, we have gone from the attitude that all of our patients are human who deserve care—no matter what their level of functioning—to believing that some people aren't people anymore," says Sharon S. Orr, a registered nurse who has spent a career caring for profoundly brain-damaged people.[2] She would know. One of her charges was a young woman named Nancy Cruzan, who was the subject of a United States Supreme Court decision that made legal history.

As we move into the twenty-first century, the once broad consensus in favor of the equality-of-human-life ethic has been substantially undermined. Not that we don't decry physical and mental abuse of the physically and mentally disabled. But a growing number of people no longer believe that cognitively disabled people possess the same inherent human worth and right to live as those of us who are able-bodied, "productive," and generally pleasing to look at. Indeed, to a disturbing degree many in the legal and medical and bioethics communities, in academia, within religious institutions, and among the general public view these helpless people as pointless and useless burdens to themselves, their families, and society. Some have always believed this, of course. What has changed is that such beliefs have become respectable and mainstream.

When a value as fundamental as the equality-of-human-life ethic is weakened, it changes our attitudes toward each other, our behavior, our concept of what constitutes a humane and compassionate society. We no longer speak of people such as Sally and Nancy Cruzan as possessing an inherent right to live. Instead, we proclaim their inalienable "right to die."

ROBERT WENDLAND

"Wife requesting transfer [of Robert] to discontinue tube feeding for euthanasia," the concerned nurse wrote in the nursing notes that became a part of Robert Wendland's medical records. "Caloric needs have increased . . . [due to] his hard work in therapies. The shock of this decision and committee approval! Is very difficult for obvious reason of his progression."[3]

In 1993, Robert Wendland, then forty-two, came home from an all-night drunk and was confronted by his wife, Rose, and his brother, Mike. An angry argument ensued. Rose told him that if he continued drinking and driving he would end up dead, kill someone else, or spend the rest of his life in a hospital, and that the family would all have to suffer for it.[4]

Robert dismissed her concerns, replying that if such a thing happened, if he could not live as a full man and support his family, he would rather be dead. Robert could not know it but these words would later be used as evidence in a bitter and angry litigation between Rose and his mother, Florence Wendland, a case that would reach the California Supreme Court, make national headlines, be covered on network television news programs such as *Today* and *Good Morning America*, and be the subject of numerous articles in some of the nation's foremost bioethics, legal, and medical journals.

One week after the argument, Robert was catastrophically injured in a terrible alcohol-related auto accident. He was unconscious, a condition from which doctors predicted he would never emerge. But doctors, being human, make mistakes. In January 1995, Robert began to stir. At first the changes were almost imperceptible: a grimace here, a hand movement there. Soon there was no doubt: Robert was conscious.

According to court testimony by his nurses and therapists, confirmed by the medical records, after he awakened, Robert's condition dramatically improved throughout the spring of 1995. He learned to maneuver a motorized wheelchair on command and avoid obstacles, and at least once he even wheeled himself out of the hospital. Just a few months after waking up, he was able to respond to requests such as "Hand me the ball" 80 to 100 percent of the time. As proved by a videotape taken of one of Robert's therapy sessions, he was able to retrieve and return colored pegs from a tray when asked to do so by a therapist, evidence of sophisticated neurological function.[5] He was able to support up to 110

pounds on one of his legs, which meant his muscle tone was returning.[6] Although unable to communicate meaningfully, he showed emotional responses to his environment. For example, his mother testified
that when asked, "Do you want to kiss my hand, Robert?" he would
sometimes take her hand to his lips and kiss her. When asked if he
wanted her to kiss his hand, he would sometimes "hold his hand up to
my lips and allow me to kiss it."[7]

By every measure Robert's cognition level and physical abilities
were far above Sally's. Yet where only ten years before, she benefited
from kind and loving care in a healthcare world where no one seriously
would have proposed taking action to end her life, Robert's doctors
and his wife, Rose, wanted to take away Robert's tube-supplied food
and fluids in order that he dehydrate to death.

In a better world, Rose's request would have been rejected out of
hand by Robert's doctors and the Lodi Memorial Hospital Ethics Committee. But illustrating the extent to which people with profound cognitive impairments are devalued in our culture and the extent to which
the equality-of-human-life ethic has already been undermined, the very
people responsible for protecting defenseless patients supported Rose's
decision. The conduct of the ethics committee is especially troubling.
Rather than giving all benefit of the doubt to life, committee members
seem to have done just the opposite. As far as is known, no one argued
on behalf of saving Robert's life. The nurses and therapists who spent
the most time with Robert—many of whom were extremely upset by
Rose's decision—were never asked their opinions. Indeed, Robert's
mother (who had visited her son almost daily since his accident) and
his sisters—all of whom would have argued against his dehydration—
were not even told that it was being contemplated. (Robert's brother,
Mike, who supported Rose, was aware of her decision.)

There were probably no disabled people on the committee who
might have better defended Robert's right to life. (The exact makeup
of the committee has been kept a closely guarded secret.) Moreover,
the county ombudsman, whose specific job was to be Robert's advo-

cate, supported Rose's decision without taking the time to learn that Robert could maneuver a wheelchair.[8] The ombudsman testified in court that her primary concern was to determine whether Rose's decision was made in haste. Once she believed that it was not, the ombudsman had no problem with the dehydration.[9]

Robert would have died then and there but for an anonymous nurse who risked being fired by blowing the whistle to one of Robert's sisters. Robert's mother, Florence, and one of his sisters, Rebekah Vinson, decided to sue to save his life. They asked the Stockton, California, attorneys Janie Hickock Siess and John McKinley to represent them. When Siess learned the facts of the case, she was stunned. "I knew from my studies in law school about the Cruzan case (see below) that unconscious people could have their food and fluids terminated, but I had no idea that anyone would ever consider dehydrating a conscious human being. But, here it was. The plans to end Robert's life had already been made. He was to be discharged from the hospital, picked up by an ambulance, brought to a skilled nursing facility, where he would be starved to death. I couldn't believe it. I thought, this can't be legal. What sane person would want to do this?"[10]

Siess and McKinley quickly obtained an injunction prohibiting the dehydration, setting the stage for a momentous six year, bitter roller-coaster court battle between Rose on one side and her mother- and sister-in-law on the other. The issue at stake: should the law permit Robert's feeding tube be removed in order that he die by dehydration?

It is important to emphasize that Robert was not terminally ill. His doctor admitted on the witness stand that there was no medical reason to withhold food and fluids.[11] His life was threatened with termination solely because it was not viewed as worth living, a view Rose claimed Robert would have shared before he was injured, and thus, she contended, his death would protect his personal autonomy. Yet whatever Robert's previous feelings about profound disability, post-injury he cooperated in his therapy, at least implying that he wanted to live. Moreover, he was sometimes able to answer yes and no questions by pushing a button ("Is your name Michael?" No. "Is your name Robert?" Yes.). When asked whether he wanted to die, intriguingly, he did not answer.[12]

In the early 1980s, when I met Sally—a young woman with even more profound disabilities than Robert Wendland—no one even contemplated taking away her food and fluids. Yet only ten years later, a hospital ethics committee unanimously recommended that a wife be permitted to order an end to her husband's life even though he was not terminally ill and did not require high tech medical life support. How can this be?

In order to understand the radical transformation of medical ethics during the last twenty years, we must discuss two related, but distinct, concepts. The first is the absolute right of all patients, no matter what their condition, to receive humane care. The other is the right of patients or their surrogates to refuse or discontinue unwanted treatment.

Humane care consists of basic non-medical services that each human being is absolutely entitled to receive in a medical setting: warmth, shelter, cleanliness, etc. No matter how ill a patient, no matter the level of his or her disability, humane care can never be withdrawn ethically— even if the patient would prefer it. For example, if a patient wanted to die by hypothermia by being left uncovered in front of an open window during a blizzard, medical personnel would have to refuse the request.

Medical treatment consists of action taken by doctors or other healthcare professionals whose purpose is to provide a medical benefit to the patient. Obvious examples of medical treatment are surgery, prescribed medications, diagnostic tests, and the like. Unlike the case with humane care, *the patient must consent to receive medical treatment* and may at any time refuse or discontinue such care. This right exists even if the refusal of treatment will likely result in death. Hence, a cancer patient is entitled to refuse chemotherapy, and the heart disease patient can refuse bypass surgery.

The differences between warmth and chemotherapy are clear examples of the distinction between humane care and medical treatment.

It was not too many years ago that food and fluids were considered humane care. That is no longer true, at least for food and water supplied through a feeding tube. Such care has been redefined as medical treatment, providing an excuse to end the lives of cognitively disabled people while retaining the pretense of ethical medical practice.

This did not just happen; it resulted from a deliberate campaign. The medical intelligentsia began to worry about the cost of caring for dependent people and the growing number of elderly. At the same time, personal autonomy increasingly became a driving force in medical ethics, and some began to look for a way to hasten the deaths of the most marginal people without seeming to be actually killing the patient and thereby arousing public hostility and opposition.

Removing food and fluids provided by tube was seen as the answer. After all, it was rationalized, the use of a feeding tube (whether in the stomach or through the nasal passage) requires a minor medical procedure. Moreover, the nutrition supplied by tube is not steak and potatoes but a liquid formula prepared under medical auspices to ease digestion. The term "artificial nutrition" was coined, making it appear that what was being withheld or withdrawn was not food and water but medicine, that is, medical treatment.

From such small beginnings—changes in definitions and terminology—have come profound consequences. The "food and fluid" cases have rippled through traditional medical ethics and public morality, undermining one of the primary purposes for which our government has been instituted: the protection of the lives of all of its citizens.

DESTINATION: EUTHANASIA

The theologian Richard John Neuhaus has written, "Thousands of ethicists and bioethicists, as they are called, professionally guide the unthinkable on its passage through the debatable on its way to becoming the justifiable until it is finally established as the unexceptional."[13] Neuhaus's point is that the loosening of ethical guidelines generally occurs first among self-described healthcare "bioethicists," theorists, philosophers, physicians, and academics long before attracting public attention. These ivory-tower types argue behind the scenes in the medical literature, in professional organizations, in universities, and at conventions about the alleged need to "reform" existing standards of morality, ethics, healthcare protocols, and public policy. The debates, which receive little if any media attention, rage for a few years and eventually culminate in a rough consensus that gives both "liberals" and "conservatives" something of what they want: an agreement that policies should change, tempered by "guidelines" to prevent abuse.[14]

The next step is usually a series of legal test cases in which the judges generally lean on the testimony of expert witnesses—often the very doctors and bioethicists pushing the new agenda—who assure the judge that the healthcare profession has worked it all through and reached an ethical consensus. Most judges decide the case along the lines of this so-called consensus. After all, the judge will reason, I am trained in law, not medicine. If doctors and professional ethicists think it is right, who am I, a mere judge, to determine otherwise? The judge's own prejudices and fears about disability or dying may also play a part in the decision.

The court's imprimatur in turn legitimizes a new morality among the public. The media pick up the baton, running sympathetic stories that play on the emotions of the moment rather than the likely consequences. Soon, public opinion polls reflect the public's increasing acceptance of policies they would once have disdained, which stimulates politicians to frame the policy as statutory law or at least deters them from leading any opposition. In the end, as Neuhaus wrote, what once was unthinkable becomes the starting point for the slide down the next portion of the slope.

This general pattern can be seen at work in the dehydration cases. The fundamental moral consensus that required the cognitively disabled to receive humane care, including nutrition and fluids for the duration of their natural lives, was attacked in this manner and eventually broken in the 1980s.[15] In March 1986, the first concrete step was taken to legitimize the intentional dehydration of unconscious, non-terminally ill patients. The American Medical Association Council on Ethical and Judicial Affairs, responsible for deliberating upon, and issuing, ethics advisories for the AMA, issued the following opinion: Although a physician "should never intentionally cause death," it was ethical to terminate life support treatment, even if "death is not imminent but a patient's coma is beyond doubt irreversible and there are adequate safeguards to confirm the accuracy of the diagnosis and with the concurrence of those who have responsibility for the care of the patient. . . . Life-prolonging medical treatment includes medication and artificially or technologically supplied respiration, nutrition and hydration."[16]

There it was. For the first time, food and fluids provided by a feeding tube were "officially" deemed a medical treatment that could be withdrawn ethically, the same as turning off a respirator or stopping kidney dialysis. The opinion, written in passive prose, appears very narrowly drawn. Only those who "beyond doubt" were permanently unconscious were supposed to be eligible for terminating the "treatment." And protective guidelines were supposed to protect against abuses. In actuality, a Pandora's box had been opened wide.

Nancy Cruzan

Once "consensus" was reached to allow intentional dehydration, at least in some situations, the issue was ripe for adjudication. Lawsuits were soon filed requesting legal sanction for making disabled patients die by dehydration. The case of Nancy Cruzan had the greatest impact. Indeed, not only did the Cruzan case open the door wide to removing food and fluids from cognitively disabled patients, but it also became intertwined with the debate on assisted suicide.

On January 11, 1983, Nancy lost control of her car on an icy road in Missouri and crashed. Thrown from her car, she landed face down in a water-filled ditch. Nancy's heart stopped, but paramedics revived her.

Nancy's injuries included profound cognitive disability. In the media and in books about her case she is usually described as unconscious from the time of the accident, but that does not appear to be true.[17] For a period of time after the accident, Nancy was able to chew and swallow food and drink fluids. Indeed, she was first put on a feeding tube to make her long-term care easier. There was also evidence that she could hear and see; she smiled at amusing stories and sometimes cried when visitors left.[18]

While the actual level of her abilities was (and still is) in some dispute, no one contends that Nancy required intensive-care hospitalization or skilled nursing care. She was not on a respirator, nor did she receive dialysis. She was not terminally ill. All she required to maintain her life was humane care: nutrition, fluids, warmth, cleaning, and turning to prevent bedsores or pneumonia.

If Nancy was unconscious, as her parents and proponents of cutting off her food and fluids claimed, then she was in no pain. The same cannot be said of her mother and father. Who can doubt that seeing a loved child so profoundly disabled over many years was agonizing for the Cruzans, a deep psychic wound that never healed. Perhaps the depth of their pain led them to consult with the Society for the Right to Die about ways to bring an end to Nancy's life.

In May 1987, the year after the AMA ethics council's opinion was published, the Cruzans filed a lawsuit seeking to force hospital employees where Nancy was living to remove their daughter's food and fluids. Hospital administrators and especially the nurses who cared for Nancy, who saw her as a living, breathing human being deserving of respect and proper care, resisted. They wanted, not to kill their patient, but to continue to care for her. However, they were unable to persuade jasper County Circuit Court judge Charles E. Teel to let Nancy live. He ordered the hospital to do as the Cruzans requested.

The Missouri Department of Health appealed the decision. On November 16, 1988, the Missouri Supreme Court reversed the trial court. The court found, "This is not a case in which we are asked to let someone die . . . . This is a case in which we are asked to allow the medical profession *to make Nancy die* by starvation and dehydration."[19]

It was on to the United States Supreme Court. The Court's decision in *Cruzan v. Director, Missouri Department of Health* dealt primarily with the evidentiary standard established in Missouri law, which was that life support could be withdrawn from an incompetent patient only if there was "clear and convincing evidence" that the person would have wanted the treatment terminated. The Court upheld this requirement as constitutional, ruling that such a strict standard was properly in keeping with the state's obligation to protect the lives of its citizens. Since no clear and convincing evidence had been offered in the trial that removing food and fluids was what Nancy would have wanted—as opposed to what her parents desired for her—Missouri could require that Nancy's life support continue.[20] (Unfortunately, the Court also accepted by implication that tube-supplied food and fluids is a form of medical treatment that can be withdrawn like any other form of treatment. Pro-euthanasia advocates often claim that this aspect recognized a new "right to die." It did not. It involved the right to refuse medical treatment, a different matter entirely.)

What at first appeared to be a victory turned sour. The Cruzans went back to the original trial court. This time, two of Nancy's former coworkers came forward to describe a conversation that, they testified, had occurred many years before, while the participants were engaged in their work activities. The details were sketchy, but the gist of the testimony was that Nancy had indicated she would not want to live in a coma. The witnesses could not confirm either her exact words or whether she had made a statement herself or simply agreed to a statement made by another. But that was all Judge Teel required to rule that the Cruzans had provided clear and convincing evidence that Nancy would want her treatment ceased.

There was no appeal. By this time, the Missouri Department of Health had abandoned the case, deciding to allow Nancy's parents to have their way. Those who opposed the ruling—and who did not believe that the testimony came anywhere near to "clear and convincing"—were not parties to the case and thus were powerless to intervene. Nancy's foods and fluids were withdrawn on December 14, 1990. She died twelve days later. The cause of death listed on her death certificate: dehydration.

In August 1996, the Cruzan family suffered another tragedy when Nancy's father, Joe Cruzan, hanged himself in the family home. Joe was described by family and friends as unable to recover emotionally from his daughter's death. Dr. Ronald Cranford, a neurologist and euthanasia advocate who often testifies as an expert witness in favor of dehydrating cognitively disabled patients (including Nancy Cruzan and Robert Wendland, as well as Christine Busalacchi and Michael Martin, whose cases I discuss below), was a friend of Joe Cruzan's. Cranford characterized Cruzan's tragic death as a "rational suicide" because, despite treatment, "He was never going to get better."[21] Joe Cruzan left behind a wife and two other children.

Christine Busalacchi

Since Nancy Cruzan's death, the starving and dehydration of cognitively disabled patients has become almost routine in hospitals and nursing homes all around the country. Moreover, such killings have definitely not been limited to people who, in the words of the AMA ethics council opinion, are "beyond doubt" permanently unconscious. When the parents of Christine Busalacchi, a twenty-year-old auto accident victim, sought permission to end their daughter's life, doctors described her condition as a persistent vegetative state (PVS). In PVS the patient has sleep and wake cycles but lacks reflex response and does not interact with his environment. The patient's eyes may be open, but he is believed to be unaware. This is distinct from a coma, where the patient's eyes are closed. Christine's father, Pete Busalacchi, believed that his daughter was "One hundred percent gone."[22] Dr. Ronald Cranford, testifying in favor of dehydrating Christine, dehumanized her by saying, "She's got a shell of a body, lying there with a brain stem."[23]

Yet nurses and medical personnel who had close interaction with Christine told a different story. Their descriptions do not come close to PVS. Some testified they had heard her grunt to indicate her choice of soap opera on television. They told of her smiling and interacting with favorite nurses. Nurse Sharon Orr recalls, "Christine was awake and alert. She would push buttons to call us. She would eat a bite and push a button, saying another bite please. We fed her with a spoon."[24] A videotape of Christine released to the media showed that she could indeed eat food by mouth, press a switch to ask for food, and obey simple requests. There is no doubt Christine was profoundly disabled, but it is highly unlikely that she was permanently unconscious.[25]

Christine's father strongly objected to the release of the videotape, claiming it was a violation of his daughter's privacy. But perhaps he was more upset because, as the old saying goes, a picture is worth a thousand words. Indeed, Rose Wendland made the same objection after KRON television in San Francisco aired a video of Robert performing simple tasks and I wrote an opinion article in the *San Francisco Chronicle* publicizing concerns about the quality of Robert's medical care.[26, 27] Rose, supported by a friend of the court brief filed by the Lodi Memorial Hospital, went so far as to unsuccessfully seek a court order from Judge McNatt imposing secrecy on the entire case.

As to the observations of Christine's nurses, Dr. Cranford discounted them, claiming that the nurses were too emotionally involved to see the truth about Christine's condition. This conforms to a pattern in these cases: judges often discount the opinions of nurses who have the closest relations with patients, while being swayed by doctors who may only have spent a few minutes examining the person.

Compelling evidence of her consciousness was not enough to save Christine's life. Nancy Cruzan had broken the ice. A new health-policy paradigm was taking control. It was not the presence or absence of consciousness that mattered. What counted was the view that death was the answer to profound cognitive disability. Since dehydration was considered appropriate for the unconscious, why not also the conscious who required a feeding tube? Christine soon followed Nancy into death by means of intentional dehydration.

The slide down the slippery slope from dehydrating the unconscious (assuming for the sake of argument that Cruzan was unconscious) to dehydrating the conscious but cognitively disabled (Busalacchi and other conscious cognitively disabled people who have met a similar fate) belies the argument that policies that permit the killing of patients can be strictly controlled. The carefully shaded moral distinctions in which the healthcare intelligentsia of bioethics and policymakers take so much pride are of little consequence in the real world of cost-controlled medical practice, in busy hospital settings, and among families suffering the emotional trauma and bearing the financial costs of caring for a severely brain damaged relative. Once killing is seen as an appropriate answer in a few cases, the ground quickly gives way, and it becomes the answer in many cases.

The deadly logic of its earlier decision to permit the withdrawal of tube feeding from unconscious people soon led the AMA to expand the list of those whose lives could be ended by dehydration. In 1994, a brief eight years after its first opinion reclassifying tube feeding as medical, instead of humane, treatment, the AMA Council on Ethics and Judicial Affairs made a crucial revision. Where once the patient had to be "beyond doubt" permanently unconscious to permit withdrawing food and fluids, now "even if the patient is not terminally ill or permanently unconscious, it is not unethical to discontinue all means of life-sustaining medical treatment [including food and fluids] in accordance with a proper substituted judgment or best interests analysis."[28]

This is a classic example of the slippery slope. When it became clear that the original guidelines were not being adhered to, the guidelines were simply expanded rather than enforced more rigorously. This, in turn, formally legitimized practices that a few years before had been deemed completely unacceptable. For example, now that the practice of dehydrating conscious cognitively disabled people is permitted in almost every state—so long as no family members object—the next step down the slope is already being taken: forced removal of feeding tubes from unconscious patients whose families want their lives sustained. This new bioethics agenda, known as "futile care theory," will be discussed in detail in chapter 6.

Proponents of dehydration contend that deaths by dehydration are peaceful. They point to the peaceful deaths of terminally ill patients who die after refusing food and water as a natural part of the dying process. But in such cases, it is medically inappropriate to force food and water upon the patient. The patients we are discussing are not terminally ill. Indeed, those who are conscious can feel hunger and thirst.

St. Louis neurologist Dr. William Burke, who opposes withholding food and water from cognitively disabled patients, claims that death by dehydration is painful: "A conscious person would feel it [dehydration] just as you or I would. They will go into seizures. Their skin cracks, their tongue cracks, their lips crack. They may have nosebleeds because of the drying of the mucus membranes, and heaving and vomiting might ensue because of the drying out of the stomach lining. They feel the pangs of hunger and thirst. Imagine going one day without a glass of water! Death by dehydration takes ten to fourteen days. It is an extremely agonizing death."[29]

Dr. Ronald Cranford, who testified in the Wendland case that he participates in withholding food and fluids from his PVS and conscious but cognitively disabled patients, reinforced such worries. Admitting that the lips, eyes, and tongue of a person being dehydrated "get extremely dry" and acknowledging that "anything that is dry for a long period of time may crack. And anything that may crack may bleed." Cranford testified that it is rare for dehydrating patients to experience

seizures. Nevertheless, even Cranford's description of dehydration reveals how awful it is. He testified that dehydration usually takes between ten and fourteen days, but in some cases up to twenty-one days:

> After seven to nine days [from commencing dehydration] they
> begin to lose all fluids in the body, a lot of fluids in the body. And
> their blood pressure starts to go down.
>
> When their blood pressure goes down, their heart rate goes
> up. . . . Their respiration may increase and then the patient expe-
> riences what's called a mammalian's diver's reflex where the blood
> is shunted to the central part of the body from the periphery of
> the body. So, that usually two to three days prior to death, some-
> times four days, the hands and the feet become extremely cold.
> They become mottled. That is, you look at the hands and they
> have a bluish appearance.
>
> And the mouth dries a great deal, and the eyes dry a great
> deal and other parts of the body become mottled. And that is
> because the blood is now so low in the system it's shunted to the
> heart and other visceral organs and away from the periphery of
> the body.[30]

To counter worries about inducing an agonizing death, doctors
generally prescribe morphine or other narcotics. But who knows
whether this precaution truly masks the patient's agony. For example,
when the lawyer Janie Hickock Siess asked Dr. Cranford what level of
morphine would have to be given to Robert Wendland to prevent him
from suffering from the symptoms of dehydration, he testified that the
dose would be "arbitrary" because "you don't know how much he's
suffering, you don't know how much aware he is. . . . You're guessing at
the dose."[31] Moreover, he stated at the trial that he would probably put
Robert Wendland back into a coma to ensure that he did not feel agony.[32]
(How tragically ironic. The patient struggles out of a sixteen month
coma and is threatened with being drugged back into one so he can be

made dead.) Thus, even according to dehydration advocate Cranford, the prospect of agony in conscious people who are dehydrated to death is very real.

Causing suffering via dehydration is only the beginning of our worries. The attitude that it is better to die than to become cognitively disabled has so pervaded the culture of healthcare that some doctors are beginning to worry about a rush to write off newly unconscious patients and consign them to death by cutting off life support before they have a chance to recover. According to Dr. Vincent Fortanasce, a board-certified neurologist and psychiatrist, too many doctors are making diagnoses of permanent unconsciousness prematurely—after only a few days or a week—when it takes at least three to six months to make a firm diagnosis.[33] "Eighty to ninety percent of the cases I see have been improperly diagnosed," Fortanasce says, "often by doctors who are not qualified to make the determination. Unfortunately, that's the real practice in medicine today."

Dr. Fortanasce recounts one example from his own practice of this rush to write off unconscious patients. A sixty-year-old patient collapsed and was diagnosed as PVS by his internist, who strongly urged the family to discontinue all life support, including nutrition. The family was reluctant, and so they sought a second opinion from Dr. Fortanasce. "I came in, took the appropriate tests. The patient was not PVS. He had experienced a severe brain seizure. I prescribed continued life support and medication. A week later, the patient walked out of the hospital in full possession of his faculties. Had the family listened to the internist, the man would be dead today."[34]

The frequency of such cases is unknown: so far, no studies have been done. In most cases the withdrawal of food and fluids is done with the consent of the families, so no notice is taken. Unless someone objects to the dehydration or the premature withholding of life support, the patients die and no one is the wiser.

DECISIONS OF LIFE AND DEATH

The legality of dehydrating the cognitively disabled has not yet been set completely in concrete. Many relatives of the unconscious and cognitively disabled refuse to permit their loved ones to be killed. A few courageous judges, such as Alabama's Pamela Willis Beschab, still hold the legal line against these killings. When relatives of Correan Salter, a stroke patient, wanted a court ruling permitting her dehydration, Judge Beschab refused, writing, "Once the state accepts a policy that some lives are not worthy to be lived and some people would be better off dead, it takes the first step on a long and slippery slope from which there can be no turning back."[35] Unfortunately, most judges and family members are swept along by the prevailing cultural tide.

The following recent cases illustrate the acute and never-ending danger to the weakest and most helpless among us.

Ronald Comeau

On June 21, 1993, Ronald Comeau, a thirty-year-old drifter, was arrested in Bennington, Vermont, accused of robbing another homeless man. Comeau grew despondent. Alone, his freedom forfeited, he had no one to turn to. It had been a very long time since he had had any contact with his father, and their relationship had never been good. His mother had no phone. He hadn't seen his brothers for nearly seven years. He was without a future, without hope. Not even the police cared enough to watch him in the station holding cell. Soon after Comeau was put in the cell, a police officer found him hanging from a noose apparently made from the trim of a cheap jail blanket.

Unconscious, Comeau was cut down. He had no pulse and didn't appear to be breathing. CPR was administered, restoring a weak pulse. An ambulance ride in the dead of night to the Southwestern Vermont Medical Center followed the arrival of paramedics and more CPR.

By the time Comeau arrived in the emergency room, he once again had no heartbeat. Doctors urgently commenced advanced life support: an injection of atropine and two pulses of electricity to the heart. After minutes of silence, the cardiac monitor began to register a heartbeat. Despite being without a pulse for about fifteen minutes, Ronald Comeau was alive.[36]

There is nothing unusual about any of this. Go to any big city hospital or small town medical center and sooner or later you will see the unwashed and unwanted who are helped as much as possible and then soon forgotten. But few who became involved with him after his suicide attempt would ever forget Ronald Comeau.

Within hours of Comeau's near death, the hospital located his father, Renald Dupois of Maine. Amy Swisher, the director of community relations for Southwestern Vermont Medical Center, says that the doctors and hospital personnel followed procedures that are standard in cases such as Comeau's: they advised Dupois that his son was severely injured and might die, requested permission for HIV testing, and asked about the possibility of organ donation, should he die.[37] There is some dispute as to the accuracy of this account. However, it is not disputed that Dupois failed to come to his son's bedside. Worse, soon after the hospital's call, his phone was disconnected.

Decisions still needed to be made about Comeau's medical treatment. Seemingly abandoned, without family available to make them, the time had come to obtain a court-appointed guardian to make decisions on his behalf. At this point, Joseph Schaaf became involved. He was well known in the local legal community because of his volunteer work as a guardian *ad litem* (a temporary representative during a court case) in local child custody matters. He agreed to serve as Comeau's permanent guardian without pay and was so appointed by Judge Doris Buchanan of Bennington Probate Court, on July 23, 1993.

Schaaf took his responsibilities to Ronald Comeau very seriously, visiting at least five days a week and discussing the case with doctors and staff as he contemplated what would be best for his ward. By mid-August, the guardian had come to a difficult decision. Comeau had been diagnosed as being in an irreversible persistent vegetative state. He was awake, he had reflexes, but he was not aware. There appeared to be no cognitive ability whatsoever. Schaaf instructed Stephen Saltonstall, his pro bono attorney in the Comeau matter, to seek permission from the probate court to remove the ventilator that aided Comeau's breathing, which he expected to lead to the young man's death.

On August 17, Judge Buchanan held a hearing. On the basis of the testimony of the attending physician, Dr. Michael Algus, and a consulting neurologist, Dr. Keith Edwards, she ruled that Comeau was a "blind quadriplegic" who was "unaware" of what was happening "around him and to him" and that there was "no reasonable possibility of recovery or improvement." Convinced it was in Comeau's best interests, she signed the order permitting the ventilator to be withdrawn.[38]

This was soon accomplished. But not only didn't Comeau die, he actually began to improve. By the middle of September the unexpected was a reality: Comeau was awake and aware. But this was not viewed as a cause for joy. Joe Schaaf was horrified by Comeau's condition. "I saw a person who could register some feelings but those feelings were pain, agony and fear," he recalls. "His hands were bent in toward his wrists. It appeared he was trying to remove his feeding tube. Whether it was a conscious act, I couldn't tell."[39]

But others sometimes saw a different Ronald Comeau. The speech-language pathologist Juanita J. Cook noted: "Seems to recognize personnel—favorite nurses. On 9/21 definitely responded with recognition today when I went in and said my name, reminding him that I was the person who came in to talk—not to do any direct care, etc.—Big smile, with overall body movement. Very different from the grimace at having hands restrained."[40] Other notes in Comeau's medical file show a man who was aware—sometimes grimacing, seemingly in pain; at other times intently concentrated on discussions about his future care.

Despite Comeau's obvious cognitive improvements, Schaaf began to discuss the issue of removing his feeding tube with doctors and other medical personnel. He says of his thinking at that time, "I thought that if it were me there, lying helpless in a bed, I hope to God that someone would help me move on from my misery to whatever comes next, because whatever comes next can't be worse than that."[41] On the basis of these personal fears, Schaaf decided to pursue the option of having Comeau's food and fluids withheld.

Not everyone approved of the proposal. Dr. Edwards, the consulting neurologist, wrote a report stating in part, "Although I would have no ethical or moral problems in letting . . . a medical complication go untreated, it is difficult to support withdrawing nutrition in a patient who is demonstrating some neurological function. . . . [I] would continue comfort care and nutritional care as currently undertaken."[42]

Psychiatrist Dr. Peter Zorach was the chairman of the Southwestern Medical Center Ethics Committee at the time of these events. In October 1993 Joe Schaaf asked the committee for its formal opinion on his plan to starve and dehydrate Ron Comeau to death. Comeau was neither terminally ill nor in an irreversible coma. He was awake and aware, if profoundly brain damaged and disabled. At the time, the 1986 AMA Council on Ethics and Judicial Affairs opinion was in effect. Indeed, it had been reiterated in 1992. Had its guidelines been followed, Comeau would not have been a candidate for dehydration.

But if the guidelines concerned the ethics committee, it was not apparent. Dr. Zorach described the subjective nature of the committee deliberations as follows: "We had a discussion. We weren't going to take a vote but Mr. Schaaf felt it would be helpful to him if he knew whether people would support his position. There were people in the discussion who had taken part in Mr. Comeau's care and who were able to express observations about what could be done. We imagined that his being in a hospital bed not able to move, might be a frustrating experience. If being in jail made him so unhappy that he wanted to kill himself, then being in a hospital partially paralyzed would also make him unhappy. People felt that he was not happy and that there was not much likelihood that he would ever be happy. His emotions usually looked like fear, anger, rage and sometimes sadness."[43] The vote was ten to three to support whatever decision Joe Schaaf might make on behalf of his ward—including completing Ronald Comeau's suicide attempt by withdrawing his food and fluids.

On November 9, Saltonstall and Schaaf appeared before Judge Buchanan for the purpose of determining whether Comeau's feeding tube should be removed. Drs. Algus and Zorach testified in support of removing nutritional care. No one argued against removal. Dr. Edwards's report recommending against this course was not mentioned to the judge. Saltonstall says he was unaware of Dr. Edwards's opinion.[44] It was disclosed that Comeau was no longer PVS and that he had improved in the weeks since the previous hearing seeking permission to remove the ventilator. But the judge seems not to have grasped the implications of the fact that the same people who argued for ending Comeau's life at that earlier time were *mistaken* when they assured her then that he would never improve. Perhaps that was because now the information presented to her was couched in graphic terms of unbearable suffering, once again with assurances that there was no hope of further improvement. Nevertheless, her apparent lack of curiosity about the accuracy of Comeau's initial prognosis is puzzling.

Judge Buchanan granted the motion, ruling that Comeau was "helpless and debilitated," and that he appeared to be experiencing "pain, terror, suffering, and horror." She further ruled that Comeau would "beyond any reasonable doubt . . . ask that artificial nutrition and hydration be terminated."[45] Food and fluids were immediately withdrawn.

If all had gone as planned, Ronald Comeau would have been dead within two weeks. But a hitch developed in the person of Reverend Mike McHugh, the minister of Grace Christian Church in Essex Junction, Vermont. A committed pro-life activist and founder of the Vermont chapter of Operation Rescue, McHugh sees it as his Christian duty to seek to preserve life, primarily the life of what he terms "preborn children." Reverend McHugh, who was not exactly known for his tact, was a very controversial figure in Vermont at the time.

Two days after Judge Buchanan ruled that Ronald Comeau's food and fluids could be withdrawn, McHugh received a phone call from someone who had heard a radio report that a young man was being legally starved to death. Was there anything Mike McHugh could do?

McHugh obtained a copy of the *Bennington Banner* issue that had run a story on the case. He was appalled. This is euthanasia, he thought, no different from a murder orchestrated by the government, especially since the decision was being made by a court-appointed guardian.[46] He knew he had to stop it and called on his network of pro-life attorneys to discuss what he could do. He then went to a prayer meeting of local pastors and sought their counsel. He came away from these discussions and his prayers and decided to be bold.

McHugh called Judge Buchanan at her home and told her he wanted a hearing so that he could petition the court to become Ronald Comeau's guardian. (Vermont law permits the clergy to intervene in guardianship cases under certain circumstances.) She agreed to convene one immediately. McHugh then decided to go high profile. He issued a press release on the case announcing that he was going to fight to save Ronald Comeau's life. A hearing was held at 8:00 p.m. on November 11, 1993. Among those present were Joe Schaaf, Stephen Saltonstall, and Mike McHugh. Also present were representatives of much of Vermont's local media. The Comeau case was about to become an event.

McHugh asked for a stay of the order removing Ron's feeding tube and asked to intervene in the guardianship case. Under cross-examination he admitted to having willfully violated a federal judge's restraining order to desist from blocking access to abortion clinics and to having been arrested twenty times in connection with his anti-abortion activities. He also admitted that he had never met Ronald Comeau and that Comeau was not part of his congregation. Judge Buchanan ruled that she could not stay her own order. Moreover, she ruled that under Vermont law, McHugh had no legal standing to enter the case. In other words, it was assumed that he had nothing at stake. Consequently, he had no legal right to intervene.

McHugh was undaunted. The next day, along with a less controversial pastor named John Goyette, he filed an appeal in the Bennington Superior Court seeking to reverse Judge Buchanan's ruling. This judge agreed with Judge Buchanan, finding that the clergymen had no direct interest in the case.

But McHugh was not done yet. He asked an attorney, Norman C. Smith, to get actively involved in the case. Smith immediately prepared and presented an emergency motion to the chief justice of the Vermont Supreme Court requesting a stay of Judge Buchanan's order removing Comeau's nutrition. On November 12 the request for a stay was granted, pending a hearing to be held the following Tuesday, November 16. The order was served on the hospital and Ronald Comeau's food and fluids were restored.

McHugh viewed the stay as a temporary reprieve of execution. When the emergency hearing started on November 16, he and Smith believed they would lose because of the issue of legal standing. After that, nothing could be done to save Ronald Comeau's life. Dejected and growing desperate, feeling the burden of Comeau's life on his own shoulders, McHugh had one last card to play. He decided to appeal to Comeau's father, Renald Dupois, even though the media had depicted the man as uncaring. To try to locate Dupois, McHugh made some phone calls to police contacts he knew and headed north toward Maine.

Later, he called one of the police contacts whom he had asked to assist him. "We found Renald Dupois," the policeman told him. "He is willing to meet you. He doesn't want his son to die."[47] For the first time since he had determined to save Comeau's life, McHugh was hopeful.

McHugh met Renald Dupois and his brother, Raymond Dupois. The men were not well educated. They wanted to know what was going on. McHugh showed them news clippings and said to Renald Dupois, "I am told you don't have an interest in this."

"That's not true," Renald Dupois insisted. He had been confused by the hospital's brief contact with him and didn't understand Comeau's status. Raymond Dupois thought that the hospital had told his brother that Comeau's was going to die. He was shocked that his nephew was still alive.

McHugh offered to pay all expenses if the two men would go back to Vermont with him and appear at the November 16 hearing. They agreed. With the help of McHugh's personal finances and contributions of other pro-life supporters, the Dupois brothers were soon in a hotel in Bennington.

If Mike McHugh's primary motive was to gain publicity for himself, as some accused, he got what he wanted. With the dramatic surprise appearance of Renald and Raymond Dupois at the Tuesday hearing, Ronald Comeau's case became a local front-page media sensation. The court continued the hearing until the Dupois brothers could visit Comeau and determine whether he was indeed their son and nephew, at which point McHugh held a news conference that quickly descended into an ugly shouting match between him and reporters when he excluded one paper from the gathering and refused to allow the brothers to be questioned directly by reporters.

An angry debate was on. Most were glad that Comeau's family was involved, but many resented McHugh's intrusion and the transformation of the young man's tragedy into a media circus. McHugh was not pulling any punches either, stating at one point that those who advocated Comeau's death were no better than "executioners." Schaaf's attorney, Stephen Saltonstall, says, "I particularly resented this allegation, since I had been one of the lawyers who had convinced the Supreme Court of Massachusetts to throw out that state's death penalty law."[48]

Each day's paper and television news reports heralded the unfolding events of the case. Editorials were flying. Strangely, the actions of

Mike McHugh seemed to be as big an issue as the life or death of Ron Comeau. A *Rutland Herald* editorial admitted that Comeau's future should be a central issue but opined "it is too bad that the sanctity of life should have as its defender a religious freebooter such as McHugh" and worried that "those involved in Comeau's case fear McHugh will succeed in manipulating Comeau's father . . . to his own ends."[49] A newspaper commentator named Jack Hoffman was furious that the press had allowed "Michael McHugh, the anti-abortion fanatic," to dictate "the terms for staging his own publicity stunts," further grousing that "the media got jerked around."[50] Meanwhile, an anonymous hospital official fretted to a reporter that Comeau's family had come under the influence of "confrontational individuals with an agenda," (as though some who push for the dehydration of cognitively disabled people don't also have their own agendas).[51]

Amid the media uproar, indications appeared that Comeau had a higher level of cognitive ability than had been previously described. After visiting his son, Renald Dupois told the press, "I said, 'This is Dad.' When he heard that, he had a smile on his face and started to move all over the place. That made me happy." Comeau's uncle, Raymond, added, "If he's in a coma, it's the funniest coma I ever saw."[52]

The case was about to take another unexpected twist. In Worcester, Massachusetts, Renald Comeau, Ron's brother, heard a news report about the Comeau brouhaha ongoing in Vermont and suddenly realized, "That's my brother!" He and his wife, Patricia, immediately left for Bennington. There they were joined by the Comeau boys' half brother, Robert DesRosiers.

The family assembled at Comeau's bedside, the first such gathering in a very long time. More evidence appeared that Comeau's condition was not as bad as previously described. When Ron Comeau was reunited with his brothers, he delighted at being shown a shirt with the Harley-Davidson logo on it. He and his brothers laughingly compared tattoos.[53]

It was clear that Comeau was able to react and communicate feelings. The brothers came away from the reunion quite upset at what had almost happened to him. "Can you imagine: They were going to kill this guy?" DesRosiers said to reporters after the reunion. "There's a lot of life there."

After that, things moved quickly. Schaaf met with Renald Comeau, and it was agreed that Renald would take over as his brother's guardian. Any thought of dehydrating Ron to death was quickly abandoned.

According to his family, in the years after Comeau's plight divided a community, his condition significantly improved. He had his bad days, sometimes becoming quite frustrated by the limitations caused by his disability. But for the most part, the news was good. He recognized family members, enjoyed listening to music, learned to sit up or roll over, use the television remote control, and clumsily push himself in a wheelchair. His personality reemerged. "He became a real flirt," Ron's sister-in-law, Patricia Comeau, told me with a laugh. "He made eyes at the nurses all the time." Moreover, he learned to communicate in one-syllable words and regained the ability to read.[54] He lived this way for several years, eventually dying naturally of pneumonia.

Joe Schaaf still believes he acted appropriately. "I have no regrets," he says, adding, "Crystal balls are hard to come by. I have thought it over many times. We did what we thought was right at the time."[55]

No doubt that is true. But why did so many well-meaning people give every benefit of the doubt to inducing Ron Comeau's death rather than protecting his life? Why were the neurologist's report opposing dehydration for Comeau and the therapist's reports about his ability to respond to stimuli not mentioned in court, even by his own temporary guardian? Why did the hospital downplay Comeau's capacities? And why were so many people so upset with Mike McHugh for trying to save Ron's life?

Once we accept the idea that some lives are not worth living, once we come to see as proper the intentional ending of lives of the profoundly disabled, once we claim the right to judge who should live and die on the basis of subjective standards such as happiness, quality of life, or dignity, we have created a disposable caste: fellow humans who can be killed without legal consequence, whose intentional deaths do not disturb a good night's sleep.

Being an honorable and compassionate people, we find it painful and difficult to admit that is what we are doing, so we are forced into pretense. We invent new terms and definitions to govern our actions: Intentional dehydration is labeled "allowing to die"—it sounds nicer that way. We twist the basic meaning of terms and concepts: abandonment of the helpless is called "beneficence," an end to suffering. We create slogans such as "death with dignity" to help us rationalize the once unacceptable. Under these circumstances, it is easy to understand why the opponents of these practices cause so much consternation. They refuse to let us deceive ourselves. When, like McHugh, they are not gentle in their approach or circumspect in their language, they outrage.

Shortly after Ron Comeau's life was saved, Renald Comeau, reflecting on how close he came to losing his brother, asked, "How many other Ronnie Comeaus are there?"[56] The answer, it appears, is quite a few.

Michael Martin

"A-F-R-A-I-D," Michael Martin, a brain-damaged forty-one-year-old man, spelled out on the alphabet board.

"Are you afraid of somebody?" asked the speech pathologist at the Michigan hospital where Michael was being cared for.

Michael shook his head no.

"Are you afraid for somebody?"

Michael nodded his head yes.

The speech pathologist asked if he was afraid for the nurses, aides, or his roommate, David.

No.

"Are you afraid for yourself?"

Yes.[57]

Martin, a profoundly disabled man, didn't know it, but he too was about to be the center of a bitter dispute over whether he should live or die by dehydration. Unlike the Comeau case, where previously estranged relatives united to save Ron Comeau's life, the Martin case deeply and bitterly divided a family. On one side was Mary Martin, Michael Martin's wife, who wanted Mike's life ended. Fighting to save him were Leeta Martin and Pat Major, Mike Martin's mother and sister.

"Do you like it here?" the pathologist continued.

Yes.

"Do you feel you get good care here?"

Yes.

"Are you afraid someone will take you from this facility?"

Yes.

The therapist then told Michael that he would be with them for "quite a while."

According to the chart notes, Michael then gave a big smile.[58] That hope was unduly optimistic. The judge of the Allegan County Probate Court, George A. Grieg, would soon issue a ruling allowing Mary Martin to order Michael's feeding tube removed in order that he die by dehydration.

What made the Michael Martin case significant was the relatively high level of Martin's functioning. Unlike Ron Comeau, when the court battle raged over Martin he was not only conscious but also interactive. For example, in April 1992 he learned how to use a communication augmentation system in which he pointed to letters so as to communicate. Through the system, he was able to say, "My name is Mike." According to the therapist's report, when asked to spell a word, "Mike spelled out the word [water]. When asked to find the character to clear this page, Mike was able to do it independently. Mike also indicated to us in response to a yes/no question, that the scanning device was too slow for him and he wanted it to be a little faster. When directed to the feelings page, Mike responded to the question of how he was feeling by indicating happy."[59] Unfortunately, Mike's current feelings would not count for anything in the coming legal drama over his potential killing.

In October 1992, as part of the court case, Dr. Robert K. Krietsch, a board-certified physician specializing in physical medicine and rehabilitation, evaluated Michael Martin. Dr. Krietsch reported:

> When I first entered the room his radio was on and he agreed to allow it to be turned off. When asked if he is able to see television and follow some shows, he indicates with an affirmative and also again, with a 'yes' head nod when asked if he likes certain types of shows. He brightened up with a large grin when asked if he liked cartoons . . . . When shown his poster with pictures of country western music stars, he again became quite animated with his expression, using a large grin, and was very cooperative in identifying by head nod and attempted to point with his right hand on questioning who were the different stars that I pointed to. . . . He was 100% accurate on identifying all of these.

In open court, Judge Grieg recalled a visit he had with Martin where he had seen for himself that Martin was conscious and interactive: "I introduced who I was, that we were having a hearing on whether or not he still needed a guardian. What did he think? Did he think he still needed a guardian? He shook his head yes. I mean it was a definite movement. It came at an appropriate time—at the end of the question." Judge Grieg related how Martin would nod yes and no when asked various questions about former coworkers and family members. He described how he then asked Martin to show volitional movements: "I asked him, 'Can you move your hand? . . . Is it your left one?' He shook his head no. I said, 'Is it your right one?' He said yes. I said, 'Can you move it for me,' and he raises it up and down."[60]

Michael Martin became disabled on January 16, 1987, when a train hit the car in which he and his entire family were riding. The accident not only disabled Michael but also killed the Martins' daughter, Melanie, aged seven. (Mary and the other two Martin children suffered injuries but fully recovered.) Michael Martin was unconscious for the first several months following the accident. Then he began to improve. By 1990, his treating neurologist, Dr. Walter Zetusky, measured his IQ between 63 and 67.[61]

Almost since the accident, Mary had believed that it was best for her husband to die. In August 1988, as Mike was slowly improving, she refused to permit antibiotics to be used to treat him for pneumonia. That, and her refusal to share information about his condition with Pat Major, his sister, and Leeta Martin, his mother, caused the two to seek Mary's ouster as Mike's guardian. That dispute ended with an informal settlement, but the conflict had created two factions in the family.

Two years later Mike developed a bowel obstruction. Mary had him transferred to Butterworth Hospital in Grand Rapids, Michigan. Unbeknownst to the rest of Mike's family, Mary asked hospital personnel to remove his feeding tube. That led to a meeting of the hospital ethics committee, which issued a statement favoring dehydration; it stated in part, "While Mr. Martin is not in a persistent vegetative state, members of the Ethics Committee felt that the persistence of his condition and the level of his functioning were equivalent to a persistent vegetative state for purposes of considering the removal of nutritional support."[62]

In defense of the ethics committee, Mike's abilities were significantly reduced from what they had been only a few weeks before. Perhaps that was because he was ill or because he was in an unfamiliar place. (Experts who work with the cognitively disabled report that they may become depressed in a new environment, leading to an apparent lowering of abilities.) Regardless of the cause, just as in the Wendland case, the committee was working with incomplete information. It made no effort to contact Mike's neurologist, Dr. Zetusky, or staff members of the New Medico Neurological Center (where Mike was cared for before coming to Butterworth), who knew Mike very well and could have told the committee that prior to his transfer he had interacted meaningfully with his environment and obtained enjoyment in life.[63] Nor were Pat Major and Leeta Martin permitted to give the committee their opinions. Thus, whether through willful ignorance, negligence, or a simple lack of facts, the committee issued a recommendation about Mike Martin's life and death without knowing the complete story.

Happily for Mike, a legal review of Mary's request had also been performed that would materially affect Mike's fate. Nervous about the previous legal scrap between Mary and her in-laws, in order to avoid litigation the lawyers recommended that the hospital should dehydrate Mike only if a court order permitted it to do so. That forced Mary to seek a judge's permission to end Mike's life, giving Pat Major and Leeta Martin the opportunity to stand up for Mike's right to live.

The case would take years. The first round went to Pat and Leeta when Judge Grieg ruled that Mike could not be dehydrated because he had not prepared a written advance medical directive indicating that that would be his desire.

Round two was Mary's. The Michigan Court of Appeals reversed Judge Grieg's decision, deciding that oral statements could constitute "clear and convincing evidence" (the standard of proof required in Michigan) of Mike's stated desires regarding his care if he were ever incapacitated. More worrisome was a ruling that pushed Michigan law down the slippery slope: The undisputed fact that Mike was conscious was not necessarily a bar to his dehydration. On the contrary, his medical condition and capabilities would be only one factor among many considered.[64]

Mary won the next two rounds also. Judge Grieg ignored plentiful evidence that Mike was currently happy, not in pain, and wanted to live. As if Mike were now a nonentity, the only thing that mattered in the decision was how Mike felt *before* he was injured. Relying on Mary's testimony concerning a private conversation she claimed to have had in which he allegedly said he would not want to live if he were incapacitated, Judge Grieg ruled that Mary could stop Mike's food and fluids. Judge Grieg did not take into account the admitted fact that

Mary would lose a substantial amount of the settlement from the railroad if she divorced Mike but not if he died, nor Mary's admitted romantic involvements after Mike was injured. Despite these apparent conflicts of interest, Judge Grieg wouldn't even appoint a neutral attorney to look out for Michael's interests. The Michigan Court of Appeals agreed with Judge Grieg, affirming the trial court's death ruling.

Mike's fate was ultimately decided in the Michigan Supreme Court, which ruled on August 22, 1995, that Mary's uncorroborated testimony was not sufficient to constitute clear and convincing evidence. Mary tried to take the case to the United States Supreme Court but was turned down.

But what if there had been clear and convincing evidence of Mike's desires before his injury? Indeed, what if he had signed a medical directive that his food should be withheld? Shouldn't the strong evidence that he was happy, not in pain, and enjoyed his life count for something? Shouldn't the benefit of the doubt be given to life, rather than death? And shouldn't the fact that Mike was awake and aware by definition preclude dehydration?

Apparently not. Although the Michigan Supreme Court's ruling saved Mike's life, it is ominous that it did not prohibit ending the lives of *all* conscious but cognitively disabled people who rely on feeding tubes, although it certainly set a strict standard of proof before such killings can take place. Indeed, Dr. Ronald Cranford groused that the Michigan Supreme Court's decision "shows how the clear and convincing evidence standard of proof can be manipulated to deny a person's liberty interest," which, he opined, should "frighten the people of Michigan."[65] In other words, according to Dr. Cranford it is wrong to give the benefit of the doubt to life.

Cut to Stockton, California, and the Robert Wendland case, where Dr. Cranford again testified in favor of dehydrating to death a conscious, interactive, cognitively disabled man—despite the uncontested fact that he had improved enough to maneuver an electric wheelchair down a hospital corridor. When asked by attorney Janie Siess why he should not give the benefit of doubt to maintaining Robert's life, Cranford coldly replied:

> The harm to continuing treatment . . . is, first of all, there wouldn't be a lot of harm per se as he is now because he has a minimal level of cognition. It's hard to talk about harm although he has some suffering.
>
> It's harmful *to the family* because . . . they know his wishes are not being observed. They know he is in limbo or living death if you want to call it that. That's not what *they* want for Robert.
>
> I think it's very harmful *for a family* to again feel like they're prisoners of medical technology about his treatment. So—you can go on and on about the psychological harm *to the family*. *I think the family should be able to go through the grieving process. Four years is enough.*
>
> And so I think for people to start functioning again—because it is *really harmful to families* when you get into a situation like this—that *the family should be allowed to live their lives.*
>
> They can still love Robert and remember Robert, *but Robert should be allowed to die so the family can grieve* and go through the normal grieving and knowing that Robert's wishes were respected.
>
> I think it is counterproductive to what medicine should be doing in an era *where we have to look at resources.* Not just money and everything, but to give futile treatment like we do in the United States in situations like this which doesn't benefit the patient and doesn't benefit the family is one major problem for healthcare costs. So, *I think it is harmful to society to do it.*
>
> I think there's a lot of harm that's done by erring on the side of caution. I think it's ridiculous to err on the side of caution when there's [no] doubt in my mind and any reputable person will say he's never going to recover. He's beyond that point.[66]

So to Dr. Cranford (and many others who support dehydrating cognitively disabled patients), apparently the issue isn't so much doing what is best for the patient, but rather, relieving family and society of the emotional and financial burdens associated with long-term care.

Such a crass, utilitarian approach to bioethics presents a clear and present danger to the most weak and defenseless among us.

Robert Wendland—Conclusion

The Robert Wendland case, as Yogi Berra once said, turned out to be déjà vu all over again. As with Michael Martin, a mother and sister faced off against a wife over whether a conscious cognitively disabled man could be dehydrated to death. And as occurred in Michigan, the state supreme court would make the final decision.

The case proved to be a bitter, white-knuckle roller-coaster ride. Robert's mother, Florence, won the first round when her attorney prevailed upon the trial judge to rule that those seeking Robert's dehydration had not presented clear and convincing evidence that he would have wanted to die under his circumstances or that dehydration would be in his best interests. That approach was reversed by the California Court of Appeals, which substantially upheld Rose's view that statutory law in California merely required her to prove her "good faith" by clear and convincing evidence. (Alarmingly, the court of appeals also ruled "there should be no presumption for continued existence" in California law.) [67]

One of the most disturbing aspects of the entire Wendland saga was the concerted effort to dehumanize and depersonalize Robert in order to make his dehydration easier for the courts to allow. Thus, instead of celebrating Robert's progress from coma to interactivity as wonderful medical victories for someone who only months before had been unconscious, expert bioethicist witnesses denigrated his interactivity as mere "trained responses," rather than truly human behavior.[68] One went so far as to contend that Robert "is unable to think at all in the manner we conceive humans do."[69] Similarly, Robert's own court-appointed appellate attorney argued that Robert "can respond to stimuli somewhat in the manner that an animal might."[70] Most disturbingly, illustrating how such dehumanizing and denigrating values can become embedded into law, the three-judge panel of the California Court of Appeals actively embraced his dehumanization in their explanation of why they wished to reverse the trial judge's ruling.

The case reached its dramatic conclusion when the California Supreme Court overruled the court of appeals and reinstated the trial judge's approach, noting, among other issues, that similarly fundamental decisions involving incompetent persons require very high standards of proof. (For example, a California conservator must prove beyond a reasonable doubt that a decision to sterilize a developmentally disabled conservatee is in the conservatee's best interests.) As Florence's lawyer argued compellingly, to "provide greater legal protections against sterilization than death is to turn the overarching purposes of constitutional safeguards upside down."[71]

Unfortunately, Robert died of pneumonia several weeks before his mother and sister's great court victory. Tellingly, the only person at his bedside as Robert died was his mother, Florence. Rose had stopped visiting her husband regularly several years before.

The food and fluids cases have desensitized people to medicalized killing, leading to a wider application of induced death as the answer to serious maladies. As we shall see in later chapters, since the cognitively disabled have a "right to die," the argument goes that the terminally ill should too. Once the terminally ill are seen to have this "right," the new "right" will be expanded to the disabled, the chronically ill, and the depressed. Thus, from relatively small beginnings that concerned approximately ten thousand people in the country who are permanently unconscious, the dehydration cases have been used as a springboard for arguments to legalize euthanasia and assisted suicide for the many.

As I write, in Pinellas County, Florida, Robert Schindler, the father of Theresa Schiavo, is locked in a bitter court dispute with his daughter's husband.[72] At stake is whether Terri will be dehydrated to death because she is profoundly cognitively disabled.

And the beat goes on.

3

Everything Old Is New Again

FOR MORE THAN TWO THOUSAND YEARS, mercy killing has been culturally disdained and illegal in the West and most of the rest of the world. Some euthanasia advocates claim that these life-affirming policies were instituted as part of some vast conspiracy by church leaders to impose religious hegemony on society and to promote suffering as a sacrament. While it is true that pragmatic concerns, humanitarian values, and religious tradition intertwined to create the particular cornerstone of Western civilization that I earlier labeled the equality-of-human-life ethic, this ethic is not in and of itself a religious belief. Indeed, the ethical precepts of modern medicine that prohibit killing date to well before Christianity to the writings of Hippocrates, a Greek physician who lived in the fifth century BC, who gave his name to the famous Hippocratic Oath, whereby doctors are to do no harm.

That is not to say, of course, that the killing of the weak and ill has never been carried out. Some ancient Greek societies, Hippocrates notwithstanding, so disdained children born with birth defects that they found a convenient way around their legal proscription against killing by exposing these unfortunate infants on hillsides. It is also true, as euthanasia advocates are fond of pointing out, that some hunter-gatherer societies traditionally expected the old and disabled to remain by the side of the trail when they couldn't keep up. Some of these cultures also routinely killed babies born with birth defects.

Unlike modern euthanasia and assisted suicide, the purpose behind these acts of killing generally involved a perception of absolute necessity: a stark choice between maintaining the life of the individual and the continued existence of the society or tribe. Infanticide also often sprang from bigotry against children who were considered abnormal, bigotry that, alas, we have not completely outgrown. These death practices—targeting the weak and "abnormal"—generally waned or ceased altogether as life became less harsh.

In the contemporary West we judge cultures as "advanced" or "civilized" in part by the manner in which they care for their weakest and most vulnerable members. Cultures that disrespect their dying, elderly, and disabled, or that do not provide for them in a caring and compassionate manner, generally are seen as backward, if not downright oppressive. Traditionally, we have measured our own progress toward a genuinely humane and enlightened society against these standards.

That may be changing. An ethical tug-of-war has emerged between those who continue to hold to the equality-of-human-life ethic and advocates who wish to replace it with a different, less egalitarian approach, sometimes described (euphemistically, in my opinion) as the "quality-of-life" ethic. I prefer to call it the "death culture." This wrestling match between what Abraham Lincoln once called "the better angels of our nature" and the utilitarian values of the death culture was described in September 1970 in a prescient editorial in *California Medicine*, published by the California Medical Association. The editors saw radical change in the offing:

> The traditional Western ethic has always placed great emphasis on the intrinsic worth and equal value of every human life regardless of its stage or condition . . . . This traditional ethic is . . . being eroded at its core and may eventually be abandoned . . . [H]ard

choices will have to be made . . . that will of necessity violate and ultimately destroy the traditional Western ethic with all that portends. It will become necessary and acceptable to place relative rather than absolute values on such things as human lives. . . . One may anticipate . . . death selection and death control whether by the individual or by society."[1]

In 1970, the very ideas of death control or death selection were utterly beyond the pale for most people. Agonizing memories were still too fresh. After the Holocaust, the equality-of-human-life ethic was at its zenith, and the watchword was "Never again!"

That was then. Now, we are confused. Many no longer believe in the traditional Western ethic. On the one hand, we feel compassion for people with developmental disabilities. On the other hand, some barely object if such people are killed. Thus, even as the Special Olympics celebrates the achievements of people with cognitive difficulties, and the Americans with Disabilities Act promotes equality for those with physical impairments, our society countenances the death by intentional neglect of infants born with Down syndrome and spina bifida and blithely accepts the premise that suicide by the disabled is "rational."[2] Even as hospice care was applauded for providing compassionate care, pain control, comfort, and emotional support for the dying and their families, juries exonerated Jack Kevorkian for assisting in the suicides of depressed, disabled, or dying people who could well have overcome the desire to die through just such humane care.

Fortunately, we don't come to this crossroads without a road map. Others in this century have walked this way, with disastrous results: the Germans and the supporters of eugenics in England and the United States. If we are wise, we will learn from that calamitous past and chart a better, more humane course as we meet the bioethical challenges of the new century.

It is a delicate matter to bring up the horrors of eugenics and the Holocaust. Many protest that those earlier proponents of the death culture were different people in a different time, many driven by intense bigotry and, in Germany at least, a fierce racial ideology that fueled the madness. And it is true: Today's euthanasia advocates are generally not overtly racist. Nor do they claim to be creating a master race. Indeed, they are far more likely to wear the mantle of compassion than of bigotry, and identify with libertarianism rather than with notions of totalitarianism embraced by the National Socialists.

These very real differences in motivation should not, however, make us any more receptive to the policies they advocate. Wicked ideas are hardest to detect in their own time, even when they are variations on a theme that has been played before. For although there are many differences between the values that drove the earlier German death culture and the ones emerging in our day, a careful analysis of the *actions* being advocated—rather than just the words used to promote those actions—leads to the uncomfortable conclusion that the differences are not as profound as many would like to believe.

USELESS EATERS

In 1806, the German physician Christoph Wilhelm Hufeland wrote, "It is not up to [the doctor] whether . . . life is happy or unhappy, worthwhile or not, and should he incorporate these perspectives into his trade . . . the doctor could well become the most dangerous person in the state." Hufeland recognized, even then, the tremendous power society gives to physicians. Modern doctors are entitled to cut people with a scalpel, prescribe dangerous drugs, and learn the most intimate and private aspects of their patients' lives. So long as physicians exercise these powers strictly for the well-being of each patient, so long as they view the lives of all patients as inherently of equal worth, then their power is unlikely to be abused.

But if doctors practice medicine in a way that imposes their own values upon their patients, the potential for abuse would be enormous. People whose lives the doctor valued would likely receive appropriate care. Those whom the doctor disdained—whether on the basis of race, age, sexual orientation, disability, or emotional state—might receive shoddy care or even no care at all.

One hundred thirty-three years after Hufeland wrote those words, his worst fears about his profession came true in Germany. Between 1939 and 1945, euthanasia made the transition from theory to practice. During those years, many German physicians participated enthusiastically in a program specifically established to kill off their most chronic patients. Euthanasia, in turn, led directly to the death camps of Auschwitz, Treblinka, and Dachau, as, in the words of the psychiatrist and Holocaust historian Robert Jay Lifton, "the medicalization of killing became a crucial . . . terrible step [toward] systemic genocide."[3] During these six years, doctors and nurses intentionally killed more than two hundred thousand helpless people: the cognitively or physically disabled, people with mental disease, infants born with birth defects, the senile elderly, even severely wounded German soldiers. German euthanasia practices were the first movement of the symphony of slaughter that took the lives of millions of Jews, Gypsies, homosexuals, communists, labor union members, Jehovah's Witnesses, Catholics, and other "undesirables" whose deaths we memorialize in the term *Holocaust*.

The medical professionals who killed their own patients did not act under duress. They were not drafted into performing euthanasia; they eagerly volunteered. "Those responsible believed in the necessity of what they were doing," writes Michael Burleigh of the London School of Economics.[4] In fact, German doctors who participated in euthanasia viewed the killing of certain patients as a final treatment—an act that compassionately served the interests of the patients as well as that of their families and the Reich as a whole.

Many people mistakenly believe that German crimes against humanity were all Hitler's idea, purely a product of Nazi ideology. In actuality, doctors who later participated in mass killing had, in Lifton's term, developed a "euthanasia consciousness," a value system that viewed some lives as unworthy of protection.[5] This unethical approach to the practice of medicine was already well developed in Germany by the time Hitler came to power in 1933. Indeed, the German medical, legal, and academic intelligentsia had aggressively promoted euthanasia as a proper and ethical public policy since the late nineteenth century, when Hitler was a child.

The first notable advocate of euthanasia in Germany was Adolf Jost, who publicized his ideas in *The Right to Death*, published in 1895. Jost considered the state to be a "social organism," a view later adopted by many Germans, Hitler included, and he argued that the life and death of each individual must ultimately belong to the collective. According to Lifton, Jost's thesis was, "The state must own death—must kill—in order to keep the social organism alive and healthy."[6]

In 1913, euthanasia was popularized and legitimized in Germany through the publication of an open letter ("Euthanasie") written by Roland Gerkan, a man dying of lung disease. Reading Gerkan's text, one would think he was a contemporary euthanasia advocate: "Why, instead of permitting us to die gently, today, do you demand that we embark upon the long martyr's road, whose final goal is certainly the same death which you deny us today?"[7] Gerkan even penned a model law legalizing euthanasia for anyone with an incurable illness, suggesting—just as modern euthanasia advocates do—that "protective guidelines" be enacted to protect against abuse, including the requirement that the person who wanted to be killed petition judicial authorities for permission, that the case be reviewed by two qualified physicians to determine the likely outcome of the disease, and that legal protection against liability be assured for "whosoever painlessly kills the patient as a result of the latter's express and unambiguous request."[8] The law would apply not just to the dying but also to the elderly and the "crippled."[9] Gerkan's thesis provoked much debate among German physicians, academics, lawyers, ethicists, and church leaders. However, the issue, then mainly seen as an intellectual exercise, was soon overshadowed by a more pressing matter for the German people: World War I.

The nation suffered terribly during the war, not only from the killing of its soldiers in battle but from the privations caused by shortages of food and other resources at home. During the war, lack of resources led to a harsh utilitarianism. Some Germans were considered expendable. Mental patients, for example, were deemed not worth feeding, which led to their intentional mass starvation.[10] It is no overstatement to say that the war and its consequences scarred the German soul.

At the end of the war, the country was reeling. Bitter in defeat, economically ruined, politically torn by factional fighting that would ultimately lead to the Nazi takeover, adjusting to the end of empire, the country desperately searched for national meaning and a way to bind its wounds. Such was the social mood when, in 1920, two venerable German professors published a book on euthanasia, *Permitting the Destruction of Life Not Worthy of Life*.[11] The book consisted of two essays, one by each coauthor: Karl Binding, an intellectual star and one of Germany's premier legal experts, and the physician Alfred Hoche, then considered one of Germany's most prominent medical humanitarians.

The importance of the publication of *Permitting the Destruction of Life Not Worthy of Life*, a full frontal attack on the equality-of-human-life ethic and described by Lifton as "the crucial work," is difficult to overstate.[12] The respectability of its authors and their explicit endorsement of legalizing the killing of weak and vulnerable Germans deeply influenced the value system of the general public and the ethics of the medical and legal communities. As a consequence, Hoche and Binding's book became a cornerstone of the intellectual foundation upon which the coming euthanasia practices would be built.

Reading *Permission the Destruction of Life Not Worthy of Life* is a chilling experience, not only because of its crass embrace of killing the defenseless, but because of the many ways in which it mirrors the concepts propounded by today's euthanasia advocates. Binding and Hoche believed that there were people living in Germany whose lives were so degraded and undignified that they constituted "life not worthy of life." Who were these "useless eaters," as they later came to be known?

First, terminally ill or mortally wounded individuals were those who "have been irretrievably lost as a result of illness or injury, who fully understand their situation, possess and have somehow expressed an urgent wish for release."[13] This view is virtually identical to that of euthanasia policies being urged upon us today.

Second, "incurable idiots," whose lives the authors saw as "pointless" and "valueless," were considered by them killable because they were an economic and emotional "burden on society and their families." Hoche put it this way: "I have discovered that the average yearly (per head) cost for maintaining idiots has till now been thirteen hundred marks. . . . If we assume an average life expectancy of fifty years for individual cases, it is easy to estimate what *incredible capital* is withdrawn from the nation's wealth for food, clothing, and heating—for an unproductive purpose."[14] Today's advocates do not denigrate the mentally retarded as "idiots," nor do most go as far publicly as Hoche and Binding did in calling for their outright killing. However, the cost of caring for those labeled as having a low quality of life is frequently noted by euthanasia advocates.

Third, the "unconscious," who, "if they ever again were roused from their comatose state, would waken to nameless suffering" and should be spared this.[15] The United States and other Western nations already ascribe to this criterion.

As euthanasia proponents always do, Binding and Hoche called for protective guidelines to govern the killing practice, including the need to make an application to an oversight board, the investigation by at least two physicians, a finding that the patients are "beyond help," with a report of the final act of killing to be given to the board.[16] Those who participated as killers, whether medical personnel, family members, or others, would, as in today's legislative proposals, be free from legal liability or criminal culpability for their lethal acts. These ideas later came to haunt Hoche; he would turn against the German euthanasia program—even though much of its rationale derived from his own writings—after one of his relatives became a victim.[17]

At the same time Hoche and Binding were urging euthanasia upon Germany, another pernicious social revolution took place in Germany as well as in the United States and Britain: the eugenics movement. Eugenicists claimed the right to determine which human traits were better than other human traits, to determine a hierarchy of "hereditary worth." They intended to promote the desirable traits through selective "breeding" using the new science of genetics. Humans with traits considered worth keeping were encouraged to procreate. Those with undesirable characteristics were discouraged and even forcefully prevented from having children. Eugenics profoundly violated the equality-of-human-life ethic, resulting in terrible oppression wherever it found official acceptance.[18]

In Germany, eugenics theory created a growing obsession with purifying and strengthening the "Nordic race." Many Germans fervently believed that unless "inferior" Germans were kept from breeding, the *Volk* would weaken and eventually cease to exist. Moreover, Jost's idea that the state, rather than the individual, was paramount also became widely accepted, popularizing the notion of forced sterilizations of those who, we might say, were deemed "useless breeders." Hitler was quite clear in *Mein Kampf* that he supported eugenics, seeing it as a method to "fight for one's own health." The alternative, according to Hitler, would be a national disaster, an end to what he called "the right to live in the world of struggle."[19]

When the Nazis took power in 1933, they quickly enacted laws authorizing involuntary sterilization. (Actually, they were years behind the United States, where some states began to pass eugenics laws in 1908.) To be kept from "breeding" were the mentally retarded, the blind and deaf, and "cripples" such as those with a club foot or a cleft palate. Relatives of such people were even urged to voluntarily sterilize themselves to prevent the "defect" from being passed to the next generation. In the end, it is estimated that up to 350,000 Germans were sterilized in the years 1933-1945.[20]

In the years following the appearance of *Permitting the Destruction of Life Not Worthy of Life*, there was much debate about the so-called right to die that had been so forcefully propounded by Binding and

Hoche. It soon became clear that the populace was in general agreement with the authors. For example, a 1925 survey of parents of children with mental disabilities disclosed that 74 percent of them would agree to the painless killing of their own children, revealing the extent to which euthanasia advocacy had already affected the population's moral values.[21] One can only imagine the attitudes of non-parents.

Well aware that the German public supported euthanasia, the new Nazi government proposed legalizing the practice in 1933. A front-page *New York Times* article described the proposal as making it possible for physicians to end the tortures of incurable patients. Protective guidelines were to be included in the law, including the necessity that the patient "expressly and earnestly" request to die, or if unable to do so personally, that relatives make the request, "acting from motives that do not contravene morals."[22]

This legislation never became law because of an outcry from the churches. But that did not stop the Nazi government from campaigning for the killing of "useless eaters." Toward this end, many propaganda films were produced depicting mentally retarded people as lower than beasts, a tactic also—not coincidentally—employed against Jews. But it was not only the cognitively impaired "idiots" who were at the receiving end of pro-euthanasia advocacy in Germany throughout the Nazi period. Various media also pushed the idea that physically disabled people also had lives not worth living and, moreover, that their deaths would be best for themselves, their families, and the state.

One notable and very popular motion picture, *I Accuse*, is a classic of this genre. *I Accuse* sympathetically depicts a physician-husband euthanizing his wife, who wants to commit suicide because she has multiple sclerosis. The picture lauds the doctor and wife for their selflessness, wisdom, and courage in deciding that she should die. To assure audiences that abuses will not occur with voluntary euthanasia, one character in the movie explains, "The most important precondition is always that the patient wants it."[23] (It is shocking how similar the values expressed in *I Accuse* are to those embraced by today's euthanasia movement. Witness the many suicides of disabled people, most with MS, facilitated by Jack Kevorkian. The reason many people state for countenancing these killings? It was what the patient wanted.)

With the German people thoroughly propagandized, all was almost ready for the horror that was to follow. All, that is, save one thing. Just as Frankenstein's monster needed a bolt of lightning to come alive, for euthanasia to become a reality in Germany one last precondition was required: the perversion of traditional medical ethics.

For millennia, physicians have owed their sole professional allegiance to their patients. That changed dramatically in Germany. Many doctors and nurses came to believe that their duty to the state took precedence in their delivery of medical services. As a consequence, as Christoph Wilhelm Hufeland had predicted, some doctors and nurses soon became among the most dangerous people in Germany.

As the 1930s came to a close, Germany had reached a dangerous point: Many physicians and most Germans believed that there was such a thing as a human life not worthy of life and that it was proper to terminate the lives of such "useless eaters." Forced sterilizations were commonplace and popularly accepted as a proper method to strengthen the state. Doctors had accepted a dual loyalty, believing they owed a professional duty to the state in their practice of medicine as well as to their patients. The ground was now prepared for mass murder.

EUTHANASIA COMES TO GERMANY

At this point it is important to acknowledge that the consequences of the abandonment by Germany of the equality-of-human-life ethic will not inevitably follow elsewhere. Nevertheless, what happened in Germany—once considered one of Europe's most civilized nations—demonstrates the grave importance strictly adhering to the equality-of-human-life ethic and the consequences that may follow should vulnerable people ever be widely viewed as having lives not worth living. In this sense, the events in Germany have much to teach us about the dangers of flirting with killing as an answer to medical difficulties.

For Hitler, the German euthanasia program was the culmination of his long-held desire to legitimize euthanasia in Germany. He had pulled back from the initial proposal at the beginning of his years as dictator for fear of opposition from the churches during a time when he was consolidating his still tenuous grasp on political power. According to Lifton, Hitler had decided that "the best time to eliminate the incurably ill" would be at the outbreak of his long-planned European war, a time when the general belief in the intrinsic value of human life could be expected to weaken.[24] But, as we have seen, many Germans were well ahead of their Führer, already accepting the idea of life unworthy of life. Indeed, by 1938, more than a year before the outbreak of hostilities, the German government had received a flood of requests from the relatives of severely disabled infants and young children seeking permission to end the lives of their little useless eaters. Requests for euthanasia of the dying and disabled also were sent, some submitted by the patients themselves and others by people who wanted euthanasia for relatives.

At the time, Hitler was looking for a good case with which to begin active euthanasia in Germany. In late 1938, the opportunity arrived in the person of "Baby Knauer," an infant born blind with a leg and part of an arm missing. The boy's distraught parents, accepting the general value system of their time, were deeply ashamed to have brought a useless eater into the world. And seeing the killing of their son as the solution to their problems, they wrote Hitler requesting permission to have their child "put to sleep."

Hitler was quite interested in the case and sent one of his personal physicians, Karl Rudolph Brandt, to investigate. Brandt's instructions from his Führer were to verify the baby's condition and, if found to be true, to assure the child's doctors and his parents that if he were killed, no one would face punishment. Brandt was then to witness the euthanasia and report to Hitler. The doctors in the case who met with Brandt agreed that there was "no justification for keeping the child alive," and Baby Knauer soon became one of the first victims of the Holocaust.[25]

By this time, Hitler, Brandt, and other Nazi social engineers had developed a detailed plan for implementing a euthanasia program. Unlike the German sterilization laws, no statute was ever enacted legalizing euthanasia. Rather, Hitler signed a decree permitting medicalized killing of disabled infants and named Brandt and a Nazi party member, Philip Bouhler, to head the program. Sympathetic physicians and nurses from around the country—many not even Nazi party members—cooperated in the horror that was to follow.

Disabled children were the first to suffer medicalized killing. Formal "protective guidelines" were created along the lines originally proposed by Binding and Hoche, including the creation of a panel of "expert referees," which judged who was eligible for killing. (The panel reviewed a questionnaire filled out by the child's doctor, not the child's actual medical records.) At first, it took a unanimous verdict of all panel referees to allow a patient to be killed. Ironically, among the selected referees was Ernst Wentzler, the inventor of an incubator for prematurely born children, who unfortunately was also a devotee of Binding and Hoche. Wentzler was so committed to euthanasia that even in 1963 he recalled his work in sorting through the euthanasia requests as "a small contribution to human progress."[26]

Beginning in early 1939, babies born with birth defects or with congenital diseases fell victim to the euthanasia program. Their doctors would admit these unfortunate infants to medical clinics, where they would be euthanized. Most of these children were voluntarily turned over to medical authorities by their own parents; some (but certainly not all) knew, or at least suspected, that their disabled children were being sent to their deaths.

The practice quickly became systematized. Regulations made it mandatory for midwives and doctors to notify authorities whenever a baby was born with birth defects. These cases would be reviewed by

euthanasia referees to determine if the children were eligible for euthanasia. Those deemed life unworthy of life were killed either by intentional starvation or an overdose of a drug, most typically a sedative
called Luminal. The euphemism for this butchery was "treatment."

Once the principle was established that some human beings could
be killed because they were disabled, it did not take long to add others
to the list of expendables: severely mentally ill and retarded adults, a
category soon expanded to include the criminally insane and people
with medical conditions such as epilepsy, polio, schizophrenia, senile
diseases, paralysis, and Huntington's disease. This was known as the T4
program. (T4 was a code name based on the address of the German
chancellery, Tiergarten 4.) As with the children's euthanasia order, the
matter was officially a secret.

The adult victims were usually killed at designated medical clinics
and hospitals, which had been turned into eradication centers. Indeed,
just as occurred in the later genocide, the T4 program became highly
bureaucratized as government workers "coldly and calculatingly organized the murder of thousands of people" and kept meticulous records
of what they were doing.[27] For example, secretaries "shared their offices
with jars of foul-smelling gold-filled teeth, listening to dictation which
enumerated 'bridge with three teeth,' 'a single tooth,' and so on."[28]
The T4 program also took the lives of many Jews. Ironically, because
euthanasia was considered a healing medical treatment, disabled Jews,
as official undesirables, were at first not included in the program. Eventually, this "discrimination" was ended. But for disabled Jews, there
were to be no protective guidelines, since, by definition, they were considered to embody "dangerous genes" in an individual medical sense
and "racial poison" in a collective ethnic sense.[29]

Disabled adults were generally killed with carbon monoxide (the
same method chosen by Jack Kevorkian for ending the lives of some of
his victims fifty years later). Eventually cyanide gas became the agent
of choice as the T4 program transformed into a dress rehearsal for the
death camps. Within this framework, experiments were performed to

determine the most efficient way to kill and dispose of masses of people, making more efficient the later slaughter at Auschwitz, Treblinka, Dachau, Buchenwald, and other genocide centers.

Modern euthanasia proponents, understandably wanting to distance themselves from these horrors, assert that German euthanasia is irrelevant to today's proposals because the German program was conducted in total secrecy. That may have been true in intent but not in actual practice. With so many people involved in the killing bureaucracy, it was not long before many Germans understood what was happening. As Hitler's henchman Heinrich Himmler put it in 1941, "This is a secret that is no longer a secret."[30] "It's hard to keep a secret when whole wards are being emptied out," notes Hugh Gallagher, an expert on German euthanasia. "Sometimes buses of those to be killed would be chased after by children who would laugh, yell and taunt the patients about their pending appointments with crematoria ovens."[31]

To their credit, the killing horrified many Germans. Some even found the courage to resist. According to Gallagher, "There were actually public demonstrations against the euthanasia program, which were anathema to the Nazis. Even some party members were appalled but they convinced themselves that the 'Führer must not know [about the program].'"[32] One of the most powerful voices in opposition to euthanasia was the Catholic archbishop Clemens August Graf von Galen, who courageously preached against the euthanasia program from the pulpit on August 3, 1941, in words still relevant today:

> If you establish and apply the principle that you can "kill" unproductive human beings, then woe betide us all when we become old and frail! If one is allowed to kill unproductive people, then woe betide the invalids who have used up, sacrificed and lost their health and strength in the productive process. . . . Poor people, sick people, unproductive people, so what? Have they somehow forfeited the right to live? Do you, do I have the right to live only as long as we are productive? . . . Nobody would be safe anymore. Who could trust his physician? It is inconceivable what depraved

conduct, what suspicion would enter family life if this terrible
doctrine is tolerated, adopted, carried out.[33]

To say the least, Hitler was not amused by the archbishop's bold-
ness. But not wishing to arouse domestic discontent by arresting the
popular clergyman—von Galen had threatened to meet the Gestapo in
full regalia if they came for him—Hitler did nothing. Still, the Führer
vowed revenge at the end of the war, promising to "balance the ac-
counts" with Archbishop von Galen, so that "no 't' remains uncrossed,
no 'i' left undotted."[34]

In response to the opposition that his euthanasia policy generated
in some quarters, in August 1941 Hitler ordered Brandt to suspend the
T4 program. (Hitler never rescinded the infanticide program.) But that
was not the end of it. Participating doctors did not need an order from
Hitler to kill their "patients." They had become true believers, convinced they were performing a valuable medical service for their "patients" and their country. The protective guidelines were cast aside as
the meaningless rules they had always been. From then until a few
weeks *after* the end of the war, some doctors went on a killing rampage.
Known today as "wild euthanasia," doctors during the later war years
killed any patient they pleased, often without medical examination,
usually by starvation or lethal injection.

It is important to reiterate that throughout the years in which euthanasia was performed in Germany, whether part of the officially sanctioned government program or otherwise, the government did not force
one doctor to kill a patient. Nor were any doctors ever punished for
refusing to euthanize a patient. The doctors themselves had become
the zealots.

Then, it was finally over. The Allies hanged Brandt and a few other
physicians after the Nuremberg Trials for crimes against humanity. But
most doctors and nurses who had been involved in mass killing went
unpunished, many continuing in their fields of practice. One physician
who appears to have participated in the euthanasia Holocaust, Dr. Hans

Joachim Sewerling, was even elected president of the World Medical Association in the 1980s. When the American Medical Association discovered his background and protested, Sewerling resigned, blaming a "Jewish conspiracy" for his troubles. However, he remains in good standing with the German Medical Association, which made him an honorary member of its board of trustees.[35]

EARLY EUTHANASIA ACTIVISM
IN THE UNITED STATES

The current efforts to legalize euthanasia are not the first in the United States, although they are certainly the most sustained. During the 1920s and 1930s this country faced the same social forces and erosion of values as Germany. Indeed, on the brink of World War II—and even for a short time into the war—euthanasia was steadily gaining respectability and acceptance among the people of the United States.

The pre–World War II American euthanasia movement sprang from the infamous eugenics movement. While not leading to mass killing as it did in Germany, American eugenics advocacy led to oppression through the legally sanctioned forced sterilization of more than sixty thousand people. Indeed, eugenics had so thoroughly polluted the moral thinking of America—especially among elites—that the legal approval for forced eugenic sterilization came from the United States Supreme Court in its notorious 1927 opinion, *Buck v. Bell.*[36]

The life story of Carrie Buck is as sad as her case was unjust. Carrie, the eighteen-year-old daughter of a prostitute, became pregnant out of wedlock, apparently after being raped by a relative of her foster father. Rather than rushing to her aid, her foster family was ashamed and had her involuntarily institutionalized in an asylum.

Rather than protecting their patient, Carrie's doctors, believing that they had a duty to protect society against the "unfit," decided to sterilize Carrie as a way to carry forward their eugenic theories. Carrie sued, and the case eventually reached the United States Supreme Court. In a ruling that demonstrates vividly how judges' own prejudices can sometimes overcome facts and logic, Oliver Wendell Holmes issued the majority opinion. "Three generations of imbeciles are enough," Holmes wrote. "We have seen more than once that the public welfare may call upon the best citizens for their lives. It would be strange if it could not call upon those who already sap the strength of the State for these lesser sacrifices [sterilization], often not felt by those concerned, in order to prevent our being swamped by their incompetence. It is better for all the world . . . [if] society can prevent those who are manifestly unfit from continuing their kind."[37]

And so the real reason Carrie Buck was sterilized, along with tens of thousands of other Americans, was not because she was somehow genetically "defective" but because she was poor, powerless, and seen as an undesirable. Later in her life, she was released from the asylum, married twice, sang in a church choir, and took care of elderly people until her death in 1983.[38] Involuntary sterilization laws remained on the books in a few states into the 1960s.

Concurrent with the general acceptance and practice of eugenics in the United States came a growing belief in euthanasia theory. This led to attempts to legalize medicalized killing. By the 1930s, several American euthanasia advocacy organizations had been formed. Like their German counterparts, these groups urged the legalization of voluntary mercy killing, which they hoped could eventually be expanded to those incapable of consent. For example, the president of the Euthanasia Society, a Cornell professor of neurology, Dr. Foster Kennedy, opined in a speech, "If the law sought to restrict euthanasia to those who could speak out for it, and thus overlooked those creatures who cannot speak, then I say as Dickens did, 'The law is an ass.'"[39] In a comment that echoes the views of some contemporary euthanasia advocates, especially Princeton professor Peter Singer, Kennedy later said that "defective children" up to the age of five should be permitted to be killed upon the request of parents or guardians, "if after careful board examination" it was determined that the child had no "future or hope."[40]

The American public responded favorably to arguments in favor of voluntary euthanasia, which then as now were couched in terms of the "right to die," a term that was first used in Binding and Hoche's *Permission to Destroy Life Not Worthy of Life* in 1920. Indeed, a 1939 public opinion poll of New York State doctors surveyed by the Euthanasia Society, published in the *New York Times*, found that 80 percent of respondents favored voluntary euthanasia for adults.[41] Whatever chance euthanasia had to become accepted public policy in the United States at that time was obliterated with the country's shock and horror over the Holocaust. After the war, euthanasia theory fell into near total disrepute and the movement grew quiescent. It did not, however, die, as the events of the last fifteen years clearly demonstrate. Indeed, many of today's euthanasia advocacy groups trace their roots back to euthanasia organizations formed in the 1930s.

HEEDING THE WARNINGS OF HISTORY

It is tempting to demonize people and public policy proposals with which we disagree by associating them with the Nazis. Such comparisons are often facile exercises that discount and cheapen the horror of the Holocaust. In that regard, the bioethicist Arthur Caplan has written, "Those who see analogies [to the Nazi period] must be specific about what they believe is similar between now and then. Blanket invocations such as . . . 'euthanasia, if legalized, will lead to Nazi Germany,' are to be avoided unless they can truly be supported in the scope of the claim being made."[42]

Caplan is right. Just because the Nazis said or believed something, or adopted certain public policies, doesn't mean, ipso facto, that the belief or policy is inherently evil. Hitler created the German autobahns, but that does not mean that President Dwight Eisenhower was wrong when he facilitated the creation of the interstate highway system.

What relevance, if any, do the euthanasia horrors of Nazi Germany bear to euthanasia proposals in our own time? Some experts see little relevance. Lifton, for one, has written, "One can speak of the Nazi state as a 'biocracy.' The model here is a theocracy, a system of rule by priests of a sacred order under the claim of divine prerogative."[43] There is no doubt that today's euthanasia advocates are not driven by the ideological madness that sees biology as destiny and the cleansing of the gene pool as a divine imperative.

Michael Burleigh, the author of *Death and Deliverance*, a study of German euthanasia policies, specifically states that he has "no axes to grind regarding contemporary discussions about euthanasia," and admits to being "sympathetic to its voluntaristic implementation." Still, Burleigh also acknowledges feeling "uneasy" about the "right to die [and] Dr. Death–style fanatics," as well as those he calls their extremist "counterparts" on the fringe of the anti-abortion movement.[44]

On the other hand, Michael J. Franzblau, MD, a clinical professor of dermatology at University of California Medical Center San Francisco and a committed Nazi hunter, who was primarily responsible for exposing Dr. Sewerling's euthanasia past, does see a "direct connection." Franzblau says, "If we codified euthanasia and assisted suicide, we would unalterably alter the relationship between physicians and patients. It is frightening to consider that many of the arguments made today by euthanasia advocates, echo almost precisely the arguments originally made by Binding and Hoche, and after them, Hitler and the Nazis as they implemented the euthanasia program. There are certain lines that should not be crossed. Permitting doctors to become killing agents is one of them."[45]

It is indeed intriguing how closely many of the concepts advocated in *Permitting the Destruction of Life Not Worthy of Life* resemble in word and rationale many of the pro-euthanasia sentiments expressed in our current debate. Examples of this can be found by comparing Binding and Hoche's text with the text of the 1996 majority opinion of the U.S. Court of Appeals for the Ninth Circuit when it ruled, in *Compassion in Dying v. The State of Washington*, that Washington State's law banning assisted suicide was unconstitutional: Binding asserts that the "freedom to end [one's] own life ... is the primary human right."[46] As Judge Stephen Reinhardt, writing on behalf of seven other jurists, put it, "There is a Constitutionally protected liberty interest in determining the time and manner of one's own death."[47]

Binding: "We are dealing with a legally permissible act of healing, which is most beneficial for patients in severe pain, and with the elimination of suffering. ... This is not a matter of killing them."[48]

Reinhardt: "We have serious doubts that the terms 'suicide' and 'assisted suicide' are appropriate legal descriptions of the specific conduct at issue here."[49]

Binding: "The permission of the suffering patient is not legally required."[50]

Reinhardt: "We should make it clear that a decision [to end a patient's life] of a duly appointed surrogate decision maker is for all legal purposes the decision of the patient himself."[51]

Binding: "It is also completely unrestricted legally for a third party to help it along and encourage a decision to do it."[52]

Reinhardt: "We recognize that in some instances, the patient may be unable to self-administer the drugs and that administration by a physician, or a person acting under his direction or control, may be the only way the patient may receive them."[53]

Binding: "The motto or rallying cry for this movement has been the expression 'the right to die.'"[54]

Reinhardt: "The terms 'right to die'. ... and 'hastening one's death' more accurately describe the liberty interest at issue here."[55]

Hoche: "I consider it less important to work out all of the details than to admit that implementing this program obviously presupposes that all conceivable safeguards along these lines must be provided."[56]

Reinhardt: "While there is always room for error in any human endeavor, we believe that sufficient protections can and will be developed by the various states."[57]

Hoche: "The idea of gaining relief from our national burden by permitting the destruction of life . . . will (from the start and for a very long time) encounter lively, strident, and passionately stated opposition."[58]

Reinhardt: "Those who believe strongly that death must come without physician assistance . . . are not free . . . to force their views, their religious convictions, or their philosophies on all other members of a democratic society."[59]

Happily, the United States Supreme Court reversed the Ninth Circuit decision in 1997 (see chapter five). But that a large majority of United States circuit judges could so closely mimic the values and attitudes expressed by Binding and Hoche—views that helped lead directly to Holocaust—is cause for sober reflection.

Many in the disability-rights community are growing quite alarmed at the similarities between current euthanasia thought and the intellectual foundations of the German experience. Carol Gill, president of the Chicago Institute of Disability Research, disabled by polio, notes that "disability has supplanted death in people's minds as the worst thing that can happen."[60] Similarly, Diane Coleman, the founder of the disability-rights organization Not Dead Yet says, "Our priorities are all mixed up. When we demand services that would help us [the disabled] to live in liberty we are resisted at almost every turn. But if we ask to die, lawyers, doctors, bioethicists, and everyone else comes out of the woodwork and are more than happy to help."[61]

These fears and prejudices about, and against, the disabled are shared by many physicians and sometimes affect their approaches to treatment. Gill notes that when "doctors don't believe the lives of disabled patients are tenable," they feel that ending the life of the patient by nontreatment (or, presumably, euthanasia) "is doing the patient and the family a favor."[62]

There can be little doubt, then, that there is a general, if not precise, analogy between the *attitudes* expressed during the pre-Nazi and Nazi periods in Germany and some in current vogue. That is not to say, of course, that we should anticipate the establishment in the United States of death camps. Nevertheless, the fact that death camps are extremely unlikely here—nay, virtually impossible—should not end the analysis. There are many other ways of falling off an ethical cliff.

Behavior is generally preceded by attitude: we tend to act as we believe. That is why comprehending how the German euthanasia program could proceed—the widespread acceptance of apportioning relative worth to different categories of human lives, the lessening of the doctor's responsibility to the individual patient—is so important. These events send messages that should resound through the decades: making a virtue out of killing will have unpredictable consequences; deforming the traditional physician-patient relationship will be at the patient's peril; degrading the inherent perceived value of some humans leads directly to their oppression.

Take the equality-of-human-life ethic. Here startling similarities between those awful times in Germany and contemporary attitudes can be found. To say, as modern euthanasia advocates do, that the lives of some should be protected by the law while the lives of others should not be, presumes that some human lives are inherently more valuable than others. This creates a subjective approach to the right to live, rather than the objective view inherent in the equality-of-human-life ethic.

Absent a strong adherence to the objective standard, decisions about life and death and access to appropriate medical care become, as they were during the Holocaust, power based. An example of a subjective approach to the right to live, albeit on a much smaller scale, is Oregon's healthcare rationing for Medicaid recipients. Under the Oregon rationing plan, a list of more than seven hundred treatments was created, and each treatment was given a number. Every year, a cutoff number is determined, reflecting the amount of money available to fund Medicaid operations. Payment is made for all appropriate treatments below the cutoff number. However, any treatment assigned a higher number will not be covered.

As first proposed, the Oregon plan placed healing treatment for end-stage AIDS patients very low on the list of treatment priorities, all but ensuring that Medicaid AIDS patients who wanted curative treatment at that stage of their disease would not receive it. AIDS activists were appropriately outraged, seeing this as a devaluation of the lives of people with AIDS. They were determined not to let Oregon abandon members of their community, no matter what the patients' prognosis. Through effective political advocacy, the activists successfully amended the plan so that AIDS patients who want healing treatment can obtain it, regardless of the stage of their disease.

If it is true that the politically powerful are better off in a quality-of-life-based system, the opposite is true for people who are less organized and less powerful. In Oregon, though late-stage AIDS patients on Medicaid need not fear being cut off from treatment, categories of patients with little or no organized power—very low-birth-weight babies and late-stage cancer patients to name two—are on the nonpayment side of the cutoff.

Are the lives of late-stage AIDS patients any more or less precious than the lives of low-birth-weight infants or late-stage cancer patients? If the equality-of-human-life ethic is followed, the answer is no. But in Oregon, with its subjective Medicaid treatment standards, the answer is yes.

We must not come to perceive killing as a virtue, as did the Germans of generations past. We have already decided that a whole class of patients, those assessed as PVS, can be killed by dehydration without consequence, and this has led directly to concerted efforts to expand the designation of those eligible for this "beneficence" to the conscious but cognitively disabled. Meanwhile, the growing public acceptance of allowing terminally ill people to be killed by doctors has already led to widespread calls for the same "right " for the nonterminal "hopelessly ill," before euthanasia is even legalized. That these policies mimic almost exactly many of the ideas and attitudes expressed by Binding and Hoche and the German medical biocracy that they helped inspire should sound an alarm. To be sure, differences between then and now should not be overlooked: German euthanasia attitudes were hate filled, based to a great degree on bigotry, concepts of racial hygiene, and collectivist notions of the state as a living organism. Contemporary advocates, on the other hand, use much more passive language, intended to reflect sober deliberation and the balancing of competing interests, with attitudes most often based on concepts of personal autonomy. Yet when one cuts through the jargon, the *acts* that are being advocated are the same as those advocated by Binding and Hoche more than eighty years ago. That they are presented in warm tones of compassion or in the bland prose of scholarship does not make them any less dangerous.

Those who sorted through the horror of the Holocaust in the years following the war earnestly wanted to learn how it could have happened and to ensure it never happened again. One man deeply involved in researching these issues with the Nuremberg Tribunal was Dr. Leo Alexander, who served with the U.S. Office of Chief Counsel for War Crimes. Dr. Alexander wrote a penetrating and important analysis of the foundation of the Holocaust in the July 14, 1949, issue of the *New England Journal of Medicine*, and its relevance is undiminished today:

> Whatever proportions these crimes finally assumed, it became evident to all who investigated them that they had started from small

beginnings. The beginnings at first were merely a subtle shift in emphasis in the basic attitudes of the physicians. It started with the acceptance of the attitude, basic to the euthanasia movement, that there is such a thing as a life not worthy to be lived. This attitude in its early stages concerned itself merely with the severely and chronically sick. Gradually the sphere of those to be included in this category was enlarged to encompass the socially unproductive, the ideologically unwanted, the racially unwanted and finally all non-Germans.[63]

Looking at the state of the culture of American medicine in 1949, Dr. Alexander warned: "In an increasingly utilitarian society these patients [with chronic diseases] are being looked down upon with increasing definiteness as unwanted ballast. A certain amount of rather open contempt for the people who cannot be rehabilitated with present knowledge has developed. This is probably due to a good deal of unconscious hostility, because these people for whom there seem to be no effective remedies, have become a threat to newly acquired delusions of omnipotence. . . . At this point, Americans should remember that the enormity of the euthanasia movement is present in their own midst."[64]

4

Dutch Treat

URING WORLD WAR II, the Germans occupied the Netherlands
for nearly five years. To say the least, it was not a happy era
for the Dutch. Yet it was also one of the most heroic times in
that nation's history. The Dutch resisted the Nazis at every turn, some
citizens risking their own lives to protect Jews and otherwise refusing
to bend to the will of their cruel occupiers.

Dutch medical professionals were major participants in the resistance. The German commander of the occupation, Arthur Seyss-
Inquart, now known derisively as "the Butcher of Holland," wanted to
remake Dutch medical ethics in the German image. Toward that end
he issued several orders, one of which required Dutch physicians to
perform their professional services as "a public task," one that he defined as assisting as "helper . . . in the maintenance, improvement and
re-establishment of [the patient's] vitality, physical efficiency and
health."[1]

At first glance the order seems rather innocuous. But Dutch physicians knew better. They widely believed that the edict was a small first
step designed to push them in the same unethical direction as had
already occurred in Germany. Accordingly, Dutch doctors unanimously

rejected the order. Some went so far as to take down their shingles rather than violate their sacred duties to heal and protect their patients and to maintain a healthy separation between private obligation to each patient and public duty to the state.

Seyss-Inquart was furious. First, he tried to coerce the doctors into compliance with his order by stripping them of their licenses to practice. The doctors paid no heed; they stopped signing birth and death certificates but never stopped treating their patients. Seyss-Inquart then took lethal action. One hundred doctors were arrested at random and shipped to concentration camps in the East, from whence few returned. Still Dutch doctors did not budge. They were literally willing to die before they would betray any of their patients.

Eventually it was the Germans who blinked in this ethical struggle. In one of history's great stories of successful peaceful civil disobedience, the Germans, unwilling to take more drastic action against the doctors of a hostile, occupied nation, eventually gave in. As a consequence, Dutch medical ethics were not subverted and euthanasia never entered medical practice in the Netherlands during World War II.

Of this episode Dr. Leo Alexander wrote: "Thus, it came about that not a single euthanasia or nontherapeutic sterilization was recommended or participated in by any Dutch physician. They had the foresight to resist before the first step was taken, and they acted unanimously and won out in the end. It is obvious that if the medical profession of a small nation under the conqueror's heel could resist so effectively, the German medical profession could likewise have resisted had they not taken the fatal first step. It is the first seemingly innocent step away from principle that frequently decides a career of crime. Corrosion begins in microscopic proportions."[2]

The Butcher of Holland was hanged after Nuremberg, in part because of his treatment of the Dutch medical community. Yet, in a painful irony, some of the very policies that Seyss-Inquart could not force upon heroic Dutch doctors during World War II have been willingly embraced by their modem counterparts—and not in microscopic proportions. Today, a majority of Dutch doctors openly accept euthanasia and assisted suicide as appropriate medical procedures.

Dr. I. van der Sluis, a Dutch opponent of his nation's euthanasia policies, told me exactly when, and how, such a radical change in ethics occurred in his country. "There was never propaganda in favor of euthanasia in my country before 1960," van der Sluis recalled. "Then came the cultural revolution of the late 1960s and early 1970s, which hit the Netherlands very hard. Traditional ethics collapsed in almost every area, including in the medical community. It got to the point that if you didn't accept the 'new ideas' you were a suspect person."[3]

A visit to Amsterdam reveals the truth of van der Sluis's woeful observations about the changes that took place in the Netherlands. On the one hand, the city is the epitome of beautiful European charm, crisscrossed by canals, filled with magnificent architecture, giving all the appearance of Old World dignity and propriety. Amsterdam, like other Dutch cities, is a model of energy conservation. People generally walk, bicycle, or take public transportation to get where they wish to go. Indeed, it sometimes seems that more people in the streets are on bicycles than in cars. The trolley system is efficient and affordable. Most notably, almost all of the people are open and friendly.

On the other hand, a walk through the city streets of Amsterdam makes clear the new course that the Dutch have embarked upon, one radically different from that of their staid forebears. Amsterdam, once a community of proper merchants, is a city where decadence has become banal. In postcard racks in front of tourist-oriented stores are cards vividly depicting the Pope defecating, along with other equally tasteless offerings. In the main downtown shopping district, where families stroll in the evenings, restaurants are situated next to open-air slot-machine casinos, which are next to clothing stores, whose neighbors are pornography emporiums that have storefront window displays of sexual toys and explicit, full-color, gynecologically oriented photographs. Then there's the famous, or infamous, red-light district, where prostitutes sit in windows to be ogled and patronized by men, like so much merchandise. "Coffee shops" abound, with names like the Grass-hopper and Mellow Yellow, where marijuana and hashish are legally sold and the pungent scent of the wares hangs in the breeze, even in the early morning, when patrons can be seen inside slumped in their chairs. Amsterdam's open hedonism has made it popular with tourists.

The Dutch pride themselves on their "nonjudgmentalism" about individual human behavior and are strong advocates of finding consensus and compromise as a way of "managing" their social problems. Thus, in an attempt to reduce the use of hard drugs, marijuana and hashish are legalized if consumed in the coffee houses. To reduce out-of-wed-lock births and abortion rates, the Dutch educational system and popular culture are very open about matters of sex, viewing it as a natural part of life, even for teenagers, while taking great pains to create a social milieu where the use of birth control and condoms is deemed an essential responsibility in the management of one's own sexuality. To reduce streetwalking, bordellos are free to operate (at least in Amsterdam) in the red-light district specifically zoned for that purpose.

The Dutch have adopted this same approach to the controversy surrounding euthanasia. Because some doctors believed that euthanasia was appropriate, it was quasi-legalized in 1973 by a court decision. The idea was to create a compromise between proponents and opponents of legalization, whereby euthanasia would technically remain illegal but would be permitted in those few cases in which, supposedly, no other method could be found to alleviate a patient's suffering. So long as Dutch doctors followed the guidelines set by the court, and later by statute, there would be no legal troubles. The idea was for euthanasia to be available as a rarely used safety valve when nothing else could be done to alleviate a patient's intense suffering.

As we shall see, however, it hasn't even come close to working out that way. Instead of the medical establishment's managing and controlling death, the reverse seems to have occurred: the death imperative is controlling the practice and ethics of Dutch medicine. In only twenty-three years Dutch doctors have gone from killing the terminally ill who asked for it, to killing the chronically ill who ask for it, to killing the depressed who had no physical illness who ask for it, to killing newborn babies in their cribs because they have birth defects, even though by definition they cannot ask for it. Dutch doctors also engage almost routinely in non-voluntary euthanasia without significant legal consequence—even though such activity is officially prohibited. And despite this abysmal record, the country formally legalized euthanasia in 2002, eradicating the last vestige of restraint in the system—the threat of prosecution, weak though it was.

To fully understand the context of the discussion, it is necessary to note the differences between the Dutch medical and legal systems and those in the United States. America's healthcare system is for the most part profit-driven, with financing primarily provided by private health insurance, although the poorest of the poor and the elderly receive government-financed healthcare benefits. This leaves some of us out in the cold. At last count, forty-four million Americans had no health insurance at any given time, which means that many receive inadequate healthcare.

In contrast, virtually every Dutch citizen is legally entitled to quality medical care from birth until death. Money is not an issue for patients, since Dutch medicine is completely socialized; medical professionals are paid salaries by the government. The majority of physicians are general practitioners, family doctors who receive compensation on a per-patient basis regardless of the level of care each patient requires. Dutch doctors are part of the broad middle class, with family doctors generally earning about sixty thousand dollars per year. Each citizen has a family doctor with whom he or she retains a long-lasting relationship. Dutch doctors even make house calls.

The Dutch legal system has its roots in the Napoleonic Code, and generally one set of statutes governs the whole country. Eugene Sutorius, the lawyer primarily responsible for pushing the Dutch euthanasia movement in the nation's courts over the last several years, described the Dutch legal approach this way: "We have professional judges and no jury system, which has a lot of consequences in the way controversial issues are dealt with. In Holland . . . the principle is that the judge is the...mouth of the law. Judges are to interpret law, not make it . . . . We are rather tied to the wording of the law. Thirdly, the system of criminal justice is centralized under the Ministry of Justice, [which] has broad discretion. . . . Prosecutions are not necessarily adversarial; prosecutors may bring cases to establish legal precedents [rather than to punish wrongdoing]."[4]

In contrast, the United States has a federal system of decentralized civil and criminal justice. Laws are made and enforced at all levels of government. Prosecutions are adversarial, based on attempts by prosecutors to punish wrongdoers, and nonprofessional juries generally decide outcomes. The United States Constitution is the supreme law of the land, superseding statutes and judicial rulings that violate its terms, but under that broad umbrella there are wide variations of law among federal, state, and local levels of government, and among the states themselves. Thus, what may be legal in one state may be illegal in another. This is not the case in Holland.

THE DUTCH SYSTEM OF EUTHANASIA

By the early seventies the Netherlands, deeply influenced by the cultural upheavals of the 1960s, cast aside traditional values and ethical norms. In this milieu, as occurred to a somewhat lesser degree in the United States, the prevailing value system was turned on its head in many cultural areas such as drug use, sexual morality, and family issues.

Unlike in the United States, however, the euthanasia movement in the Netherlands quickly established a strong beachhead, finding respectability and broad public acceptance, at least in theory. Euthanasia became a popular topic of discussion and analysis, and many doctors and laypeople came to accept euthanasia as an appropriate response to the few cases at or near the end of life where suffering could supposedly not be alleviated.

These new attitudes profoundly affected Dutch law, beginning with a 1973 case in which Geetruida Postma, a Dutch physician, was charged with murder after she terminated the life of her seriously ill mother by giving her a lethal injection.[5] Postma appears to have intentionally used her mother's death to legitimize euthanasia. Indeed, it is unlikely that the matter would have come to the attention of the authorities had she not insisted that her actions be made known.[6]

During the trial, an unrepentant Postma testified that she acted out of compassion, stating that her mother was partly paralyzed, could hardly speak, had pneumonia, and was deaf. She further asserted that she killed her mother at the elder woman's request.

The highly visible case soon became a cause celebre, much discussed and debated throughout the country, a rallying point for legalizing euthanasia, and the catalyst for the establishment of Holland's first voluntary euthanasia organization, the Voluntary Euthanasia Society. Postma's case generated such support that during the proceedings, doctors in her province signed an open letter to the Netherlands minister of justice stating that euthanasia was commonly practiced among physicians.[7]

The court found Dr. Postma guilty of murder. However, the court also accepted the premise that most Dutch doctors supported euthanasia in some cases. That being so, the court reasoned, the law should follow the medical consensus rather than the democratically enacted statute. In a departure from the usual Dutch practice that requires changes in law to be made exclusively by members of Parliament, the court decided instead to issue a legal precedent permitting euthanasia in some cases.

Postma received only a one-week suspended sentence and a year's probation. To justify its action, the Dutch court relied heavily on expert testimony by the district's own medical inspector (illustrating the non-adversarial nature of the trial), who set forth certain conditions under which the average physician allegedly thought euthanasia should be considered acceptable. These conditions established the first boundaries for euthanasia practice in the Netherlands. Among these were the requirements that the patient be considered incurable, implying that the patient must suffer from a physical illness; that the patient's suffering be subjectively unbearable; that the request for termination of life be in writing; and that there should be adequate consultation with other physicians before euthanasia was carried out.[8] Inclusion of these conditions in the court's decision, which was not appealed, became the basis for subsequent public and government acceptance of euthanasia in the Netherlands.

With the Postma decision, the Dutch stepped boldly onto a steep slippery slope. Other court decisions soon followed, each widening the boundaries of acceptable medicalized killing and further expanding the conditions under which euthanasia would not be punished. Thus, even though killing by doctors remained technically illegal, it soon became entrenched in Dutch medical practice.

In 1993, the Dutch Parliament established a regime of euthanasia by statute, drafting "guidelines" to which doctors were required to adhere if they wished to avoid punishment for euthanizing or assisting the suicides of patients.[9] These guidelines included the following:

- The request must be made entirely of the patient's own free will and not under pressure from others.

- The patient must have a lasting longing for death:

- The request must be made repeatedly over a period of time.

- The patient must be experiencing unbearable suffering.

- The patient must be given alternatives to euthanasia and time to consider these alternatives.

- There must be no reasonable alternatives to relieve suffering than euthanasia.

- Doctors must consult with at least one colleague who has faced the question of euthanasia before.

- The patient's death cannot inflict unnecessary suffering on others.

- Only a doctor can euthanize a patient.

- The euthanasia must be reported to the coroner, with a case history and a statement that the guidelines have been followed.[10]

In practice these guidelines offered scant protection for the weak, vulnerable, and despairing; nor, as we shall see, did they keep doctors from euthanizing patients who fell outside the guidelines' parameters.

At this point it is important to recall that when euthanasia was first accepted in the Netherlands, it was supposed to be a rare event, to be resorted to only in the most unusual cases of "intolerable suffering." The guidelines were designed specifically to keep euthanasia occurrences few and far between by establishing demanding conditions that had to be met, at the risk of criminal prosecution. Over time, however, doctors began to interpret the conditions loosely and even ignore them. In the few circumstances where the law took notice, it accommodated expanded euthanasia through a progressive loosening of the guidelines.

This is the typical pattern of the euthanasia movement. Killing by doctors is always presented to the public as a "rare" occurrence, undertaken only when nothing else can be done. Proponents assure a doubtful public, as the New York euthanasia advocate Dr. Timothy Quill puts it, that euthanasia will be restricted to "the patient of last resort, [to be] taken only when hospice care stops providing comfort and dignity," when "all alternatives have been exhausted."[11] Unfortunately, when put into actual practice, as the Dutch experience clearly demonstrates, it quickly ceases to be rare or resorted to only when all else fails. Instead, in the words of Dr. K. F. Gunning, perhaps the most notable Dutch opponent of euthanasia, "Once you accept killing as a solution for a single problem, you will find tomorrow hundreds of problems for which killing can be seen as a solution."[12]

In the twenty-plus years since euthanasia was redefined in the Netherlands as a legitimate medical practice, cultural biases have changed. No longer constrained by conscience or culture, Dutch doctors now terminate categories of people whose assisted deaths would have once provoked outrage, and they do so in numbers that were not anticipated when the practice was first promoted in 1973. "Since my country came to accept euthanasia, there has been a steady increase in the categories of people who can be killed," says Dr. Gunning. "The numbers of cases in which doctors consciously cause their patients' death in my country is frightening."[13] Rather than being rare, statistics show that doctors intentionally kill almost 9 percent of all of the Dutch people who die each year.

THE REMMELINK REPORT

In 1990, responding to the heated debate about Dutch euthanasia and the many anecdotes being told internationally about involuntary killings of patients by doctors, the Dutch government decided to determine how euthanasia was actually being carried out and appointed an investigative committee. Called the Committee to Investigate the Medical Practice Concerning Euthanasia, it was commonly known as the Remmelink Commission, after the committee's chairman, Professor J. Remmelink, then attorney general of the Dutch Supreme Court.

The Remmelink Commission conducted three studies. In the first, a retrospective study, more than four hundred physicians were interviewed about their opinions on the practice of euthanasia. Then for six months the same physicians were asked to record and report their actions in cases with a fatal outcome. Finally, a representative sampling of deaths was taken from the register at the Central Statistics Office, and the physicians who had been involved in the care of the deceased were asked to provide information about the cases. In all three instances, the doctors' anonymity was guaranteed.

The commission's two-volume report, known as the Remmelink Report, was issued in 1991.[14] It was not written objectively; rather, the Remmelink Report was written to assure that euthanasia was rare and that the existing guidelines were effective in controlling the practice. This was done, in part, by severely restricting the definition of "euthanasia" to deliberate termination of another's life at his or her request, usually accomplished by a lethal injection of a sedative and a curare-like poison. Cases that did not explicitly fit this category were not called euthanasia. A doctor's lethally injecting a patient without request, which as we shall see is not an uncommon occurrence in the Netherlands, was called, not involuntary or non-voluntary euthanasia, but rather "termination of life without patient's explicit request." (Some Dutch doctors call the act "life-terminating treatment," proving that the Dutch are not above resorting to euphemisms.) Other acts of intentional killing, such as purposefully overdosing a patient with pain-control medication to kill him, also fell outside the Remmelink Report's working definition of euthanasia. Why? Because the drugs used in pain control, when properly applied, are palliative rather than lethal agents—unlike curare, which is always a lethal agent. Even if they were used to intentionally cause death, their use in killing was not labeled euthanasia.

Although it dubiously narrowed the definition of euthanasia, to its credit the Remmelink Report did include the complete statistical data upon which it based its conclusions. Independent analysis of this rich source of information had a profoundly negative impact on the world's view of Dutch euthanasia. According to the Remmelink Report, about 130,000 people die each year in the Netherlands.[15] Of these, approximately 43,300, or about one third, die suddenly—from catastrophic heart attacks, stroke, accidents—thus precluding decisions about end-of-life care.[16] That leaves approximately ninety thousand people each year whose deaths involve end-of-life medical decisions.

With that in mind, here are the figures about euthanasia-related deaths in 1990, derived from the Remmelink Report's published statistical data:

- 2,300 patients were euthanized (killed) by their doctors upon request, and 400 people died through physician-assisted suicide, for a total of 2,700 doctor-induced deaths.[17] That is approximately 3 percent of all deaths involving end-of-life medical care. The equivalent percentage in the United States would be approximately 41,500 deaths.

- 1,040 died from involuntary euthanasia, lethal injections given without request or consent—three deaths every single day.[18] These deaths constitute slightly more than 1 percent of all cases involving end-of-life medical care. The equivalent in the United States would be approximately sixteen thousand involuntary killings per year.

- Of these involuntary euthanasia cases, 14 percent, or 145, were fully competent to make their own medical decisions but were killed without request or consent anyway.[19] The equivalent in the United States would be over two thousand. Moreover, 72 percent of the people killed without their consent had never given any indication they would want their lives terminated.[20]

- 8,100 patients died from an intentional overdose of morphine or other pain-control medications, designed primarily to terminate life.[21] In other words, death was not a side effect of treatment to relieve pain, which can sometimes occur, but was the *intended result* of the overdose. Of these, 61 percent (4,941 patients) were intentionally overdosed without request or consent. The equivalent in the United States would be around seventy-eight thousand.

These figures are startling. Of the approximately ninety thousand Dutch people whose deaths involved end-of-life medical decisions in 1990, 11,140 were intentionally killed (euthanized) or assisted in suicide—or 11.1 percent of all Dutch deaths involving medical decisions. This is approximately 8.5 percent of Dutch deaths from all causes. Of these killings, *more than half were involuntary* (1,040 involuntary lethal injections and 4,941 involuntary intentional overdoses). Applying those percentages to the U.S. death rate would mean more than 170,000 deaths each year caused by euthanasia or assisted suicide, and about eighty-five thousand of these involuntary, more than the current number of U.S. suicides and homicides combined.[22]

It should also be kept in mind that the Remmelink statistics probably underestimate the actual number of deaths caused by euthanasia and assisted suicide. A study conducted by the Free University at Amsterdam revealed that two thirds of Dutch general practitioners have certified a patient's death as resulting from natural causes when in fact it was euthanasia or assisted suicide.[23] Another Dutch study arrived at a similar conclusion, finding that only 28 percent of doctors were honest about their euthanasia killings when filling out death certificates.[24] Moreover, in a study conducted by the Medico-legal Group of Limburg University in Maastricht found that 41.1 percent of doctors admitted to having engaged in involuntary euthanasia.

A more recent Dutch study, published in the *New England Journal of Medicine* in November 1996, found that only 41 percent of all euthanasia deaths were reported to the authorities. This same study revealed that 23 percent of physicians had killed patients without an explicit request. Moreover, at least half of Dutch physicians take the initiative by *suggesting* euthanasia to their patients.[25] It is no wonder, then, that an analysis of these and other Dutch euthanasia statistics, published in the *Journal of Medical Ethics*, concluded that the Dutch promises of "effective regulation ring hollow" and that killing by doctors in the Netherlands "remains beyond effective control."[26]

GUIDELINES THAT DO NOT PROTECT

The Remmelink Report and other research into Dutch euthanasia practices suggest that guidelines do not protect and do not restrict. One reason is that guideline violations are rarely punished, and even when they are, the sanctions are almost never meaningful. For example, a Dutch nurse was given a two-month sentence for killing an AIDS patient.[27] Meanwhile, when doctors kill people who have not asked to die, they generally receive no punishment of any kind. The *British Medical Journal* reported on a general practitioner who killed his elderly comatose patient with a lethal injection and was convicted of murder but received no penalty of any kind despite having violated virtually every protective guideline.[28]

But the issue goes much deeper than law enforcement authorities refusing to enforce the rules. What euthanasia really did to the Dutch was to profoundly alter the nation's conception of right and wrong. With the widespread acceptance of a euthanasia consciousness in the Netherlands, the guideline limitations became mere window dressing that made little actual difference at the bedside to doctors or, indeed, to much of the general public. Finding the proverbial exception to the rule became a standard practice which, in turn, soon changed the exception into the rule. The official guidelines then expanded to meet the actual practice.

These cases have real faces. Dr. Gunning tells of one such tragic circumstance: "A friend of mine, an internist, was asked to see a lady with terminal lung cancer, who had a short time to live and was very short of breath. After the examination, he asked the patient to come to the hospital on Saturday for a few days so that be could alleviate her distress. She refused, being afraid of being euthanized there. My friend assured his patient that he would be on duty and that no such thing would happen. So the lady came. On Sunday night she was breathing normally and feeling much better. The doctor went home. When he came back on Monday afternoon, the patient was dead. The doctor's colleague told him, 'What is the sense of having that woman here? It makes no difference whether she dies today or after two weeks. We need the bed for another case.'"[29] In other words, the woman was euthanized, against her explicit wishes simply to accommodate the killing doctor's priorities.

The psychiatrist Dr. Herbert Hendin, medical director of the American Foundation for Suicide Prevention, is one of the world's foremost experts on Dutch euthanasia. Over the last several years, Hendin has held extensive discussions with Dutch doctors who euthanize patients and has reviewed the records of actual cases. Dr. Hendin believes that many doctors in the Netherlands feel justified in performing involuntary euthanasia, because a system that permits them to kill "encourages some to feel entitled to make [euthanasia] decisions without consulting the patient."[30] As an example, Hendin recounts his interview with a pro-euthanasia doctor who justified killing a nun who had requested not to be killed on the basis of religious belief, because *he felt* she was in too much pain.[31]

It is not only the many involuntary killings that violate Dutch guidelines. Dr. Hendin describes his conversation with a Dutch doctor who has euthanized between fifty and one hundred patients. One of the cases in which he consulted was that of an elderly woman who wanted to die, not because she was ill, but because she was haunted by memories of being a concentration camp survivor.[32] How could this case possibly meet the guidelines? The woman was not ill. The doctor in question was a family practitioner, not a psychiatrist, and there appears to have been no sustained attempt to alleviate the poor woman's anguish. Despite this, in an act that reeks of tragic irony, the doctor put her to death and is now afflicted himself by his memory of her.[33]

To prove the existence of cases that violate the official guidelines, it is not necessary to rely on anecdotes. Such cases have even been documented in euthanasia-friendly documentaries originally produced in the Netherlands and later shown in the United States. One such documentary, broadcast in 1993 over public television on the program *The*

Health Quarterly, revealed how broadly the Dutch guidelines are interpreted—that is to say, how commonly they are ignored.[34]

One case documented in the film concerns a man named Henk Dykema, who at the time of filming was asymptomatic HIV-positive. Dykema feared the afflictions that he expected to befall him and had been asking his doctor to kill him for more than a year. The film shows the doctor telling Henk that he might live for years at his current stage of infection, but the patient wants none of it. The doctor, a general practitioner, then discussed Henk's case with a colleague, also a general practitioner. Significantly, no psychiatrist was consulted. Finally, the doctor agreed to provide a poisonous drug cocktail to Dykema, even though he was not suffering any significant physical symptoms.[35]

Dykema's assisted suicide was clearly not a last resort, as required by the Dutch guidelines. He and his doctor did not explore all other possible options, such as psychiatric treatment, which could well have alleviated his anxiety and depression. Nor was he told of the actions the doctor could have taken to relieve his suffering when he did become ill. The doctor didn't even wait until Henk had actual symptoms of AIDS. As Dr. Carlos Gomez, a specialist in hospice medicine at the University of Virginia and an expert on euthanasia issues, aptly put it, Dykema's physician was "responding to anticipation of suffering . . . which may or may not have been true. In a sense the physician was saying, 'You're absolutely right, your end is going to be a disaster.'"[36] Dr. Hendin, analyzing Dykema's case from a psychiatrist's perspective, commented, "The patient was clearly depressed. The doctor kept establishing that the man was persistent in his request, but did not address the terror that underlay it."[37] Now consider this: had the doctor called in suicide prevention experts to help Henk instead of helping to kill him, Dykema might well have survived long enough to benefit from the drugs that now extend the lives of HIV patient for many years. There is a word for that kind of "care": abandonment.

The documentary shows another patient who was euthanized, a psychiatrist named Jan Stricht, who asked for euthanasia because he had blood clots on the brain. The malady was not terminal. Dr. Stricht, the viewer is told, might have lived "one year or twenty years."[38] Nor had the affliction caused significant physical pain. Rather, Dr. Stricht was emotionally upset at his greatly reduced physical capacities, caused primarily by significant difficulties in depth perception and other such motor deficiencies.

Dr. Stricht's own physician, a general practitioner, described the case as one of "mental suffering." The depressed man was feeling the effects of being dependent on others for the necessities of life: "I can depend on other people to do things, but the bad thing is they want to do it their way and not my way, so they don't help me. . . . I have to eat what they decide that I have to eat, which I don't want to eat at all . . . Or, I want to drink, and they say, 'You drink too much. It's wrong to do.'"[39] Dr. Shricht's upset at his growing dependence is seen by the doctor as legitimate reason to provide euthanasia. Tellingly, the doctor took no effort to address and correct Dr. Stricht's legitimate complaints about the quality of his caregiving.

The documentary also shows Maria, a twenty-five-year-old woman with anorexia nervosa, asking for euthanasia. She is in remission but fears a recurrence of her malady, stating: "I've thought about dying day and night, and I know that if relief does not come, I will return to the old pattern, the pattern of self-punishment, hurting myself. I know it. I feel it, and therefore I hope the release will come soon and I die."[40] Maria's doctor agrees to euthanize her, stating, "It is not possible to have a good quality of life for her." This case was even too much for the authorities, who brought charges against the doctor. However, the euthanasia consciousness had so permeated the justice system that a judge ruled that Maria's killing was justified because her suffering had made her life unbearable.

Similar tragedies can be found in many published investigations of Dutch euthanasia. For example, the *Oregonian* reported on a woman with skin cancer who was euthanized. She was not in pain, nor was she in a terminal stage of her illness. Rather, she was upset by the scars on her face and demanded euthanasia from her doctor, or else—the threat being that she would "jump from the balcony." Her doctor, to his later expressed regret, accommodated her wish to die.[41]

Studies indicate that families, rather than patients, generally decide when the time has come for euthanasia. According to Dr. Hendin, doctors called in such cases "usually advocate euthanasia," because they "support the relatives' desire to be free from the burden of caring for the patient."[42] One such case occurred when a wife told her husband to choose euthanasia or a nursing home. Not wanting to be cared for by strangers, he chose death. The doctor killed him, despite knowing of the coercion.[43]

Dr. Gunning tells of another such case related to him by a close physician friend of his who supports euthanasia. A man was hospitalized with terminal cancer and was in great pain. His son came to his father's doctor and said that the family wanted to bury the old man before they went on holiday. The doctor agreed and overdosed the man with pain-control medication. The next day, much to his shock, the old man was sitting up, feeling great. The intended overdose had not killed him but had killed the pain.[44]

Dancing With Mr. D, a revealing book written a few years ago by a Dutch doctor, Bert Keizer, demonstrated how farcical the protective guidelines have become in the Netherlands. Keizer works in a nursing home, where he cares for—and sometimes kills—disabled, elderly, and dying people. He looks upon euthanasia as a necessary and proper, albeit distasteful, part of his job. As depicted in the book, so do his colleagues, patients, and their families.

Keizer is brutally honest in revealing his own attitudes about his patients. He depicts the lives of frail and dying people as pointless, useless, ugly, grotesque. Those with whom Keizer interacts all seem to share these views, including his colleagues, family members of patients, and the patients themselves. This allows Keizer to kill patients without and consequence other then having a few bad dreams.

And kill his patients Keizer does, again and again. One man he euthanizes probably has lung cancer but the diagnosis is never certain. A relative tells Keizer that the man wants to be given a lethal injection, a request later confirmed by the patient. Keizer quickly agrees to kill the man. Demonstrating the utter uselessness of "protective guidelines," he never tells his patient about treatment options or how the pain and other symptoms of cancer can be palliated effectively. He never even checks to see if the man has been pressured into wanting a hastened death or is depressed. Keizer doesn't even take the time to confirm the diagnosis with certainty. When a colleague asks, why rush, and points out that the man isn't suffering terribly, Keizer snaps: "Is it for us to answer this question? All I know is that he wants to die more or less upright and that he doesn't want to crawl to his grave the way a dog crawls howling to the side walk after he's been hit by a car."[45]

Keizer either doesn't know or doesn't care that with proper medical treatment, people with lung cancer do not have to die in such unmitigated agony. The next day, he lethally injects his patient, telling his colleagues as he walks to the man's room to do the deed, "If anyone so much as whispers cortisone [a palliative agent] or 'uncertain diagnosis,' I'll hit him."[46]

Another of Keizer's patients is disabled by Parkinson's disease. The patient requests to be killed but before the act can be carried out, he receives a letter from his brother, who uses a religious argument to urge him to change his mind. The letter causes the man to hesitate, upsetting Keizer, who writes: "I don't know what to do with such a wavering death wish. It's getting on my nerves. Does he want to die or doesn't he? I do hope we won't have to go over the whole business again, right from the very start."[47]

Keizer has the nursing home chaplain assure the man that euthanasia will not upset God. The man again thinks he wants to die. Keizer is quick with the injection, happy the man has "good veins," and the man expires before his uncertainty can disturb his doctor's mood again.

The book is rife with such stories. In Keizer's world, his patients' lives are inherently undignified. Medical professionals view those in their care with disdain. Family members are mostly selfish, stupid, greedy, and unloving.

Keizer consults with patient who wants to commit assisted suicide because he has Lou Gehrig's disease. But Keizer objects—not because he values the man's life and wants to convince him to find a better way to deal with his disease—but fearing the man will botch his own death, he wants to do the killing personally. So Keizer involves a social worker, a longtime acquaintance of the distraught man, who tells him coldly: "Your life is one of the most terrible things I know of and I do believe that it would a great relief to you if it would end. But I cannot believe that you will have the strength to take the overdose in the event the doctor will hand it to you."[48]

The guidelines clearly protect nobody in the Netherlands. But when you think about it, that is not their purpose. Their real purpose is to allow the Dutch people to ignore reality and pretend that killing can be controlled. But if doctors aren't punished for violating the killing regulations, if physicians like Keizer can kill patients when a cancer diagnosis isn't even certain, if a young anorexic woman can be assisted in suicide because she fears she will again abuse food, if a doctor kills a woman on the basis of what the doctor himself called "a case of vanity," if they allow families to push the death agenda regardless of the desires of their sick relatives, whom can they protect?

The answer is very clear to anybody willing to look beyond the romantic myths of euthanasia to the way it actually works in the real world: nobody.

DEATH ON DEMAND COMES
TO THE NETHERLANDS

The Dutch psychiatrist Boutdewijn Chabot has written, "If one accepts, as I do, that persistently suicidal patients are indeed terminal,

then one must ask whether a persistently suicidal state can be diagnosed as an incurable disease. I believe in some cases, like that of my
patient, it can."[49]

Hilly Bosscher was just such a deeply depressed and suicidal woman.
She had lost her two sons, one to suicide in 1986 and the other to brain
cancer in 1991. Her marriage, never very good and often abusive, took a
turn for the worse after her first son's death and was dissolved in 1990.
Bosscher had briefly received psychiatric treatment years earlier for the
depression and suicidal thoughts she experienced after her son's suicide. On the day her second son died, she failed in an attempt to kill
herself. She still wanted to die but hesitated at self-destruction for fear
that she would be hospitalized if she tried and failed again. However,
she moved the graves of her two sons to the same cemetery and purchased a burial plot for herself so she could be buried between them.[50]

Bosscher began to attend meetings of the Dutch Euthanasia Society, where she met Dr. Chabot, who attended meetings to troll for patients. She told Chabot that she didn't want therapy, "because it would
loosen the bonds with her deceased sons."[51] Chabot took her as a patient anyway and met with her on four occasions between August 2 and
September 7, 1991. Chabot did not attempt to treat her. Rather, he interviewed her to determine her prognosis. After these interviews and
his consultations, despite the absence of any physical illness, he agreed
to help Bosscher kill herself, which he did on September 28, 1991.

Chabot was charged with the crime of assisted suicide, which is
less dramatic than it sounds. As I mentioned earlier, Dutch trials are
not based strictly on the adversary system. Prosecutors sometimes file
cases not to punish wrongdoers but rather to establish a legal precedent
permitting a specific activity. This is the primary method by which euthanasia guidelines have been steadily loosened in the Netherlands.

Dr. Chabot's lawyer was Eugene Sutorius, a charming man with a
quick smile and a sharp legal mind any attorney would admire. Sutorius
was no stranger to euthanasia cases, being a legal adviser to the Dutch
Voluntary Euthanasia Society and the lawyer primarily responsible over

many years for pushing the boundaries of euthanasia in the Dutch courts. Sutorius recalled his legal argument on behalf of Dr. Chabot:

> My . . . plea was [that] the doctor acted justifiably in [a situation of] a conflict of duties, one, the preponderant duty, which is preserving human life, and the second is fighting suffering or preventing it. . . . In this case, the duties could not be reconciled, one could not be fulfilled without violating the other. . . . So, I said, he could not escape the [patient's] request, and the request would be reasonable and understandable and it would be according to his prognosis, inevitable that the suffering would just continue. . . . So, I argued that a doctor may, under very strict circumstances, be justified in giving the priority to the other duty, the duty to relieve suffering. And that, they [the court] accepted.[52]

According to Sutorius the prosecutor vigorously presented the case, but even so there was never much question of Chabot's actually being meaningfully punished: "The public prosecution, as a body, sees that this is not criminality in the normal sense. That he [the prosecutor] is not fighting real criminals here; he is fighting doctors that encounter a problem. . . . So, even the prosecutor, while bringing the case, he's more interested in making sure that we have strict definitions and order than he is in punishing the professional. He's trying to create a precedent. It's either yes or no, but he wants to make sure that there's order in society and that these things are done decently."[53]

Both the prosecutor and Sutorius got what they were looking for in the Chabot case. The lower court refused to punish the psychiatrist in any way, a decision blessed by the Dutch Supreme Court, with the minor caveat that Chabot erred by not having a colleague independently examine the patient. The basis of the ruling was that the law cannot distinguish between suffering caused by physical illness and suffering caused by mental anguish—which, of course, is where the logic of euthanasia leads inevitably. Thus, Dutch guidelines now permit doctors in the Netherlands to kill their depressed patients on the basis of patient demand caused by depression, even if the patient refuses treatment that might overcome the suicidal fixation. In other words, in the Netherlands, people with a significant depression can obtain death virtually on demand.

KILLING BABIES

In the Netherlands, infants are killed because they have birth defects, and doctors justify the practice. One Dutch pediatrician explained, "Some patients, if you withhold or withdraw treatment, the child will not die immediately. It might take hours or days or weeks. And then, I think it's better to support the child to die, and to help the child to die, and that's actually what we are doing, of course, in very rare occasions."[54]

Thanks to another "prosecution" of a doctor who euthanized an infant, the courts have begun to open the door for euthanasia to legally enter the pediatric ward. Dr. Henk Prins killed a three-day-old girl who was born with spina bifida, hydrocephaly, and leg deformities. The doctor—a gynecologist, not a pediatrician or a medical expert in such cases, although experts were consulted—was defended by Sutorius. Prins testified in the trial court that he killed the child, with her parents' permission, because of the infant's poor prognosis and because the baby screamed in pain when touched. Yet the child was in agony because she was neglected medically. The open wound in her back, the primary characteristic of spina bifida, had not been closed, nor had the fluid been drained from her head, even though these medical treatments are standard in spina bifida cases and would have substantially reduced her pain. The trial court refused to punish the doctor. Indeed, the judge praised Dr. Prins for "his integrity and courage and wished him well in any further legal proceedings he may face."[55]

A 1997 study published in the British medical journal, the *Lancet*, reveals how deeply pediatric euthanasia has already metastasized into Dutch neo-natal medical practice. According to the report, doctors kill approximately 8 percent of all infants who die each year in the Netherlands. That amounts to approximately 80 to 90 each year. Of these, one-third would have lived more than a month. At least 10 to 15 of these killings involve infants who did not depend on life-sustaining treatment to stay alive. The study found that 45 percent of neo-natologists and 31 percent of pediatricians who responded to study's questionnaires have killed infants.[56]

A 1990 report of the Royal Dutch Medical Association (KNMG), *Life-Terminating Actions with Incompetent Patients*, set forth "require-ments for careful medical practice" when ending the lives of handi-capped newborns. The standard for euthanasia is based on what Dutch doctors call an "unlivable life."[57] If this sounds familiar, it is: it differs little in its bigoted view of the value of disabled people from the atti-tudes expressed by Binding and Hoche in 1920 in *Permitting the De-struction of Life Not Worthy of Life*.

According to current Dutch medical ethics, the "livableness" of a life depends on a combination of factors, including the following:

- The expected measure of suffering (not only bodily but also emotional—the level of hopelessness);

- The expected potential for communication and human rela-tionships;

- Independence (ability to move, to care for oneself, to live in-dependently);

- Self-realization (being able to hear, read, write, labor);

- The child's life expectancy.

If the infant's "prospects" don't measure up to what the doctor and parents believe is a life worth living, the child can be neglected to death or, if that doesn't work, killed. It is stunning how similar these views are to those expressed by Karl Brandt—who was executed after Nuremberg—to the father of Baby Knauer in 1939 in justifying the baby boy's infanticide: "From then on, we wouldn't have to suffer from this terrible misfortune, because the Fuhrer had granted us the mercy killing of our son. Later, we could have other children, handsome and healthy, of whom the Reich could be proud. . . . He [Brandt] was like a savior to us—the man who could deliver us from a heavy burden. We thanked him and told him how grateful we were."[58]

It is noteworthy that the Remmelink Report did not include figures on the incidence of pediatric euthanasia, which was already an accepted practice among most Dutch pediatricians by 1990. Nor did it include cases in which disabled children were allowed to die by medical neglect, the preferred Dutch method of killing newborns with birth defects. For example, children with Down's syndrome are commonly born with a bowel obstruction easily corrected with surgery. To refuse this treatment for a "normal" child would be considered an outrageous crime. But in the Netherlands, it is acceptable to leave the obstruction in place if the infant has Down's syndrome, resulting in the baby's starving to death. One doctor has justified this form of killing by saying that the Down's child would suffer if allowed to live because he or she "would always be dependent" and find it "very difficult to establish normal social relations, to create or bring up a family."[59] It is estimated that at least three hundred Dutch infants die from intentional medical neglect each year.[60] (Such deaths also occur in the United States.)

These barbaric policies have been rationalized by Dutch doctors and ethicists on a number of grounds. A few resort to hard utilitarianism, asserting that the value of a life "depends on how valuable that life is for other people."[61] However, most justifications of Dutch infanticide are couched in more compassionate tones, stressing that the killing is in the best interests of the child. Thus, the State Committee on Euthanasia of the KNMG declared support for killing newborns—as well as minors, mentally retarded persons, and the demented elderly—if "one can suppose that were the patients to express their will, they would opt for euthanasia."[62] It is doubtful that actual disabled people are often permitted to participate in decisions about whose lives are livable and whose lives are better off ended.

Infants are not the only children who are eligible for euthanasia. Pediatric oncologists have provided a *hulp bij zelfoding* (self-help for ending life) program for adolescents since the 1980s, in which poisonous doses are prescribed for minors with terminal illness.[63] Moreover, children who want physician-assisted death may be able to receive it without the consent of their parents. A 1986 report issued by the Central Committee of the Royal Dutch Medical Association explained its position on euthanasia of older minors:

> The Central Committee is not in favour of including an exact limit in the law with respect to the 'rights' of parents in the case of a minor making a request for euthanasia. Nor is the Central Committee in favour of giving a right of veto to one or both parents in such cases. The Central Committee does hold the view, however, that the physician should always consult the parents about their child's request for euthanasia. But with a view to the child's own good, *this does not imply that parents have the power of decision*. It goes without saying that where a young child is concerned, the state of affairs will be different from those where an older child is concerned.
>
> We would like to advocate not to include a separate age limit in the law, as it may be impossible as well as unjust in our opinion to lay down an exact age limit in this matter. Sometimes, a 15-year-old child can have a mature judgment. At all times, it will be a matter of acting carefully in medical respect.[64]

Where next for Dutch euthanasia? Any pretense of control and "limits" are evaporating before our very eyes. In 2000, a Dutch doctor was found to have acted properly when he euthanized an eighty-six-year-old man who wanted to die because he was "living a pointless and empty existence." The man was depressed about the deaths of friends and his own "physical decline." In other words, the euthanasia was justified by the social decline of the patient. Despite this, the doctor was acquitted of any crime, the court ruling that the man's "hopeless existence" justified the euthanasia.[65]

In 2001, despite the many problems—only some of which have been described in this chapter—the Netherlands formally legalized euthanasia. The guidelines that have proved so inadequate to their protective task remain. Only now, doctors don't even have to report their killing activities to a prosecutor, but only to a medical board.

But even this broad license isn't enough for the death fundamentalists that drive the Dutch euthanasia agenda. On the day after the new law took effect, Els Borst, the Dutch minister of health, suggested that elderly people "who are tired of life" and who not otherwise qualify for euthanasia should be given access to a "suicide pill," to end their lives. Borst cited two ninety-five-year-olds she knows as a reason for the Department of Justice to permit the distribution of a suicide pill: "They were bored stiff, but alas, not bored to death."[66]

DRAWING CONCLUSIONS

One of the pioneers of Dutch euthanasia, Dr. Pieter Admiraal, who has killed more than one hundred patients, told me, "Of our doctors, eighty-four percent will give euthanasia, while sixteen percent will not. Of these sixteen percent, most will send patients to another doctor for euthanasia. Only a few will not participate either directly or indirectly . . . If you come to euthanasia like we did, you will come to the same result."[67] I doubt that the Dutch physicians who died resisting Nazi pressure to begin killing their weakest and most vulnerable patients would admire Dr. Admiraal and his colleagues today. They would be horrified and appalled.

Unlike the Dutch, Americans do not come to the decision whether to accept legalized euthanasia blindly. We have the Dutch experience to guide us. On the basis of their experience with euthanasia, what can we learn about the death culture? First, the slippery slope is very real. As Dr. Gunning put it, the Dutch have proved that once killing is accepted as a solution for one problem, it will be seen as the solution for many other problems. Once we accept the killing of terminally ill patients, as did the Dutch, we will invariably accept the killing of chronically ill and depressed patients, and ultimately, even children.

Second, the substantive differences between the Dutch and U.S. healthcare systems mean that the U.S. experience with the death culture would likely be far *worse* than that in the Netherlands. Recall that the Dutch have virtual universal health coverage. We, on the other hand, have tens of millions of Americans without health insurance, which by definition means they often receive inadequate healthcare. Moreover, for-profit health maintenance organizations are putting great financial pressure on the healthcare system and are imposing a financial conflict of interest between patients and their own doctors by punishing physicians financially if they provide too much care (which I will discuss in chapter six). Although cost containment is an issue in the Netherlands, financial pressures to hasten death are much more muted there than they would likely be here.

Third, the Netherlands is a much more tolerant society than we are, generally more accepting of differences among people, such as those of race, gender, and sexual orientation. Nevertheless, these attitudes filter into their medical practice; it is to be expected that our prevailing prejudices would filter more strongly into our medical practice. An editorial in the *New England Journal of Medicine* cited a plethora of studies that uncovered significant race-based inequality in the delivery of healthcare in the United States and opined that the disparities in the delivery of healthcare apparently caused by racism need to be focused upon with the "rigor and attention given to other health concerns of similar magnitude."[68] These and other factors make it likely that legalizing, and especially "routinizing," euthanasia in the United States would be especially dangerous for marginalized populations.

A legitimate question is, If euthanasia is so bad, why do a majority of the Dutch people support their country's policy? I put that very question to the Dutch ethicist W. C. M. Klijn, a retired professor of medical ethics who served as a member of a government-appointed committee that investigated whether euthanasia should be formally legalized and wrote the minority report recommending against legalization. Professor Klijn told me: "We Dutch pride ourselves on our history. We see ourselves as having been good in the past; therefore, we believe that we will always be good. It is an arrogance of goodness. Thus, even though there are striking resemblances to our euthanasia practices and those the Nazis sought to impose upon us, we assure ourselves: We resisted the Nazis. We are sophisticated, humane. We can't be doing wrong! To admit we are wrong on euthanasia would be to say that we are not the compassionate, sophisticated, enlightened people we think we are. It is very hard in the Dutch character to do that."[69]

Professor Klijn also believes that, much like the people of the United States, the Dutch have an almost reflexive response to arguments based on "personal autonomy." Because this concept is so deeply ingrained in the Dutch and U.S. value systems, upon hearing the magic word "choice," many people make up their minds and don't have the time or inclination to dig deeper. They don't see the whole picture: the abuses, the destruction of family cohesiveness, or the paternalism inherent in euthanasia because the decision as to whether one lives or dies often depends more on the doctor's values than on the patient's.

Dr. van der Sluis, a secularist opponent of his country's euthanasia policies, raises another point germane to the debate in the United States. Many Dutch accept euthanasia so as not to be perceived as overly religious. "The proponents of euthanasia have falsely, but successfully, cast the argument as one of religion versus rationality," Dr. van der Sluis told me. "They assert that only fundamentalist Christians oppose euthanasia and since few Dutch are fundamentalist Christians, they tend to support euthanasia." [70] Dr. Pieter Admiraal verified this when he told me, "The only way to deny euthanasia is based on religion. Most Dutch are nonbelievers, and thus, they must support euthanasia."[71]

Dr. Herbert Hendin discovered another interesting reason why euthanasia may be accepted by the Dutch: the case studies, only some of which are recounted here, are not widely discussed in the Netherlands out of "loyalty to the system" and in order not to threaten the delicate consensus that has developed among the Dutch concerning the practice. Dr. Hendin writes that several Dutch euthanasia proponents admitted that they are not candid in their discussions about euthanasia "for political considerations." They don't want to "play into the hands of the Christian Democrats," the minority opposition party that opposes euthanasia.[72] Moreover, Dr. Hendin discovered that the Dutch are exquisitely sensitive to being criticized and that "savage criticisms" of Dutch euthanasia policies by "physicians in the rest of Europe" have "forced the Dutch into a defensive position."[73] He also noted, "Virtually all of those who have played a role in advancing the cause of euthanasia [in the Netherlands] on humanitarian grounds were concerned about the problems in implementation yet seemed disinclined to express their doubts publicly."[74] Hendin confronted one such proponent who had published an article in favor of euthanasia that broadly contradicted his private conversations with Hendin. The doctor justified his hypocrisy on the basis of not "wish[ing] to be critical of the system or perhaps to be viewed as being so in a culture in which uncritical support for Dutch euthanasia policies is politically correct."[75]

More than twenty years of legitimized euthanasia may also have desensitized the Dutch to activities that they once would have found abhorrent. One documentary televised on the Dutch television network showed the actual killing of a man with amyotrophic lateral sclerosis, generally known in this country as Lou Gehrig's disease, by his doctor. Even this documentary, intended to promote the legitimacy of euthanasia, showed how the Dutch euthanasia guidelines offer little actual protection. For example, the doctor who provides the required second opinion tells the patient bluntly, "You have an incurable disease which will soon end in death, and unless there is some intervention you will experience terrible suffering. You will probably suffocate."[76] In fact, according to Dame Cecily Saunders, the creator of the English hospice movement, if people with ALS receive proper care, *they do not suffocate.* She has helped more than three hundred such patients die with dignity in hospice, so she should know. (I have confirmed this assessment with several U.S. neurologists and hospice doctors.) Yet neither the patient's doctor nor the rubber-stamp consultant bothered to tell the patient this news that might have caused him to change his mind about being killed. (An edited version of this documentary was shown in the United States on December 8, 1994, on ABC's magazine show *Prime Time Live*.)

Another example of the desensitization of a nation to indecency was a program aired on Dutch television that was partly financed by the Dutch ministry of health, called *A Matter of Life and Death*. The broadcast consisted of six segments; in each one, two seriously disabled patients were pitted against each other. Both tell the audience about themselves and their respective illnesses and describe their current prognosis. The audience then votes on which of the two should receive life-prolonging treatment and which should not. The Dutch government defended the show as an effort to stimulate discussion about reducing healthcare costs.[77]

Then there is the case of the little girl who fell into a lake and drowned. Normally, that would not be national news. But in this case, "Two hundred people stopped eating sandwiches, playing Frisbee, or walking the dog, and stood. Some moved to the bank and watched the girl drown. No one tried to help."[78] The little girl's death, captured on video, shook the Netherlands in much the same way the Rodney King video did in this country, as the Dutch, "in a rare moment of self-examination," wondered and worried about the decline of their culture.[79]

Of course, these anecdotes do not prove that euthanasia has adversely affected the Dutch national character. It is interesting to note, however, that some Dutch no longer trust their doctors. The Dutch Patients Association, a patients' rights group with sixty thousand members, distributes a wallet card to protect members from being involuntarily euthanized. The card specifically states that it is "intended to prevent involuntary euthanasia in case of admission of the signer to the hospital" and instructs that "no treatment be administered with the intention to terminate life."[80]

Nevertheless, Dutch proponents and opponents of euthanasia agree: disaster lies ahead if the United States follows their country's lead. Dr. Pieter Admiraal told me: "I am totally against euthanasia in the U.S. as matters now stand. Before you have euthanasia, you have to have quality of care for terminally ill people, and the U.S. doesn't have that. Unless the U.S. can obtain it, it would be silly—ridiculous—for euthanasia to be legalized."[81]

Eugene Sutorius, certainly no shirker when it comes to advancing euthanasia in his country, agrees. He believes that "in the States, euthanasia will become a substitute for care": "I think that a society that doesn't start with care cannot talk about euthanasia. I don't mean this as arrogance, but I think that care in Holland is in the center of what we feel that doctors should do and be there for. And I think doctors in a large degree mirror that. Because in Holland, the technological side didn't overthrow the care side. We didn't destroy the relationship between doctor and patient."[82]

Sutorius chuckled as he told me that he now rarely receives invitations from U.S. proponents of euthanasia to come to the States and speak, largely because of his belief that policies he has worked so energetically to create in his country would be a terrible thing for America.

One pro-euthanasia book, which was underwritten by the Dutch government, put it thus: "Given the fact that euthanasia . . . can only be tolerated by society in [a] context where on the whole all human life is valued highly . . . in situations where the value of life becomes more uncertain due to violence, high suicide rates, disasters, economic uncertainties, etc., the basis of mutual trust on which this [euthanasia] decision-making should be founded cannot be sufficiently guaranteed."[83]

In the United States, with its declining belief in the equality-of-human-life ethic, with its high rates of violence, significant suicide levels, pronounced economic uncertainties, divisions of race, gender, religion, sexual orientation, class, and the concomitant lack of mutual trust, euthanasia would be an ethical and moral catastrophe.

But the euthanasia virus is catching. As these words are written, Belgium, which borders the Netherlands, have followed the Dutch as the world's second nation to legalize euthanasia. Even though studies show that 3 out of 100 deaths in Belgium's northern Dutch speaking Flemish region are caused by doctors killing patients who have not asked to be euthanized. Moreover, already 10 percent of Belgian deaths appear to result from euthanasia.[84] Considering that legalizing the practice will, in all likelihood, only increase the number of people doctors kill, the government of Belgium seems bent on following its neighbor off the ethical cliff. Indeed, it is worth noting that the first reported case of euthanasia in Belgium—that of a patient with MS—appears to have violated that nation's protective guidelines. As of this writing (April 2003), no legal action has been taken against the attending doctor.[85]

5

Inventing the Right to Die

I N 1992, JACK KEVORKIAN SERIOUSLY PROPOSED in the *American Journal of Forensic Psychiatry* that a pilot program of death clinics be established in Michigan. The clinics, which he called "obitoria," would be staffed by physician-killers known as "obitiatrists," who would be permitted legally to terminate patients who request it, in a procedure Kevorkian then called "medicide" but now labels "patholysis."[1] Kevorkian foresaw that the first "patients" to receive medicide would be the terminally and chronically ill. However, he looked forward to the eventual widening of obitiatry to include people he labeled "patients tortured by other than organic diseases."[2]

At the time such an idea seemed fantastic, appropriate to science fiction movies such as *Soylent Green,* rather than serious intellectual discourse. Not anymore. Euthanasia is no longer confined to debates in ethics classes or late-night musing among friends over drinks. Indeed, in the last fifteen years determined and never ending political and legal actions undertaken by euthanasia advocates and their lawyers brought assisted suicide to legal reality in Oregon and to the verge of being declared a national constitutional right. Opponents can no longer afford the luxury of assuming that "it can never happen here."

If we are to counter the euthanasia juggernaut we must carefully analyze the history and tactics of euthanasia advocates that have proved surprisingly successful in recent years.

INITIATIVE 119 AND PROPOSITION 161

It is quite shocking to realize that the modern euthanasia movement has only been with us since 1988, when the first attempt was made to qualify a euthanasia legalization initiative on California's ballot. And that effort failed miserably; proponents were unable to obtain enough signatures to qualify for the ballot.

If death fundamentalists are anything, they are indomitable. Rather than being discouraged by their California failure, they redoubled their efforts. In 1991 they tried again, this time succeeding in qualifying a euthanasia legalization initiative in the state of Washington. Known as Initiative 119, the proposal would have permitted doctors to lethally inject patients under some circumstances. The early polls had the proposal far ahead, with some polls exceeding 70 percent approval. But that was before the anti-119 forces were able to present the reasons why legalizing euthanasia is a dangerous and unwise idea. In the end, support for euthanasia plummeted in Washington, and Initiative 119 lost by 54 percent to 46 percent.

Encouraged by the relatively narrow margin of their loss, euthanasia advocates got right back to work. Again California was targeted, and Proposition 161, a proposal that was almost identical to Initiative 119, successfully qualified for the November 1992 ballot.

The campaign over Proposition 161 was a virtual replay of the earlier Washington struggle. Once again, early polls showed public support in the 70-percentile range. But as usually is the case in debates over euthanasia, the more California voters learned about euthanasia and the more they considered the consequences that would follow from permitting doctors to kill, the less they liked Proposition 161. Following Washington's lead, California rejected legalized euthanasia 54 to 46 percent. Next, it was on to Oregon, where a different political strategy would lead to a dramatic victory for the death culture.

OREGON'S MEASURE 16

After the narrow passage of Oregon's Measure 16 in 1994, the first law in modern history explicitly legalizing physician-assisted suicide (PAS), one would have expected suicide guru Derek Humphry to be ecstatic. He was not, warning in a letter to the *New York Times*: "The Oregon law, which forbids infections, could be disastrous. . . . Evidence I have accumulated shows that about 25 percent of assisted suicides fail. . . . The new Oregon way to die will work only if in every instance a doctor is standing by to administer the coup de grace, if necessary."[3]

Needless to say, Humphry's doubts about Measure 16 were not disclosed to Oregon voters during the campaign for its passage. Not once did Humphry, an Oregon resident, warn his fellow citizens, as he did the readers of the *New York Times*, that "the only two 100 percent [effective] ways [of] accelerating dying are the lethal injection of barbiturates and curare or donning a plastic bag."[4] Rather, Humphry professed great enthusiasm for the proposal, writing in a fund-raising letter on behalf of the initiative, "A break-through in Oregon will start a domino effect of law reform on assisted dying throughout America."

And so it came to pass. Euthanasia proponents received that deeply longed-for breakthrough—albeit with a bare 51 percent of the Oregon vote—and nothing has been the same since.

The passage of Measure 16 illustrates the step-by-step political tactic that euthanasia advocates believe offers their best hope of establishing a broad euthanasia license: When necessary, take a half step back in order to propel the euthanasia cause two steps forward. But never stop agitating. Never stop pushing. Never stop propagandizing. Wear down opponents until they tire of the fray.

Realizing that Initiative 119 and Proposition 161 had been too ambitious in seeking to authorize doctors to lethally inject patients, as occurs in the Netherlands, Measure 16 was written in minimalist terms to make it appear less threatening and radical. Instead of lethal injections, doctors would "only" be permitted to write lethal prescriptions that the patient would self-administer.

This was a purely pragmatic decision. Despite the death culture's successes, the prospect of doctors actively killing people remains a daunting idea. (For example, in the same year that Oregonians would be voting on Measure 16, the Kevorkian gang in Michigan was unable to gather enough signatures to qualify an initiative to legalize euthanasia for that state's ballot—despite a very public and well-publicized petition drive seeking support.) For the same reason that Humphry didn't share with Oregon voters his belief that Measure 16 would be a disaster, the initiative's backers also didn't tell Oregonians what a lawyer arguing on behalf of the new law later told U.S. District Court judge Michael R. Hogan: that they viewed Measure 16 as merely a "first step."[5]

The Political Campaign

Both sides in the debate over legalizing euthanasia entered the Measure 16 campaign with reason for optimism. Opponents, buoyed by the victories in Washington and California, believed that an appropriately hard-hitting campaign would convince the people of Oregon to reject physician-induced death. Proponents believed that the measure's minimizing text had sufficiently weakened the potent "abuse" issue, which had so damaged their cause previously. Moreover, initial polls showed support for the initiative in the high 60 percent range.

The "Yes on 16" campaign led by Oregon Right to Die wasted no time getting out their emotion-driven appeal. Their poster woman was a nurse named Patty A. Rosen, head of the Bend, Oregon, chapter of the Hemlock Society. Rosen claimed in commercials to have helped her daughter, who was dying from bone cancer, to kill herself some years before. In the ads she labeled herself a "criminal" because she had obtained the pills for her pain-racked daughter to swallow and asserted that she had done so because her daughter "couldn't bear to be touched." Her voice cracking with emotion, Rosen recounted, "As she slipped peacefully away, I climbed into her bed and I took her in my arms for the first time in months." It was a poignant, touching bit of advocacy that left few viewers unmoved and fewer still thinking about the vital issues of the campaign, such as the potential for abuses, societal consequences, the availability and underutilization of compassionate caregiving opportunities like effective pain control (effective even for bone cancer when properly applied), and the issues of whether doctor-induced death would really reduce human suffering—not to mention where passage of the law might lead next.

Emotionalism and fear mongering about suffering and death were not the only tactics of Measure 16's proponents. There was also an unsubtle appeal to Oregon voter's reputed parochialism, mixed in with a strong dose of Catholic bashing.

The Catholic Church was very closely associated with the "No on 16" campaign, as it had been with the campaigns to defeat Initiative 119 and Proposition 161. Catholics provided significant funds to the "No on 16" campaign, and clerical-collar-wearing church representatives were often selected by the media to express anti-Measure 16 sentiments. Soon, as had occurred in the Netherlands more than twenty years before, a false premise became the controlling paradigm, that Measure 16 was a battle between rigid religionists and compassionate rationalists.

In furtherance of this strategy, the "Yes on 16" campaign created ads that stank of anti-Catholic bigotry. One ad asked, "Are we going to let one church make the rules for all of us?" A notable pro–Measure 16 radio commercial was more specific in its anti-Catholic appeal:

> Who do you politicians and religious leaders think you are, trying to control my life? It's none of your business, so back off and back off now. I'm voting yes on 16 because what we have are some politicians and religious leaders who are playing politics all getting together to control my life. Listen, if I'm terminally ill I don't want my family to be forced to drain their savings for unnecessary

costly medical care while I suffer just because the politicians and religious leaders say that's the way it has to be. And don't buy the garbage the Catholic Church is putting out. The safeguards in 16 are as long as your arm. Multiple medical opinions, two oral requests, and a written request that can be canceled at any time, a fifteen-day waiting period, and another forty-eight-hour waiting period. You know, there are just some people who believe they have a divine right to control other people's lives, and they'd better back off because it's none of their business. Vote yes on 16.[6]

Another complained that Catholics were financing the opposition: "Their opposition is theological. They believe suffering is redemptive and that preserving physical life is always valued higher than relief of suffering, no matter how humiliating and intolerable that physical life is. And they apply that standard not only to themselves but also to every Oregonian. They want to impose their unique theological perspective on the entire state."[7]

It was not true, of course. Opponents of Measure 16 were not asserting that people have a duty to suffer. Nor were they seeking to impose some religious hegemony on the people of Oregon. But what did facts matter? If recent American political history proves anything, it is that negative ads work.

In contrast to the proponents' hardball, pull-out-all-the-stops advocacy, the opposition forces, under the umbrella of the Coalition for Compassionate Care (ccc), took more of a surprisingly wiffle-ball approach to the campaign. The ccc ran a fine commercial of a woman who had been misdiagnosed as being terminal within six months, warned of mistakes if Measure 16 passed, and financed rebuttals to the false assertion propounded by the "Yes on 16" crowd that only the Catholic church opposed the initiative. But the campaign did not go for the emotional jugular vein, as had opponents of Washington's Initiative 119 and California's Proposition 161. In California, for example, the political consultancy firm of Cavalier and Associates had created an award-winning television ad depicting a Kevorkian-esque doctor entering an elderly woman's room carrying a euthanasia syringe with which to kill her. That ad had resonated with voters, causing support for Proposition 161 to drop like a rock. But no similar advertisements were run in Oregon against Measure 16. Consequently, although support for Measure 16 dropped nearly 20 percent from original poll numbers, the ccc was never able to drive support for the measure below the crucial 50 percent mark.

Critics contend this go-soft approach was a form of unilateral political disarmament leading directly to the measure's narrow passage. One experienced political strategist (who asked to remain anonymous) who has run many initiative campaigns and who watched the Measure 16 campaign closely is convinced that the initiative could have been defeated. "For whatever reasons, the opposition campaign decided to softball their campaign," this strategist says. "They simply chose not to use their most potent arguments, even though history proves that these arguments work."[8]

This lack of aggressiveness is perhaps best illustrated by a crucial lapse during the critical last week of the campaign. Information surfaced that Patty Rosen had been, to put it kindly, less than candid about the death of her daughter in her commercials in support of Measure 16. In these ads, Rosen stated that her daughter had died from taking an overdose of pills. But a tape recording and transcript of a speech Rosen had made in California two years previously on behalf of Proposition 161 revealed that she claimed to have actually given her daughter an injection because she feared the pills were not going to work.

Here was an opportunity rarely found in campaigns of this sort. Measure 16 proponents assured voters that passage of the measure would benefit the dying. Yet the poster woman for the campaign had stated earlier that she feared pills alone would not be sufficient to kill her dying daughter. If Patty Rosen's credibility could legitimately be questioned in the minds of voters (she admitted in a newspaper article that she had given her daughter an injection), then so could the veracity of all the arguments supporting Measure 16. But no attempt was made to exploit Rosen's yawning credibility gap, even though the opposition campaign was well aware of her deception and still had money in the bank. As a result, the matter was barely mentioned in a few low-key, inside-page newspaper stories.

In the end, it was a tragic matter of "so close, yet so far." Support for Measure 16 plummeted, as had support of Initiative 119 and Proposition 161—but not quite far enough. A bare 51 percent of Oregon's voters formally gave a state's formal imprimatur to physician-assisted suicide, for the first time in history.

The Nuts and Bolts of Measure 16

Measure 16, formally called the Oregon Death with Dignity Act, classifies a prescribed fatal overdose of drugs as a medical treatment. It authorizes patients who have been "determined by the attending physician and consulting physician to be suffering from a terminal disease" to make a written request for "medication for the purpose of ending his or her life."[9] The following "safeguards" were written into the act.

The attending physician shall:

- Make the initial determination of whether a patient has a terminal disease, is capable, and has made the request voluntarily;

- Inform the patient of

    a. His or her medical diagnosis;
    b. His or her prognosis;
    c. The potential risks associated with taking medication to be prescribed;
    d. The probable result of taking the medication to be prescribed;
    e. The feasible alternatives, including, but not limited to, comfort care, hospice care, and pain control;

- Refer the patient to a consulting physician for medical confirmation . . . and for a determination that the patient is capable and acting voluntarily;

- Refer the patient for counseling, if appropriate (counseling is required only if depression or another mental condition causes "impaired judgment");

- Request that the patient notify next of kin;

- Inform the patient that he or she has the opportunity to rescind the request at any time . . . and offer the patient an opportunity to rescind at the end of the 15-day waiting period;

- Verify, immediately prior to writing the prescription . . . that the patient is making an informed decision;

- Fulfill the medical record documentation requirements;

- Ensure that all appropriate steps are carried out in accordance with this Act.

The law also requires a waiting period of fifteen days between the initial request "and the writing of a prescription."[10]

As for the so-called safeguards, they are mostly smoke and mirrors designed, like those in the Netherlands, to give the appearance of control. Measure 16 proponents insist that the only people eligible for doctor-hastened death are people at, or near, the brink of death. This is not true. The law defines terminal illness as "an incurable and irreversible disease that . . . will, within reasonable medical judgment, produce death within six months." The measure thus assumes that doctors who diagnose a terminal condition can be accurate in predicting the expected time of death. But that is just plain wrong. Many people who have been told they were going to die within months have lived for years. Indeed, some "terminally ill" people never die of the diagnosed disease at all. As an Oregon hospice doctor, Gary L. Lee, put it, "The 'six months to live' provision is bogus. Doctors usually can't predict the time of death in that fashion. I have had the experience where people were supposed to die, and didn't. I have seen cases where cancer suddenly cleared up for no apparent reason. You never know who is going to die. You just never know."[11]

Ira Byock, former president of the American Academy of Hospice and Palliative Medicine, agrees: "No one's life is over simply because a terminal prognosis has been given. There are people who don't die. Some people enter a hospice because of a terminal diagnosis, stabilize, and leave the hospice. Some live far longer than anyone ever anticipated. I had a patient who wanted to commit suicide because of the prognosis that he would soon die. Not only didn't he kill himself, he didn't die."[12]

Another telling lapse in the initiative's language is that nothing in the definition of terminal illness requires that death will occur despite appropriate medical treatment to weed out people who will be unlikely to die if they receive proper medical care. Nor is there any requirement that assisted suicide be the only option to alleviate suffering.

Worries about doctors killing patients are assuaged in Measure 16 with the blithe assurance that under the law doctors can't do the deed, that patients have to kill themselves. Yet nowhere in the initiative is there an explicit requirement that the lethal dose be self-administered or, indeed, is there a prohibition against a physician's administering a lethal dose. The law merely says that it doesn't specifically authorize such action.

Worries that self-administered assisted suicide would eventually lead to physicians' lethally injecting those who cannot swallow prescribed poison were validated after Measure 16 went into effect. In 1999, ALS patient Patrick Matheny committed assisted suicide after obtaining a lethal prescription—which he received via Federal Express.[13] According to media reports, Matheny's brother-in-law provided "help" after Matheny had difficulty self-administering the poison. That is not supposed to happen under the protective guidelines.

Matheny's death led to a minor contretemps. Law enforcement officials conducted a perfunctory investigation to see whether the self-administration provision of Oregon's assisted suicide law had been broken, but were so lacking in curiosity that they didn't even question the brother-in-law who admitted helping Matheny. Then David Schuman, an Oregon deputy attorney general, opined that the state constitution and the Americans with Disabilities Act would likely require the state to offer "reasonable accommodation" to "enable the disabled to avail themselves of the [Death With Dignity] Act's provisions."[14]

What would "reasonable accommodation" be in this context? Well, if someone has a legal right to be dead, and can't make themselves dead, than someone else would have to do it for them—in a word the very type of killing that Measure 16 supposedly prevents. Thus, the active euthanasia of dying disabled people may only be one lawsuit away in Oregon.

Proponents also assure us that depressed people will not be helped to die under Measure 16 because doctors are supposed to refer for "counseling" those they believe to be depressed. Yet the medical literature makes it clear that most doctors are not adept at identifying depression in their dying patients.[15] That means that many depressed people could easily slip through the Oregon suicide machinery without referral to a mental health professional.

But suppose a doctor believes a suicidal patient is depressed and refers him for counseling. Even that "safeguard" is more mirage than substance, given Measure 16's definition of counseling: "Counseling means a consultation between a state licensed psychiatrist or psychologist and a patient for the purpose of determining whether the patient is suffering from a psychiatric or psychological disorder, or depression causing impaired judgment."[16]

Nowhere does the law mandate a formal psychiatric evaluation of the type required to accurately diagnose depression. Even if depression is diagnosed, there is no requirement that it be treated. Moreover, since depressed patients are not prevented from killing themselves, so long as they do not have "impaired judgment"—at best a vague and undefined legal term—assisted suicides of depressed people are very likely to take place under Measure 16. Indeed, the very first person to legally commit assisted suicide had been diagnosed as depressed by a physician who had refused to participate in the woman's medicalized killing.

There's more. Incompetent patients might be allowed to receive a lethal dose of drugs under the act, since the doctor need only determine that the patient is "capable" before assisting in a suicide, not that a patient is "competent." This is a crucial distinction. Under the act, every person is capable who is not "incapable," defined as lacking "the ability to make and communicate healthcare decisions." Thus the ability to communicate decisions replaces the necessity of being competent to make decisions. Besides, depression is a mood disorder, not a thought disorder. Depressed people know they are not Napoleon or Cleopatra. They know that two plus two equals four. But because they are depressed, they are likely to make self-destructive decisions—decisions that they can justify with apparent rationality but that they would not make were they free of depression.

Measure 16's consulting-physician protection is also a joke. To be a consulting physician, a doctor need only be "qualified by specialty or experience in making a professional diagnosis and prognosis of the patient's disease."[17] That's no different from requiring that the consulting doctor be licensed, since the fact of licensure, by definition, means that the doctor is "qualified to make a professional diagnosis." (That is why it is legal for ob/gyns, for example, to perform plastic surgery, often with regrettable results.) A doctor like Jack Kevorkian who possesses few skills and little up-to-date training could make a specialty out of rubber-stamp death consultations. And as for being an attending physician, any doctor obtains that status as soon as a patient or surrogate decision maker asks him or her to become the patient's primary doctor. Thus, under Measure 16, a doctor with only a brief and superficial relationship with the patient can prescribe the deadly doses of drugs. (As we will see below, Kevorkian-style death doctors have written the bulk of lethal prescriptions in the wake of Measure 16 going into effect.)

With so much missing from Measure 16's guidelines, they can hardly be called strict. Nor, as we shall see, do they protect. What they do, like all euthanasia guidelines, is to give false assurance.

The Court Case

Shortly after Measure 16 passed, Dr. Gary Lee and others, including a man dying of AIDS and a diabetic, filed suit against Oregon's Death With Dignity Act. The suit was based on the belief that "Oregon's new assisted suicide law rests on a judgment that the lives of terminally ill and disabled patients are less deserving of protection than others." The plaintiffs contended that the law "violates the constitutional guarantees to terminally ill and disabled individuals of equal protection of the law and due process with regard to the right of an individual to life."[18]

The lawsuit succeeded at the trial court level. United States District Court judge Michael Hogan ruled that Measure 16 is unconstitutional, because it creates a two-tiered system of justice. In his decision he wrote: "Measure 16 singles out terminally ill persons who want to commit suicide and excludes them from protection of Oregon laws that apply to others. Residents of Oregon are entitled to protection from committing suicide if found to be a danger to themselves, and after evaluation by a psychiatrist or other state certified mental health specialist. . . . Under Measure 16, the very lives of terminally ill persons depend on their own rational assessment of the value of their existence, and yet, there is no requirement that they be evaluated by a mental health specialist."[19]

Judge Hogan noted that doctors must treat their patients with medical competency but that Measure 16 established a lower standard of care for the terminally ill: "Treating physicians may not be sufficiently qualified alone to evaluate mental impairments for the general public, but are given the significant role of deciding whether their patient may be suffering from a 'psychiatric or psychological disorder or depression causing impaired judgment.' . . . Contrary to the physicians 'reasonable' standard of care [the minimum level of competence required of physicians] for other patients, under Measure 16 there is no bar to a physician acting negligently [in assisting suicides]."[20]

Hogan also believed that the law left the terminally ill open to coercion, exploitation, and victimization after the time the lethal prescription is filled by the patient, ruling: "Measure 16 abandons the terminally ill person at the time the physician provides a lethal prescription. It fails to even acknowledge the most critical time, that of death. It provides a means to commit suicide to people who may be competent, incompetent, unduly influenced, and/or abused at the time of death. There is no distinction."[21]

Judge Hogan ruled that Measure 16 violated the United States Constitution and issued an injunction against its enforcement, stating that Measure 16's "safeguards are inadequate to bar incompetent, depressed but treatable, judgment-impaired, or unduly influenced terminally ill patients from committing suicide."[22] In reaction, Derek Humphry, who himself had labeled Measure 16 "disastrous" in a letter published in the *New York Times* shortly after its passage, grumped that "the Oregon law is as sound as any law in the world."[23]

Judge Hogan's decision was appealed to the U. S. Court of Appeals for the Ninth Circuit. The Court of Appeals could have tackled the substance of the decision, setting up a determination by the United States Supreme Court as to whether states may legalize assisted suicide. Instead, they issued a procedural ruling, reversing Judge Hogan on the basis that the plaintiffs in the case did not have "standing" to sue because they were not suicidal.[24] This "catch-22" ruling prevents the Oregon law from ever being judicially reviewed. In order to seek a review of the law, a plaintiff must be terminally ill and suicidal. But such a plaintiff won't want a review of the law. Thus, Measure 16 may have made legal history by becoming the first American law whose constitutionality is incapable of being judicially determined.

Legalized Killing Comes to Oregon

In September 1997, the Oregon Death With Dignity Act went into effect. So how is the law working? It is hard to tell. Psychiatrist Gregory Hamilton, president of Oregon's Physicians for Compassionate Care, says, "Rather than being an open experiment as promised by proponents, the actual practice of assisted suicide in Oregon is practiced in darkest secret," a bureaucratic stonewall opponents deride as "the iron shroud." [25] There are no independent investigations conducted by the state into actual assisted-suicide deaths; nor are any attempts made beforehand to ensure that the guidelines are followed. Almost the only information the state receives comes from forms filled out after the death by the doctors who lethally prescribe—sources not likely to tell the state if they break the law. Even the Oregon Health Department (OHD) admits that it doesn't know if these physicians honestly or fully report on their activities.

We do know from the forms filled out by lethally prescribing doctors that more than one hundred people have legally committed assisted suicide since the law went into effect. Euthanasia advocates claim that the information supplied by these death doctors demonstrate that the law is working well. But what little information that has come to light that has not been controlled by willfully naive OHD bureaucrats, gives the lie to the stream of blithe assurances issued routinely by assisted- suicide advocates.

In order to get voters to vote yes on Measure 16, Oregon advocates promised that physician-assisted suicide would be limited strictly to those rare cases in which patients were in "severe, unrelenting, and intolerable suffering," that could not be otherwise relieved. [26] Moreover, hastened deaths were only supposed to take place "in the context of a meaningful doctor-patient relationship," and then only after a deep and thorough discussion of all options between trusting patients and devoted physicians. [27]

But from the very beginning that has not been the actual practice. Much is known about the first reported legal assisted suicide because the assisted-suicide advocacy organization, the misnamed Compassion in Dying (CID) held a press conference shortly after the death to provide details. According to CID, "Mrs. A" had terminal breast cancer. She did not swallow physician-prescribed poison because of unbearable suffering and agony. Rather, in her own words played on audiotape posthumously at the CID news conference, she wanted to "be relieved of all the stress I have."[28] But stress caused by dying and growing debilitation, while certainly a very real and substantive medical issue that needs to be taken seriously by caregivers, is a treatable condition that does not require killing to alleviate.

A subsequent in-depth analysis of this case by medical and bioethics experts revealed an even more detailed account of these troubling events. Upon receiving her terminal diagnosis, the woman asked her treating doctor to assist in her suicide. The doctor refused. She consulted with a second doctor who also declined and diagnosed her as depressed. She then contacted CID, whose medical director, Dr. Peter Goodwin, spoke with her twice on the telephone, after which he decided that she wasn't depressed but merely "frustrated." Goodwin then referred her to a doctor he knew would be willing to write a lethal prescription.

That doctor referred her to a psychiatrist who saw her only once, and to a second doctor to confirm the terminal diagnosis. He also conducted a "cursory" discussion with the patient about alternatives to assisted suicide. When she voiced fears of being kept alive by artificial nutrition if she did not kill herself, the death doctor failed to assure her that she had the right to refuse such care—perhaps a crucial factor in her decision to commit assisted suicide. The woman did not know her prescribing doctor well and, indeed, died less than three weeks after their first meeting, at a time when she was not in pain and still looked after her own house.[29] That wasn't careful medical practice. That wasn't killing as a last resort when nothing else could be done to alleviate suffering. It was pure *Kevorkianism.*

Then there was the Kate Cheney travesty, reported in the Portland *Oregonian*, which provided a sickening glimpse of how easily supposedly protective guidelines are circumvented.[30] Cheney, aged eighty-five, was diagnosed with terminal cancer and sought assisted suicide. But there was a problem: Cheney was probably in the early stages of dementia, raising significant questions about her mental competence. So, rather than prescribe lethal drugs, her doctor referred her to a psychiatrist.

Her daughter, Ericka Goldstein, accompanied Cheney to the psychiatric consultation. The psychiatrist found that Cheney had a loss of short-term memory causing the psychiatrist to write in his report that while the assisted suicide seemed consistent with Cheney's values, "she does not seem to be explicitly pushing for this." He also determined that she did not have the "very high capacity required to weigh options about assisted suicide." Worse, the person who seemed most intent on Cheney's committing assisted suicide wasn't the elderly patient herself but her daughter. Accordingly, the psychiatrist refused to provide the lethal prescription.

Advocates of legalized assisted suicide might, at this point, smile happily and point out that such refusals are the way the law is supposed to operate to protect the vulnerable. But that wasn't the end of Kate Cheney's story. According to the *Oregonian* report, Cheney appeared to accept the psychiatrist's verdict but her daughter most certainly did not. To circumvent the rejection of assisted suicide, Goldstein merely did what anyone in Oregon wanting assisted suicide can do if refused by one physician: she went doctor shopping.

Kaiser Permanente, Cheney's HMO, acceded to Goldstein's demand for another opinion. This time, the psychiatric consultation was with a clinical psychologist rather than a psychiatrist. Like the first psychiatrist, this psychologist found that Cheney had significant memory problems. For example, she could not recall when she had been diagnosed with cancer. The psychologist also worried about familial pressure, writing that Cheney's decision to die "may be influenced by her family's wishes." Still, despite these reservations, the psychologist determined that Cheney was competent to commit suicide.

The final decision to approve the death was made by a Kaiser HMO ethicist and administrator named Robert Richardson. Dr. Richardson interviewed Cheney who told him she wanted the poison pills, not because she was in irremediable pain, but because she feared not being able to attend to her personal hygiene. After the interview, satisfied that she was competent, he approved the lethal prescription.

It is important to reiterate that whatever protection that guidelines provide in Oregon end with the writing of a lethal prescription. At that point, no doctor was required to be at the patient's bedside. Indeed, the law does not require that anything be done thereafter to determine if the patient is competent when swallowing poison or to prevent that patient from being coerced into taking the pills. In short, once Kate Cheney received the prescription, under the law she was on her own.

What happened next in the Cheney case illustrates the potential for problems after the lethal prescription is issued. Cheney did not take her lethal drugs right away. According to the *Oregonian* report, she first asked to die immediately after her daughter had to help her shower after an accident with her colostomy bag. But she quickly changed her mind. Then, Cheney was sent to a nursing home for a week so that her family could have some respite from care giving.

The time spent in the nursing home may have pushed Cheney into wanting immediate death. As soon as she was brought home she declared her desire to take the pills. Her grandchildren were quickly called to say their goodbyes, and Cheney swallowed her prescribed poison. She died with her daughter at her side, telling her what a courageous woman she was.

If Cheney was depressed when she swallowed the poison, there was no doctor available to diagnose it. If she was coaxed or pressured into taking the pills (which was not contended or implied in the *Oregonian* story) there were no witnesses from outside the family to protest. Indeed, other than what family members told the *Oregonian* reporter, we don't know what happened at Kate Cheney's death since the Oregon guidelines do not require any independent assessment of assisted suicide deaths.

Assisted suicide advocates when faced with the examples cited above simply point to the OHD yearly reports, which they claim validate their cause. But a close reading of these compilations of data reveals that rather than providing assurance, the data actually affirm the concerns of assisted suicide opponents.

For many years, we have been told repeatedly by assisted suicide advocates that legalized mercy killing would be a "last resort," applied only when nothing else can be done to alleviate "severe, unrelenting and intolerable suffering."[31] Yet, it appears that none of the Oregonians who committed assisted suicide during the law's first four years in effect were in that desperate condition. Pain was a factor only in a few cases. Indeed, rather than unbearable agony, the primary reasons for assisted suicide in the overwhelming majority of these deaths were:

- Losing autonomy—85 percent;

- Decreasing ability to participate in activities that make life enjoyable—77 percent;

- Losing control of bodily functions—63 percent;

- Being a burden on family, friends, and caregivers—34 percent.[32]

These are issues that require loving attention—not suicide support—from caregivers, friends, and relatives. Rather than cold "choice," dying people need to know that their lives are cherished even if they can't, at the moment, value themselves. In the words of the late Robert

Salamanca, who lived for years with ALS before dying from the disease peacefully in his sleep:

> Euthanasia advocates believe they are doing people like me a favor. They are not. The negative emotions toward the terminally ill and disabled generated by their advocacy is actually at the expense of the "dying" and their families and friends, who often feel disheartened and without self-assurance because of a false picture of what it is like to die created by these enthusiasts who prey on the misinformed.
>
> What we, the terminally ill, need is exactly the opposite—to realize how important our lives are. And our loved ones, friends, and indeed society, need to help us feel that we are loved and appreciated unconditionally.[33]

Disability rights advocates, who often echo these sentiments, are appalled by the message that the Oregon statistics send about the perceived value of their lives. In testimony before the California Assembly Judiciary Committee, disability rights activist Paul Longmore addressed this crucial aspect of the Oregon experience, pointing out that legalized assisted suicide hasn't really been about compassion for the dying but about validating fears about becoming disabled: "Fear of disability typically underlies assisted suicide. . . . The advocates play on that horror of 'dependency'. . . . If needing help is undignified and death is better than dependency, there is no reason to deny assisted suicide to people who will have to put up with it for six or sixteen years, rather than just six months. Not that we favor assisted suicide if it is limited to terminally ill people. We simply want to ask, has this country gotten to the point that we will abet suicides because people can't wipe their own behinds?"[34]

Another significant problem with assisted suicide in Oregon, rarely explored by a compliant media, is the number of patients who barely knew their lethally prescribing doctors. Cheney had less than a three-week relationship with the doctor who wrote her lethal prescription.

Her case was more the rule than the exception. The yearly OHD reports have shown that many assisted suicide victims went to more than one doctor to obtain their lethal prescriptions and that many knew the prescribing doctors for only a few weeks before committing their deaths.

Assisted suicide proponents told us this wouldn't happen either. They assured that assisted suicide would only occur after a deep exploration of values between patients and doctors who had long-term relationships. But we now know that in many cases death decisions are being made by doctors the patients barely know, many being referred by assisted suicide advocacy groups after primary care physicians have refused to assist their patients' suicides. These "death doctors" are thus not chosen to treat the patient or to palliate their symptoms. They may not even specialize in treating the condition causing the patients' illnesses. They have one job—to write lethal prescriptions. This isn't careful medical practice—it is rampant *Kevorkianism*, in which doctors are selected, not for their medical expertise, but their ideological willingness to help end their patients' lives.

There are also material omissions in the reports that detract from their empirical usefulness. The primary information about the people who committed assisted suicides comes from death-prescribing doctors—not necessarily the most reliable sources, considering their ideological predispositions and their sometimes brief relationships with their patients. Doctors who actually treated patients, but who did not participate directly in ending their patients' lives—doctors who knew their patients longer than those who assisted the suicides—were not interviewed. Nor were other doctors who refused to write lethal prescriptions. Family members were often not contacted either. Furthermore, the investigators did not disclose whether any (or all) of the prescribing doctors were affiliated with assisted suicide advocacy groups, a matter of some importance if we are to judge whether the decisions to prescribe lethally were ideological. (Press reports indicate that at least some were.) Moreover, none of the patients were autopsied to determine whether they were actually terminally ill.

The OHD studies warn us that Oregon has started down same destructive path previously blazed by the Netherlands. It is clear for those who are willing to see: assisted suicide is not only bad medicine but even worse public policy.

MAKING UP RIGHTS AS THEY GO ALONG

Euthanasia advocates did not put all of their advocacy eggs into a legislation basket. They also sued and sued again seeking to establish federal and state constitutional rights to assisted suicide. Happily, every such effort was eventually unsuccessful.

The most famous of these cases made it to the United States Supreme Court. In 1994, the assisted suicide advocacy group Compassion in Dying joined with three dying patients and five physicians to challenge Washington's law banning assisted suicide. Their record of success prior to reaching the high court was mixed: they won in the trial court, then lost in the U.S. Court of Appeals for the Ninth Circuit, where a three-judge panel ruled that Washington's law was constitutional. But then the Ninth Circuit granted an en banc hearing by eleven judges, which by an eight to three decision found that Washington's law against assisted suicide as it applied to the terminally ill was unconstitutional. The United States Supreme Court ultimately overruled the Ninth Circuit.

Despite never becoming law, the decision of the en banc court, written by Chief Justice Stephen Reinhardt, is worth pondering. The majority quickly and hubristically dismissed the court's obligation to apply the law as written and to depend on previous rulings: "We must strive to resist the natural judicial impulse to limit our vision to that which can plainly be observed on the face of the document before us, or even that which we have previously had the wisdom to recognize."[35]

Thus freeing themselves of the usual constraints that serve to limit the scope of judicial rulings, Reinhardt and seven of his colleagues, in effect, licensed themselves to create new constitutional rights from whole cloth. The United States Constitution, judicial precedent, and the vote of the people of Washington carried little weight.

The Compassion in Dying opinion relies on polls for justification; it blurs sensitive and vital distinctions; and the opinion is rife with factual error. For example, the eleven-judge panel found that "Unlike the depressed twenty-one-year-old, the romantically devastated twenty-eight-year-old, the alcoholic forty-year-old . . . who may be inclined to commit suicide, a terminally ill, competent adult cannot be cured." Yet, as noted earlier, no clear definition of terminal illness is medically or legally possible, since only in hindsight is it known with certainty when someone is going to die.

Judge Reinhardt also wrote, "While some people who contemplate suicide can be restored to a state of physical and mental well-being, terminally ill adults who wish to die can only be maintained in a debilitated and deteriorating state, unable to enjoy the presence of family or friends." But there are many experts who disagree with this despairing and nihilistic view of the process of dying. Dr. Ira Byock, a hospice physician with extensive experience in these matters, says: "Every life-stage has value, including the time of dying. Obviously, it can be wrenching and require an abrupt adjustment, but over time, if treated with respect, compassion and expertise, dying people often achieve a sense of mastery. It is an arduous time but a very personal and extraordinary time. It should not be dismissed as unimportant or not worth living."[36]

Factual inaccuracies are a minor problem compared to the rest of Judge Reinhardt's decision. Officially, the case stood for the now defunct proposition that there is a fundamental liberty interest in the United States Constitution in allowing citizens a "right to die." Unlike other constitutional rights, however, this "liberty interest" would not have been available to all people. Rather, deciding who possessed or did not possess it would have been measured on a sliding scale. According to Reinhardt, the state had an interest in protecting the lives of the "young and healthy" against suicide, but not much interest at all in protecting the lives of people "who are diagnosed as terminally ill." So

long as the dying were not coerced into choosing death and were mentally competent (extremely questionable propositions), Reinhardt and
his seven colleagues would have granted them an almost absolute right
to choose to be assisted in their suicide by a doctor.

Judge Reinhardt shared the restricted view of many assisted suicide advocates of the state's obligation to protect its citizens, according
to which the state doesn't protect lives by prohibiting assisted suicide,
but in Reinhardt's words "forces" people to stay alive. The state may
engage in this totalitarianism against the young and healthy because
"forcing a robust individual to continue living does not, at least absent
extraordinary circumstances, subject him to 'pain . . . and suffering that
is too intimate and personal for the state to insist on.'"

Note that if "extraordinary circumstances" exist, perhaps even young,
healthy lives would not be protected. Moreover, if "suffering" is the primary issue justifying assisted suicide, if it is somehow "wrong" for the
state to "force" suffering people to stay alive, Reinhardt's decision could
be interpreted to permit members of an oppressed minority to petition
for suicide assistance because they could no longer stand to live as victims of injustice. To be consistent, the court would have to permit the
killing if the minority member demonstrated sufficient anguish that
was "too intimate and personal for the state to insist on."

Judge Reinhardt's decision would also have specifically opened the
door to hastening the deaths of the disabled: "There are . . . subtle
concerns . . . advanced by some representatives of the physically impaired, including the fear that certain physical disabilities will errone-
ously be deemed to make life 'valueless.' While we recognize the
legitimacy of these concerns, however, we also recognize that seriously
impaired individuals will, along with nonimpaired individuals, be the
beneficiaries of the liberty interest asserted here—and that if they are
not afforded the option to control their own fate, they like many others
will be compelled against their will to endure protracted suffering."

Judge Reinhardt also legitimized money worries as a reason for
seeking medicalized suicide: "While state regulations can help ensure

that patients do not make uninformed, or ill considered decisions, we are reluctant to say that, in a society in which the costs of protracted healthcare can be so exorbitant, it is improper for competent, terminally ill adults to take the economic welfare of their families and loved ones into consideration."

Not only that, but Judge Reinhardt's decision endorsed non-voluntary killings of the incompetent—which by definition includes children, who generally are not allowed to make their own healthcare decisions—people who want to die because they receive inadequate access to healthcare, and even outright euthanasia:

> We should make it clear that a decision of a duly appointed surrogate decision maker is for all legal purposes the decision of the patient himself.
>
> One of the prime arguments [in favor of laws prohibiting assisted suicide] is that the statute is necessary to protect the poor and minorities from exploitation. . . . In fact, . . . there is far more reason to raise the opposite concern: the concern that the poor and the minorities, who have historically received the least adequate healthcare, will not be afforded a fair opportunity to obtain the medical assistance [with suicide] to which they are entitled.
>
> . . . .
>
> We agree that it may be difficult to make a principled distinction between physician-assisted suicide and the provision to terminally ill patients of other forms of life-ending medical assistance, such as the administration of drugs by a physician . . . or a person acting under his direction or control.

Judge Reinhardt's opinion was so extreme that some of his colleagues took the extraordinary step of trying to have all twenty-four active judges of the U. S. Court of Appeals for the Ninth Circuit rehear the case. When that failed, several justices filed dissents, which, among other criticisms, complained that Judge Reinhardt and his cohorts nullified "the public will" of Washington's voters, who had voted in 1991 not to allow assisted suicide. One judge, Diarmuid E. O'Scannlain, labeled the decision "embarrassing judicial excess" and a "shockingly broad act of judicial legislation."[37]

In the weeks following the Ninth Circuit's en banc decision in *Compassion in Dying*, the U. S. Court of Appeals for the Second Circuit, whose jurisdiction includes New York State, also ruled on the constitutionality of state laws that prohibit assisted suicide. The lawsuit had been filed by Dr. Timothy Quill, one of the nation's foremost euthanasia proponents, along with other physicians and terminally ill patients. The suit sought a ruling to declare unconstitutional New York's over one hundred-year-old law prohibiting assisted suicide. The trial court had dismissed Dr. Quill's suit as without merit. But the matter was appealed to a three-judge panel of the U.S. Court of Appeals for the Second Circuit.

The Second Circuit explicitly repudiated the Ninth Circuit's en banc decision by specifically ruling that assisted suicide is not a fundamental liberty interest founded in the United States Constitution. Unfortunately, the judges found a different constitutional justification to permit legalized suicide: equal protection of the law.[38]

The equal protection clause of the Fourteenth Amendment requires that similarly situated citizens must be treated alike under the law. Thus, requiring all six-year-old children to attend school treats similarly situated persons—six-year-old children—alike, whereas a law compelling six-year-old boys but not six-year-old girls to go to school would be to treat similarly situated persons differently, which would be a violation of the equal protection clause.

The Constitution does not require the law to treat matters that are not the same as if they were. Generally, the decision to decide what is a similar situation is up to lawmakers, requiring only that the distinctions made in law be "rationally related to a legitimate state interest."[39] In the example above, even though boys and girls are not exactly the same, the state would not be able to demonstrate a rational basis for allowing young girls and not young boys to stop attending school. But a law allowing seventeen-year-old minors to quit school would probably pass equal-protection muster, even though it treats some minors differently from others, the state having a rational basis for treating six-year-old minors and seventeen-year-old minors differently. In contrast, if a law restricts an activity deemed a fundamental liberty interest, such as freedom of speech (or in the Ninth Circuit's *Compassion in Dying* opinion, the right of an ill person to be killed by a doctor), the state can interfere with the activity only if it has a "compelling state interest," an extremely difficult legal standard to meet.

In the Quill case, the court of appeals decided that

- Terminally ill patients who require life support and those who are dying but who do not require life support are similarly situated persons;

- Since it is legal for people to reject the medical treatment of life support, terminally ill people who are on life support and want to die can do so quickly by refusing such care;

- Terminally ill people who do not require life support are forced to stay alive, even if they want to die quickly, since rejecting treatment would not immediately accomplish that goal;

- Therefore, those who cannot die by refusing treatment should have the right to assisted suicide, to fulfill the requirement that the law treat them in a manner similar to their terminally ill counterparts who are on life support (in other words, by allowing patients to refuse life support, the state has created a right to die quickly that should apply to all terminally ill people);

- The state serves no rational interest in preventing the terminally ill from killing themselves, since their lives are all but over anyway.

According to the court, since similarly situated people—the terminally ill—are being treated differently under the law, the assisted-suicide ban as applied to terminally ill people must fall.

As the United States Supreme Court would later rule, the decision exhibited faulty logic. Dying a natural death, which may happen if life support is terminated, is not the same thing as being killed. The former is by natural processes, while in the case of assisted suicide, a death-causing agent intentionally induces death. Moreover, when life-sustaining medical intervention is withheld or withdrawn from a patient, the result is uncertain: death may or may not come. In an assisted suicide, on the other hand, death is inevitable and will occur immediately following the injection or ingestion of the poisonous agent.

Here are just two examples. A young woman named Karen Ann Quinlan overdosed on drugs and alcohol and became permanently unconscious. After several years, her parents sued Karen's hospital to compel her doctors to stop the unwanted medical treatment of machine-assisted breathing. Eventually, the New Jersey Supreme Court properly approved their request, and Karen was taken off the respirator.[40] But Karen didn't die. Indeed, she lived for ten years, finally succumbing to an infection.[41]

In the Ron Comeau case discussed in chapter two, when Comeau's respirator was cut off he too was expected to die. But he didn't: his condition began to improve. That was why the guardian decided to have him dehydrated!

The court of appeals decision in the Quill case also applied the wrong comparison. There is no analogy between a patient's right to refuse unwanted life-sustaining treatment and being killed by assisted suicide. It is freedom from treatment, not freedom from life, that has consistently served as the legal and ethical underpinning for the right-to-refuse-medical-treatment cases, from Karen Ann Quinlan to Nancy Cruzan. This distinction is rational and vital. It protects people from unwanted physical intrusions. It does not, however, create a right to be killed with all of the dangers and potential for exploitation and abuse that such a right would entail.

THE CONSTITUTIONAL ISSUE IS DECIDED

In June 1997, the Supreme Court unanimously ruled that there is no right to assisted suicide to be found in the United States Constitution. The two contemporaneous decisions, *Washington v. Glucksburg* and *Vacco v. Quill*, were both thorough and far-reaching.[42] Chief Justice William Rehnquest penned both majority opinions. (There were also multiple concurring opinions.)

In Glucksburg, the Court determined that assisted suicide was not a fundamental right. First, the court reviewed the laws surrounding suicide and assisted suicide during the last seven hundred years of Anglo-American jurisprudence, finding that assisted suicide is not a "fundamental liberty interest " protected by the due process clause.[43] That being so, all that the State of Washington had to demonstrate was that its anti-assisted suicide law "be rationally related to legitimate government interests."[44] This, the Court ruled, Washington had "unquestionably" accomplished. The Court then set forth these interests over several pages of text:

- The State's "unqualified interest" in the preservation of human life, "even for those near death";

- Suicide is a "serious health problem," especially among "persons . . . in vulnerable groups." That being so, states have the right to pass laws, including laws criminalizing assisted suicide as a matter of suicide prevention;

- Those who commit suicide, including the terminally ill, "often suffer from depression or other mental disorders." Because depression can often be effectively treated—and its causes such as pain significantly ameliorated—"legal physician assisted suicide could make it more difficult for the State to protect depressed or mentally ill persons, or those who are suffering from untreated pain, from suicidal impulses."[45]

- The State has "an interest in protecting the integrity and ethics of the medical profession." Legalized physician-assisted suicide could "blur the line between healing and harming."[46]

- "Next, the State has an interest in protecting vulnerable groups—including the poor, elderly, and disabled persons—from abuse, neglect, and mistakes." If physician-assisted suicide were permitted, "many might resort to it to spare their families the substantial financial burden of end-of-life healthcare costs."[47]

- "The State's interest here goes beyond protecting the vulnerable from coercion; it extends to protecting disabled and terminally ill people from discrimination, negative and inaccurate stereotypes, and 'societal indifference.' . . . The State's assisted-suicide ban reflects and reinforces its policy that the lives of terminally ill, disabled, and elderly people must be no less valued than the lives of the young and healthy; and that a seriously disabled person's suicidal impulses should be interpreted and treated the same way as anyone's else's."[48]

- "Finally, the State may fear that permitting assisted suicide will start it down the path to voluntary and perhaps even involuntary euthanasia."[49] In this regard, the decision made much of the experience in the Netherlands with termination without request and consent—an issue discussed at length in chapter four.

But what about the often made assertion by euthanasia advocates, adopted by the Second Circuit Court of Appeals, that assisted suicide is the legal equivalent to refusing unwanted life-sustaining medical treatment and that permitting one but legally prohibiting the other, therefore, violates the right to equal protection of the laws? Not so, the Court declared in *Vacco v. Quill*: refusing life-sustaining medical treatment and killing are not the same things at all. Noting that, "when a patient refuses life-sustaining medical treatment, he dies from an underlying fatal disease," the Court ruled:

> [A] physician who withdraws, or honors a patient's refusal to begin, life sustaining medical treatment purposefully intends, or may so intend, only to respect his patient's wishes to cease doing useless and futile degrading things to the patient when the patient no longer stands to benefit from them. . . . A doctor who assists a suicide, however, must necessarily and indubitably, intend primarily that the patient be made dead. Similarly, a patient who commits suicide with a doctor's aid has the specific intent to end his or her own life, while a patient who refuses or discontinues treatment might not . . . [and] may instead fervently wish to live, but to do so free of unwanted medical technology, surgery, or drugs.[50]

In other words, the right to refuse unwanted medical treatment is not a "right to die" but a right to be free from unwanted bodily intrusions. Accordingly, the Court decided that New York's law prohibiting assisted suicide was perfectly constitutional.

Glucksburg and *Vacco* were devastating losses for the assisted suicide movement. (Euthanasia advocates did, however, successfully spin the media that their unanimous defeat was almost akin to a victory due to a comment by a concurring justice that states were free to continue to experiment with end of life issues.) It was now clear that any attempt to transform the United States into a suicide nation would require intense state-by-state political struggle rather than a sweeping declaration from the judiciary.

Or was it? Determined to prevail regardless of the laws or even the beliefs of the populace, euthanasia advocates also mounted legal challenges in selected state courts, claiming that state constitution privacy provisions preclude laws prohibiting assisted suicide. Here too, however, the movement hit brick walls. First, Michigan refused the constitutional claim in a case involving Jack Kevorkian.[51] In 1997, the Supreme Court of Florida rejected claims that the Florida constitution guarantees terminally ill patients a right to be made dead.[52] Finally, in 2001, the Alaska Supreme Court made a similar ruling.[53] The assisted suicide movement's dream of prevailing in one fell stroke via judicial fiat has all but evaporated.

THE STRUGGLE CONTINUES

The years since the passage of Measure 16 have not generally been successful ones for the assisted suicide movement. They have repeatedly and unsuccessfully sought to pass legislation in many state legislatures to legalize assisted suicide. Jack Kevorkian was imprisoned for murder after he video taped himself killing an ALS patient and then aired the killing on *60 Minutes*. In 1998, Michigan assisted suicide activists sought to pass an initiative legalizing assisted suicide in Kevorkian's home state and lost by an overwhelming 71 to 29 percent. In 2000, Maine, a state with demographics remarkably similar to Oregon's, rejected assisted suicide by 51 to 49 percent.

Why this turnaround when assisted suicide threatened to sweep the country? Prior to Measure 16, the moral and legal struggle over euthanasia was largely—if inaccurately—viewed as a contest between religious conservatives and modern rationalists. But the passage of the Oregon law and the general approval of Jack Kevorkian's assisted suicides changed that. A remarkable and robust alliance, made up of disability rights activists, hospice professionals, religious groups, advocates for the poor, pro-lifers, and medical and nursing associations, came together to combat the culture of death. Many who disagree about other controversial issues agree that doctors should not be licensed to kill their patients. This diverse coalition has proved much more successful at conveying the anti-assisted suicide message to the public.

Still, if euthanasia activists have proved anything it is that they are indomitable. They never stop; they never rest; they never give up. They never cease their war of attrition against the equality-of-life ethic and the values of the Hippocratic oath, a war they hope to win simply by exhausting their opponents. Indeed, despite their many recent setbacks, the American euthanasia movement is today more powerful then it has ever been, now consisting of a plethora of local organizations and several national groups such as the Hemlock Society, Death With Dignity Education Center, and the Compassion in Dying Federation (CDF). Not only do they have committed activists to perform the daily tasks of trying to change a culture, they now have ample money to spend on advocacy, some generously bankrolled by several notable foundations. For example, in 1997, CDF received $100,000 from George Soros's Open Society Institute (OSI), more than $300,000 from the Gerbode Foundation between 1995 and 1999, a $300,000, three-year grant in 1998 from the Columbia Foundation, and $50,000 from the Donald A. Pels Charitable Trust in the same year. Funding for the Death With Dignity Education Center has also been generous, including grants from OSI ($100,000 in 1997), the Gerbode Foundation ($544,900 since 1996), the Columbia Foundation ($200,000 since 1998), and the Walter and Elise Haas Foundation ($57,500 during 1996-97).[54] This level of giving seems to have continued to the present moment.[55]

These funds make for political and media clout. As Rita Marker, president of the International Task Force on Euthanasia and Assisted Suicide says, "Influencing public opinion is an expensive endeavor. It requires a virtual non-stop public relations campaign, including frequent contact with the media, a lobbying presence in government centers, presence at policy-making forums, and an energetic public information component. It requires professional spokespersons to be available to be seen and heard. All of this is very costly, but very effective, often enabling assisted suicide activists to set the agenda."[56]

With their ample funding and emotional commitment to their cause, assisted suicide advocates will not be going away any time soon. Indeed, Hawaii came very close to passing an assisted suicide law in 2002. Like a chronic low grade fever that threatens at any moment to become a full-blown medical crisis, it is now quite clear that euthanasia will remain a significant threat for many years to come.

6

The Betrayal of Medicine

I MAGINE A WORLD where everyone receives optimum healthcare, regardless of financial means. Imagine a world where all seriously ill or disabled persons are surrounded by a loving and supportive community of family, friends, and professionals dedicated solely to their welfare, where elder abuse is a problem of the past and all are welcomed wholeheartedly as equal members of the human community. Imagine a world where family members are ever supportive and never pressure, intimidate, manipulate, or abandon their loved ones. Imagine a world where everyone has altruistic motives. Imagine a world where depression is immediately recognized and treated. Imagine a world where disabled people are universally valued and are provided the services they require for full participation in the community. Imagine a world where health choices are all made with due deliberation and rational analysis, where people do not act in haste and are free of duress, menace, coercion, or fraud.

Anyone who believes that such a world exists has gone to one too many Grateful Dead concerts. But don't tell that to death fundamentalists, because this is the environment in which they claim euthanasia would be practiced.

Read the words of Dr. Timothy Quill: "Assisting death either by direct or indirect methods is not something to undertake without careful assessment of mental status and exploration of all alternatives. It is the path of last resort, taken only when hospice care stops providing comfort and dignity, and when there are no good options for regaining quality of life."[1, 2]

Read the words of Jack Kevorkian: "The medical profession must display the moral virility expected of that once noble calling by taking absolute control of its ethical prerogatives. The ideal doctor, armed with a good medical education and practical training . . . with strong character . . . with honesty and common sense . . . and with a completely free mind. . . can handle any medical challenge. . . . This can be true only if . . . the highest respect is given for the personal autonomy . . . of every patient. . . . Under those conditions of patients' autonomy coupled with medical competence and honesty, how could any overwhelming or insuperable bioethical problem arise?"[3]

The self-proclaimed "death counselor" and pro-assisted suicide author Stephen Jamison, PH.D., has written: "I believe it [hastened death] will be reserved for extraordinary cases that fail to respond to efforts at palliative care. Moreover, it should be provided in such a way that promotes an ideal of medical intervention that carefully looks at each case and balances a patient's suffering with the principles of beneficence, nonmaleficence, autonomy, and justice. . . . [A] team approach to implementation [would] ensure that a patient has received the best quality of pain management and comfort care available."[4]

Lonny Shavelson, a photojournalist and emergency-room physician whose book, *A Chosen Death*, I discussed in the first chapter, states, "Assisted suicide, active euthanasia, and even passive euthanasia should be available only to patients who have first had the fullest chance to control the suffering of dying by every possible means other than by bringing on their own death."[5]

Even if these authors believe their naive assertions, the actual practice of euthanasia and assisted suicide in the Netherlands and Oregon belie such idealized descriptions of medicalized killing as restricted to "last resorts" when "nothing else can be done to alleviate suffering." Indeed, a close look at the societal context within which these agendas would be practiced demonstrates that assisted suicide and euthanasia could only result in abuses of the powerless and abandonment of the defenseless.

A DYSFUNCTIONAL HEALTHCARE SYSTEM

Euthanasia advocates almost always ignore, or perhaps choose not to see, that the conditions under which they assert euthanasia should be undertaken simply do not exist in our money-driven healthcare system. They don't take into account the difficulties and stresses of family life, the vulnerability to pressure and coercion of people who are depressed or in pain, or indeed the reality of human nature as it too often relates to money issues such as inheritance or life insurance. Nor do they acknowledge that it is likely that some physicians, perhaps those with a bias in favor of assisted suicide, may become death doctors whose primary "practice" degenerates into the killing of patients.

Death doctors would be very unlikely to have the kind of long-term patient-physician relationships that Dr. Timothy Quill and Stephen Jamison envision. Rather, they would more likely resemble Jack Kevorkian, not treating patients or seeking to relieve their suffering, but only being there to help kill them. Indeed, this is precisely what has come to pass in many of the cases in of legal assisted suicide in Oregon.

Ironically, legal assisted suicide and euthanasia are not only unlikely to be intimate and compassionate affairs but, in fact, are likely to cause more misery and suffering than they would ever alleviate. This was the conclusion of the twenty-five-member New York State task force on Life and the Law, a permanent commission created by Governor Mario Cuomo in 1985. The task force spent more than a year intensely investigating whether assisted suicide should be legalized. Despite having some members who supported assisted suicide and euthanasia in theory before beginning their investigation, the group's recommendation was unanimous: euthanasia and assisted suicide should not be legalized.

The task force's report, *When Death Is Sought: Assisted Suicide and Euthanasia in the Medical Context*, remains highly relevant and is still required reading for anyone interested in the euthanasia debate.[6] One of the most striking features of the report is that it does not rely on abstract notions of religion, morality, or philosophy but, rather, focuses extensively on practical analysis of the world as it really is: "In light of the pervasive failure of our healthcare system to treat pain and diagnose and treat depression, legalizing assisted suicide and euthanasia would be profoundly dangerous for many individuals who are ill and vulnerable. The risks would be most severe for those who are elderly, poor, socially disadvantaged, or without access to good medical care."[7]

When Death Is Sought effectively rebuts the naive account of assisted suicide offered by euthanasia advocates. According to the task force, the "good case," that is, in which all "safeguards would be satisfied . . . bears little relation to prevalent social and medical practices."[8] In other words, despite their advocacy of high ideals, the world envisioned by euthanasia advocates simply doesn't exist—and will not exist in the foreseeable future. Many social risks inherent in euthanasia were also cited by the task force as a reason not to legalize euthanasia:

- Euthanasia would be practiced through the "prism of social inequality and bias that characterizes the delivery of services in all segments of our society, including healthcare."[9] Racism, ageism, sexism, bigotry against disabled people, and socioeconomic status would all materially affect killing decisions, just as they do other issues of American life. Moreover, the quality of care given a Jackie Kennedy who requested hastened death would be quite different from that of a dishwasher without health insurance.

- "Most doctors do not have a long-standing relationship with their patients or information about the complex personal factors" that go into a request to be killed. Moreover, "neither treatment for pain nor diagnosis of and treatment for depression is widely available in clinical practice."[10] Yet untreated pain and depression are the primary reasons patients request physician-assisted suicide.

- "As long as the [killing] policies hinge on notions of pain and suffering, they are uncontainable," because "neither pain nor suffering can be gauged objectively, nor are they subject to the kind of judgments needed to fashion coherent public policy."[11] Legalized killing based on "unbearable suffering" cannot logically be limited to the dying and, if legalized, would soon be available to anyone who claimed to be in agony. As we saw in chapter four, this inexorable widening of killing categories has already occurred in the Netherlands, to the point where patients desiring to die do not need to be physically ill.

Perhaps most important, the task force found that euthanasia and assisted suicide are unnecessary to relieve suffering. "Contrary to what many believe," the report noted, "the vast majority of individuals who are terminally ill or facing severe pain or disability are not suicidal. Moreover, terminally ill patients who do desire suicide or euthanasia often suffer from a treatable mental disorder, most commonly depression. When these patients receive appropriate treatment for depression, they usually abandon the wish to commit suicide."[12]

Indeed, the task force noted that techniques to control pain, treat depression, and provide support for patients and families already exist. The problem isn't with whether these truly beneficent care opportunities work: if properly applied, they do in nearly every case. Rather, society still must overcome the "numerous barriers" that exist to their proper application, "including a lack of professional knowledge and training, unjustified fears about physical and psychological dependence, poor pain assessment . . . and reluctance of patients and their families to seek pain relief."[13] That will require dedicated effort and sustained energy, which too often are diverted from these important tasks to the struggle over legalizing euthanasia.

The New York State task force is not alone in making these points. When Dr. Timothy Quill began his assisted suicide crusade, his colleagues at the University of Rochester Medical Center conducted a study of the issue. After more than a year's investigation, which included significant input by Dr. Quill, the University of Rochester task force unanimously recommended against legalization, for reasons similar to those detailed by the New York State task force, including the existence of "practical treatments and management techniques available at the present time which should prove adequate for palliation of suffering in virtually all clinical situations."[14] The Rochester report also noted that doctors have done an insufficient job of treating dying and suffering patients and recommended greater attention be paid to these vital care issues.

The conclusions of these studies are echoed by discussion within the medical profession, which has finally come to realize its partial responsibility for the fear and anxiety over suffering at the end of life felt by many of their patients, and the scandalous undertreatment of pain and depression, major sources of the energy driving the euthanasia movement.

For example, the *Journal of the American Medical Association* has stated "inadequate treatment of pain continues to be a problem despite more knowledge about its causes and control and despite widespread efforts of governments and multiple medical and voluntary organizations to disseminate this knowledge. . . . All types of pain in all parts of the world are inadequately treated."[15] *American Medical News* editorialized, "Evidence suggests that there is a significant gap between the most effective pain treatment and what most patients actually get."[16] And the authors of a special report on pain control in the *New England Journal of Medicine* wrote, "Undertreatment of cancer pain is common because of clinicians' inadequate knowledge of effective assessment and management practices, negative attitudes of patients and clinicians toward the use of drugs for the relief of pain, and a variety of problems related to reimbursement for effective pain management."[17] Yet despite more than ten years of such intense pushing by the medical establishment, it is not an overstatement to state that "untreated and under treated pain is nothing short of a national scandal."[18]

If doctors currently do such a poor job, generally, of relieving the pain and depression of suffering people when doctor-induced death is illegal, what kind of a job would they do if killing a patient were considered just another "treatment option," and a less expensive and time-consuming option at that? To put it another way, why would we trust doctors to kill us, when too often they don't do an adequate job of caring for us? With so many Americans uninsured, the "last resort" scenario is a virtual impossibility.

DEADLY FINANCIAL INCENTIVES

To assert that money drives the American healthcare system is like stating that seals like fish. Doctors' fees generally amount to hundreds of dollars an hour. One day in the hospital alone can cost thousands of dollars, and that doesn't include the "extras" for which hospitals also charge, such as intensive care, oxygen, bandages, and aspirin. If your condition requires a few weeks of hospitalization followed by extended follow-up care, the tab could easily rise into six figures.

This money imperative and the sheer cost of medicine in the United States makes euthanasia even more dangerous here than it is in the Netherlands. At last count, forty-four million Americans had no health insurance. Almost by definition, being uninsured means that one lacks sustained access to quality healthcare services. Most doctors refuse to accept new patients who do not have health insurance, and most private hospitals will only help uninsured ill people when required to do so by law in a life-threatening emergency.

Being uninsured means that healthcare, when it is received, is generally delivered in a public hospital emergency room, where, after hours of waiting, a harried doctor (often in training) will be assigned to deal as quickly and cheaply as possible with the problem. Those with chronic conditions often face similar barriers to effective care, relying on free clinics or emergency rooms where the lack of consistent treatment can cause complications requiring an expensive emergency response later.

With the near geometric growth of for-profit hospitals and healthcare financing systems, even this meager measure of care for the uninsured poor is now threatened. According to Bruce Hilton, director of the National Center for Bioethics, a study in Florida indicated that for-profit hospitals, which make up more than half of that state's healthcare institutions, only supply 8 percent of the state's charity care.[19]

In this context, euthanasia would be a potential form of oppression against the uninsured, the working poor, divorced persons, minorities, the unemployed, the mentally ill, and those lacking education who may not even speak English. For these people, the presumption that assisted suicide would be considered only after every other conceivable method of care has been tried is, to put it politely, unrealistic. Hospice, extended pain control, psychiatric treatments for depression—services essential to the "last resort" scenario—are usually inaccessible to the uninsured. If euthanasia advocates really believed that doctor-hastened death should be performed only if there is no other way to alleviate suffering, they would put their issue on the shelf until the structural flaws in American medicine are solved.

In these circumstances, many who would want to live were they to receive proper care might, out of desperation, express a desire to die when they have difficulty obtaining it. Doctors might be tempted to follow the line of least resistance by going along with such desires. Such a scenario is not purely imaginary. In July 1996, Rebecca Badger, aged thirty-nine, traveled from California to Michigan to become Jack Kevorkian's thirty-third known assisted-suicide victim. In a KEYT-TV (Santa Barbara) television interview taped only days before her death, Badger, who believed she had multiple sclerosis and who lost her private health insurance after a divorce forced her onto MediCal (California's Medicaid program), complained bitterly about five-hour hospital waits to see a doctor and explained that the reason she was going to Kevorkian was her constant, unrelieved pain. Badger also said that if her pain were only relieved, she would want to live.[20]

According to press reports, at least one doctor who cared for Rebecca, when contacted by a self-identified Kevorkian associate, did nothing to try to protect his patient but rather "presumed they [Kevorkian and associates] would talk her out of it."[21] The Kevorkian contact either did not thoroughly investigate Badger's reasons for wanting to commit suicide or, if he did, didn't provide the pain relief she specifically said would transform her desire to die into a will to live.

According to Badger's autopsy report, she did not have MS at all. Dr. Ljubisa J. Dragovic, a neuropathologist with specialized training as a pathologist in detecting neurological conditions and thus an expert in detecting MS, performed Badger's autopsy. He told me, "Rebecca Badger had no sign of the disease. The findings are completely negative. The problem with MS is that a lot of conditions can simulate MS and MS can simulate a lot of conditions."[22]

What Badger did suffer from was diagnosed depression and abandonment by the healthcare system just when she needed compassionate treatment of her ailments the most. According to her daughter, Badger, a recovering alcoholic who was addicted to prescription medications, had lost faith in the medicine and believed that her maladies would never be taken seriously. In despair, she took her final, fatal trip to Michigan.[23]

A DEADLY COMBINATION

The uninsured aren't the only ones who are threatened by the commercialization of healthcare and the approach of legalized euthanasia. We all are, for it is no secret that healthcare costs are skyrocketing. In 2000 the total spent on healthcare, including research, topped $1.2 trillion, or approximately 13.2 percent of the nation's entire gross domestic product.[24] Controlling unnecessary costs and improving the efficiency of healthcare delivery is both desirable and necessary. But cost cutting in a medical system in which assisted suicide and euthanasia were legal would be a lethal threat to us all.

Recent changes in the economics and financial incentives of American medicine have made the legalization of euthanasia especially hazardous. In recent years, we have evolved from a health system based on "fee for service" to one dominated by HMOs and managed care, in which money is made not by providing services but primarily by controlling costs. In the former system an insured, seriously ill person generally made profits for hospitals and physicians. Today, they may cost money. Such a shift turns the traditional presumptions about healthcare financing and the delivery of medical services inside out.

The cost-cutting agendas of managed care are now rife throughout private and publicly financed healthcare. HMOs are ubiquitous. Payments to physicians who treat Medicaid (the federal and state funded and state-administered health insurance for the poorest of the poor) and Medicare (the health insurance plan for the elderly and some disabled) recipients are increasingly being squeezed to the point where there is nothing left to give. Indeed, Medicare now pays doctors so little in compensation for their services that many physicians now refuse to take on Medicare recipients as new patients.[25]

Now, consider these intense pressures to cut costs in the context of legalized euthanasia. If killing patients because they are seriously ill or disabled becomes viewed as merely another "treatment," the lives of patients who require expensive care will be endangered. Remember, for HMOs, profits come not through providing services but through limiting costs, which in real life often means reducing services. Now, imagine the money that could be saved—and thus profits earned—by not treating cancer patients, by not treating AIDS patients, by not treating MS patients, by not treating quadriplegics, all because they "choose" instead to be killed.

This disturbing possibility is one reason why managed care is now called "managed death" by those who worry about legalized euthanasia in a healthcare system dominated by HMOs. As Dr. Daniel P. Sulmasy, of the Center for Clinical Bioethics at the Georgetown University Medical Center, has written in *Archives of Internal Medicine*, we may be heading toward a healthcare system where cost control and the killing of patients go hand in hand:

> As providers of managed death, many physicians will be sincerely motivated by respect for patient autonomy, but the cost factor will always lurk silently in the background. This will be especially true if they are providing managed death in a setting of managed care. A perilous line of argument might then emerge: . . . 1) Too much money is spent on healthcare; 2) certain patients are expensive to take care of (i.e., those with physical disabilities and the elderly); 3) these patients appear to suffer a great deal, lead lives of diminished dignity, and are a burden to others; . . . 4) recognizing the diminished dignity, suffering and burdens borne by these persons and those around them, their right to euthanasia or assisted suicide should be legally recognized; and 5) the happy side effect will be healthcare cost savings.[26]

Lending credence to Dr. Sulmasy's warning is the intense pressure already placed on doctors at the clinical level to cut costs. One of the hallmarks of HMO care is the dual role of the plan member's primary-care physician (PCP). First, the PCP, usually an internist, family-care specialist, or for children, a pediatrician, is the plan member's personal doctor, in charge of preventive care, managing chronic conditions, providing inoculations, and the like. The PCP also serves a function on behalf of the HMO as cost-cutting "gatekeeper," the person in charge of controlling the cost of each patient's care.

It is the gatekeeper function that has so many physicians and consumer advocates worried about financial conflicts of interest between doctors and their patients. Doctors in many HMOs are paid individually (or as part of a small group) on a capitation basis. That means that the PCP (or the group) receives a flat monthly fee for each patient, regardless of the frequency of care the patient requires. (HMO defenders point out that some patients rarely see the doctor and so the capitation system evens out, with the doctor compensated for care he or she is never called upon to provide.)

That a doctor receives no extra compensation for additional effort isn't the primary worry about capitation. The real concern is that some companies impose a capitation system in which the PCP is held *personally financially responsible* by the HMO for any referrals made outside his or her group, to specialists or for tests. In such contracts, the PCP receives a higher-than-usual capitation payment, perhaps forty dollars per month per patient, but in return must personally pay for each patient's lab tests, consultations with specialists, and emergency care, up to a maximum per patient that may be as high as five thousand dollars, after which the HMO pays.[27] In a system where doctors lose money every time they refer a patient out of house, they may be reluctant to allow their patients to consult specialists, including pain-control experts or psychiatrists, physicians who are crucial to the proper care of many dying or chronically ill patients. Without such treatment, these patients might turn in despair to a death doctor—or ask their PCP to become one—in search of relief.

These and other financial pressures by HMOs on doctors in clinical practice may already have life-and-death repercussions. Take the case of the Christie family of Woodside, California. In 1993, Katherine and Harry Christie joined an HMO known as TakeCare Health Plan. They chose the Palo Alto Medical Clinic as their primary medical group, a group of doctors of varying specialties who would be responsible for the family's medical care. At the time, Carley, the Christies' nine-year-old daughter, was having significant kidney problems. According to a petition to assess civil penalties filed by the California Department of Corporations, the agency in charge of regulating HMOs in the state, Carley's PCP, Dr. Susan Smith, referred her to Dr. James Bassett, a Palo Alto Medical Clinic colleague, for consultation, despite the fact that Dr. Bassett had little experience in pediatric urology.[28]

Dr. Bassett diagnosed Carley with a rare and life-threatening cancer known as Wilms' tumor. Having no experience in treating Wilms' tumor and knowing that he was not the doctor to adequately care for Carley, Dr. Bassett suggested that the Christies take Carley to Dr. Michael Link, a pediatric urologist with extensive experience in treating Wilms' tumor, which often requires surgery, chemotherapy, and radiation. Dr. Link and other members of his specialized team were not part of the Palo Alto Medical Clinic group practice.

Under the HMO contract with the Christies, any out-of-group referral needed the go-ahead of Carley's PCP, Dr. Smith. Refusing to abide by what the Department of Corporations called "good professional practice," Dr. Smith refused to authorize a referral to Dr. Link and instead insisted that her colleague Dr. Bassett, with no experience in Wilms' tumor surgery or treatment, perform the surgery.[29] Adding to the outrageousness of this decision was the worry that Dr. Bassett may have worsened Carley's condition previously during a biopsy by "causing spillage of the tumor [into other parts of her body]. This spillage triggered an additional nine months of painful chemotherapy."[30]

The Christies were in a dreadful bind: their daughter needed immediate surgery to save her life, yet they faced paying for it themselves unless they permitted an unqualified doctor to provide the care. As the clock was ticking toward the time surgery would have to be performed, Dr. Smith's position softened: Dr. Bassett would have to assist at the surgery if the referral were to be made. The Christies agreed, but he declined to participate.[31] Their daughter's life being paramount, the

Christies transferred Carley's care to the experienced medical team. The surgery was successful. Carley's life was saved.

TakeCare soon informed the Christies that it would not pay for Carley's treatment, "in retaliation," according to the Department of Corporations, "for the Christies' choosing a qualified pediatrician surgeon to remove Carley's tumor."[32] The HMO also refused to pay for the cost of hospitalization, which represented $47,000 of the $55,000 total cost of Carley's care, despite the fact that the same hospital would have been used regardless of which doctors treated Carley. Thus, in addition to worrying about their daughter's recuperation, the Christies were now facing pronounced financial difficulty.

The Christies entered the contractual grievance process of the HMO (a binding arbitration clause prevented them from suing.) They obtained an arbitration award recovering their medical expenses and arbitration fees, but not their legal fees. They then filed a complaint with the Department of Corporations, alleging that the HMO had violated the California Health and Safety Code. The Christies were not after a monetary settlement for themselves but, rather, hoped the DOC would fine the company to set an example for all of the state's HMOs. An administrative fine of $500,000 was levied against TakeCare, which was upheld on appeal. As of early 1997, TakeCare had not decided whether to pursue further appeals.

The DOC contends that a primary reason Carley was refused referral to a qualified specialist was the HMO's capitation agreement with Palo Alto Medical Clinic, which required the physicians group to pay for Carley's surgery out of its own funds if it were performed by nongroup physicians, money that would have been saved by keeping her care in-house.[33] The HMO denied the charge.

The Christie family story was not a tale of euthanasia. But if a capitation-based financial conflict may have put a nine-year-old girl with a good chance of recovery at significant risk, imagine what these financial conundrums would mean to elderly cancer patients, disabled persons requiring long-term specialized care, or dying people who require intensive and perhaps costly pain control. In order to save their own money, unscrupulous PCPs might deny expensive specialized care to their most needful and vulnerable patients, leading to unrelieved suffering and despair. This in turn could propel patients toward wanting euthanasia. Indeed, the doctor could legally recommend the killing as a "treatment option." This is an especially worrying scenario considering the depth of trust and hope seriously ill patients place in their physicians and the ease with which physicians could maneuver suffering patients toward requesting euthanasia.

What would it be like to know that the doctor who is licensed to kill you also benefits financially from the act? Or to know that a doctor who recommends suicide for your spouse could be financially punished for providing him or her with "too much" care? What would happen to the trust between you and your doctor? How would potential financial gain affect your doctor's attitude toward your care if you develop a problem that requires specialized treatment? Would you have ready access to pain control, psychiatric treatment, hospice, and other care opportunities that would be more expensive than euthanasia? Moreover, if killing the weak and sick becomes a major area of cost cutting—and thus a profit center in the immensely powerful healthcare industry—what would happen to medical ethics overall? And would legalized killing change society's attitudes toward the value of the lives of people deemed eligible for hastened death: the dying, the ill, the elderly, and the disabled? With HMOs becoming the norm, these questions must be answered before we embrace euthanasia or take seriously the "last resort" scenarios spun by death fundamentalists.

Most euthanasia advocates like discussing these financial issues about as much as cats like to jump in rivers. But a rare few are quite candid about the money agenda behind the euthanasia movement. Indeed, none other than Derek Humphry admits that saving money is the "unspoken argument" in favor of legalizing physician killing of patients. In the book *Freedom to Die*, which Humphry co-authored with pro-euthanasia attorney Mary Clement, the authors wrote:

> A rational argument can be made for allowing PAS [physician-assisted suicide] in order to offset the amount society and family spend on the ill, *as long as it is the voluntary wish* of the mentally competent terminally and incurably ill adult. There will likely come a time when PAS becomes a commonplace occurrence for individuals who *want* to die and feel it is the right thing to do by their loved ones. There is no contradicting the fact that since the largest medical expenses are incurred in the final days and weeks of life, the hastened demise of people with only a short time left would free resources for others. Hundreds of billions of dollars could benefit those patients who not only *can* be cured but who want to live.[34]

Humphry and Clement assert that economic necessity will "continue to drive the right to die movement largely because of its appeal to common sense." They then assert that "Economic realty, therefore, is the main answer to the question [about the emergence of the euthanasia movement], 'Why now?'"[35] For perhaps the only time in his death-purveying career, Derek Humphry has it exactly right. In the end, legalized assisted suicide and euthanasia—at least in the United States—would not be about compassion and altruism: it would be about money.

THE SILENT EPIDEMIC

Another disturbing truth about our healthcare system routinely overlooked in euthanasia advocacy is the "silent epidemic" of medical malpractice.[36] According to Charles Inlander, president of the People's Medical Society, one of the nation's largest patient advocacy groups, with more than one hundred thousand dues-paying members, "Between 136,000 and 310,000 people a year are injured or killed due to medical mistakes by their doctors," a figure Inlander called "conservative."[37]

An authoritative study published in 1991 by the Harvard Medical Practice Study Group, conducted at Harvard's School of Public Health and one of the most comprehensive and objective investigations of medical malpractice ever performed, found that more than ninety-eight thousand patients in hospitals located in New York State suffered "adverse events," injuries from medical care rather than disease, in one year, 1984. Twenty-seven percent of these adverse events were the result of medical negligence, causing 6,895 patient deaths in the state's hospitals that year.[38] Projecting these figures nationwide, the study's authors project that at least 80,000 people are killed in hospitals each year by medical malpractice, more than deaths caused by suicide, homicide, and AIDS combined. These figures only represent deaths in hospitals— and don't reflect the potential for a significant worsening of the situation in recent years caused by nursing staff cuts and other cost-cutting measures that have hit the hospital industry like a perfect storm under the pressure of managed care economics. They also do not measure misdiagnoses, failure to properly alleviate pain or depression, or other failings in the clinical setting that bear on the euthanasia issue.

Between 5 and 15 percent of the physician population are believed to be "incompetent or dangerous," and these doctors would be as entitled as any other physician to kill patients were euthanasia legalized.[39] Indeed, some might be attracted to euthanasia "practice," as legalization proposals provide civil and criminal legal immunity to doctors who kill their patients. Legalizing killing by doctors could even become a way for a few very unscrupulous doctors to cover up their malpractice or limit damages from lawsuits, by killing the victims they have injured in the name of "death with dignity" and the "right to die."

A euthanasia case that occurred in San Francisco several years ago illustrates how easy it would be for a doctor to kill a patient as a means of covering up malpractice. In March 1995 a nine-year-old girl with a neurological condition that affected her physical development was admitted into the University of California Medical Center for elective surgery to realign her jaw. The surgery, which required that her jaws be wired shut, went well, but afterward an apparent case of medical malpractice led to the girl's jaws not being unwired when she became nauseated. The girl aspirated on her own vomit and was left with severe brain damage.[40]

The girl had been unconscious for a few weeks when a pediatrician specialist, an employee of the hospital who was not the cause of the girl's aspiration-caused injury, undertook her care for a couple of hours. A different doctor had previously convinced the girl's mother to suspend life support, but the girl hadn't died. After being removed from a respirator she began to breathe spontaneously, after which, apparently, the hospital refused to support the girl nutritionally. A few hours after the decision to cut off food and fluids, the pediatrician injected the child with potassium chloride, which paralyzed the girl's heart and killed her. (A legal dispute later arose over whether the girl's distraught mother had asked the doctor to administer the lethal injection.)

This intentional killing of a child did not result in criminal prosecution. Nor, as far as is publicly known, did the California Medical Board discipline the doctor, although one source told me the case is still being investigated. Nevertheless, three nurses who blew the whistle on the doctor were suspended without pay, allegedly because they delayed reporting the incident. (The nurses' suspension was overturned on administrative appeal. One of the lawyers in the case told me that they were all reassigned to other duties, prompting at least one nurse to quit her job and move to another city.) The pediatrician, however, only had her hospital staff privileges suspended but did not lose pay.

An astonishing level of secrecy was imposed on the case from the beginning, depriving the public of very important information about the quality of care being rendered in an important local public hospital, about the professional competency of the doctors involved, and about the intentional killing of a nine-year-old child. The hospital's press release on the killing referred to it as "an atypical" case of "withdrawing life support."[41] The doctor's name was not publicly disclosed, nor was the name of the killed child or her mother. Even the nurses' names remain a secret, and two of them weren't even on duty when the girl was killed.

The killing doctor has claimed, in anonymous interviews, that her decision to inject the girl was motivated solely by a "compassionate" desire to end the girl's suffering at the request of the mother.[42] Perhaps. But what if her motive had actually been venal, to reduce the malpractice legal exposure of her hospital or, say, to protect a friend who had actually injured the girl? What if she had been the original malpracticing doctor (which she was not) and her motive was self-protection? Who would know? She could claim she was acting as an angel of mercy to provide "death with dignity," when her actual motive was to reduce the monetary damages, since the "value" of a case involving a dead child is usually less, perhaps far less, than a malpractice case involving a child who will require a lifetime of assisted care. (In the former, the damages generally are limited to the emotional anguish of the parents and the loss of love and companionship, certainly no small matter, and to awards to compensate pain and suffering, which in many states are capped by law. In the latter case, the expenses associated with providing a lifetime of medical care for the injured child are added to the distress damages, meaning that such cases are usually worth many millions of dollars.)

The malpractice civil suit brought by her mother involving the girl's post-surgery injury and subsequent killing was settled quickly for an undisclosed amount. If the terms of the settlement were those usually used in legal settlements of this kind, the hospital and doctors involved did not admit liability or wrongdoing. My request to the University of California Medical Center for an interview with the killing doctor was refused, nor would it release the name of anyone involved.

Euthanasia advocates often use cases such as this to support their contention that euthanasia is common and, as Dr. Quill put it, must be "brought out of the darkness into the light." In fact, there is no reliable information on the frequency or infrequency of euthanasia in the clinical setting. No one knows whether, or how often, doctors actually kill their patients.

Surveys of doctors taken on this issue tend to rebut the claim that euthanasia and assisted suicide are common occurrences. For example, in the wake of the passage of Measure 16, Oregon doctors were surveyed by the *New England Journal of Medicine* to determine their attitudes and experiences with assisted suicide. Only 7 percent of the responding doctors had ever written a lethal prescription for use in a patient's suicide, 187 out of 2,761 doctors surveyed.[43] A similar study published in the same journal in 1994 found that only 9.4 percent of physicians had taken action to "directly" cause a patient to die (not necessarily euthanasia or assisted suicide), and only 3.7 percent had provided information that would cause a patient's death.[44] The polling also suggests that physicians, while reflecting society's deep divisions about legalizing assisted suicide, are generally quite worried about its application in the real world. The Oregon poll found that more than half of Oregon physicians would be unwilling because of moral objections to prescribe an overdose. Adding to their unease was the fear felt by more than ninety percent of the doctors that their patients would seek hastened death so as not to be a burden on others. This fear was born out once legal assisted suicide began in Oregon, as described in the last chapter.

The *New England Journal of Medicine* study was so significant that one of its authors, Diane E. Meier, changed her position. Where she once viewed legalization as a way to regulate a supposedly common clinical practice, once it became clear to her that doctors do not commonly kill patients, she opposed legalization out of fear that it would "become a cheap and easy way to avoid the costly and time-intensive care needed by the terminally ill."[45]

Meier's opposition to the legalization of assisted suicide and euthanasia echoes the official positions of almost all professional medical organizations and other healthcare groups. The American Medical Association opposes euthanasia and assisted suicide. So does the National Hospice Organization, which certainly understands the issues involved with end-of-life care. The American Nurses Association is also staunchly opposed.

It is worth reviewing some of the official statements of some of these groups. The AMA's opinion states in part: "The medical profession will not tolerate being put in a position to judge the value of human lives. . . . To allow or force physicians to participate in actively ending the lives of patients would so dramatically and fundamentally change the entire patient/physician relationship that it would undermine the principles we, as a society, hold most dear. We must never lose sight of the caveat that physicians are healers, and where we cannot heal, our role is to comfort."[46]

The medical profession around the world almost universally shares these views. The British Medical Association (BMA), like its American counterpart, has consistently maintained firm opposition to assisted suicide and euthanasia. In the early 1980s, the BMA responded to calls for a policy change by undertaking a study of euthanasia in the Netherlands. The study resulted in a 1988 report, reiterated in 1993, which concluded: "The law should not be changed and the deliberate taking of a human life should remain a crime. This rejection of a change in the law to permit doctors to intervene to end a person's life is not just a subordination of individual well-being to social policy. It is, instead, an affirmation of the supreme value of the individual, no matter how worthless and hopeless that individual may feel."[47]

Similarly, the World Medical Association, whose members are physicians from forty-one countries, has also adopted a position opposing physician-induced death. It states: "Physician-assisted suicide, like euthanasia, is unethical and must be condemned by the medical profession. Where the assistance of the physician is intentionally and deliberately directed at enabling an individual to end his or her own life, the physician acts unethically."[48]

Advocates of euthanasia like to quote polls that show doctors split on the issue. Yet, despite the intense public campaign to legitimize and legalize assisted suicide and euthanasia, despite the unremitting "educational" efforts by bioethics institutes, which regularly present the pro-euthanasia point of view in professional symposia, doctors cannot be said to have come anywhere close to endorsing the culture of death.

REFUSING WANTED TREATMENT

So far, we have seen that euthanasia advocates largely appeal to patient autonomy to promote their wider agenda. So too has the dehydration of cognitively disabled people been justified as a matter of respecting the personal values and decision making of the patient or their surrogates. In a culture steeped in individualism, there is no question that such appeals resonate with many who cherish personal autonomy and the right of "choice."

This raises an interesting and important question. Do these purveyors of assisted death really believe in "choice"? For example, what if the seriously ill or disabled patients or their surrogates wish to continue treatment that many in bioethics and among the medical intelligentsia believe should be stopped? What if the patient's personal value system holds that it is right and proper to fight for life until death can no longer be held at bay?

As a matter of consistency, one would expect that decisions to resist dying—even with the use of heroic measures—would be deemed as sacrosanct as the decision to seek death or refuse life-sustaining medical treatment. But consistency and autonomy are not necessarily the point. Now that the "right to die" has sunk its hooks into the culture, those who assert the concomitant "right to live" are increasingly being told that autonomy has its limits.

While society and the media have focused on assisted suicide and the right to refuse unwanted treatment, little attention has been paid by the media to concurrent efforts promoted in bioethics to disregard patient autonomy when dying or profoundly disabled patients want their lives sustained. This is the emerging bioethical debate over "futile care" (sometimes called "inappropriate care"), in which many bioethicists, academics, members of the medical intelligentsia, and social engineers argue that requests for life-sustaining treatment may, and should, be disregarded if the patient's life is deemed not worth living.

Futile care advocates, whom some call "futilitarians," often act as if the struggle against medical paternalism over the last twenty years had never happened. "The decision about futile therapy cannot and should not be abdicated by the physician to the patient, family, surrogate, court, or society in general," says Allen J. Bennett, MD, vice chairman of the Committee on Bioethical Issues of the Medical Society of the State of New York. "To abdicate a decision about the futility of a procedure or medical treatment is to abdicate professional responsibility for the patient. . . . Futility decisions should be left to physicians."[49] More succinctly, the California Healthcare Foundation, stated in a written objection to anti-futile care legislation in California: "The provision of medical care must be left in the hands of treating providers to do what is best for patients . . . Decisions to provide or withdraw care *must be made by the appropriate medical personnel* on a case-by-case basis and not limited or extended by law."[50]

Futile care theory, as it is sometimes called, proposes that the old, the dying, those on the margins, and the profoundly disabled can be pushed out of the lifeboat in order to allow others in or, indeed, to keep the boat afloat. Thus, futile care can be accurately described as a first cousin to euthanasia in that it rejects the equality-of-human-life ethic in favor of a subjective value system that determines whose lives are worth protecting and whose lives are not.

The theory behind futile care theory goes something like this: When a patient reaches a certain stage of age, illness, or injury, any further treatment other than comfort care is futile and should be withheld or stopped. That the patient may *want* the treatment anyway because of deeply held values or a desire to improve his condition is not decisive; the doctors involved have the right to refuse treatment unilaterally.

At this point, let me make it clear that I am not talking about treatment that is truly and objectively "futile." If a patient requests a medical intervention that would provide no physiological benefit, the doctor can, and should, refuse. To use an extreme example, if a patient afflicted with a simple ear infection requested an appendectomy to cure it, the doctor could and should refuse to perform the surgery because it would have no effect on the earache.

But this is not the kind of futile care that futilitarians promote. Rather, they espouse a radical view of healthcare decision making that would allow the values of healthcare professionals, health insurance company executives, or even community "consensus" over what should be done to, and for, the patient to take precedence over patients' own wishes for their care.

Futile care theory has quietly gained momentum in the last several years. Mandatory treatment guidelines have already been drafted by bioethics think tanks and are beginning to be implemented in hospitals around the country. These are not rules intended to define minimum allowable standards (which are desperately needed in this age of HMOs), but rather to serve as guidelines and procedures for denying wanted life-sustaining care.

The first targets of what developed into the futile care movement were patients diagnosed with persistent unconsciousness. For example, in 1994, Dr. Marcia Angell, then executive editor of the *New England Journal of Medicine*, editorialized that current presumptions in favor of life as they apply to the permanently unconscious must be changed so that "demoralized" caregivers won't have to provide care they believe is futile—or waste "valuable resources."[51]

Dr. Angell offered three proposals that would permit care to be withdrawn. The first would be to broaden the definition of death to include diagnosis of permanent unconsciousness. (This approach is also seen by some in bioethics as a way to increase the supply of transplantable organs.)[52]

There are currently two primary and appropriate definitions of death in use: brain death, the total cessation of all measurable electrical activity in the brain, and complete cessation of heartbeat and respiration.[53] Dr. Angell's radical suggestion would be to take living people with functioning bodies, including brain systems, and for utilitarian purposes to pretend that they are deceased. Demonstrating the illogic of the suggestion, Dr. Angell, noting that these "patients do not 'look dead," admits "it would, paradoxically, be necessary to withdraw life-sustaining treatment, including artificial feeding, to stop the cardiopulmonary function." In other words, the "dead" patients would have to be made actually dead so that their treatment could cease.

Dr. Angell's second proposal would allow legislatures to pass laws prohibiting life-sustaining medical treatment for the unconscious after the passage of a specified period of time. Under this approach the decision to make a person die by withholding nutrition would be made in advance by society without regard to any individual case. Thus, according to Angell, the family who wanted care to continue could at least be comforted by the knowledge that the decision to terminate their loved one's life was not personal. This is an example of futilitarianism.

The third and "less sweeping" proposal, favored personally by Dr. Angell, would create a legal presumption that persons who are unconscious would not want treatment after a specified time. In that way, a family that held the "idiosyncratic" view that their loved one should not be dehydrated to death would have to prove that the patient had expressed a specific desire to be treated under these specific circumstances. In other words, the current, though weak, presumption in favor of life for the profoundly cognitively disabled would be changed to an explicit legal presumption in favor of death.

Dr. Angell and many others who agree with her, assert that *their* personal beliefs that unconscious patients do not have lives worth living should trump the values of patients or families who see unconscious people as fully human and worthy of love and care. Ironically, their reason for stopping the "treatment" of food and fluids would not be because the treatment was failing but because it was succeeding in keeping patients alive—to futilitarians, an unacceptable outcome. Or to put it another way, in futile care theory, it isn't the treatment that is actually dismissed as futile—but the *patient*.

This is rank hypocrisy. If a family requests death by dehydration for their unconscious loved one, their request is now granted out of respect for patient autonomy. But under futile care theory, if the same family should instead rebel against the prevailing ethos and desire to keep their loved one alive, many in the medical profession lose their ardor for autonomy.

Note, too, the values expressed in Dr. Angell's editorial. As Thomas Marzen of the National Center for the Medically Dependent and Disabled, a legal advocacy group for the profoundly disabled, says, it seems that we "have lost the virtue of caring for people simply because they are people."[54] Indeed, nowhere does Dr. Angell speak of unconscious patients as people. Rather, she views them as problems, patients who "demoralize" caregivers and waste resources.

There is another flaw in Dr. Angell's thesis. She gives short shrift to the fact that people diagnosed by doctors as permanently unconscious often aren't actually unconscious. According to a growing body of medical literature, misdiagnosis of the persistent vegetative state is common. For example, a study published in the June 1991 *Archives of Neurology* found that of eighty-four patients with a firm diagnosis of PVS, fifty-eight percent recovered consciousness within a three-year period. Studies also show that researchers have been unable to identify objective "predictors of recovery," to differentiate between those who may awaken and those who most likely will not. Moreover, some supposedly unconscious patients who later awaken report that they were not unaware as is supposed, but rather had "visions" or "out-of-body experiences," or were aware and emotionally responsive to everything going on around them, but were unable to communicate.[55] A study in

Great Britain revealed that perhaps 40 percent of patients diagnosed with PVS actually are conscious.[56] If these and other similar studies were accurate, Dr. Angell's proposed ethic, if accepted, would likely cause the deaths of some people who would have recovered consciousness given sufficient time. It also means that those dehydrated to death on the assumption that they were completely unaware and hence unable to suffer could die in a most agonizing manner, whether or not they or their families wanted that outcome.

Unconscious patients aren't the only ones threatened by futilitarianism. So too are the elderly, physically disabled people, and others with serious chronic conditions. The influential bioethicist Daniel Callahan offered several rather vague definitions of futility in his 1993 book *The Troubled Dream of Life*. It exists, he wrote, when:

- "there is a likely, though not necessarily certain, downward course of an illness, making death a strong probability"; or,

- "successful treatment is more likely to bring extended unconsciousness or advanced dementia than cure or significant amelioration"; or,

- "the available treatments for a potentially fatal condition entail a significant likelihood of extended pain or suffering"; or,

- "the available treatments significantly increase the probability of a bad death, even if they promise to extend life"[57]

In such cases, Callahan urged that a presumption against medical treatment, other than comfort care, be created and that people who insist on these futile treatments be required to pay for it themselves.

FUTILE CARE ARRIVES

Forcing people off of wanted life-sustaining treatment isn't a fantasy. A few futile care cases have already reached the courts. The first such case occurred in 1990-91 in a case that pitted the husband of Helga Wanglie, an elderly woman in a permanent coma with multiple organ failure, against her doctors and hospital. Helga was dependent on a ventilator, and her doctors received permission from her husband to place a DNR ("do not resuscitate") order on her chart. But he refused to permit them to withdraw the ventilator. As a consequence, he was sued.

According to physician and bioethicist Steven Miles, a bioethics consultant who became the public spokesman for the hospital, there were three reasons why Helga's physicians wanted to stop her treatment. "The palliative aspects of her care would not work because she was incapable of feeling the benefit of having the ventilator relieve air hunger; the continued provision of the respirator would not keep open the possibility that she would return to any type of minimally rational life; and, the use of the respirator would not allow her to have a relational life in the present."[58] I asked Miles whether her continued life, in and of itself, was considered a benefit to her. "Yes," he replied, "but we did not have a way to help her acquire a quality of life that she herself could value." Mr. Wanglie's position was that his wife valued life for life's sake and that she would want to remain alive under these conditions. The question presented to the court: whose ultimate moral values should prevail, the husband's or wife's—or those of the medical professionals?

Dr. Miles brought a court case to have Mr. Wanglie removed as his wife's medical decision maker. (Miles told me he became the petitioner after Helga's treating physician was forced to withdraw due to a death in the family.) The trial was to be held in two parts: first, to decide who should decide about Helga's care, Mr. Wanglie or an independent person to be selected by the court as a guardian ad litem; and second, whether Helga's physicians had to continue her treatment despite the desires of Mr. Wanglie, were he named by the court to be his wife's medical decision maker.

After a hearing, the court refused to oust Mr. Wanglie as his wife's medical surrogate, ruling that as her husband of many years, he was

the best person to make Helga's healthcare decisions.[59] The ruling
only settled the first part of the case. Still to be decided was whether
the doctors had to continue to treat Helga with a respirator despite
their view that the treatment was futile. This issue was never adjudi-
cated because Helga died and the matter was dropped.

A similar scenario unfolded in Flint, Michigan, in 1993, where Baby
Terry was born prematurely at twenty-three weeks gestation. (The normal gestation for a human infant is thiry-eight to forty weeks.) Baby
Terry, weighed one pound, seven ounces at birth and was desperately
ill. Deprived of oxygen, his brain had been damaged, and he required
a respirator to stay alive.

Doctors at Hurley Medical Center advised Terry's parents, Rosetta
Christle, aged twenty-one, and Terry Achtabowski, aged twenty-two,
that Terry's life support was futile. But Christle and Achtabowski disagreed. They weren't ready to give up. Their baby had gained a pound
and successfully resisted a bacterial infection, and they wanted him to
have every opportunity to fight for his life.

The parents' refusal to accept treatment termination was unacceptable to Baby Terry's doctors and the hospital administration. They called
in the Michigan Department of Social Services, which quickly brought
court action to strip the young parents of their right to make decisions
over their son's medical treatment. (Such drastic action is usually taken
only when parents refuse needed medical treatment for their children.)
A hearing was convened and testimony elicited. The physicians were
unanimous in their desire to terminate care, testifying that Terry was in
pain, although relieved by morphine, that his bodily systems were slowly
breaking down, and that he had no chance of long-term survival. The
Hurley Hospital ethics committee weighed in on August 9, 1993, opin-
ing that granting the parents' wish for continued treatment "would be
contrary to medical judgment and to *moral and ethical beliefs of physicians* caring for the patient."[60] In other words, when it came to choosing between the values of Baby Terry's parents, based in large part on

their religious faith, and the values of doctors and the hospital, the state argued that only the latter opinions mattered.

Solely on the basis of their refusal to permit treatment to end, Judge Thomas Gadola of the Genesee County Probate Court found Christle and Achtabowski unfit to make proper health-care decisions for their baby and stripped them of their rights as parents. He then awarded temporary custody of Baby Terry to his maternal great-aunt, who had previously stated her willingness to obey the doctors and cut off life support.

Legal wrangling continued. Before the case concluded and a final decision was made as to who should have final authority over the care of Baby Terry—his parents or his doctors—the infant died in his mother's arms, aged two and a half months. Lawyers for Christle and Achtabowski still wanted a formal court decision overruling the trial court. But the court of appeals dismissed the case as moot.

Baby Ryan Nguyen was born in Spokane's Sacred Heart Hospital on October 27, 1994. At just twenty-three weeks gestation, he was very premature. His kidneys were not working well so doctors put him on dialysis. But when the doctors determined that Ryan was not a good candidate for kidney transplantation, they decreed that continuing his treatment was futile.

In the face of the physician's taking their child off of life support, Ryan's parents retained an attorney who quickly obtained a temporary court order compelling Ryan's treatment to continue. Unhappy that their will had been thwarted, and perhaps inspired by the Baby Terry case which had occurred the previous year, hospital administration reported Ryan's parents to child protective services, accusing the Nguyen's of "physical abuse" and "physical neglect"[61] for obtaining the injunction. When that tactic didn't fly, administrators and doctors fought the parents in court. Despite the fact that there "are few statements made in medicine based on flat certainty," only probabilities,[62] Ryan's physician's swore under oath that "Ryan's condition is universally fatal" and that the infant had "no chance" for survival, and that treatment could not "serve as a bridge to future care." Based on these contentions, Ryan's doctors urged the judge to permit them to cease his continued treatment and a violation of *their* integrity, values, and ethics.[63]

The court never decided who had ultimate say over Ryan's care—his parents or medical professionals—because his treatment was transferred to Emanuel Children's Hospital in Portland, Oregon, under the care of a different doctor who did not view Ryan Nguyen as a futile patient. The new doctor, not the original physicians, had it right. Ryan was soon weaned from dialysis and survived for more than four years, a time in which he was a generally happy, if sickly, child who liked to give "high fives." Had his original doctors successfully imposed their futile care philosophy on their patient and his parents, Ryan would have died before he had a chance to live.

Another family was forced to go to court to obtain wanted treatment in a more recent case in Winnipeg, Canada. Andrew Sawatzky, aged seventy-nine, had late-stage Parkinson's disease and had experienced debilitating strokes. His doctors decided to place a DNR order on his chart over the objections of Helene, Sawatzky's wife. When Helene could not get the doctors to remove the DNR order, she sued. The court granted a temporary court order removing the DNR order, pending further investigation of whether the doctors or the Sawatzkys would determine Andrew's level of care. The case became moot when Andrew's condition improved so much that he was able to return home.

In England, the courts sided with doctors in a futility case when parents sought similar relief, with very frightening implications for the most weak and vulnerable members of British society. David Glass, aged twelve, was a mentally retarded boy, who was blind and quadriplegic. He was also greatly loved by his parents and siblings, who cherished him as an integral part of his family.

In October 1998, David was admitted to St. Mary's Hospital in Portsmouth with respiratory failure. Instead of trying to save his life, doctors unilaterally withdrew curative treatment and injected him with a palliative agent, telling the parents their son was dying and nature should be allowed to take its course.

The parents refused to stand by and watch their son die because doctors did not perceive his life to be worth living. They instituted resuscitation on their own and saved David's life. One doctor later testified that he objected strenuously to the parents actions because their action "had prevented him from dying."[64] Clearly, if family members could save David without the expertise of formal treatment, the refusal of care was more a matter of physician bias than compassionate allowing of nature to take a sad but inevitable course.

David's parents sued to prevent such an awful abandonment from being repeated. Unexpectedly, they lost. The trial and appeals courts both ruled that doctors, not parents, have the ultimate say over David's life and death. This ruling is in line with a recent ethics opinion published by the British Medical Association, which established an ethical protocol granting doctors the ultimate power to determine when and if treatment will be terminated.

The uncertain outcome of court rulings inspired futilitarians to create formal futile care hospital protocols designed to create administrative processes by which to decide whether doctors should be permitted to withdraw wanted life-sustaining treatment. The August 21, 1996, *Journal of the American Medical Association* described one such policy created by a collaboration of Houston-area hospital ethics committees, which have been adopted by the participating hospitals with the intent that "professional integrity and institutional integrity" would serve as a counter balance "to patient autonomy."

The Houston policy created an eight-step "conflict resolution mechanism"—essentially a quasi-adversary system between doctors and patients—to resolve disputes in which patients or family refuse to accept a doctor's decision that continued treatment (other than comfort care) is "inappropriate." These eight steps are:

1. Careful discussion with the patient (or surrogate decision maker) why the attending doctor believes that the treatment in question is "medically inappropriate." Alternatives to treatment, such as hospice and palliation, should be discussed.

2. If the patient or surrogate still wants the treatment, the physician is to discuss the option of transferring to another physician or hospital, or of obtaining an independent medical opinion.

3. If agreement is still not reached, other hospital resources, e.g., chaplaincy, patient-care representatives, social workers, biomedical ethics committee, etc., are called in.

4. If agreement is still not reached the doctor may call in "an institutional interdisciplinary body" to make a determination about the propriety of the disputed treatment.

5. The patient or surrogate is notified that the decision-making process has been invoked, with the date and time set for the administrative proceeding.

6. During "the institutional review process" the physician and patient or surrogate are encouraged to present their perspectives together and to suggest alternative plans of care.

7. If a finding of medical inappropriateness is made, the treatment may "may be terminated." (The policy allows hospitals to replace the word "must" for the word "may.") A new plan of comfort care will then be instituted.

8. Once the determination of futility has been made, the patient may transfer to another hospital. However, if another doctor is willing to provide the desired treatment in the same hospital, the treatment will "not be allowed."[65]

This is how the Houston process might work in real life:

Assume your eighty-five-year-old grandmother, already partially disabled by a stroke, is transferred from her nursing home to the hospital with a high fever and breathing difficulties. She is very ill and chances of her survival are estimated to be 15 percent, with a return to her previous functioning level deemed highly unlikely. The doctor in charge of her care decides that giving her antibiotics and respiratory assistance is "futile," because in his opinion, even if she lives she will never regain a quality of life that would be of benefit to her.

You protest. You and your grandmother have discussed end-of-life issues at great length. She signed an advance directive naming you as her surrogate decision maker. She instructed you that she does not want treatment discontinued because she is disabled or unconscious. She doesn't view life with disabilities and pronounced frailties as being undignified but an "opportunity to make lemonade out of lemons."

Unable to pressure you into allowing them to cease life-sustaining treatment, her doctor initiates the futility process by calling in nurses, chaplains, social workers, or other hospital "resources" to attempt to resolve the dispute. You are told you are causing your grandmother unnecessary suffering. If you are religious, you are accused of making irrational choices. Some claim you are acting out of guilt or misplaced emotionalism. In ways great and small, you are pressured, cajoled, and pleaded with to follow the doctor's advice.

You still refuse to give in. A second doctor is brought in to examine your grandmother and render an opinion. She agrees that treatment is "inappropriate." The hospital ethics committee is then contacted and a formal hearing to adjudicate the dispute is scheduled.

The hearing is held seventy-two hours later. You appear and explain why you want treatment to continue. The doctor and others explain why they believe the treatment is futile. The ethics committee courteously thanks you for attending and assures you that your grandmother will not be abandoned but that the decision will be made to promote her best interests. You leave, and the committee takes a secret vote. It sides with the doctor.

Your grandmother's treatment is about to be stopped over your objection. You are now left with two options. Under the hospital's protocol, you can accept the decision and make sure your grandmother receives comfort care until she dies, using a different doctor within the hospital if you desire. Or, you can transfer your grandmother to another hospital, assuming you can find one willing to accept responsibility for her care. After making several calls, you discover that no other hospital is willing to admit her.

In desperation, you speak with another doctor. You are thrilled when she agrees to provide the desired treatment in the hospital. You ask that responsibility for your grandmother's care be transferred to the new doctor. The hospital tells you that the new doctor will not be permitted to render life-sustaining treatment. The ethics committee has ruled. Under the hospital's futile care policy, any further treatment other than comfort care in the hospital is now forbidden. There is no appeal. Treatment, other than comfort care, is withdrawn over your objections.

Your grandmother is now too weak to be moved to another hospital, even if you could find one willing to accept her care. You hold her hand as her temperature rages at 105 degrees. She is given comfort care consisting of analgesics. She becomes delirious and soon expires. You are left with the bitter feeling of having been abandoned and betrayed.

For obvious reasons, hospital publicists don't hold press conferences to announce that they have granted themselves permission to refuse wanted life-sustaining treatment. Thus, nobody really knows which hospitals have adopted futile care protocols and which have not, or indeed, whether protocols are actually being applied against patients and their families. But it does appear that the futile care agenda is spreading. A very disturbing survey published in the fall 2000 edition of the *Cambridge Quarterly of Healthcare Ethics* reported that twenty-four out of twenty-six California hospitals that were surveyed "defined non-obligatory treatment" in terms that were not "physiology based." Twelve of these hospitals surveyed prohibit treating people diagnosed with permanent unconsciousness (other than comfort care) based on these patients' supposed inability to know they are being treated. Only seven of the hospitals left the final decision about whether to continue the treatment in the hands of the patient or family.[66]

A primary purpose of these futile care protocols is to head off at the pass families and patients who sue to receive wanted treatment. The idea is to present judges with the protocols as a defense to lawsuits demanding treatment, in effect telling the courts that the bioethicists and doctors have already worked things out, that futile care is ethical and widely accepted, and that the patient received due process via the administrative process established by the futility protocols. At that point, the $400-per-hour lawyer for the hospital would argue, "Judge, how can you, a mere lawyer, gainsay what the medical profession has carefully considered over several years and determined to be medically appropriate?" Futilitarians expect judges would respond positively to this argument and allow treatment to be withdrawn.

Unfortunately, that's probably a good bet. For as the authors of the *Cambridge Quarterly* study put it, "Hospitals are likely to find the legal system willing (and even eager) to defer to well-defined and procedurally scrupulous processes for internal resolutions of futility disputes."[67]

But is this approach something that the people—who, after all, are the very ones who would be most affected by medical futility—support? Since so little has been written and broadcast in the mainstream press about futile care theory, that is hard to know. However, the rise and fall of a futile care think tank, the Colorado Collective for Medical Decisions (CCMD), provides an important clue.

CCMD's former director, Dr. Donald J. Murphy, hoped the work of CCMD would empower doctors, hospitals, nursing homes, and health-care financing entities all over the country, including for-profit HMOs, to refuse "futile" medical treatment, even when the care was desired by the patient. According to the group's published preliminary guidelines, "futile care" would have included, among other things: food and fluids and other forms of life support for persistently unconscious people; CPR—even when requested—for the "frail, institutionalized elderly";

and CPR for people with a "terminal illness" where there is "less than a 5 percent chance of surviving to discharge after CPR," if the patient is "receiving hospice care," and if more than "seven minutes pass from the cardiac arrest before CPR can be initiated."[68]

The stated purpose behind CCMD futilitarianism was to save healthcare resources for those whom "society" deems more worthy of consuming them. The advocates of such changes maintain that such quasi-rationing would better promote overall "health," a concept that Dr. Murphy asserted includes broad community issues of "education, transportation, and recreation, as well as medical care."[69] If that meant sacrificing the ill, the elderly, even people who would have a "5, 10, or even 20 percent chance of surviving," according to Dr. Murphy, that difficult decision would just have to be made.[70]

CCMD's idea was to develop the guidelines and then introduce them at a series of community forums for approval. When the public learned that CCMD wanted permission to impose its values upon the sick and their families, futile care theory fell flat on its face.

Murphy approached The Colorado Trust, a philanthropic foundation dedicated to funding projects designed to promote "accessible and affordable healthcare programs." The Trust granted CCMD $1.3 million to develop its guidelines. "It was a unique grant," said Nancy Baughman Csuti, Senior Evaluation Officer for The Colorado Trust. "It was not done in response to a Request For Proposals. Dr. Murphy just came in as the leader of his organization and made a strong presentation asking for the money."

CCMD used The Colorado Trust's donation to convene community focus groups intended to determine—and hopefully to mold—the public's attitudes toward end-of-life care. Murphy's purpose was to generate so much public agreement with CCMD's proposed guidelines that hospitals, HMOs, and physicians would be emboldened to immediately begin the widespread withholding of "inappropriate" care. But to Murphy's chagrin, "the community" generally rejected futile care theory.

"It became clear that people believe that they should be in control of their own care," Csuti told me.

Seeing the writing on the wall, The Colorado Trust ceased funding CCMD and used the information gleaned from the focus groups to help craft a new Palliative Care Initiative by which the trust hopes to promote better and more humane medical treatment at the end of life—a program *not* based on a coercive model. Why the change? Says Csuti: "Our foundation believes that the community must buy into new approaches to medicine. It became clear that the guidelines would not fly. So, the Foundation is now pursuing a different path."

The loss of The Colorado Trust's funding dealt a deathblow to CCMD. The organization is no longer active, and Dr. Murphy has moved on to new endeavors.[71]

FOLLOW THE MONEY

A primary purpose behind futile care theory—as with the rarely stated but clear impetus driving assisted suicide—is to save medical resources for patients who are deemed to have a greater claim or to help pay for expanded access to health insurance.

But this belief, that the healthcare system will be destroyed unless we cease spending so much money on dying people, is fundamentally misguided. End-of-life care takes up only 10 to 12 percent of the entire healthcare budget. So, unless we refuse to treat every patient as soon as the terminal diagnosis is given, savings from futile care theory will not produce significant savings.[72] As Dr. Joanne Lynn, professor of medicine and of community and family medicine at the Center for the Evaluation of Clinical Sciences, Dartmouth Medical School, explained in testimony before the Senate Finance Committee in 1994: "There is a widespread myth that enormous resources are wasted on the dying. The evidence for this is actually quite frail. About one-quarter of payments under Medicare are directed at the care of those who die during that year. This seems to be a reasonable proportion—after all, persons are commonly quite sick in the year before they die. . . . Very few dying persons now have resuscitation efforts or extended stays in intensive care."[73]

"The Economics of Dying," an article published in the *New England Journal of Medicine* in 1994, is even more to the point. Its authors, Drs. Ezekiel Emanuel and Linda Emanuel, reviewed studies of the cost savings that could be achieved by Medicare if more people signed advance directives (such as durable powers of attorney for healthcare), if there were broader use of DNRs, if futile care guidelines were enacted, and the like. Although the studies were not definitive, the Emanuels concluded: "The amount that might be saved by reducing the use of aggressive life-sustaining interventions for dying patients is at most 3.3 percent of total national healthcare expenditures. In 1993, with $900 billion going to healthcare, this savings would amount to $29.7 billion. . . . We must stop deluding ourselves that advance directives and less aggressive care at the end of life will solve the financial problems of the healthcare system."[74] Even rationing advocates admit that there is little money to be saved by denying people end-of-life treatment.

Dr. Murphy of the late, unlamented CCMD admitted to me that imposing futile care would not save the healthcare system a lot of money. So why try to impose it upon a reluctant society? Permitting doctors to refuse "futile" care is only the first step in the proverbial thousand-mile journey. In the end, many futilitarians hope to arrive at a rationed healthcare system where "community consensus" determines the parameters of medical treatment. Indeed, Dr. Murphy told me that the next step after futile care would be to "restrict marginally beneficial care." Where, he claimed, "greater resource savings are to be found."[75] What would an example of marginally beneficial care be? According to Dr. Murphy, "mammograms for women over 80" or medical treatment that the community finds inappropriate for some people because of, say, age or state of health, but which the community considers acceptable for those it deems more deserving of care.[76]

Considering the similar value systems at play in both assisted suicide and futile care, we shouldn't be surprised. For many involved in these end-of-life issues, patient autonomy in end-of-life decision making isn't the ultimate goal—the death of certain patients is. If patient autonomy obtains that end, well and good. But if patients or families want to "rage, rage, against the dying of the light," then the theory of futile treatment will be applied. Clearly, assisted suicide and futile care theory have no place in a moral, compassionate healthcare system.

~ 7 ~

Euthanasia as a Form of Oppression

T HE IDEA THAT LEGALIZED EUTHANASIA would be a form of oppression will undoubtedly offend believers in "rational suicide" who equate assisted suicide and euthanasia with individual liberty. While it is not my intention to give offense, I believe that the contrary is true, indeed, that legalized assisted suicide would create a new form of oppression.

Let's explore this premise for a moment. In order to oppress others and still get a good night's sleep, we must first divide those who are to be oppressed from those deemed to deserve full human rights. This task requires the creation of false distinctions that permit us to distinguish "us" from "them," toward the end of dehumanizing those deemed the "other." Once some people are seen as "different," the path is opened to oppression.

In human history such invidious distinctions have been based on race, nationality, tribe, religion, age, gender, sexual orientation, and ideology, and disability, just to name a few. Now perhaps, we will have to add state of health or happiness to this woeful list.

Oppression is especially insidious when formalized into law. For example, in the United States, the Jim Crow statutes in the Old South, explicitly legitimized discrimination based on race. These laws not only gave African-Americans extremely short legal shrift but actively promoted a racist culture by granting the states' imprimatur to bigotry. This, in turn, encouraged the overt, extra-legal racism then common in Southern society. Thus, discriminatory public policies, such as those requiring segregated schools, added fuel to the fire of hatred, leading directly to extra-legal forms of bigotry such as lynching.

So too would it be if the state created a doctor's legal right to help kill his patients based on poor state of health or disability. The law's wording would be couched in words of compassion and liberty, but language—for example, "separate but equal"—does not always mean what it says. By making assisted suicide a legally recognized and enforceable right, the state would be proclaiming that not all human lives are of equal inherent worth, that some of us (the healthy, able-bodied, and relatively happy) are worth protecting, even from self-destruction, while others (the "hopelessly ill") are of such little use that their deaths are best for all. The impact of such a proclamation would be no different from that of legally institutionalized racism: to create a new basis for dividing humans into privileged and oppressed classes, thereby influencing cultural outlook as well as the state's legal obligations toward its citizens. In other words, "rational suicides" would be not only permitted but could eventually become actively encouraged. Indeed, one of the hottest issues in contemporary bioethics discourse is whether people deemed burdensome, such as the frail elderly and those with profound cognitive disabilities, have a "duty to die."[1]

PREJUDICE AGAINST THE DISABLED

Increasingly, disabled people are in the crosshairs of the euthanasia movement, which views them as potential "beneficiaries" of the right to be killed by a doctor. Many in the disability-rights community have a dramatically different view. Rather than seeing euthanasia as a guarantee of "liberty," they view legalization as a dire threat and a form of

bigotry against disabled people that sends the loud message that disabled people's lives are worthless. Paul Longmore, a nationally respected
disability-rights activist, writer, and associate professor of history at
California State University at San Francisco, says,

> Current euthanasia activists talk a lot about personal autonomy
> and choice. Well, for people with disabilities who have opted for
> assisted suicide, it was a spurious choice. These are people who
> have been denied the ability to choose about virtually every other
> option in their lives: They have been segregated out of society;
> they have been denied the right to work; they have been discrimi-
> nated against in getting an education; they have been blocked from
> expressing themselves romantically and sexually; they have been
> penalized for marrying by having public benefits shut off, includ-
> ing desperately needed health insurance; they have been shunned
> by loved ones and friends. In virtually every case in which a per-
> son with a disability has sought legal assistance in ending their
> lives, they have been discriminated against in most if not all of
> these ways.[2]

The late Evan Kemp, a political conservative with different political opinions from Longmore, who served as chairman of the Equal
Employment Opportunity Commission under former president Bush,
worked assiduously against assisted suicide during his last years. About
hastened death, he stated bluntly, "Euthanasia is nothing more than
human beings—often doctors—killing disabled, ill, or elderly people."[3]
Diane Coleman, founder of Not Dead Yet, the noted disability-rights
organization that campaigns against assisted suicide and other forms
of anti-disability discrimination, has written:

> The widespread public image of severe disability as a fate worse
> then death is not exactly a surprise to the disability community.
> Disability rights activists have fought against these negative ste-
> reotypes of disability for decades in the effort to achieve basic civil
> rights protections. What has been a surprise for many advocates
> is the boldness with which these stereotypes are asserted as fact by

proponents of assisted suicide, and the willingness of the press and the public to accept them, without even checking them against the views of people who themselves live with severe disabilities ....These stereotypes then become grounds for carving out a deadly exception to longstanding laws and public policies about suicide prevention.[4]

Those of us who are able-bodied may think that the worst form of discrimination that disabled people generally face is having their "handicapped" parking spaces taken by those who have no right to use them. Actually, hate crimes against disabled people are a pervasive problem (so bad that the law now requires the FBI to gather statistics on them). Disabled people not only face the danger of physical assault but hurtful insults and thoughtless comments by friends, neighbors, and even total strangers. "Every day I run into people who will say, 'If I were you, I'd give up,'" says Kathi Wolfe, a writer who is legally blind. "A taxi driver recently refused to pick me up, telling me he won't allow handicapped people in his cab. A few months ago, when I was heading for the subway, someone took my cane and threw it down the escalator, hissing at me, 'You people belong in a concentration camp.' I've even had a doctor tell me that if he were blind like me, he would kill himself."[5]

Longmore, who can't use his arms because of polio, has curvature of the spine, and frequently requires a respirator, tells a similar story. "Strangers have come up to me on the streets telling me that they would rather be dead than in my position, that before they would be disabled, they would kill themselves. A lot of people would rather not see us and be reminded that life is fragile and not totally within our control. They wish we would just go away."[6]

"Disability has supplanted death in people's minds as the worst thing that can happen," says the psychologist Carol Gill, a disability-rights activist and head of the Chicago Institute on Disability Research. "These prejudices are sometimes shared by physicians, ethicists, and others in the healthcare hierarchy. That can be frightening. If a doctor doesn't think that a life with disability is tenable, they think they are doing a [disabled] patient a favor by advocating an end to treatment [so death will occur]." As detailed in the last chapter, such refusals of care are becoming systemic via futile care theory. If active euthanasia were legalized, such pressures could only increase.

"Kevorkian and other 'death with dignity' proponents are broadening the definition of 'extreme human suffering' to encompass mental and physical disabilities that leave individuals unable to live life unassisted," a disability rights journal noted early in Kevorkian's killing spree. "Activists fear that such thinking will reinforce society's acceptance of healthcare rationing and the denial of adequate funding for assistive technology and personal assistance services. One activist attending a recent meeting on disability and euthanasia scoffed, 'Dignity my eye; all that concern about dignity boils down to society's contempt for people who need help to go to the bathroom!'"[7]

These prejudices seep into the delivery of healthcare that those of us who are able-bodied take for granted. Examples of such biases are routinely reported in disability-rights literature. The following excerpt from an article in the disability health and wellness journal *One Step Ahead's Second Opinion* is typical of the impediments placed in the paths of disabled people: "Robert Powell has lived with partial paralysis since childhood and learned two years ago he has a heart condition. . . . [The] hospital staff repeatedly asked him how much he wanted done to save his life should his condition fail to respond to routine treatment. Having barely reached middle age, he assured them he wanted aggressive measures to save his life. Staff continued to question him about his decision. They finally requested a psychiatric consult because they felt he was 'having trouble accepting death.'"[8]

Facing and overcoming this type of prejudice is difficult enough in a healthcare system whose official ethics still value all lives equally. But now, with the equality-of-human-life ideal under attack from the euthanasia movement and bioethics, and in the context of society's prejudice against people with disabilities, many in the disability-rights movement are very concerned that they will be victimized by legalized euthanasia. One prominent disabled disability-rights activist, extremely alarmed by society's apparent acceptance of euthanasia, told me, "I don't expect to die a natural death."

William G. Strothers, the former editor of *Mainstream* magazine, a monthly serving the disabled community, issued a call to anti-euthanasia activists after two women with multiple sclerosis were assisted in suicides, one by Jack Kevorkian and one by a man named George Delury, who participated in his wife's death. Strothers wrote: "What's troubling is that medical professionals and others are eager to pursue assisted suicide as a viable option when they and society at large have a fairly limited understanding of life. For example, negative stereotypes of disability as a fate worse than death persist, even among people with disabilities. . . . As active participants in society, people with disabilities have the opportunity to counter Kevorkian and be evangelists for life. We had better get to it quickly."[9]

Some disability activists are doing just that. Disability rights organizations such as Not Dead Yet work tirelessly to stop the legalization of assisted suicide. "Not Dead Yet is declaring war on the ultimate form of discrimination, euthanasia," Coleman asserts strongly. "We've watched over the last decade as our brothers and sisters have been denied suicide prevention that non-disabled people take for granted. We've watched as families have been allowed to withhold food and water from their disabled children. We are acting before it is too late."[10]

Activists of Not Dead Yet engage in demonstrations and other educational efforts around the country to alert the general public to the threat euthanasia poses to disabled people. Fittingly, the organization's first demonstration, in June 1996, was in front of the house of Jack Kevorkian, whom Not Dead Yet considers a bigot because of his disdainful statements about disabled people and because he has helped so many depressed disabled people kill themselves.

Not Dead Yet next targeted a medical ethics conference where a keynote speaker advocated limiting medical treatment for certain disabled people as "exoticare." Rather than endure the adverse publicity of people in wheelchairs demonstrating against discrimination, the ethicists invited representatives of Not Dead Yet to address the convention. What could have been a confrontation became an educational opportunity. "We asked the ethicists how many of the hospital ethics committees had disabled people as members," Diane Coleman recalls. "Only two out of forty or fifty of the people raised their hands. When we asked if the disabled people who were represented had knowledge and experience in independent living, no one raised their hands. Yet, these committees continually make decisions about life and death based on the perceived quality of disabled people's lives."[11]

Members of Not Dead Yet also were fittingly present in Jack Kevorkian's last trial. On trial for murdering Thomas Youk, a man disabled by the terminal illness ALS, members of the organization sat daily in the public section of the courtroom, a silent witness against Kevorkian's bigotry against their community.

The Robert Latimer Case

Few events illustrate the anti-disability attitude that afflicts society better than the reaction of much of Canada to the murder of twelve-year-old Tracy Latimer, who had a severe case of cerebral palsy. Her father, Robert, killed Tracy one Sunday when the rest of the Latimer family was at church. After the family had left, Latimer carried Tracy to the garage, put her inside the cab of the family pickup truck, turned on the ignition, and closed the garage door. He then walked away leaving his daughter to die alone, choking on carbon monoxide fumes.

Robert Latimer was arrested, convicted of second-degree murder, and given a sentence of life in prison, of which he would have to serve a minimum of ten years. The Latimer case caused a national uproar, but not against the father. Rather, his conviction and jail sentence outraged many Canadians. The case turned into a cause célèbre for legalizing euthanasia. One columnist asked, "Where were the doctors when Robert Latimer needed them?" and advocated, in the guise of sharing a correspondent's opinion, that "a committee to make life and death decisions" be formed when "life becomes intolerable and death may be the most compassionate thing."[12]

Supporters donated tens of thousands of dollars to the Latimer legal defense fund and the pro-Latimer uproar was crucial in obtaining Robert Latimer's release from prison, pending appeal. One judge, dissenting from an earlier court of appeals decision affirming Latimer's sentence, even included in the text of his dissent letters from outraged citizens demanding that Latimer be freed rather than punished for his "act of love."[13]

Within months of Tracy's death, an American parent, Susan Smith, killed her two sons by pushing her car into a lake with the boys firmly buckled into their car safety seats. Like Tracy, the Smith children died alone as their murderous parent watched from only a short distance away. But unlike Tracy's case, the entire country leapt to the posthumous defense of the Smith boys. Susan Smith was branded a monster and had to be protected from an angry crowd, while Robert Latimer was widely hailed as a loving father.

Why the difference? There is only one explanation: Smith's children were able-bodied and pleasant to look at, and therefore had a right to their lives. Tracy Latimer was disabled and unphotogenic, and therefore she was seen by many as better off dead.

That was certainly the message received by another Canadian youngster who took Tracy's killing and Robert Latimer's popular support quite personally. His name was Teague Johnson. Teague and Tracy had a lot in common. They were about the same age. Both had severe cases of cerebral palsy. Both were quadriplegic. Both were often in pain and required various treatments to alleviate their discomfort. Both had severe communication difficulties. Unlike Tracy, Teague had learned facilitated-communication techniques that allowed him to express himself to his close relatives and friends.

"I remember Teague was very distressed by the idea that a father could take it upon himself to choose death for his disabled daughter,"

Teague's father, Larry Johnson, recalls. "And he was distressed that so many Canadians reacted with sympathy for the man who killed a daughter who differed from Teague only in the fact that five or six people in Teague's life had been able to help him say his own words and clarify his own wishes."[14]

Teague was so anguished by Tracy's murder and the widespread approval of it by his fellow Canadians that he wrote an opinion column, which was published in the *Vancouver Sun* on December 9, 1994:[15]

> My name is Teague. I am 11 years old and have really severe cerebral palsy. The Latimer case . . . has caused me a great deal of unhappiness and worry . . . I feel strongly that all children are valuable and deserve to live full and complete lives. No one should make the decision for another person about whether their life is worth living or not. . . .
>
> I have to fight pain all the time. When I was little life was pain. My foster Mom Cara helped me to learn to manage and control my pain. Now my life is so full of joy. There isn't time enough in the day for me to learn and experience all I wish to do. I have a family and many friends who love me. I have a world of knowledge to discover. I have so much to give.
>
> I can't walk or feed myself but I am not "suffering from cerebral palsy." I use a wheelchair but I am not "confined to a wheelchair." I have pain but I do not need to be "put out of my misery."
>
> My body is not my enemy. It is that which allows me to enjoy Mozart, experience Shakespeare, savor a bouillabaisse feast, and cuddle my Mom. Life is a precious gift. It belongs to the person to whom it was given. Not to her parents, nor to the state. Tracy's life was hers "to make of it what she could" [quoting the Latimer trial judge]. My life is going to be astounding.[16]

Teague's loved ones helped him communicate his values of love, mutual connectedness, and universal equality to people all over the world on the Internet. In a letter to a friend dated April 4, 1994, facilitated by Teague's foster mother, "Ca," Teague wrote:

I am really working hard these days to be strong and healthy. I really want to live a long, long time because I have so much to do. There is so much I want to learn and many people who need me. My Ca loves me and really needs me to be her foster boy. That's right, I used to think that I needed my Ca but she really needs me. I thought really I was a burden to my Ca. But really, I discovered that the best place for my Ca. to be is living with me. My Ca needs me to be really happy. My L. [Larry, Teague's father] needs me to really help him with his master's thesis. Really, without me these grownups would actually stop learning new things. And I have lots to teach the world. I am going to be an important teacher.[17]

Another note from Teague:

I am working on helping the world understand that children with disabilities are really the same as other children and need love and a good education. Really people shouldn't make assumptions on what someone is like based on what they look like. I hope [to show] people that those assumptions about people based on religion and race and sexual orientation are really wrong too. I am doing this by talking to people, and making speeches, and writing articles for newspapers. This is really my mission. And really if one segment of the population, like . . . people with disabilities, are considered second class citizens, then that makes it easier for people to start treating other segments of the population too.[18]

Facilitated communication is a matter of some controversy. Some experts contend that the disabled person isn't doing the actual communicating, but rather that well-meaning facilitators are unconsciously supplying words and thoughts that are not really there. Other experts accept facilitated communication as genuine.

Be that as it may, the sentiments expressed by Teague are important and meaningful. For, as Paul Longmore says of the Tracy Latimer case, "One of the serious dangers to all disabled people is that there is an ideal, a standard, a norm, against which people with disabilities are measured. The further you depart from the ideal, the less human you are deemed, until you get to people who are nonverbal and quadriplegic, where many see the disabled person as literally nonhuman. That appears to be driving the public attitudes in the Tracy Latimer case."[19]

Teague Johnson died in his father's arms from natural causes at age twelve. "Teague never doubted that his own life was worth living," Larry Johnson says. "He was excited about the future, and he continually made plans to advance his education and to engage in new and exciting projects. He lived to communicate his thoughts to the people and to help them understand that peace, love, and joy were possible for every human being."[20]

As for Robert Latimer, who had a different view of the value of his daughter's life, he remained free on bail for several years while his case was on appeal. He was granted a new trial because the prosecution asked jury members about their feelings toward assisted suicide before the trial, which is not permitted under Canadian law. Once again he was convicted. That case finally went to the Supreme Court of Canada where it was affirmed. He is now doing his ten years. Even after all this time, there are websites and continual petition gathering and political agitation by Latimer's many supporters to obtain clemency for the murderer.[21]

It now appears that the public's reaction to Latimer may have increased the number of developmentally disabled children being killed by a parent in Canada. This is the conclusion of Professor Dick Sobsey, Director of the JP Das Developmental Disabilities Centre at the University of Alberta in Canada. Sobsey reviewed homicide statistics in the United States and Canada involving the killing of developmentally disabled children:

> After correcting for population Americans with developmental disabilities were 2.5 times as likely to be killed by the parents as Canadians. From 1994 to the present [the end of 2001] we found 21 cases in Canada and 101 cases in the United States. [The U.S.

has ten times the population of Canada.] This means that suddenly Canadians with developmental disabilities were 84% more likely than Americans to be killed by their parents [in the wake of Latimer].

Another way to look at this is that in the United States the per cent of homicide victims with developmental disabilities did not change significantly since 1994—less than 1%. In Canada, it increased 88.5% since 1994.[22]

If Sobsey's research is accurate, if indeed public support for Latimer led to additional homicides of disabled children, why would such a phenomenon occur? "Social learning theory is one of the most time-tested theories of psychology," Sobsey explains. "Basically, it says that when people witness violence that is socially endorsed, they are likely to imitate it. In this case, we are talking about parents who for many different reasons are close to the edge of the abyss of killing their own children. Presenting them with a model that says in some cases this is the right thing to do *for* their child, helps them overcome the guilt that would normally hold them back."[23] This is hardly surprising when murder is called "altruistic" by a judge and deemed an act of love by a large segment of the population. When many Canadians commended Robert Latimer for killing Tracy, their social sanction might have provided other parents of disabled children with the rationalization they needed to overcome their own consciences.

Elizabeth Bouvia

Few cases enrage disability-rights activists and prove to them as convincingly the bigotry faced by disabled people as does that of Elizabeth Bouvia. In the early 1980s, Bouvia became suicidal after undergoing one devastating emotional crisis after another over two years: her brother died, she was in deep financial distress, she left graduate school because of discrimination, she had a miscarriage, and her marriage dissolved. She checked herself into a psychiatric hospital and declared her desire for pain-control medications that would assist her to commit suicide by self-starvation.

Normally, such a request would be rejected out of hand; it would be deemed a cry for help, and medical professionals and other compassionate and involved persons would have attempted to help Bouvia find a reason to go on living. But some thought this case was different. Why? Bouvia's stated reason for wanting to die was that she had cerebral palsy and was quadriplegic.

Ignoring the profound emotional blows Bouvia recently had experienced, blows that individually and collectively could produce a desire for suicide in almost anyone, the American Civil Liberties Union took up her cause. The lead ACLU attorney in the case, Richard Scott, had been the first legal counsel of the Hemlock Society. The expert mental health professional testifying in support of her dying was Faye Girsh, later the executive director of the Hemlock Society.

The trial court refused Bouvia's request. She left the hospital, and after an unsuccessful trip to Mexico to seek aid in dying, she again began to eat. Her suicidal impulse seemed to have abated, but it later returned. She again checked into a hospital and stopped eating, and attorney Scott returned to court. To keep her alive, the hospital put in a feeding tube.

The second trial judge again refused her request for assisted suicide. The ACLU appealed the decision. But a new era was about to arrive on the food and fluids front, and consistent with the emerging ethic, the California Court of Appeals judge saw Bouvia's case in a different light and decided that this was not a matter of assisted suicide but of refusing medical treatment. In language dripping with the pervasive societal prejudice that death is better than disability, Judge Lynn Compton wrote: "In Elizabeth Bouvia's view, the quality of her life has been diminished to the point of hopelessness, uselessness, unenjoyability, and frustration. She, as the patient, lying helplessly in bed, unable to care for herself, may consider existence meaningless.

She is not to be faulted for so concluding. . . . We cannot conceive it to be the policy of this State to inflict such an ordeal on anybody."[24]

On the surface, Judge Compton's thesis may sound reasonable. But it really expressed the insidious abandoning philosophy of "rational suicide." After all, *anybody* who wants to commit suicide believes that his or her life is "meaningless," "useless," and "hopeless," forever to be without joy. Otherwise, the person would not want to die. Yet when the cause of such despair is the end of a love affair, the death of a child, loss of reputation, and the like, no court would rule (at least not yet) that the suicide wish should be accommodated because it is wrong for the "state to inflict such an ordeal on anybody." Solely because Bouvia's stated reason to die was her disability, the court viewed her differently: Of course she wanted to die. Who wouldn't? She was disabled; hence, her hopelessness and despair were perceived as permanent conditions, unlike feelings caused by the loss of career or death of a loved one.

The late Mark O'Brien, who was a quadriplegic from his early childhood because of a severe case of polio, lived for the last forty-four years of his life in an iron lung. He not only graduated from the University of California at Berkeley but also was a published poet, a journalist, and an author. O'Brien said of the court's reasoning: "It is false to say quadriplegics can never have a meaningful life. [Bouvia] had more mobility than I do. To link disability with worthlessness and uselessness, as too many people do and as the court of appeals did, is pure superstition. These attitudes are based on fears and false presumptions held by people who aren't disabled."[25]

Bouvia's life was clearly not foreordained to uselessness. She had lived on her own and had attended San Diego State University.[26] She once volunteered as a social worker and might well have continued in that field to a paying position had she not quit college in a dispute over her studies, after which the college had refused to readmit her.[27]

Paul Longmore, who has written extensively on the Bouvia case, agrees with Mark O'Brien's assessment. "When we [in the disability-rights community] tried to point out that Elizabeth's depression was caused in large part by society's unwillingness to give us the assistance that would allow us to live independently, to work, to be free from discrimination, we were contemptuously dismissed by the court and in the media. Yet, in the end, everything we said was right and everything the ACLU said was wrong."[28]

Longmore's point is this: Elizabeth Bouvia didn't die. Instead of killing herself, she chose to go on, and now many, sometimes difficult, years later, she is living independently, with the help of a personal assistant, in California. Ironically, her lawyer, Richard Scott, was the one who ended up committing suicide.

Larry McAfee

The Bouvia case was not unusual in its reasoning or result. Other disabled people have asked successfully for court help in committing suicide by starvation, usually because their aspirations for independent living have been blocked, not because of their physical limitations. Joseph Shapiro, in *No Pity*, wrote about a young man named Larry McAfee, disabled in a motorcycle accident, who wanted to die because "every day when I wake up, there is nothing to look forward to."[29] The court agreed that his disability made his life hopeless and not worth living and sanctioned pulling his feeding tube in 1989.

Shapiro convincingly demonstrates what the court seemed unable to grasp: McAfee felt useless because he was "being handled like a piece of radioactive waste," forced unnecessarily to live in nursing homes solely because of his quadriplegia while denied life-enriching opportunities for independent living.[30]

For reasons quite relevant to this discussion, McAfee's story had a happy ending. After McAfee's case made headlines, he received assistance—not in dying but in living. He was given a computer, which he worked by using his head and which allowed him to pursue his interest in architecture and engineering. Then, when he finally had the opportunity to have attendants to assist him, people he hired and could fire, his spirits rallied, and he decided he definitely wanted to live. He was able to leave the nursing home and he lived for several more years in a shared-living arrangement with other disabled young men. He died from natural causes in 1996.

What if euthanasia and assisted suicide were legalized for disabled people like Elizabeth Bouvia and Larry McAfee, who request "rational suicide" out of despair caused in large measure by societal discrimination and disdain? What if, rather than having to go through lengthy court proceedings, Bouvia and McAfee had been required only to wait fifteen days from their request before being given a lethal injection or poisonous potion? In such a world, both of these people would have been dead and buried long before their spirits rebounded and they moved on to the next phase of their lives.

A review of the professional literature supports the contention of disability-rights activists that disability is more of an emotional problem for the general community than it is for most disabled individuals. One study, which compared the attitudes of disabled people to those of medical professionals, found that 86 percent of spinal-cord-injured high-level quadriplegics rated their own quality of life as average or better than average, while only 17 percent of the doctors and nurses surveyed thought they themselves would have an average or better-than-average quality of life if they became disabled.[31] Interviews and tests administered to 133 persons with severe mobility disabilities revealed no differences between them and the non-disabled norm on psychosocial measures. Another study found no significant difference on quality-of-life measurements between persons with severe disabilities and persons without any disabilities.[32] Hospital personnel consistently overestimated their disabled patients' level of depression, whereas self-rating of depression by these patients found levels similar to that of the general population.[33]

We must therefore ask ourselves: Would legalizing assisted suicide and euthanasia for disabled people—too many of whom are cared for in medicalized or nursing home settings that devalue their lives, and in a healthcare system increasingly concerned about cost of care—truly be "compassionate"? Or would it be an expression of the general community's own fears, prejudices, and—in Mark O'Brien's apt term— superstitions about disability? If it were indeed the latter, as many in the disability-rights community strongly assert, wouldn't the facilita- tion of disabled persons' deaths actually be to abandon them? Calling such "chosen" deaths exercises in liberty or death with dignity would not change that reality.

The extent to which society accepts the belief that death is better than disability is aptly illustrated by the case of Dr. Gregory Messen- ger, a Michigan dermatologist who, fearing that his son Michael would suffer and be disabled because of being born prematurely, at twenty-six weeks, took him off a respirator with the intent that the boy should die. Dr. Messenger unilaterally took this deadly action, even though Michael had not been examined, even though necessary diagnostic tests to de- termine his likely prognosis had not been conducted, even though his wife's doctor estimated the chance of Michael's survival before the emergency birth at 30 to 50 percent, even though a significant number of babies born at twenty-six weeks survive, many without significant impairment. Michael Messenger died at age eighty-two minutes.[34]

Everyone can deeply sympathize with Dr. Messenger's grief, worry, and fear about his baby. But did that give him the right to end his baby's life before his son had a chance to fight for his own survival? According to the jury, apparently so. After only four hours' delibera- tion, they acquitted Dr. Messenger of manslaughter charges, a verdict some delighted bioethicists called a blow for parental rights.[35]

Compare Dr. Messenger's exoneration to what happened to the parents of Baby Terry and Baby Ryan. The father who took away his son's right to live was widely viewed as a loving and caring parent only trying to prevent his son's suffering. But parents who wanted to give their prematurely born children every chance for life were turned over to the authorities by doctors and hospital administrators as child abusers and, in the Baby Terry case, were stripped of parental rights. There is a paradox here—unless these cases are seen in the broader context of a culture increasingly looking to death as the answer to the medical difficulties and disability potential associated with premature birth.

The Messenger case also has about it the noxious odor of the euthanasia advocate Peter Singer's theory that parents and doctors should have the legal and ethical right to have doctors kill unwanted disabled infants, as currently exists in the Netherlands. Singer states in *Rethinking Life and Death* (a reiteration of the same thoughts that he has presented in other forums): "Both for the sake of 'our children' [other healthy children, whether or not they have yet been born], then, and for our own sake, we may not want a child to start life's uncertain voyage if the prospects are clouded. When this can be known at a very early stage of the voyage ... we can still say no, and start again from the beginning."[36]

THE ANTI-FAMILY VALUES OF EUTHANASIA

Even the most loving and supportive families are plunged into emotional crisis when a family member is catastrophically ill or injured. Sadly, too many families approach health crises or tackle long-term-care challenges without adequate information about services and products that would assist them. For example, many people who care for elderly parents are unaware of the many social service options that exist to help them, such as respite centers, adult day care, hospice, group homes, support groups, and the like.

The national culture can also be a barrier to effective caregiving. Caregivers report that many people look askance at their friends and neighbors who sacrifice personal pursuits in order to give sick and dying loved ones the loving care they need and deserve. This sad truth was illustrated by Lucette Lagnado in a *Wall Street Journal* article titled

"Mercy Living" in which she wrote about the reactions of her friends and acquaintances when she brought her elderly, disabled mother home rather than keep her in a nursing home. Noting that "mercy killing is increasingly de rigueur," Lagnado wrote, "In the two years I cared for Mom at my home, if friends didn't make me feel that I was somehow mishandling—even wasting—my life, then the 'professionals' did. . . . Forced to rely on a battery of neurologists, cardiologists, gastroenterologists and pulmonologists . . . I learned to steel myself for that cold look, the shake of the head that meant there was not much hope for her, so why bother?" One doctor even yelled at Lagnado. "What was I doing keeping a sick mother at home, he thundered. Posing a question as loaded as it was insidious, he asked: 'Is she really alive?'"[37]

Lagnado's experience is not unique. Increasingly, many see caring for people who are elderly, profoundly disabled, or seriously ill as a burden that wastes time and resources that would be better spent "productively." This subversive message is delivered throughout society, in personal conversations, in the attitudes of the youth culture, in the media, sometimes even in advocacy for the "right to die," in which dependency and disability are commonly equated with a lack of dignity and human worth.

This milieu of fractured communities, of societal indifference, of isolation, of dysfunctional families, of widespread ignorance of caregiving and pain management, of patients worrying about being burdens is the one in which families would face "rational" decision making about euthanasia and assisted suicide. Even in the best of families, those with only loving and altruistic motives, such "crisis atmospheres" would not be conducive to reasoned decision making about killing as a perceived answer to difficulty. If legalized euthanasia were brought as a "solution" into a family crisis among people who are not loving or mutually supportive, or where there was substantial money at stake, the lethal danger to the ill and vulnerable is hard to overstate.

Myrna Lebov

The tragic assisted suicide of the author and editor Myrna Lebov is a case in point. Disabled by multiple sclerosis, Lebov committed suicide on July 4, 1995, at the age of fifty-two, with the active assistance of her husband, George Delury, a former editor of the *World Almanac,* who was soon charged in her death.

As soon as the news broke about Lebov's death and Delury's arrest, many in the death-on-demand movement rushed to his support. The Hemlock Society created a legal defense fund for Delury. William Batt, chairman of the New York chapter, expressed confidence that Lebov had not been coerced, since most people would want to die if they were in her condition.[38] The case was widely seen within the assisted-suicide movement as a breakthrough that would move their cause forward. (Note that these advocates supported Delury even though there was no indication that Lebov was terminally ill.)

Initially, the media reported about the assisted suicide in its usual facile and breathless manner. Most reports accepted at face value Delury's claim that he was merely a compassionate husband doing what his totally debilitated and suffering, but courageous, wife desperately wanted. The *Charleston Daily News,* for example, under the headline, "Writer Wanted Relief," reported: "She knew her future was without hope. Instead of withering in a nursing home, Lebov, fifty-two, swallowed pills and died in her Manhattan apartment."[39]

Delury became an instant "victim-celebrity." He made numerous television appearances, a speech before the American Psychiatric Association, and signed a book deal. Far and wide, he was acclaimed as a dedicated husband willing to risk jail to help his wife achieve her deeply desired end to suffering. He was allowed to quickly plead guilty to a minor crime and served only four months in jail.

But a few months later, *Forward,* a Jewish weekly, reported that all was not as George Delury wanted it to seem. For example, Delury repeatedly claimed that Lebov's life had been reduced to the merely "biological" by her disease. Yet *Forward* reporter discovered that only a week before she died, Myrna swam twenty-eight laps with the help of a therapist.[40] The paper also discovered that Delury had convinced Lebov to accept a buyout of her monthly disability insurance payments by accepting a check for fifty thousand dollars, which he then cashed against her express wishes.[41] Lebov's sister, Beverly Sloane, appalled at the sympathy and support she perceived her former brother-in-law was receiving among the public and in the press, publicly countered Delury's characterizations of Lebov's final months, describing her sibling as engaged in life, albeit struggling against depression caused, in part, by an emotionally unsupportive husband.

The lid blew off Delury's claim of selfless altruism when the New York district attorney's office released the contents of his diary. It revealed that Lebov did not have an unwavering and long-stated desire to die, as Delury had alleged. Rather, as often happens with people struggling with serious illnesses, her moods waxed and waned. One day she would be suicidal but the next day, Delury's diary revealed, she would want to engage life. Moreover, the diary clearly demonstrated that it was Delury, *not* Lebov, who had the unremitting suicide agenda.

Delury admitted that he encouraged his wife to kill herself, or as he put it, "to decide to quit." He researched her antidepressant medication to see if it could kill her, and when she took less than the prescribed amount, which in and of itself could cause depression, he used the surplus to mix the poisonous brew that ended her life.

But he went further than that. He helped destroy her will to live by making her feel worthless and a burden on him. Beverly Sloane says, "There was definitely psychological coercion involved [in Lebov's death]. He was telling her in front of others, including my daughter, . . . that she was exhausting, she was a burden, that in two years he would be dead [from taking care of her]."[42]

Delury's own diary supports Sloane's recollections. On March 28, 1995, Delury wrote in his diary of his plans to tell his wife the following: "I have work to do, people to see, places to travel. But no one asks about my needs. I have fallen prey to the tyranny of a victim. You are sucking my life out of my [sic] like a vampire and nobody cares. In fact, it would appear that I am about to be cast in the role of villain because I no longer believe in you."[43] Delury later admitted on NBC's *Dateline* that he had shown Lebov this very passage.[44]

That Delury wanted Lebov to kill herself is beyond dispute. On May 1, he wrote: "Sheer hell. Myrna is more or less euphoric. She spoke of writing a book today. [Lebov was a published author.] She's interested in everything, wants everything explained, and believes that every bit of bad news bas some way out. . . . It's all too much. I'm not going to come out of this in one piece with my honor. I'm so tired of it all, maybe I should kill myself."[45]

On May 27, Delury wrote: "Myrna's mood was erratic today. Subdued in the morning, focused and realistic in the afternoon, rather more assertive in the evening—all definitely forward looking and without any indication that she wants to die. On the contrary, this evening she suggested that I was the only one who wanted her to die."[46]

On June 10, Delury's diary entry described an argument with Lebov that started after she left a message to her niece that "things are looking splendid": "I blew up! Shouting into the phone that everything was just the same, it was simply Myrna feeling different. I told Myrna that she bad hurt me very badly, not my feelings, but physically and emotionally. 'Now what will Beverly think? That I'm lying about how tough things are here.' I put it to Myrna bluntly—'If you won't take care of me, I won't take care of you.'"[47]

July 3, the day before Myrna's death, Delury wrote: "Myrna is now questioning the efficacy of solution, a sure sign that she will not take it [the overdose] tonight and doesn't want to. So, confusion and hesitancy strike again. If she changes her mind tonight and does decide to go ahead, I will be surprised."[48]

Finally, on July 4, Delury got what he wanted: his wife's death. After postponing an earlier suicide date that her husband had advocated, the couple's anniversary, Lebov swallowed the overdose of anti-depressant medicine that her husband prepared for her, and died. George Delury did not wait for her death by her bedside, but according to his diary, went into another room and went to sleep. The next morning he wrote, "Slept through the alarm. It's over. Myrna is dead. Desolation."[49]

In an interview with *Dateline*, Lebov's swimming therapist disclosed that she had indeed discussed suicide with her during their therapy sessions, although she subsequently told the therapist that she had decided to live. Lebov's self-described reason for wanting to self-destruct on July 4, Independence Day, was that she wanted to give her husband, George Delury, the freedom from her that he so fervently desired.[50] As one police official put it, George Delury put Myrna Lebov out of *his* misery.

And how was this man treated—a man who emotionally abandoned his disabled wife, a man who did nothing to seek treatment for his wife's intermittent suicidal thoughts but instead helped push her into choosing an early grave? Delury became something of a hero within the euthanasia movement, often speaking at assisted suicide conventions. His book, *But What if She Wants To Die*, was published.[51] Despite the abandonment revealed by Delury's diary and the disclosure made in his book that he had put a plastic bag over his wife's head to make sure she died, Susan Cheever, the reviewer for the *New York Times*, described Delury as a loving husband and the history of the marriage a "love story."[52]

Myrna's sister remains appalled by the widespread support for Delury. "People were quick to accept George's excuse for ending Myrna's life," she told me. "But in my opinion, he used the assisted suicide controversy as an alibi for intentional homicide. Her disease did not change the essence of Myrna. She was a loving, intelligent, warm, compassionate, sensitive, giving human being. She was a joy to talk to and be with. She was making plans for the future. She was not in pain. She was not terminally ill. She should still be alive enjoying the love of her family and he should still be in jail."[53] (Sloane and other family members sued

Delury for the "wrongful death" of Myrna Lebov. The case settled, with Delury promising to pay approximately $14,000 plus interest.)[54]

Gerald Klooster

Similar dynamics can be seen at work in a case that made national headlines and was featured on *60 Minutes*. Dr. Gerald Klooster was a retired physician from Castro Valley, California, who had Alzheimer's disease. When Klooster's son, Gerald (Chip) Klooster II, learned in August 1995 that his mother was about to take his father to Jack Kevorkian, he immediately flew to Florida, where his parents were visiting friends, and quickly whisked his father to safety. Chip then moved Gerald into his own home in Michigan, and after a psychiatric examination showed that Gerald was medically incompetent; he sent the finding to Kevorkian through his attorneys, pleading, "Please do not harm my father, he definitely does not want to end his life."

Chip then obtained temporary guardianship in his home state of Michigan and sought permanent custody of his father in a court battle that pitted him against his mother and siblings. Michigan judge Richard Mulhauser heard five days of testimony: Gerald's wife, Ruth, took the Fifth Amendment, and testimony was presented that Gerald was not in pain, enjoyed his family, and had years left to live. Moreover, according to witnesses, Gerald repeatedly expressed a desire to live, not die, a statement he repeated on *60 Minutes* on February 25, 1996."[55]

At the end of the five-day trial, Judge Mulhauser granted temporary custody of his father to Chip, ruling that "there is overwhelming evidence in the record of this case that Ruth intended to pursue the ending of Gerald Klooster's life through either the use of fatal drugs... or by taking him to Dr. Kevorkian in Michigan"; that "Ruth's children, except son 'Chip,' proved incapable of protecting Gerald"; that "it must be presumed that Ruth still intends her husband's suicide," that "Ruth was on a mission and that mission was the end of her husband's life because she believed it was the right thing to do"; and that "Chip likely saved his father's life."[56] In other words, according to the judge, Gerald's hastened death was Ruth's agenda, not Gerald's. She was the one who contacted Kevorkian and made arrangements to bring her husband to him, a visit that would probably have been a one-way trip.

The Klooster case soon turned into a bitter interstate custody struggle between Chip, in Michigan, and his siblings and mother, in California. In Alameda County, California, Judge William McInstry, who had not heard the evidence presented to Judge Mulhauser, granted custody of Gerald to Chip's sister, Kristen Hamstra, and ordered Gerald returned to California, threatening Chip with jail and a five-hundred-dollar-per-day fine. Meanwhile, Chip was ordered by Judge Mulhauser to keep Gerald in Michigan. The interstate battle soon ended in federal court, where a mediator helped the family reach a settlement, in which Gerald was returned to California after Chip's mother and siblings specifically agreed in writing that Gerald would not be euthanized or assisted with suicide, even if such practices become legal. Ruth also agreed to counseling to help her cope with her husband's ailment. Chip's sister, Kristen Hamstra, was named as her father's conservator.

Gerald lived with Kristen for several months. Then, over Chip's strenuous objections, Judge McInstry allowed Gerald to live with Ruth, who solemnly promised there would be no attempt to hasten the death of her husband.

A few months later, Chip's worst fears were realized. Gerald lay in a hospital near death from an overdose of alcohol and sleeping pills. The police treated the case as an "attempted suicide with suspicious circumstances," in part because Ruth had attempted to prevent resuscitation by paramedics after she called 911 and because of the family history. After a hearing, Judge McInstry returned custody of Gerald to Kristen, ignoring Ruth's pleas that she "would never hurt Gerald."[57]

Gerald recovered from the overdose. On February 7, 1997, Judge McInstry granted Ruth's request that her husband live with her after she hired a live-in helper and took other court-requested actions designed to protect Gerald's safety. (The police investigation was unable to determine whether there was wrongdoing involved in Gerald's near fatal overdose.) Gerald Klooster eventually died of natural causes. After having repeatedly accused Chip of being in the case for the money, Ruth Klooster sold the rights to her story, and it was made into a made-for-television movie.

Judith Bement

Susan Randall, the distraught daughter of Judith Bement, asked her stepfather, John Bement, an excruciating question: "When you put the [plastic] bag on mom's head, was she awake? I mean, did she know you were doing that? I just need peace of mind."

Bement did not realize that Susan was cooperating with a police investigation into her mother's death or that she was taping their conversation and conversations with her sister, Cynthia, who had been present for part of the assisted killing. Bement replied, "I don't know. I don't know. She was not totally out but she wasn't conscious."

Bement told Susan, the tape transcript reveals that years previously, when Judith was first diagnosed with ALS, he promised to assist his wife's suicide. He claimed that placing a plastic bag over Judith's head after she took twenty Seconals was simply the keeping of that promise.

But Susan didn't see it that way. She had been with her mother on the night of her death and Judith was happy. She said, "But when I left, we were joking around and everything was fine and it was a split second and everything just went to hell. Do you know what happened?"

"Well, what she wanted was the pills. . . . I read that book and . . ."

"What book?"

"*Final Exit.*"

"I never saw it."

"It's a book this guy wrote. So he says whenever you take these drugs that after the person is unconscious, you slip the bag over their head—kind of like insurance because, you know, somebody could survive." Bement then rationalized his actions: "She wasn't going to get any better. If it wasn't then it would be a month later, two months later."[58]

Susan is convinced that her mother was not suicidal on the night she died and that she had not given up on life. "My mother had made plans for the future," she told me. "Her moods fluctuated sure, but they were dictated by the quality of care she was receiving. When she felt valued and loved, she wanted to live. When she was made to feel like she was a burden, she grew despondent. She was not going to die soon. She had not qualified for hospice care because they said she would not die within six months. What mom needed was quality care and to know that she was loved, not a plastic bag over her head to suffocate the life out of her."

What shocked Susan was not only the manner of her mother's death but her stepfather's actions afterwards. "John began to date immediately after mom's death. His entire lifestyle changed. When mom was alive and needed him, he would often not come home at night, he said, because of his job as a local truck driver. I know because I stayed with her. As soon as she died, suddenly he started coming home every single night. I would drive by her house and his vehicle was always there."

Even worse for Susan, the townsfolk of Springville, New York, in her words "were conned into believing his sad story of acting out of love for his wife. Before and during John's trial, all the sympathy went to him, even though he never took the stand in his own defense. I was ostracized for awhile and only because I tried to stand up for my mom."

Had Judith ever expressed a desire to die? "Yes," Susan says. "When she was first diagnosed, a neurologist in Buffalo told her, 'You are a lost cause. You might as well go home, sit in a chair and wait to die.' She became despondent after that. Who wouldn't? For two years, she gave up on life. But then, my daughter was born, and she started seeing things differently. She had an active life again. Sure, she sometimes got depressed, but she would bounce out of it and get on with life."

Despite Bement's conviction of second-degree manslaughter, the local media and public opinion generally supported John, as did apparently, the judge. A jury convicted him of second-degree manslaughter. But despite his never having testified at either his trial or sentencing hearing—which would have allowed the district attorney to challenge his motives on cross-examination—Bement was sentenced to only two non-consecutive weeks in jail.

Susan is bitter. "With that sentence, the law confirmed what that awful doctor told my mother. Her life had no value. Her death wasn't worth worrying too much about. That was an insult to my mother and to all sick people. I hope that if I ever get into a position where I am vulnerable like mother was, that there is a law that protects my life and prevents others from getting rid of me and then saying it was okay because it was all about compassion."[59]

THESE LAST TWO CHAPTERS demonstrate a disturbing truth: Legalized euthanasia would be a volatile, dangerous, and toxic social policy, rather than the compassionate, "last resort" beneficence imagined by euthanasia ideologues. *In the real world*, doctors routinely undertreat pain and fail to diagnose clinical depression in their dying, chronically ill, and disabled patients. *In the real world*, managed-care doctors are under tremendous financial pressures that can result in inadequate care and could lead to killing as a means of protecting their pocketbooks. *In the real world*, chronic inequalities and animosities within our society—racism, sexism, ageism, homophobia, prejudice against disabled people—affect the delivery of medical care as much as they impact other areas of society. For example, African-Americans are less likely to receive adequate cancer pain control and have higher cancer death rates than whites. *In the real world*, people without private health insurance, such as the unfortunate Kevorkian victim Rebecca Badger, are driven to suicide by suffering caused by inadequate care. *In the real world*, relatives abandon their ill loved ones, have venal motives, or crack under the pressure of providing care. *In the real world*, as illustrated by the Klooster, Delury, and Bement cases, vulnerable, catastrophically ill, and disabled persons are easily manipulated into a hastened death not necessarily of their own choosing.

If we want to avoid these tragedies in the future, we must, as Chip Klooster puts it, "throw the whole idea of euthanasia out the window."[60] We must get on with the important task of finding truly humane ways out of the healthcare dilemmas we face, without resorting to killing as an answer to our difficulties.

8

Common Arguments for Euthanasia

P UBLIC POLICY CONTROVERSIES are a bit like the music business:
just as some songs are played so often that they become standards, some arguments made in political debates are so ubiquitous that they too can be called standards. This is certainly true in the
euthanasia debate. Raise the issue, and sooner rather than later, one or
more of the euthanasia standards will be played. For example, a talk-
show caller may assert, "We put our animals to sleep when they get
sick, don't humans deserve the same humane treatment?" Or a euthanasia proponent in an Internet chat-room debate may write, "The only
reason to oppose euthanasia is religious. Laws opposing legalization
violate the separation of church and state." Or a television interviewer
may ask, "If abortion is legal, shouldn't euthanasia be legal? After all,
both are about 'choice.'"

The reason music standards endure is that people like them. Similarly, euthanasia standards are perennial favorites because they represent ideas and concerns that normal people who are not euthanasia
activists or death-culture ideologues respond to and take very seriously.
Since it is real people, and not activists, who will ultimately decide
whether the country adheres to the equality-of-life ethic or discards it

in favor of the death culture, these common opinions, thoughts, feelings—and, yes, passions—about euthanasia need to be carefully and respectfully addressed.

EUTHANASIA STANDARD NO. I
Euthanasia is a religious issue.

"There are no grounds for denying euthanasia other than religion," the Dutch doctor Pieter Admiraal, who has personally killed more than a hundred patients, told me. "But I am not a believer, so what do they have to tell me?"[1] Similarly, proponents of Measure 16 painted opposition to the initiative as religious oppression and accused their political adversaries of seeking to impose sectarian religious beliefs on the people of Oregon. During his reign of death, Jack Kevorkian and his representatives always labeled their opponents "religious fanatics" and accused them of engaging in Salem-style "witch-hunts" when efforts were made to enforce the law against assisted suicide. (Kevorkian also said that the only way he would be stopped would be by being "burned at the stake," an unsubtle allusion to the Spanish Inquisition and the religious intolerance that historical event represented.) Derek Humphry, Peter Singer, and others have all claimed the crown of rationalism for euthanasia, in contrast to their opponents' thoughtless religiosity.

This refrain of euthanasia advocates is as inaccurate as it is clever. "Proponents try to paint euthanasia as an issue of religious belief because they perceive accurately that most people don't want to be told what to do by churches," says the noted civil libertarian thinker and writer Nat Hentoff, who writes a nationally syndicated column and appears weekly in the *Village Voice*. "In that way, they hope that people won't look to the substance of the issue but rather, will accept euthanasia as a means of opposing church-state involvement."[2]

That is not to say that religious groups do not oppose euthanasia. Many Christian churches, representatives of Orthodox Judaism, Islamic groups, Buddhist organizations, and others have issued policy positions opposing euthanasia. But many of these same religious groups also support the civil rights movement, oppose legislation or laws they consider anti-environment, take strong stands on immigration, and express opinions on many other controversial public policy issues such as welfare reform and the death penalty without being accused of imposing religious hegemony over the land. As Rita Marker, president of the International Task Force on Euthanasia and Assisted Suicide, notes, "Legislation that prohibits sales clerks from stealing company profits also coincides with religious beliefs, but it would be absurd to suggest that such laws be eliminated because they conflict with the separation of church and state."[3]

The false claim that opposition to euthanasia is only about religion also ignores reality. In truth, the primary reason that assisted suicide has had little success in the United States since the passage of Measure 16 is that it is now opposed by a robust and diverse coalition of strange political bedfellows. This alliance includes many distinctly secular, pro-abortion-rights, and generally liberal organizations and individuals—disability-rights groups, professional medical, nursing, and hospice associations, and advocates for the poor—who willingly work alongside the Catholic Church and conservative members of the pro-life movement to prevent doctors from ever again being granted a legal license to kill.

This coalition has been effective and successful. In 1998—just one year after Oregon voters reaffirmed Measure 16 by a 60 percent vote—Michigan euthanasia supporters qualified Measure B, an assisted suicide legalization initiative, for the November ballot. Early polling showed wide support for the plan. But then the coalition went work and their strategy worked beautifully. Voters who distrusted the pro-life movement had plenty of pro-choice advocates arguing against assisted suicide. Those who were liberal politically found other liberals in the "No on B" corner as well, making it easier for them to hear the reasons why it is bad public policy to legalize assisted suicide. For those who wanted medical opinions, doctors, nurses, and hospice workers were active in anti-assisted suicide campaign. Meanwhile, people who respond to religious arguments could find those views expressed as well. The result was that not only did Measure B fail, it was swamped by an overwhelming vote of 71 percent!

The same pattern worked to defeat a Maine legalization in 2000. Early polls reported that voters would vote yes to assisted suicide in the 70 percent range. But by the time the coalition was finished, Maine voters rejected assisted suicide despite supporters' greater financial resources in pushing their cause.

This phony allegation that only religious reasons exist for opposing assisted suicide is reminiscent of the 1960 presidential campaign, in which some political opponents of John F. Kennedy, well aware that most Americans strongly supported the separation of church and state, sought to create a rift between non-Catholic voters and Kennedy by claiming the Pope would call the shots if JFK were elected. It was not true—but truth was not the point; politics was. The same is true in the euthanasia debate.

"The euthanasia debate is about what will happen to all of us, sooner or later," says Nat Hentoff. "It's a moral issue, an ethical issue, an issue involving medical ethics and managed care. It is a political issue about who has power and who does not, who is expendable and who is important. It is an issue about protecting the most weak and vulnerable among us. When you are near death is when you are the most vulnerable to coercion, intimidation, and to powerlessness. Allowing euthanasia would victimize the poor, the uneducated, minorities, and anyone without the ability or support to insist on receiving the best of medical care."[4]

Hentoff has it exactly right. Euthanasia is not a religious issue: it is a vital public policy issue. As I have made clear—without making one religious argument—at stake in this debate are our most fundamental mores and ethical concepts and determining the public policy that best promotes the highest good for individuals and society. This is why most of the prominent opponents of euthanasia, regardless of their individual religious beliefs—or lack thereof—use secular arguments against as-sisted suicide. These include Dr. Herbert Hendin, psychiatrist and di-rector of the American Foundation for Suicide Prevention; the legal scholar Yale Kamisar, a "fervent agnostic"[5] who first wrote against le-galizing euthanasia in 1958 based specifically on nonreligious concepts;[6] Diane Coleman, a disability rights activist and co-founder of Not Dead Yet; Dr. Joanne Lynn, perhaps the most prominent physician involved in end-of-life medical care; Dr. Ira Byock, past president of the Ameri-can Academy of Hospice and Palliative Medicine; Rita Marker, direc-tor of the nonprofit and nonreligious educational organization the International Task Force on Euthanasia and Assisted Suicide; and of course, the writer Nat Hentoff; just to name a few. Indeed, when I asked Hentoff about this facet of the debate, he laughed and told me, "I can't base my opposition to euthanasia on religion. I am an atheist!"[7]

EUTHANASIA STANDARD NO. 2
Guidelines can prevent abuses.

This book has documented the many dangers, abuses, and opportuni-ties for oppression inherent in legalizing and legitimizing euthanasia and assisted suicide. Euthanasia advocates recognize these concerns and have a facile answer: "We'll enact strict protective guidelines to protect against abuse." But a look at the record reveals that these assur-ances are hollow. Everywhere euthanasia or related policies have been instituted, in every country in which they have been tried, the result has been the same.

Germany

As we have seen, both in the pre-Nazi era and during Hitler's rule, the Germans assured themselves that "protective guidelines" would pre-vent euthanasia abuses. Indeed, the medical profession, the driving force behind euthanasia in prewar and wartime Germany, established the policy under supposedly rigorous guidelines. But the guidelines, such as they were, soon broke down, leading to "wild euthanasia," where doctors killed any disabled patient they wanted to kill—even though the euthanasia policy had been partially canceled by Hitler, even though their activities violated previous methods of determining who received "treatment," and eventually, even though the war had ended.

The Netherlands

The Netherlands recently became the first nation in modern times to formally legalize euthanasia. The mainstream media stories about legalization frequently asserted with a straight face that euthanasia would be governed by strict guidelines to prevent abuse. Well, we've been hearing that little ditty for decades about Dutch euthanasia, but as I detailed thoroughly in chapter four, the vaunted guidelines do not even rise to the level of paper tigers.

The newly enacted killing regulations are virtually identical to those that have governed Dutch euthanasia for many years under which euthanasia remained technically illegal but was not prosecuted so long as doctors followed the guidelines. (The only substantial difference between the former regime and legalized euthanasia is that doctors will no longer have to notify coroners after they kill a patient.) Not only have these guidelines failed to protect vulnerable patients, but they have been violated so often that they might as well not exist at all. Here are the guidelines followed by a brief description of how each has been violated in actual practice:

- When ending a life a physician must be convinced that the patient's request is voluntary, well considered, and lasting.

Study after study of Dutch euthanasia practice have shown that Dutch doctors routinely kill patients who have not asked to be poisoned. In the Netherlands this practice is known as "termination without request or consent" and is not even formally considered euthanasia in the statistics compiled by the government.

The evidence of decades demonstrates that such involuntary euthanasia is rampant. Indeed, in its 1997 ruling refusing to create a constitutional right to assisted suicide (*Washington v. Glucksberg*) the United States Supreme Court quoted a 1991 Dutch government study finding that in 1990 doctors committed "more than 1,000 cases of euthanasia without an explicit request" and "an additional 4,941 cases where physicians administered lethal morphine overdoses without the patients' explicit consent." That means in 1990, nearly 6,000 of approximately 130,000 people who died in the Netherlands that year were involuntarily euthanized—approximately 4 percent of all Dutch deaths. Moreover, babies are also killed for being born with disabilities. By definition, babies cannot ask to be killed. So much for the guideline requiring "choice."

- The physician must be convinced the patient was facing unremitting and unbearable suffering.

Notice that this guideline does not require that the patient be dying or, for that matter, even be actually ill. Indeed, there have been several documented cases of euthanasia based on depression or suicidal ideation. For example, a Dutch documentary reported on the euthanasia of a young woman in remission from anorexia. Worried that her eating disorder would return, she asked her doctor to kill her. He did and the authorities refused to prosecute.

The most infamous case of this sort involved a physically healthy woman who had become obsessed about being buried between her two dead children. As readers will recall, Hilly bought a cemetery plot, had her children buried one on each side of her planned grave, and then asked a psychiatrist named Boutdewijn Chabot to assist her suicide. He met with her four times over approximately five weeks and never attempted treatment. He then assisted her suicide. The Dutch Supreme

Court refused to punish him, ruling that suffering is suffering, and it does not matter whether it is physical or emotional.

Another documented euthanasia that violated this and other guidelines was depicted in a Dutch documentary played in this country on the PBS program the *Health Quarterly*, in 1993. Henk Dykma had asymptomatic HIV infection. Fearing future afflictions that might befall him, Henk asked his doctor to kill him. The film shows the doctor telling Henk that he might live for years at his current state of seemingly healthful living. When Henk still proclaims a desire to die, the doctor speaks with a colleague but never consults a psychiatrist or psychologist. He then helps kill Henk on July 28, a date, we are told, which had symbolic importance for the patient.

This killing, like those of the anorexic young woman and the bereaved mother, was clearly not a matter of last resort, as the guidelines claim to require. Henk and his doctor did not explore all other options available to him before ending his life. Indeed, psychiatric treatment, which might have alleviated Henk's obvious anxiety about being HIV-positive, was never even discussed or attempted. Nor was Henk advised of the steps that could be taken to alleviate his suffering should he fall ill. The doctor didn't even wait until Henk had symptoms of AIDS. There is a word for that level of care—abandonment—and it demonstrates the utter hollowness of the Dutch protective guidelines.

- The physician must have informed the patient about his situation and prospects.

This guideline presumes that the physicians involved will have sufficient expertise to adequately inform the patient about his condition and options for treatment or palliation. But the Dutch medical system is unlike ours. It is primarily made up of general practitioners, rather than specialists, who may not have the training, expertise, or desire to know the many treatment alternatives that may be available. Moreover, there are few hospices in the Netherlands, meaning that the many compassionate and dignified methods of alleviating suffering in the dying may never be discussed with patients who ask to be killed.

As described earlier, a good example of this phenomenon can be found in the memoir *Dancing with Mr. D*, written by a Dutch nursing-home doctor named Bert Keizer. Keizer writes about a patient who had been tentatively diagnosed with lung cancer. A relative tells Keizer that the man wants to be given a lethal injection, a request later confirmed by the patient. Keizer quickly agrees to perform the killing. Demonstrating the utter uselessness of "protective guidelines," Keizer never tells his patient about treatment options that may be available or how the pain and other symptoms of cancer can be palliated effectively. He never checks to see if the man has been pressured into wanting a hastened death or is depressed. Indeed, Keizer doesn't even take the time to confirm the diagnosis with certainty or to prepare a prognosis about the expected course of the disease. When a colleague asks, why rush, and points out that the man isn't suffering terribly, Keizer snaps: "Is it for us to answer this question? All I know is that he wants to die more or less upright and that he doesn't want to crawl to his grave the way a dog crawls howling to the side walk after he's been hit by a car." (Perhaps Keizer did not know or care that with proper, attentive medical care, such an awful death need not happen to cancer patients.) The next day, Keizer lethally injects his patient, telling his colleagues as he is about to do the deed, "If anyone so much as whispers cortisone [a palliative agent] or 'uncertain diagnosis,' I'll hit him."[8]

- The physician must have reached the firm conclusion with the patient that there was no other reasonable alternative solution.

The cases already described illustrate the hollowness of this guideline. Another example of its uselessness is the killing by Dr. Henk Prins of a three-day-old infant born with spina bifida and limb anomalies.

Spina bifida is a spinal condition in infants that may cause disability or death. Prins—a gynecologist, not a pediatrician or expert in spina

bifida—killed the child at the request of her parents, because, he later
testified, the baby screamed in agony when touched. No wonder the
baby was in pain! Prins never closed the wound in her back. In other
words, the doctor killed his patient without first attempting *proper medical treatment*. Yet, rather than punishing Prins, the trial judge praised
him for his "integrity and courage," wishing him well in any further
legal proceedings he might face.

- The physician must have consulted at least one independent
  physician, who has examined the patient and formed a judgment about the above points.

The idea of independent physicians acting as a check and balance
to prevent abuses sounds good. But in practice, it offers little actual
protection. Proof of this is found in a Dutch euthanasia documentary—
played in the U.S. on the ABC television program *Prime Time Live*. It is
the euthanasia of Cees van Wendel, a patient disabled by ALS (Lou
Gehrig's disease). As depicted in the film, the driving force behind the
euthanasia appears to be the man's wife, Antoinette, who does all of the
talking for her husband (who is able to communicate). This also proves
true during the second opinion consultation, which is cursory and perfunctory. Suicide expert New York psychiatrist Dr. Herbert Hendin,
perhaps the world's preeminent expert on Dutch euthanasia, in his
book *Seduced by Death*, describes that the "consultation" was more an
"orchestrated event" than a truly independent review of the case: "The
consultant, who practices on the same block as the doctor, also makes
no attempt to communicate with Cees alone, and he too permits the
wife to answer all the questions put to Cees. When the consultant asks
the pro forma question if Cees is sure he wants to go ahead, Antoinette
answers for him. The consultant seems uncomfortable, asks a few more
questions, and leaves. The consultation takes practically no time at
all."[9] Can we all say "rubber stamp"?

Dutch euthanasia is a human rights disaster masking as compassionate medical practice. Not only does it victimize ill and despairing people, but it also alters the views of society for the worse about the value of those who are sick or disabled. How else explain the shrug of the shoulders of Dutch doctors, government leaders, and indeed of wider society to the consistent and routine violations of the guidelines. As Hendin wrote in a recent book, *The Case against Assisted Suicide*:

> I was troubled, as were other foreign observers, by what we regarded as Dutch indifference to their system's failure to protect patients and their physicians' failure to follow their own euthanasia guidelines. I found that while some physicians supportive of euthanasia were willing to admit abuses in general, and even to concede that in a particular case euthanasia should not have been performed or that a wrongful death had taken place, they did not express anger or indignation that a life had been taken unnecessarily. The common attitude was that the doctor may have been mistaken but was entitled to his or her judgment of the matter. This casualness, often rationalized by the Dutch as tolerance, appears to a foreign observer to border on callousness.[10]

This proves that guidelines don't work. Worse, they lead people to believe that active killing can be controlled, dulling the moral sense against it. We ignore the lessons of the Netherlands at our own peril.

The United States

U.S. euthanasia advocates, when they will admit there is anything wrong with Dutch euthanasia practices, blithely assure us that this country will learn from the Dutch mistakes so that such abuses never happen here. There's only one problem with that assurance: violations and erosion of euthanasia-type guidelines have already happened here.

Take the issue of food and fluids. In 1986 and again in 1992, the American Medical Association's Council on Ethical and Judicial Affairs issued ethical opinions designed to define the circumstances under which terminally ill and permanently unconscious patients could ethically be starved and dehydrated. These guidelines permitted "technologically supplied" food and fluids to be withdrawn from terminally ill people "whose death is imminent" and from unconscious patients whose coma or persistent vegetative state is "beyond doubt irreversible."[11]

Despite these easily understood restrictions, people who were neither terminally ill nor unconscious soon had their "medical treatment" of food and fluids withheld. This expanded practice was never seriously opposed and eventually received the approval of some courts. The AMA then expanded the guidelines to comport with actual clinical practice.[12] A classic example of the slippery slope in action.

Jack Kevorkian also repeatedly stated that he governed his participation in assisted suicide by adhering to strict, self-imposed "guidelines." He and a small group of doctors formed a group they call Physicians for Mercy. The group published a set of rules under which it claimed to operate, requiring, for example, that people who wished to die because of a specified disease consult with a specialist in that condition prior to their suicide, and that if pain is an issue in the desire for suicide, the person had to be directed to a pain-control specialist before a member assisted their suicide. Yet when Rebecca Badger wanted to kill herself because her purported multiple sclerosis pain was so severe she wanted to die, no news account, public statement by Kevorkian or his attorneys, or comment by Ms. Badger's children made any mention of Kevorkian referring her to a pain-control specialist or even to a specialist who treats MS.

Oregon too has already begun to experience the slippery slope despite assisted suicide having been legal only for a few years. Recall the case of Kate Cheney, the woman dying of cancer who received assisted suicide despite having dementia, described in detail in chapter five. Not only is it questionable whether Cheney had the cognitive capacity to "rationally" commit assisted suicide—she could not remember recent events or people, including the name of her hospice nurse—but according to the two mental health professionals who examined her, she was under internal family pressure to decide to die. As Oregon psychiatrist Dr. Gregory Hamilton wrote in *The Case against Assisted Suicide*, the Cheney case "illustrates how once assisted suicide is legalized, there is no way to protect those who are vulnerable and mentally ill from social or even financial pressures."[13]

Protective guidelines give the appearance of normalcy and protection while offering no actual shelter from abuse. Worse, they act subversively to hide the truth about the victims of euthanasia and seduce society into accepting an ever expanding license for doctors to kill. In short, guidelines serve no useful purpose other than to provide false assurances to the public.

EUTHANASIA STANDARD NO. 3
Euthanasia would be only for the "hard cases."

The "hard cases," those in which a patient's pain is resistant to effective alleviation, or in which a patient is suffering so much that he or she is literally begging to die, are the people around whom the euthanasia debate often swirls. Proponents use the sympathy we all feel for seriously ill people, and our own fears of being similarly situated, to plead for a broad permissiveness. Yet as our previous discussions of Dutch euthanasia and assisted suicide in Oregan clearly demonstrate, the truly "hard cases" are most rare. At the same time, it must be admitted, euthanasia opponents occasionally act as if hard cases don't really exist. So the question has to be asked: What do we do about the hard cases?

"When any person is suffering, that's a hard case for that individual and the family," Rita Marker, the director of the International Anti-Euthanasia Task Force, says. "We simply must work harder to let people know that not only can something be done to alleviate suffering, but that it is the responsibility of the medical profession to do so."[14]

Marker also notes that the widespread, but erroneous, belief that suffering cannot be alleviated can of itself lead to a suicidal desire.

"There's often a mistaken perception that nothing can be done. This can lead to people feeling trapped into 'choosing' assisted suicide [as the only way out]. The tragedy is that the activities and attitudes of euthanasia activists make the news, eclipsing the realistic message of hope and caring that people want and deserve.

Medical experts verify Marker's statement. Dame Cicely Saunders, who established the model hospice St. Christopher's in London in 1967 and who has supervised the treatment of thousands of dying people in the last thirty years, points out that "the alternatives for the dying patient are not inevitable pain or a quick lethal injection," as is often asserted by euthanasia advocates. Rather, Saunders asserts, "If a patient asks to be killed, someone has failed him."[15] Dr. Ira Byock, past president of the American Academy of Hospice and Palliative Medicine, agrees with this great hospice pioneer, adding that the reason there are "hard cases" at all is because "undertreatment and maltreatment at the end of life is endemic. It is the exception rather than the norm for dying patients to receive good care at the end of life, to have their physical symptoms adequately addressed and their human needs met. Given the decay in even basic care, including shelter, nutrition, assistance with bowel and bladder functions, we must be extraordinarily cautious in responding to the resulting suffering in any class of people by eliminating sufferers."[16] In other words, the hard cases exist primarily because we *allow* them to exist.

Dr. Linda Emanuel, the American Medical Association's vice president for ethics standards and the director of its Institute for Ethics, also sees the problem as one of inadequate care. She told the *New York Times Magazine*, "I simply have never seen a case nor heard of a colleague's case where [euthanasia] was necessary. If there is such a request, it is always dropped when quality care is rendered."[17] This truth was amply illustrated in Australia recently when Nancy Crick, a woman dying from cancer, publicly proclaimed her desire to be assisted in suicide by euthanasia proponent Dr. Philip Nitschke. A date for the death was selected and publicized. The Australian media was abuzz, even asking to be present when the assisted killing occurred. But after the woman received adequate palliative care, the date of the suicide came and went without her dying. As of this writing—months after she was supposed to commit assisted suicide—the woman remains alive and comfortable thanks to receiving proper medical treatment.[18]

The pain-control specialist and hospice medical director Dr. Eric Chevlen acknowledges that difficult circumstances exist, but that does not mean we must resort to killing. "The hard cases by definition are hard," he told me. "But that does not make them impossible. It is these very hard cases that require an experienced clinician, knowledgeable in the management of the physical symptoms of advanced illness." Chevlen adds, "It is striking that so many people are ready to cross the country for a lethal injection and yet will not put out that same effort to take their loved ones to one of the many world-class pain clinics associated with university hospitals across the country."[19] Often, this is because people are unaware that such clinics exist.

It is our lack of knowledge that suffering can be substantially alleviated that causes cases to harden. "A century ago, *all* the cases were hard cases," Dr. Chevlen notes. "And there was little outcry for euthanasia then. Yet now, when truly hard cases are growing fewer and fewer, there is less reason . . . for euthanasia than ever before in history. The hard cases are the pretext, not the reason, for legalization."[20]

A classic example of this systemic failure can be seen in the undertreatment of the pain caused by AIDS, an affliction that can lead to neuropathy (nerve pain), terrible headaches, and severe abdominal cramps, among other painful conditions. (I recall visiting an AIDS patient whom I had to hold in my arms to keep him from pounding his head into a wall, his head hurt so badly. Yet his doctor had prescribed only mild medication for his pain. Not coincidentally, this patient had little formal education, was living in a single-room occupancy hotel, and had no family, no assets, and no private health insurance.)

Despite the suffering AIDS pain causes, AIDS patients' pain is notoriously under-palliated. A report at the Eighth World Congress on

Pain disclosed that 80 percent of AIDS patients receive inadequate analgesia (non-narcotic pain-control agents). Only 6 percent of AIDS patients experiencing severe pain receive a strong opioid, often necessary to control pain that analgesics don't alleviate. Women and those with less education are the most likely to be undertreated.[21]

Euthanasia advocates often point to the pain associated with AIDS as a reason to legalize assisted suicide. Yet, as these appalling statistics demonstrate, inadequate pain control is the source of a tremendous amount of suffering that could be alleviated. Obviously this needs to change. The question is: Will this situation change if killing becomes just another form of "comfort care"? Considering that killing is far cheaper and quicker than providing adequate medical treatment, and in light of the widespread marginalization and isolation of AIDS victims by society, it seems unlikely that the profound failure to adequately treat AIDS pain will be corrected if euthanasia is legalized. Legalizing euthanasia does not solve the problem of suffering, but surrenders to it.

Sadly, there are a very few among the dying for whom no palliation effort sufficiently eases agony—but that does not mean that they must continue to suffer. For these patients, palliative sedation throughout the balance of the dying process is a viable solution.

If people accept sedation as an acceptable answer to the very few cases of irremediable suffering that exist, the euthanasia movement will deflate. This is why euthanasia advocates brand sedation as unacceptable and somehow less dignified than euthanasia. But how is entering a state of deep sleep any less dignified than being killed by poison? Indeed, sedation has all of the "benefits" of euthanasia—an end to individual suffering—without any of the dangers inherent in the death culture. That so many euthanasia proponents disdain this very real and available beneficence of last resort in favor of killing suggests that establishing the values of the death culture, rather than actually ending suffering, may be their primary goal.

EUTHANASIA STANDARD NO. 4
We put suffering animals to sleep, so why not people?

Another argument one occasionally hears is that since we routinely put ill and dying dogs, cats, and other animals to sleep out of compassion, we owe human beings the same consideration. It seems to me that what this argument really asserts is that we should treat people as we treat animals. This euthanasia standard assumes an equivalency between the moral value of the life of an animal and that of a human being.

Most dogs and cats that are put to sleep are not killed because they are sick, but because they are abandoned. Thousands of pets are euthanized each year simply because they are unwanted. To follow this euthanasia argument to its logical conclusion, then, would be to countenance the mercy killing of despairing homeless people because society is unwilling to care for them—a ridiculous notion. Similarly, we may legally shoot a horse when it breaks a leg, but we would never accept that we could kill a similarly injured human. Dogs and cats—as delightful and loving as they are—are not people. They are animals, and in the end, society permits them to be treated like animals.

Few people believe that animal deaths are the moral equivalent of human deaths. That is the reason society permits animals to be killed, whether for food, sport, purposes of population control, or at times out of compassion. While most pet lovers who have put a beloved sick or injured pet to sleep have done so because they didn't want their beloved friend to suffer, many have also chosen euthanasia for their animal because they didn't want to spend the time, effort, and money to provide their ill pet with curative treatment, pain control, or palliation that would materially reduce their suffering without killing them. Others euthanize pets when they cease to be fun as a result of illness or incontinence. Others have animals killed just because they don't want them anymore.

Interestingly, a few death fundamentalists, most notably Peter Singer, do not accept any moral distinction between human life and animal life. In addition to being a euthanasia advocate, Singer is one of the world's most preeminent animal-rights activists. He believes that "species membership alone is not morally relevant," in determining rights, including the right to live.[22] He believes that some "non-human animals" (his misanthropic term designed to create a moral equivalency between humans and animals), specifically pigs, dogs, cats, dolphins, and elephants—are "persons" and should have the same "rights" currently reserved for humans. At the same time, he proposes that some humans—newborn infants, cognitively disabled people, those diagnosed as permanently unconscious—be denied the status of persons and the attendant rights. Singer writes, "Since neither a newborn human infant nor a fish is a person, the wrongness of killing such beings is not as great as the wrongness of killing a person."[23] In other words, to Singer, a newborn child is the moral equivalent of a tuna, and killing a pig is more wrong than killing a human infant.

Singer is not alone in his misanthropy. Some prominent euthanasia advocates wrote favorable reviews of Singer's book *Rethinking Life and Death*, in which he expresses his animal rights and pro-infanticide philosophy. For example, the book review in the Hemlock Society newsletter, *Hemlock TimeLines*, approved Singer's thesis, stating, "Mr. Singer's new ethic is built [among other 'cornerstone' concepts, such as euthanasia] with enlightening discussions of speciesism and the ongoing argument about differences between human life and all other life."[24]

EUTHANASIA STANDARD NO. 5
*There is no difference between "choice"
in abortion and "choice" in euthanasia.*

Euthanasia advocates take every opportunity to identify with the pro-choice side of the abortion debate.[25] They believe that by making euthanasia the caboose to abortion's locomotive, they can gain the same public acceptance for euthanasia that they perceive currently exists for the right of a woman to terminate her pregnancy.

Many supporters of the pro-choice position who are convinced that maintaining the legality of abortion is essential to women's freedom have fallen for this gambit. For example, the National Organization for Women supports legalizing euthanasia, ignoring the sexism within the medical system that sometimes causes women to receive inadequate care, a key issue in the euthanasia debate. Officials of Planned Parenthood have likewise stated "choice is choice," accepting a moral equivalency between abortion and being personally killed by a doctor. The media often feed this misperception by portraying euthanasia opponents as "pro-lifers," a group whom pro-choice advocates almost reflexively oppose, regardless of the topic under discussion.

Euthanasia and abortion are not the same. Certainly there is substantial opposition to euthanasia among pro-lifers. But there is also opposition to euthanasia among pro-choicers. Almost every medical organization in the world opposes euthanasia and assisted suicide. Yet, most of these same groups support abortion rights.

Linkage of the two issues is a legal fiction, according to the University of Michigan law professor Yale Kamisar, one of the nation's most renowned legal scholars and a strong supporter of *Roe v. Wade* and abortion rights: "In *Roe v. Wade*, the Court cleared the way for its ultimate holding [finding a right to abortion] by rejecting the argument that a fetus is "a person" within the meaning of the Constitution. . . . But terminally ill persons, for example, a cancer patient who despite our best medical efforts, is likely to die in four or five months, is incontestably a 'person' or 'human being.'"[26] Kamisar also notes that legal scholars who do view the fetus as a "person" but who think there is a right to abortion anyway have "maintained that the right to abortion is grounded on principles of sexual equality, rather than due process or privacy," an issue not involved in the euthanasia controversy.[27]

For pro-choice advocates there is also a tactical problem in linking abortion rights with euthanasia. The liberal *Washington Post* columnist E. J. Dionne notes that linking euthanasia and abortion tends to highlight some of the very arguments anti-abortion advocates have made over the years about the societal impact of accepting legalized abortion. "The pro-choice movement should be very wary of embracing physician-assisted suicide," Dionne says. "Right-to-lifers have always argued that there is a slippery slope between abortion rights and euthanasia. By accepting the same arguments for both issues, pro-choicers could give philosophical validation to what their opponents have claimed all along."[28]

The abortion debate divides this country like no issue since the war in Vietnam. Mention the topic and people immediately go to their usual corners, the bell rings, and the fighting begins. Euthanasia is similarly emotional and divisive, but unlike abortion, public opinion is fluid and still forming. That is why euthanasia advocates want people to see their cause as a "choice" issue, like abortion; they believe it will create unthinking support for euthanasia among pro-choice advocates and thereby save them from having to deal with the substance of the issue.

Euthanasia is a policy that should be decided on its own merits, regardless of one's opinion about abortion. One can be pro-choice and still oppose euthanasia. Indeed, it is an issue around which pro-choicers and pro-lifers have often found desperately needed common ground.

EUTHANASIA STANDARD NO. 6

*Polls show that people support
euthanasia, so legalization is inevitable.*

Many have argued on the basis of polls that euthanasia and assisted suicide enjoy wide support in the United States and that it is foolish to resist legalizing a practice that the people want. The evidence that doctors are kindly disposed to euthanasia is extremely thin, so it should come as no surprise that the proof of widespread popular support for the practice is also flimsy.

With the exception of the Netherlands and Belgium, euthanasia is universally outlawed (although the Swiss turn a blind eye toward pri-

Common Arguments for Euthanasia

vate assisted suicides.) Here in the United States, only Oregon has legalized physician-assisted suicide. The longtime criminalization of these forms of killing in Western democracies and throughout the world reflects the near universal recognition that euthanasia and assisted suicide substantially undermine the equality-of-human-life ethic and endanger vulnerable populations.

Public opinion polls often show widespread support for legalization of assisted suicide or euthanasia, often in the 70 percent range, at least for the terminally ill. Yet when Americans have the chance to actually vote, support for such a law invariably plummets. Even in Oregon, assisted suicide received only 51 percent of the vote after initially being supported, according to contemporary polls, by about 70 percent of the electorate. Moreover, the various polls that have been taken on the issue sometimes disagree. For example, an October 1996 Gallup Poll that asked 1,007 adults "Should it be legal for a physician to participate in assisted suicide?" found that support and opposition to legalization are narrowly divided, with 50 percent in favor and 41 percent opposed. (The margin of error was plus or minus 3 percent.)[29] More recently, an ABC News/Beliefnet poll found that more people oppose assisted suicide than support it. When half of the poll's respondents were asked simply "if it should be legal for doctors to help terminally ill patients commit suicide with fatal drugs," 48 percent said no, while 40 percent said yes. When the other half of respondents were asked the same question after the provisions of the Oregon law were described, 48 percent still said no, and 46 percent said yes.[30]

Some of the support for legalization has to do with confusion over terms. Many people confuse refusing unwanted treatment—"pulling the plug"—with active killing. Some confusion may also have to do with the way the polls are conducted. Poll questions about legalizing euthanasia often start with the false premise of the dying person's being in unrelievable agony and then ask whether that person should have the "right to die."

Regardless of the reasons for current poll results, concrete evidence indicates that popular sentiment in favor of euthanasia is probably loosely held rather than deeply ingrained. When a concrete opportunity to officially sanction euthanasia occurs, support for legalization generally plummets. This is illustrated by the several attempts to legalize euthanasia or assisted suicide by means of ballot referendums over the last decade:

- California, 1988: Proponents of a proposal to legalize active euthanasia of the terminally ill did not obtain sufficient signatures to qualify the initiative for the ballot.

- Washington State, 1991: An initiative to legalize active euthanasia of the terminally ill lost 54 to 46 percent, even though polls showed more than 70 percent support for the measure.

- Michigan, 1994: Jack Kevorkian and some of his associates proposed an initiative to legalize euthanasia for the terminally ill and disabled, but collected insufficient signatures to qualify it for the ballot.

- Oregon, 1994: A proposal to permit doctors to issue lethal prescriptions for the terminally ill began with nearly 70 percent approval in the polls but passed only 51 to 49 percent.

- Oregon, 1997: An attempt to rescind passage of Measure 16 lost 60 to 40 percent, but was seen as indicating resentment by voters at being forced to revisit the issue.

- Michigan, 1998: A proposal to legalize assisted suicide for the terminally ill began with more than 70 percent approval but lost 71 to 29 percent.

- Maine, 2000: A proposal to legalize assisted suicide for the terminally ill began with more than 70 percent approval but lost 51 to 49 percent.

What do the differing polls and the outcome of these legalization attempts teach us? That rather than being overwhelmingly supportive of legalization, the public is profoundly ambivalent and deeply divided. Indeed, if actual legal change is any indication, Americans oppose legalization. Three states—Iowa, Louisiana, and Rhode Island—have banned assisted suicide since the passage of Measure 16, and no other state has legalized it. If left to the democratic process, legalization is anything but a sure bet.

EUTHANASIA STANDARD NO. 7
Euthanasia is needed to prevent doctors
from keeping patients alive for too long.

One of the driving forces behind the euthanasia movement is the conviction that modern medicine is too impersonal, too technologically driven, more interested in keeping the body's biological functions operating than in treating patients as people. This belief is not irrational. Too many people have seen their loved ones "hooked up to machines" against their will, treated as if they were slabs of meat, and otherwise chewed up and spit out by an unresponsive medical system.

Euthanasia advocates are well aware of these fears. Indeed, they take every opportunity to exploit the anxiety of patients and their families about the consequences of unwanted medical treatment and falsely accuse euthanasia opponents of being "vitalists," extremists who insist that doctors should do everything that can be done in every case to keep people alive for as long as possible, regardless of the suffering the procedures cause or of the patient's desires.

That charge, often made, is untrue. "No one should be forced to accept unwanted medical treatment," says Rita Marker. "Insisting that death be postponed by every means available is not only against current laws and practice, it is also cruel and inhumane. Patients have a right to say, enough is enough, and to refuse curative medical treatment they don't feel is appropriate."[31]

But saying that one has a right to refuse care is one thing; actually getting it done in the clinical context is sometimes a different matter. Even healthy patients sometimes face medical situations and procedures that begin benignly or with a positive prognosis, but do not end that way. If a patient is in an accident, or unforeseen or unlikely medical complications arise, families and doctors may be faced with situations that require split-second decisions about treatment options where the patient's desires are unknown. That is why all states permit patients to prepare written legal documents known as advance directives. The most common of these are "durable powers of attorney for healthcare" and "living wills."

With an advance directive, all competent adults can leave instructions about their future medical care—whether they want treatment or not and under what circumstances—for use in the event they become incapacitated and therefore unable to give informed consent. (Informed consent is the right of the patient to accept or refuse medical treatment on the basis of adequate information provided by the doctor.)

Advance directives have the potential to be a positive antidote to overzealous doctors keeping patients alive by rendering undesired treatment, although with the new financial imperatives of managed care the danger is greater that desired treatment would be withheld. Unfortunately, proponents of the death culture use advance directives to promote their agenda. In the discussions of advance directives, the only choice generally considered or encouraged is to terminate or withhold life-saving treatment. The desire to fight for life—as legitimate as the decision to allow nature to take its course by not artificially prolonging life—almost always receives short shrift or goes unmentioned.

Evidence of this agenda can be seen in the advance directives themselves, which are drafted to make refusing treatment easy. Some "form" advance directives only permit one choice: nontreatment. On others, all you have to do is check a box if you don't want treatment. But if your decision is to fight for life, it can get complicated, often requiring you to create your own detailed treatment instructions—a daunting task.

Even more worrisome is that many healthcare professionals appear to be confused about the legalities surrounding advance directives, sometimes leading to misapplication of the directive and the denial of care to people with treatable medical conditions. One such case was that of Martha Musgrave, a seventy-three-year-old woman who in 1993 decided to undergo a hip replacement. After being discharged from the hospital and upon being admitted to an interim-care facility, she was given a form advance directive to sign along with the other usual admission documents. Musgrave either did not know what she had signed or thought so little about it that she didn't even mention the fact to her daughter, with whom she shared every important decision.[32]

Musgrave seemed well on the road to recovery, then she suffered a cardiac arrest caused by an unexpected embolism, a complication of her surgery. Rather than attempt to save her (she was not otherwise terminally ill), the staff assumed that because she had signed a living will, she wanted to die if faced with a grave medical condition. Thus, Musgrave was given no medical assistance whatsoever. The hospital staff just stood there and watched as she died, a process that took about twenty minutes. Her daughter was not even notified of the problem or asked for permission to "do nothing." The first she found out about her mother's crisis was when she was informed of her mother's death.[33]

Another case involved a nursing-home resident from Washington state who was accidentally given the wrong medication by a staff nurse. Though the mistake was quickly discovered, the patient was not advised of the mishap, even though she was mentally competent. Why? She had signed a living will instructing that she not be resuscitated if she suffered a cardiac arrest. It was thus assumed she would not want to be treated for a condition that might (and did) lead to her death, even though she was capable of making that decision herself.[34]

Even more disturbing are the "gotcha" cases, where people who have signed living wills were not allowed to explicitly or implicitly change their minds about refusing care. One such case is that of Marjorie Nighbert. Nighbert had signed a durable power of attorney giving her brother Maynard the authority to make her healthcare decisions should she become incapacitated. While visiting her family in Alabama, Nighbert had a stroke, which caused some disability. After she was stabilized, she seemed well enough to benefit from rehabilitation.[35]

Nighbert was transferred to the Crestview Nursing and Convalescent Home in Florida, where doctors attempted to teach her techniques used by stroke patients to eat and drink. Unfortunately, she had difficulty with the technique. Worried that she would aspirate and die, doctors performed the minor surgery of placing a feeding tube in her abdomen so she could be safely nourished. (Feeding tubes are commonly used for people who have difficulty eating. Rose Kennedy at age ninety-four had a gastrostomy tube inserted "to correct a nutritional problem," which aided her for the last ten years of her life.)[36]

This presented a problem for Nighbert's brother. Although she had not said so in her power of attorney granting him authority to make her medical decisions, Nighbert had previously stated in conversations that she would not want to use a feeding tube. Thus, even though she was not terminally ill, her brother asked the doctors to cease all food and fluids, a request to which they consented.

Twenty days later she should have been dead, but she was not. Members of the staff were apparently sneaking food to her. "She was saying things like, 'Please feed me,' 'I'm hungry,' 'I'm thirsty,' and 'I want food,'" says attorney William F. Stone, who later became Marjorie's guardian ad litem when her case went before a judge.[37] In response to Nighbert's utterances, staff members were feeding her, ignoring a doctor's order to dehydrate her to death.

The pressure of feeding Nighbert in the face of the doctor's order eventually was too much for one distraught staff person (who remains anonymous). This person blew the whistle, leading to a state investigation and a temporary restoration of nutritional support. (One person at the Crestview Home was later fired as a result of the Nighbert case.)

Stone was appointed Nighbert's temporary guardian by Okaloosa County (Florida) Circuit Court judge Jere Tolton, who gave him only twenty-four hours to conduct an investigation into the matter. Stone was unable to explain the need for the rush. "My authority was limited to determining whether she had the legal capacity to revoke her durable power of attorney," Stone told me. "I stayed up until after four AM trying to interview all involved." After his rushed investigation Stone reported back to Judge Tolton that Nighbert did not *at that time* "have the capacity to revoke her advanced medical directive" (in other words, to ask for the "medical treatment" of food).[38] Stone also specifically noted that he was unable to determine what her capacity had been before she was malnourished for twenty days. Furthermore, in the brief time he had to issue his report to the court he was unable to determine what, if any, financial issues might have been involved in the decision to dehydrate Nighbert, who had once been the head of the Cincinnati Chamber of Commerce, or whether any conflict of interest might exist, for example, with regard to inheritance. Stone did tell me that Nighbert's brothers were emotionally distraught over their sister's impending death.[39]

With Stone's report in hand, Judge Tolton ordered the starvation to continue. Stone considered an appeal but before he could determine the legal and ethical issues, Nighbert died, on April 6, 1995. "I was disturbed by Marjorie's case," Stone says now. "I had no problem with the judge's ruling concerning her then legal capacity, because at the time I did my investigation [after twenty days of undernourishment] she didn't have capacity to revoke her advance directive. I did feel, however, from a public policy point of view, that the issues I raised were not adequately addressed by the court."[40] Stone was convinced that the decisions implementing Marjorie's advance directive did not comply with Florida law.

The case has also changed Stone's approach to his own legal practice. "It has made me change the way I prepare advance directives," Stone says. "There are difficult moral and practical issues involved. I have told my mother and father not to sign advance directives supplied to them at hospitals upon admission. People need to think carefully about these issues in advance and realize their seriousness and what they might actually mean."[41]

Marjorie Nighbert imagined that she would not want a feeding tube. But when the time came, even though she specifically asked for food and water, at a time in which she might very well have been legally competent (not that strict legal competence should matter if someone asks to be fed), her wishes were ignored because she had made contrary statements in the past. Her earlier expressed sentiments ended up costing the nonterminally ill Nighbert her life.

A similar controversy ensnared a Colorado woman named Mary Theresa Corrao, aged fifty-nine, and her family. Mary, a breast cancer patient, was placed in the Hospice of Metro Denver by her doctors, having signed an advance directive that she did not want medical treatment once she entered the dying stage of her illness. Later, her brothers Paul (a board-certified pathologist) and Marc, Mary's designated healthcare decision makers, decided that her advance directive had been misapplied because she was not actually in the final, dying stage of her condition. They were also upset that at the hospice Corrao developed a kidney infection and a very large bedsore and, they claimed, was overmedicated.

Paul and Marc Corrao, as Mary's duly designated healthcare decision makers, insisted that she be returned to the Columbia Aurora Presbyterian Hospital for further treatment. (The hospital and Mary Corrao's insurance company are owned by the for-profit Columbia/HCA Health Care Corp., the largest in Colorado and one of the largest in the country.) Mary improved under the treatment she received at Columbia Aurora Presbyterian, becoming alert and interactive. She then decided to accept curative medical treatment and eschew further hospice care, a sentiment she later reiterated in the media.[42]

But the hospital and Mary Corrao's doctors disagreed. Doctors conceded that Mary's immediate condition had materially improved. Indeed, her cancer had not grown or progressed in some time. They also conceded that she had changed her mind about wanting hospice care and refusing curative treatment. However, they contended that her mental capacities were so reduced that she was incapable of making such a "complex decision." They also insisted that she be transferred back to the hospice or to a nursing home so that her hospital bed could be saved for a "salvageable case."[43] In other words, they wanted to hold her to her previous advance directive instructing doctors not to provide curative treatment, even though that was no longer her desire.

The fact that Mary had signed a new advance directive containing a "presumption for life" and requiring ongoing treatment made little difference to the hospital or her doctors. They claimed she remained incompetent to make medical decisions, and they were bound and determined to hold her to her previous directive for withholding curative treatment. Columbia Aurora Presbyterian decided to make an example of Mary and her brothers. With vastly superior financial resources, they sicced their corporate lawyers on the family and filed a lawsuit that requested, among other things, that Paul and Marc Corrao be stripped of their rights as medical decision makers for their sister and that the hospital be allowed involuntarily to discharge her back into the hospice or a nursing home. Adding to the pressure on the Corraos, the insurance company then sent a notice that it would pay for only six of seventy-eight days of hospitalization, presenting the family with financial ruin.

Not coincidentally, a member of Columbia's Colorado Division Ethics Committee is the medical futilitarian Dr. Donald J. Murphy, of the Colorado Collective for Medical Decisions (CCMD). Dr. Murphy urged Columbia Aurora Presbyterian onto the legal battlefield, saying, "This conflict could be a landmark in medical history. This case has the potential to affect much of what we do, if it gets solved."[44] The court appointed Susan Fox-Buchanon, the legal counsel for Dr. Murphy's CCMD, as Mary Corrao's guardian ad litem—hardly a likely candidate to make objective decisions about her care. (The Corraos' lawyer had stipulated that Fox-Buchanon could serve as guardian ad litem, apparently not knowing of her CCMD affiliation. When the Corraos learned of her connection with CCMD, they asked her to step aside. But Fox-Buchanon refused to recuse herself, despite the apparent conflict of interest.)

If Mary Corrao's newly desired treatment did not medically require acute hospitalization for its safe and effective delivery, the hospital was within its rights to request that she be discharged to a more appropriate setting for her continued care, paid for by her health insurance. As the controversy unfolded, there was discussion of moving her to a ward within the hospital that provided less acute care, since her bedsore still required treatment. But if the hospital and insurance company sought to bind Mary to the terms of her former advance directive—as appeared to be the case, despite her obvious change of mind—or if the hospital and insurance company took action successfully to preclude further medical treatment on the basis of their value judgments about her life, the Corrao case would be a profoundly dangerous watershed event. If the hospital and doctors could refuse legally to provide treatment that Mary Corrao desired, it would become difficult for healthcare consumers to have their desires for treatment heeded if they sign an advance directive eschewing care but later change their minds after they become seriously ill. Such a precedent would threaten the very purpose for which advance directives were created, gutting the value of patient autonomy that the documents are supposed to protect. The Corrao matter was never resolved legally. Mary Corrao died in September 1996 after surgery to treat her bedsore.

EUTHANASIA STANDARD NO. 8
Only conservatives oppose euthanasia.

Many so-called progressive supporters of legalizing euthanasia try to make the case that this issue is one that liberals must embrace as they embraced the civil rights movement and the pro-choice view in the abortion issue. With euthanasia, however, the usual liberal-conservative paradigm does not apply. The controversy cuts across the usual political differences. People on the "religious right" generally oppose euthanasia—and so, too, do many on the "secular left." On this issue former 2000 Reform Party presidential candidate Pat Buchanan agrees completely with 2000 Green Party presidential candidate Ralph Nader, who agrees with former president Bill Clinton, a Democrat, who agrees with current president George W. Bush, a Republican. Similarly, the left-wing political commentator Nat Hentoff, one of the nation's foremost liberal civil libertarians, agrees with Charles Krauthammer, a staunch conservative political commentator.

The nationally syndicated *Washington Post* columnist E. J. Dionne told me why he, a Democrat, opposes euthanasia and assisted suicide. "Above almost everything else, liberals are supposed to be allied with the powerless, the disabled, the poor, the infirm, and the dying, and it is the powerless who could be victimized by euthanasia. We are also supposed to understand how individual decisions can be less than free if they are made under unfair or unreasonable constraints. Considering the growth of managed care, legalizing physician-assisted suicide would place people in the weakest and most vulnerable positions under excruciating pressures to do things they don't want to do and shouldn't be asked to do."[45] Add in other such liberal voices as those of Matthew Rothschild, the editor of the *Progressive*, and Donna Shalala, former secretary of health and human services, and it can be safely said that opposing euthanasia is neither a "liberal" nor a "conservative" position: it is a human position.

EUTHANASIA STANDARD NO. 9
There is no difference between pain control and euthanasia.

One of the more disturbing standards sung by euthanasia advocates rests on the "double effect" scenario in pain control. Pain control, which often requires powerful drugs, can have the effect, not only of controlling pain, but also—sometimes—of hastening death. Thus, euthanasia proponents argue, since death might be hastened by the use of pain control, and since euthanasia is designed (they allege) to reduce suffering, there is no difference between aggressively applied pain palliation and intentionally hastened death.

This is an intentional misapplication of the principle in ethics called the "double effect." There are occasions when a person may intend to do a good thing, recognizing that a bad result might occur despite his good intentions. Even if the bad outcome occurs, so long as the intention was good, then the action is morally acceptable. But in order for "double effect" to apply—meaning an act that produces a bad result is still considered to be ethical—four conditions must be met:

1. The action taken (in this case, treating pain) is good or morally neutral.

2. The bad effect (in this case, death) is not intended.

3. The good effect (in this case, the relief of suffering) cannot be brought about by an act designed to intentionally cause the bad effect (death).

4. There is a sufficiently grave reason to perform the act (in this case, the presence of severe pain).

If properly applied pain control *accidentally* hastens death, the palliative act remains ethical on the basis of the principle of double effect, since the bad result, death, was not intended. Euthanasia, on the other hand, fails the third requirement that the hoped-for good—relief of suffering—was accomplished by *intentionally causing the bad effect*, death. As the pain-control expert Dr. Eric Chevlen notes, "Euthanasiasts have tried to stand the concept of double effect on its head, arguing that the killing of the patient is done with the intention to relieve suffering, and that therefore it is morally acceptable under the doctrine of double effect. This is casuistic nonsense. When a doctor purposely kills a patient, the fact that the doctor liked the patient and didn't want him to suffer does not change the fact that he has acted wrongly. Only if the bad outcome is *possible* and *undesired* rather than *certain* and *intentional* does the doctrine of double effect come into play. Sadly, in the hands of euthanasiasts, the only thing certain is that there will be one more corpse by the end of the day."[46]

Although the use of pain-control drugs such as morphine, like surgery or most other medical treatments, can have serious side effects, including death, pain control, if properly applied, rarely hastens death; in any event, it is in no way akin to intentional killing. "Effective application of pain control is not euthanasia," says the Oregon hospice physician and pain-control expert Gary Lee, MD. "People receiving pain control at the very end of their lives to preserve comfort are in the dying process. As folks relax, and there is less drive to breathe and fight the pain, they fade off. That happens in the natural course of dying anyway. People become weak or drowsy; because of their advanced disease they cough less and develop pneumonia and die. From a practical standpoint, you can't really tell if the patient died earlier because of the pain control or not." Dr. Lee adds, "We don't see respiratory depression in patients not on the brink of death already, unless the intent is to cause respiratory depression. That is what euthanasia advocates are interested in. Causing these effects 'earlier' than they would occur in the natural processes, including when they would happen even with the proper application of proper pain control techniques."[47]

Dr. Chevlen agrees. "Certainly, the doctor prescribing morphine must be knowledgeable about its safe use to avoid adverse effects. But fortunately, patients become tolerant to the respiratory effects of morphine. Those patients who have been taking the drug for a fair while experience very little, if any, suppression of respiratory drive on the doses of morphine needed to control pain, which can be increased as time goes on. When morphine is used properly in the last hours of life, it eases the anxiety and discomfort the patient might otherwise have, but it does not hasten death."[48]

Another aspect of the false equation of pain control and euthanasia is that many well-meaning and compassionate people accept the legalization of euthanasia because they believe that killing patients is sometimes the only way to alleviate suffering. This is a false premise. There are abundant opportunities for compassionate and empowering caregiving. If these were fully accessed and competently implemented, human suffering would be alleviated significantly. This in turn would allay the public's fear of dying in agony—perhaps the primary reason many reluctantly support legalizing doctor-induced death. These important issues will be addressed in the last chapter.

EUTHANASIA STANDARD NO. 10
Assisted suicide is medicine.

In April 2002, to the cheers of editorial writers throughout the country, a federal judge enjoined Attorney General John Ashcroft from revoking the federal license to prescribe controlled substances of Oregon doctors who legally assist in a patient's suicide.[49] The Oregon lawsuit was filed in 2001 when Ashcroft issued a directive in the Federal Register, proclaiming that assisted suicide was not a "legitimate medical purpose" under the Controlled Substances Act (CSA). But United States District Court judge Robert E. Jones ruled that once Oregon determined that assisted suicide was a legitimate medical act, the federal government was bound to accede to the state's determination even when enforcing federal law.

During this same time, the European Court of Human Rights issued a ruling in another assisted suicide case, the facts of which seem to have great bearing on whether assisted suicide is a medical act.[50] The case involved a terminally ill woman named Diane Pretty disabled by Lou Gehrig's disease (known as motor neurone disease in Europe). Mrs. Pretty wanted to commit suicide, but her disease had progressed to the point where she could not do the deed on her own. So in 2001, she filed suit in Britain seeking a court order guaranteeing that her husband would suffer no legal penalty for helping her kill herself, even though Britain's law prohibits assisted suicide.

Consider the relief Mrs. Pretty requested from the British and EU courts: She wanted her *husband*, Brian, to help kill her legally. Not her doctor; her husband who, relevantly, is not a physician and has no medical training other than what he may have picked up as a caregiver for his wife.

Pretty's lawsuit was treated with great respect in the British and European courts. The trial court first gave its permission to bring the case and then spent a great deal of time hearing evidence and pondering the law before ultimately rejecting the claim. The House of Lords, the British equivalent of the Supreme Court, took the appeal and held a hearing that treated her arguments with utmost solemnity and seriousness. Then, when the Lords ruled against Mrs. Pretty, the EU court agreed quickly to take up the matter to see if Britain's anti-assisted-suicide law violated the European Rights Convention.

Now imagine what would have happened if this case had not been about assisted suicide but about Mrs. Pretty wanting her husband to be allowed to perform surgery upon her, such as the minor procedure required to insert her feeding tube into her abdomen. Or, what if she had brought the case requesting that her husband be allowed to decide the proper medication for her to take to alleviate the symptoms of her disease. She would have been laughed out of court, because those are actions that are clearly medical: only licensed medical professionals can perform surgery or prescribe medications. Thus, the case would be deemed utterly frivolous and a waste of the court's time.

Notice also that Mrs. Pretty did not sue to prevent her husband from being prosecuted for practicing medicine without a license if he assisted her suicide. The very idea of such a suit is so ludicrous that no doubt it never occurred to her attorneys. Of course, the reason for this is because assisting a suicide isn't really medicine.

Further proof of this is found in the advocacy of the euthanasia movement, which has established a cottage industry in suicide devices. For example, Derek Humphry, co-founder of the Hemlock Society, started NuTech, which is devoted to promoting suicide facilitation devices. As reported breathlessly in the December 6, 2001 *Economist*, among these contraptions is the "DeBreather," a face-mask apparatus that recycles a suicidal person's own carbon dioxide toward the end of cutting off all oxygen. How-to-commit-suicide videos Humphry promotes (and stars in), also extol the use helium and a plastic bag to bring life to an end.[51]

Now ask yourself this question: Should Medicare pay for the expense of obtaining and using a DeBreather if the patient is over sixty-five? Or should your local HMO provide the device to patients as if it were durable medical equipment akin to an oxygen tank or a kidney dialysis machine? Indeed, should helium be considered a palliative medical agent? The entire concept is preposterous, ridiculous. Why? Because killing isn't medicine.

A few years ago, Berkeley Assemblywoman Dion Aroner authored legislation to legalize physician-assisted suicide in California. At a public forum I confronted her and made these points. Aroner acknowledged candidly that she would have preferred to keep doctors out of it. But, she said, she believed it necessary to bring assisted suicide under a medical umbrella for political reasons. Otherwise, her bill would have no chance of passage.

So what is the point of doctors' involvement in assisted suicide? It offers a false appearance of respectability. Advocates know that their ad hoc approach to killing will never catch on. However they also know that the public, lawmakers, and judges tend to defer in matters involving healthcare public policy to the medical profession. Thus, if they can invoke the physician's authority in medicalize killing and use "medicine" to cause death, assisted suicide advocates hope to overcome society's resistance to their agenda.

Calling killing medicine doesn't make it so. Assisted suicide activists intentionally redefine, distort, and subvert medicine, medical ethics, and the morality of healthcare public policy in pursuit of their dream of obtaining the right to "choose the time and manner" of their own deaths.

9

Hospice or Hemlock?

EUTHANASIA IS ON THE CUTTING EDGE of twenty-first-century social trends. This is not surprising. Few other issues so perfectly reflect the public gestalt of our times: Euthanasia is justified by claims of compassion, appeals to raw emotionalism, and paeans to "choice." But in light of the consequences that could flow from the legalization and legitimization of euthanasia, we should all think deeply about what accepting the values of the death culture would really mean.

Social libertarians argue that the state has no interest in preventing suicide, because each person's body is exclusively his or her own. Therefore all of us must be free to do exactly as we please with our own body—even destroy it if that is what we want. But do we really want to live in a society that accepts the abandoning premises inherent in "rational suicide" and whose public policies would require authorities to stand back and watch deeply depressed persons jump off a bridge or shoot themselves in the head?

Some would say that legalizing physician-assisted suicide (PAS) and euthanasia wouldn't prevent police from stopping bridge jumpers who want to die. It would, however, prevent us from stopping doctors from killing patients who want to die. But what is the difference between a jump off a bridge and a lethal injection? In both cases, the despairing person wants to die for reasons that are compelling at that moment. It thus seems to me that if we are to create a noninterference policy toward the one, we must also stand back and permit the other: if we stand back to let a physician kill, then we must stand back to let a person kill himself.

That being said, suicide per se is not the issue. Jumping off a bridge is an individual act. Being killed by a doctor or committing PAS is a joint endeavor between two or more people, a conspiracy if you will, to commit a form of homicide. The point is not the propriety of suicide itself, but whether we should have the legal right to have ourselves killed by another person. Looked at from another angle, the question is whether the broad prohibition against killing by private persons, self-defense and defense of others being the exceptions, should be discarded to permit third parties to collaborate and participate in the deaths of sick, disabled, or incompetent people—and this on the basis of beliefs that certain lives are not worth living.

This question is of monumental importance. If we remain a society of "ordered liberty" envisioned by the Founders, a nation created to promote the greatest common good while allowing for as much individual liberty as is consistent with this broader purpose, we will reject euthanasia and assisted suicide as a danger to vulnerable persons, as a threat to basic institutions, and as a dangerous frayer of the social fabric. If, on the other hand, our nation above all else exists primarily to maximize the autonomy of the individual, regardless of its overall impact, indeed, if the state's purpose is merely to prevent one autonomous individual's fist from hitting another autonomous individual's nose, then legalized euthanasia makes sense.

But, as Charles Krauthammer has warned, if choosing to be killed by others is a matter of individual liberty, then what "private" activities are there that can be proscribed? If individuals cannot be prevented from arranging their own killing, then how can we logically outlaw a pregnant woman taking crack cocaine? What could possibly be more personal than what one chooses to put into one's body? What is more intimate than one's chosen state of consciousness? Similarly, if we accept euthanasia as a basic liberty the state cannot proscribe, would the laws that prohibit the selling of human organs for transplants fall too, perhaps as an adjunct to legalized assisted suicide.

Such a policy could easily fall into the "choice" category as well as fit into the increasing commercialism of our culture; it is also likely such a policy would create a marketplace in human organs leading to the catastrophic exploitation of the poor and to a medical system where transplants would go to the highest bidders.

Some of the most notable physicians and bioethicists in the organ transplant community already envision assisted suicde dovetailing with organ donation. Robert W. Arnold and Stuart J. Youngner wrote in the influential bioethics publication *Kennedy Institute of Ethics Journal*: "If active euthanasia—e.g., lethal injection—and physician-assisted suicide are legally sanctioned…patients could couple organ donation with their planned deaths; we would not have to depend only upon persons on life support. This practice would yield not only more donors but more types of organs as well, since the heart could not be removed from dying, not just dead, patients."[1]

Never mind that the prospect of organ donation could induce despairing people to commit suicide. And never mind the ghoulish prospect of taking vital organs from living people. If all that matters is "choice," this prospect should be of no significant concern—after all, "true freedom" has its costs.

How we decide the euthanasia controversy will determine the kind of society we live in and the one we will create for our children. Seen in this light, the issue transcends what may or may not be good or bad, right or wrong, for individuals. It defines who and what we are as a society, a culture, and a people.

Change isn't necessarily progress. As the victims of the French and Russian revolutions discovered to their dismay, change can be violent

and culturally destructive. Since we are dealing with the most fundamental issue, life and death, we should not make changes lightly or
base them on emotionalism or sound-bite rationales and slogans. Legalizing euthanasia would cast aside twenty-five hundred years of accumulated wisdom, ethics, and morality, and dramatically burden our
culture with foreseen and unforeseen consequences. We only should
risk such consequences if it is rational to do so.

I propose a three-pronged test to judge the rationality of creating a
"right to die": First, is there a need for this proposed revolutionary
change? Second, are the expected benefits of the change worth the foreseeable risks of the change? Third, would the change be progress? I
believe that a rational analysis of the euthanasia issue demonstrates
that the answer to all three questions is a resounding no.

IS THERE A NEED TO LEGALIZE EUTHANASIA?

Pain Can Be Controlled

The most emotionally compelling arguments in favor of euthanasia are
that euthanasia is needed to help relieve human suffering caused by
illness and prevent people from dying in agony that cannot be controlled. But this is a false premise. Too many patients die in unrelieved
pain: but this isn't because we *can't* provide relief but because we *don't*.

The difference between "can't" and "don't" is a vital part of this analysis. If relief of pain and suffering is the reason for legalizing assisted
killing, and if medical science has the wherewithal to relieve pain and
significantly reduce suffering, then there is no real need to legalize euthanasia. Rather, there is a need to improve the delivery of proper medicine by making the currently available relief universally accessible.

This is fact: Nearly all pain can be effectively treated and controlled,
including pain associated with arthritis, cancer, AIDS, and multiple sclerosis. Regardless of the cause of pain, severity of condition, or type of
disease or affliction, with proper medical treatment nearly every pa-

tient can exercise "power over pain," adding tremendously to the quality of his life—and even to its length. The beneficent potential of pain control through palliative care cannot be overstated.

Of course, some conditions are more difficult to palliate than others. For example, one of the most painful diseases known to medicine is bone cancer. The pain can be unbearable. Bones grow brittle and break easily. The patient may be unable to bear simply being touched. But even this pain can be significantly relieved, though it takes multiple strategies and hard work and concerted effort by dedicated doctors.

Dr. Robin Bernhoft, a Washington surgeon, has seen such an effort succeed in his own family. That is one of the reasons he opposes euthanasia. Dr. Bernhoft told me the following story:

> People who say bone cancer pain cannot be relieved are mistaken. My brother died of multiple myeloma [a bone-marrow cancer] when he was forty-one. His cancer destroyed his spine and ribs. He had fractures all over his chest that moved when he breathed. It was as painful a case of cancer as I have seen since I became a surgeon in 1976. But Larry was lucky. He was at the Mayo Clinic, where doctors knew how to take care of such horrible pain, even back in 1981. Throughout his illness, he remained very comfortable, and very alert, because they knew how to treat such pain. Pain can almost always be controlled and without putting people into a drugged stupor. Pain medicine—even morphine—goes straight to the pain. If the dosage is properly controlled, the patient will not feel drunk, drugged, and most importantly, will not be in pain.[2]

The bad news, of course, is that too many patients are not given the proper treatment that Larry Bernhoft received. We have a choice: do we improve the training of doctors in the areas of pain, depression, disability, and the needs of the dying, and demand that their professional performance meet the highest standard, or do we lower our medical standards, in Dr. Bernhoft's provocative words, to "veterinary levels" and allow doctors off the hook by permitting them to kill?

If we want the former, we have a lot of work to do. When it comes to pain control, doctors are notorious underachievers. As discussed earlier in the book, in the United States alone tens of millions of people—cancer patients, AIDS patients, MS patients, rheumatoid arthritis patients, and others—receive inadequate pain relief, causing unnecessary suffering and giving impetus to the euthanasia movement. According to the medical literature, there are several reasons for this failure of modern professional medicine.

1. *Too many doctors did not receive sufficient training in pain control in medical school and have not pursued the subject since graduation.* As a consequence, they don't even know about the newest pain-control techniques, thus depriving their patients of relief that should be theirs.

2. *Too many doctors fear that pain medicine will cause drug addiction.* This is a false fear. When used appropriately for pain control, and when applied properly, narcotic agents are virtually never addictive. That means that narcotics can be used liberally, relieve pain and suffering, and not add to the country's drug-abuse problem.

3. *Patients also fear becoming addicted, sometimes leading to their refusing readily available pain control.* I have faced this problem with my own family. My father was dying of colon cancer. I came to visit him in the hospital after surgery to clear his bile duct of tumor. The surgeon had not only botched the job but Dad was lying in bed, writhing in pain, an ice pack held against his wound.

I was appalled. "Didn't they give you something for the pain?" I demanded.

"They did son, but I refused."

"What? Why?"

"I don't want to become addicted," he replied in the firmest voice he could muster.

Dad had been a top sergeant in the army before receiving battlefield promotions to captain during World War II. He prided himself on being strong. But this was a false bravado that was causing him unnecessary suffering. I said, "Dad, you're a tough guy. You won't get addicted but even if you do, I know you're strong enough to beat it. For goodness sake, take the [bleeping] pain medicine!"

Dad looked up at me gratefully. "Okay," he said sheepishly.

Apparently my father had just needed permission to take strong drugs. We called the nurse into the room, and he was soon comfortable. For the remaining months of dad's life he never had problems with pain.

4. *Pain control is often an innocent casualty of the war on drugs.* Many state laws designed to curb drug abuse instead make it difficult or inconvenient for doctors to effectively treat their patients' pain. But this is beginning to change. Several states have passed laws explicitly setting forth in law that aggressive pain control is a proper medical act— even if it leads to the accidental death of the patient. As a consequence, morphine use in these states has soared. For example, after Iowa passed such a law in conjunction with a new state law banning assisted suicide, morphine use increased 136% as of 1998. Rhode Island passed a similar law and saw morphine use increase 164% as of 1998.[3]

5. *Too many doctors are excessively concerned about side effects that sometimes occur with pain control.* These can include constipation, nausea, and drowsiness. Yet, like pain, these side effects can almost always be controlled. For example, patients on morphine should take laxatives to relieve constipation. Nausea can usually be limited with medication or by changing from morphine to some other opioid. Drowsiness will usually abate after a few days on morphine. But if it doesn't, the doctor can prescribe medication to promote wakefulness.[4]

6. *Too many doctors believe that only the severest pain requires treatment, thereby abandoning many chronic pain sufferers to their misery.*

7. *Too many doctors treating patients for painful conditions do not take the time or effort to reevaluate their patients' pain on a regular and continuing basis.* Some doctors never even ask their patients about their pain.[5] Patients, too, are often reluctant to tell their doctors that they hurt. There are several reasons for this: Some patients believe that the presence of pain means that they are going to die or that their illness has

worsened—which isn't necessarily true. Or some patients believe that "good patients" don't bother their doctors by reporting pain. In fact, the opposite is true. Good patients let their doctors know what is going on. Otherwise their doctors may be prevented from providing optimal care.[6]

8. *Patients also know too little about the benefits of pain control.* They and their loved ones do not know that they are suffering unnecessarily, and consequently they may come to believe that death is the only way to obtain relief. Like doctors, patients sometimes eschew pain control for fear of becoming addicted to drugs. It needs to be reiterated: Morphine and other pain-control agents, when used in appropriate doses to stop or prevent actual pain do not cause addiction. Nor, again assuming proper application, do they usually cause mental confusion, pronounced drowsiness, personality change, or stupor.[7]

Hospice Care Already Provides "Death with Dignity"

Many dying people who consider assisted suicide are afraid of future pain, abandonment, or a "medicalized" death hooked up to machines in a cold, sterile institutional setting. While some patients do still die this way, dying does not have to be so impersonal and burdensome. Over the last few decades the hospice movement has slowly reversed the over-medicalization of death.

Hospice is less a place than a concept. According to the *Harvard Health Letter*, "The hospice philosophy is that dying should be accepted as a unique part of life, not resisted with every weapon in medicine's armamentarium. When nothing more can be gained from [curative] treatment, hospices focus on making people as comfortable as possible."[8]

The goal is to provide whatever care patients need to enable them to die naturally, in peace, and with dignity. This means that no efforts are made to extend the patient's life. Instead, the focus is on providing whatever treatment is necessary to control pain and alleviate symptoms, while at the same time taking a holistic approach by providing emotional support for the patient and the family.

Hospice uses a team approach to better ensure that the patient's and family's entire needs are met. A typical team includes a physician, such as the hospice physicians interviewed for this book, Drs. Eric Chevlen, Ira Byock, and Gary Lee. But the doctor is only the beginning. Hospice nurses make house calls to check on patients and provide needed medical services. Social workers are available to assist the patient and family and assess their needs. Psychological therapists and bereavement counselors provide valuable grief counseling and emotional support. Volunteers work creatively to fill caregiving niches for the benefit of patient and family. Respite care is also available to aid families needing a short break from the intense effort of caregiving. Since most hospice care occurs in the home (although there are hospice facilities), once a patient enters hospice, usually when the life expectancy is six months or less, he can say goodbye to the impersonal hospitals and being "hooked up to machines" that so many of us fear.

The beneficence of hospice, for those patients who desire to cease life-prolonging medical treatment and transition peacefully into death, cannot be overstated. "Hospice is often misunderstood as limited to controlling a dying person's symptoms," says Dr. Ira Byock. "Symptom control is the first priority of hospice, but it is not the ultimate goal. The fundamental purpose of hospice is to enhance the quality of life for the dying individual and the family, to give the opportunity for the patient to live as fully as possible in community with his or her friends or family, to get affairs in order, to deepen and complete relationships. Hospice is about the completing of a life, and in that context, it is . . . wonderfully human."[9]

Euthanasia advocates usually give lip-service support to hospice but contend that hospice providers should also be in the business of hastening their patients' deaths—called by the euthanasia advocate Lonny Shavelson "hospice and hemlock."[10] This idea is anathema to most hospice professionals as the antithesis of the hospice philosophy.

The message of hospice is that each patient is valuable and important, that dying is an important stage of life that is worth living through

and growing from—until death comes through natural processes. As Dame Cicely Saunders has recently written, hospice asserts on behalf of the dying patient his "common humanity and personal importance" to the moment of natural death.[11] No wonder hospice has become a valued institution worldwide.

The euthanasia philosophy is just the opposite. By definition, euthanasia is a statement that life is not worth living, not worth protecting, not worth spending the time to "suffer with," the true definition of compassion. Worse, the euthanasia philosophy claims that the answer to dying, disability, or other "hopeless illness" is to artificially induce death and "get it over with." No wonder the world's most notable hospice professionals disagree with the hemlock approach.

Dr. Carlos F. Gomez, assistant professor of medicine at the University of Virginia School of Medicine and a hospice physician of national repute, firmly opposes mixing hospice with hemlock as an easy way out of truly caring for dying patients. He told a congressional committee looking into the assisted-suicide issue: "We now have it well within our technical means to alleviate, to palliate and comfort and control the worst symptoms of those of our fellow citizens who are terminally ill. The question before . . . the country at large is whether we have the heart, the courage, and the will to make it so, or whether we will opt for expediency and call it mercy."[12]

Dr. Gary Lee also strongly opposes mixing hospice with hemlock. "I am there to take care of the patient," he says. "You can't move the line in hospice to allow the killing of patients. It would destroy the line." Dr. Byock puts it even more succinctly: "The hospice focus is on life and the alleviation of suffering," whereas "the goal of assisted suicide and euthanasia is death."[13]

From this perspective, euthanasia threatens the hospice movement. "Hospice commits to the patient and the family that we will take care of them, to non-abandonment," says Dr. Lee. "But if euthanasia becomes a standard of practice, too many times there would be a real incentive to do it. There are some patients whose proper care requires time and effort, professional services that aren't necessarily paid for by insurance companies. I might say, 'There has to be an easier way.' I could too easily find myself seeing euthanasia as the simple answer; one that is less time-consuming and the least expensive. If accepted, euthanasia could very easily take the place of proper patient care."[14]

The Dutch experience with hospice lends credence to Dr. Lee's concerns. Studies show that hospice-style palliative care is stunted in the Netherlands. There are very few hospice facilities, very little in the way of organized hospice activity, and few specialists in palliative care, although some efforts are now under way to try and jump-start the hospice movement in that country. One reason for the lack of hospice opportunities in the Netherlands is the general-practitioner style of medical delivery, in which doctors make house calls and care for citizens from birth until death—a hands-on approach to medicine that the hospice movement is reintroducing to American healthcare. However, the widespread availability of euthanasia in the Netherlands may be another reason for the stunted growth of the Dutch hospice movement. As one Dutch doctor is reported to have said, "Why should I worry about palliation when I have euthanasia?"

Hospice can be provided in the home, in a nursing home, or in a hospice facility. Medicare and most health insurance policies cover the cost of hospice treatment.[15]

Independent Living Eliminates Despair

As we have learned from people such as Paul Longmore, Diane Coleman, and Carol Gill, disabled people usually seek out assisted suicide because they have suffered the kind of crisis that can afflict anyone or because their desire to live freely and independently has been needlessly stymied, leading to feelings of despair and hopelessness. As with untreated pain and undesired medicalized dying, this need not be so. Increasingly, the disability-rights and independent-living movement works on behalf of disabled people and their families to help overcome hurdles that needlessly interfere with their living full and productive lives. The movement provides disabled people with personal assistants who help them learn independent-living skills and help perform tasks their disabilities prevent or make difficult. It also provides other forms of peer counseling and deals with issues of housing advocacy, disability-rights advocacy, transportation, and most important of all, information and referral. By law, the centers for independent living must have at least 51 percent control by people with disabilities, ensuring that the perspective of disabled people is amply considered in decision making. There are independent-living centers all around the country.

Independent living makes a tremendous difference. Take the late Mark O'Brien, the Berkeley, California, journalist-poet described earlier in the book. O'Brien contracted polio at the age of six and was a quadriplegic for forty-four years. The polio so profoundly disabled him that he was dependent on an iron lung for the rest of his life. He rarely left the machine for more than a few hours a month to make personal appearances at lectures near his home in Berkeley, when he was able to survive in a supine position on a ventilator for an hour or so. Otherwise, from the age of six to his death just before his fiftieth birthday in 1999, Mark spent his entire life inside his yellow iron lung, which dominated the living room of his one-bedroom loft apartment.

Jack Kevorkian has said that those among us who have significant physical impairments, people such as O'Brien, are "certifiably pathological" if they are not in despair.[16] Nothing could be more wrong. Mark did not despair and he was definitely not "certifiable." While he faced considerable challenges, he enjoyed his life and lived it to the fullest—in large part because of the independent-living movement. "Before I lived on my own," O'Brien told me, "I was afraid my life wouldn't amount to anything, that I couldn't do anything, that I would never be able to contribute to society. But because of independent living, I now have my own career, work at it, and live my own life. Because of independent living, I paid income taxes for the first time in my life.

Most disabled people could achieve at least partial self-sufficiency with the appropriate services made available to them."[17]

O'Brien strongly believed that: "The idea of disabled people being stuck in nursing homes for life is not only wasteful of resources, it is wasteful of people, and little better than slavery. We know how to assist people to live independently, it is cheaper than warehousing people, we are just not doing it sufficiently to be of assistance to most disabled people. I consider the cause of independent living to be the moral equivalent of the civil rights movement of the 1960s."[18]

Another example of the difference that independent living can make for even the most profoundly disabled was brought to my attention by an attorney named Beth Roney Drennan of Baraboo, Wisconsin. Drennan was appointed guardian ad litem for David W Domenosky, a young man whose brain was injured in an auto accident. Domenosky awakened from a six-month coma with quadriplegia. Despite his medical records' showing that he has no intellectual impairment, and despite his being able to communicate by blinks and stares, Drennan was shocked to learn that doctors had discussed withholding antibiotics from Domenosky should he develop an infection. His parents refused to authorize discontinuing treatment for their son.

When Drennan asked about this, one of Domenosky's nurses nonchalantly admitted that the idea was for him to die if he should ever develop pneumonia.[19] When Drennan asked a supervising nurse at a different facility (where she was thinking of placing Domenosky) her views on this matter, the woman asserted that she too believed treatment should be withheld from Domenosky because he "is no longer experiencing life." The nurse then asked Drennan, "Do you want your tax dollars supporting people like this forever?"[14]

Appalled at what she considered the cavalier attitude about Domenosky's life on the part of some of his caregivers, worried that "David would be killed without his mother being consulted" (as we have seen, this is not an unreasonable fear), and believing firmly in her client's right not only to live but to thrive, Drennan spent more than a year, in her words, "fighting blindly" to get Domenosky out of the nursing home and into a better placement.

Eventually, Drennan's care for Domenosky and her tenacity led her to a disability-rights group committed to the independent-living concept. With the group's help, she has overcome "budget cuts, recalcitrant bureaucrats and overburdened case workers," and placed David into his own apartment.

Domenosky's release from the nursing home was only the beginning of Drennan's plans for her friend and client. "David will get communication therapy," Drennan told me excitedly in 1995. "He will receive vocational training so he can work or otherwise involve himself in projects, plus, he will receive physical therapy to improve his physical abilities." According to Drennan, Domenosky is almost as charged about his upcoming new life as she is. "He is most excited about 'getting back into the culture,'" Drennan says. "He can hardly wait to listen to his own style of music, watch current movies on video, create a new life for himself outside of a nursing home setting."[18]

In May 2002, I decided to see whether Drennan's plans for Domenosky panned out. "It all turned out better than we even thought it would be!" Drennan told me:

> All our work was a complete success: David did move into a beautiful new home right after your book [the first edition of *Forced Exit*] came out. He was always positive that that getting into his own place would be the key to his happiness and he was right. He is so happy, and it has been several years now. He was given a similarly challenged roommate his own age right at the start and that has worked out fine. He has fabulous caregivers and his cheerful attitude wins everyone over. He communicates excellently by blinking. He has gained a little weight and looks adorable. He is about 30 now, still has a little "tail" of long hair in back of his head to keep the cool look. Best news: He is eating now by mouth! The tube is used only for medications. All those years he couldn't

even taste food and now, last time I saw him he was eating a cookie—and laughing at the same time. He has a new van and a busy social schedule, his caregivers tell me. He went to one of his caregiver's college graduation, he goes shopping, all kinds of things.[20]

Compare Drennan's understanding of human compassion to the mindsets of so many others—doctors, euthanasia advocates, well-meaning relatives of disabled people—who proclaim that some lives are simply not worth living, that for the good of the patient, to ease the burden on the patient's family and relieve society of a financial burden, disabled people like Domenosky can ethically be dehydrated to death, assisted with suicide, or, indeed, fatally injected. To this Drennan responds:

> In our culture, I think that many people see affection as something that occurs *post hoc, ergo propter hoc* [after something and therefore because of it]. They believe there must be a "cause" for affection; that the cause comes first. If there is enough cause then the effect follows that if the person is deserving or has certain attributes, then that is a cause for having affection for them. But I believe that real affection for each other is inherent in our natural state, and that if we do nothing to block that affection, it will flow through us toward others, at least in some degree. No cause is required, no attributes of mind or body, not earned by conditions, but not lost by them either. Not even old age, loss of teeth, loss of hair, loss of physical beauty, or ability to move the body due to quadriplegia, can make the affection go away. Those of us who have affection for David, see the beauty and infinite value of his life—and that affection is not conditioned on the state of David's body. David is wonderful, just as and because he is.[21]

Mark O'Brien, David Domenosky, and disabled people like them are "cases" of "suffering" that pro-euthanasia types would consider "hopeless conditions," people who, in Jack Kevorkian's words, are "pathological" if they are not in despair and whose killing should therefore be deemed "rational" and, again in Kevorkian's words, "a standard medical service."[22] Yet given access to independent living rather than abandoned to "warehousing," most disabled people lose the desire to die, much less to be killed, and instead get about the adventure of life.

IS THE EXPECTED BENEFIT OF EUTHANASIA
WORTH ITS CONSIDERABLE RISKS?

Euthanasia is akin to "destroying the village in order to save it." There are far better ways to serve people in need, care opportunities that dramatically reduce suffering and pain while simultaneously increasing the sense of personal dignity and self-worth in virtually all ill or disabled people. If we applied these treatment and caregiving strategies universally, people's fear of suffering, the driving force behind the advance of the idea of euthanasia, would virtually disappear. At this juncture in the debate, death fundamentalists will usually say, "But what about the few who, despite the best of care, would still want euthanasia rather than to await a natural death or live a life with the limitations of disability, or chronic disease? Shouldn't they be given the opportunity to have their lives ended as they choose?"

Again, that depends on what one believes the purpose of society to be, as expressed through its public policy. Is it to best serve the forest, or is it to make sure that each tree has maximum autonomy? In the latter case there isn't really a forest, but merely a bunch of trees in close proximity to each other. Should the morality, ethical concepts, and laws that protect and benefit the many be cast aside because a relatively small group of people does not want to abide by them?

Certainly, there are times when the rights of even one person override the views of the rest of society. One of the geniuses of our system is that at such times, special legal niches can be created to accommodate and protect the rights of small groups. For example, the law in most states requires universal education to age sixteen. Yet Amish parents have the legal right to remove their children from public school before they reach sixteen.

The niche created to accommodate the Amish has little if any impact on the general society. Nor does it endanger non-Amish children. The same cannot be said of euthanasia. As we derive rights from our community, so too we bear responsibilities. That is what it means to be part of a community. Even though a few people would undoubtedly wish to hasten their deaths despite receiving the best medical treatment and care that exists, asking to be killed should be viewed in the same way as someone threatening to jump off the Golden Gate Bridge: as a request for help. The compassionate answer must be to render assistance, not give the suicidal person a "helpful" push off the rail.

Moreover, what message would be sent to others with similar illnesses as people receiving assisted suicide? One day when I went to visit my hospice friend Bob, who died of ALS, he was so angry he was spitting nails. The year was 1997, and the United States Supreme Court was about to hear arguments as to whether the United States Constitution provided a "right" to assisted suicide.

The media was all over the story. *Nightline* presented the case of a Rhode Island man with ALS, who claimed to want assisted suicide. Bob believed that the entire program had been biased in favor of allowing the man to be killed. "How do you think that makes *me* feel," he demanded. "That my life isn't worth protecting or living." Bob was so angry he wrote an opinion article published in the *San Francisco Chronicle* entitled "I Don't Want a Choice to Die," in which he wrote:

> Euthanasia advocates believe they are doing people like me a favor. They are not. The negative emotions toward the terminally ill and disabled generated by their advocacy is actually at the expense of the 'dying' and their families and friends, who often feel disheartened and without self-assurance because of a false picture of what it is like to die created by these enthusiasts who prey on the misinformed.

What we, the terminally ill, need is exactly the opposite—to realize how important our lives are. And our loved ones, friends, and indeed society, need to help us to feel that we are loved and appreciated unconditionally.[23]

Bob was right. Legalization would not increase the compassion and equal treatment of dying people. It would a step backward, sending the loud message that certain lives just are not worth living.

The history of the West in general, and this nation in particular, has been largely about the epic struggle to transform the equality-of-human-life ethic from an ideal into a reality. Equality requires us to shed our social smallness and distance ourselves from past and present discrimination based on race, creed, gender, physical ability, religious beliefs, sexual orientation, and status of health. Toward that end great strides have been made, profound evils have been overcome. Yet for many, true equality remains an elusive dream.

As long as some remain on the outside looking in, the struggle will continue. How can it not? Equality is the bedrock foundation of our culture. But as this vital work continues, as we rid ourselves of false concepts and phony distinctions, let us not make the mistake of replacing current groups of oppressed people with a new collection of "others"—this time based on our fears and prejudices about health, age, disability, and death. As we rejected Jim Crow, let us also reject the inherent discrimination of futilitarianism. As we open our arms to those whom we have traditionally rejected, let us not turn our backs on the dying, the disabled, and the chronically ill. In short, as we painfully achieve true equality, let us not undo our work by countenancing the killing of the weakest and most vulnerable among us.

WOULD THE CHANGE BE PROGRESS?

I believe it is fair to assert that this book has demonstrated that legalizing euthanasia would not be a step forward for society but rather a giant leap backward in our desire to serve and assist those among us who have been affected by a terminal diagnosis, disability, chronic pain, the debilitation of advanced years, the despair of depression—indeed, everyone and anyone experiencing what euthanasia advocates call "hopeless illness." It would be to countenance their killing, in essence to legalize murder. It would inevitably lead, as it has in the Netherlands, to involuntary euthanasia. This is especially dangerous for those among us who are less powerful: African-Americans and other minorities who too often receive a lower standard of healthcare, such as the poor and the uneducated, those with little understanding or ability to assert their rights to quality healthcare in an increasingly commercialized medical milieu. It would be to make a virtue out of abandonment and accelerate the country's tendency to isolate those most in need of community.

This last point was brought home to me in a forceful manner recently in my work as a hospice volunteer. I turn once again to the wisdom of my hospice friend Bob. I visited Bob once a week for almost two years. During that time, we spent many hours discussing his feelings about dying, about becoming disabled, indeed, about the purpose and meaning of life. Our many conversations were profound, inspiring, and rewarding.

Bob's experience vividly made clear the isolation faced too often by dying and disabled people. "For the first two and a half years after my diagnosis I wanted to kill myself," Bob told me early in our acquaintance. "It was not the illness so much that depressed me but the reaction of the people around me. First they stopped visiting, then they stopped calling to speak to me, and then they stopped calling. I found myself completely isolated. I felt like a token presence in the world."[24]

Jack Kevorkian was first making headlines during this time, and Bob took acute notice. He told me that he listened to the newscasts carefully and that they definitely impacted his thinking about suicide. "During my worst moments, the idea of a quick demise had an appeal," he recalls. "I didn't want to be a burden, and I figured it would be the best thing for everyone." If Kevorkian didn't plant the suicide seeds in

Bob's consciousness, his activities and their coverage certainly watered the sprouts.

Suicide thoughts and Bob eventually parted company as he, his wife, and their children pulled together and kept on going through the difficulties caused by his inability to work and the distress of his weakening condition. When he joined the Mormon Church he found a new community whose members rallied to his side. Church members visited Bob every day. Two and a half years after his diagnosis he "came out of the fog," as he put it. He discovered that life held a very special meaning for him and that for as long as nature permitted, he deeply wanted to live.

Bob lived for nearly five years after he was expected to die. He spent his final days happy to be alive, relishing each day. He wrote a novel, invested on the Internet, and used the computer to collect art. He was especially proud of a Dali lithograph he purchased at an online auction. "Believe me, this time has been a blessing," he once told me, "I have grown. I have come into my own. I know myself better than I ever thought I would. I understand more about life than I ever thought I could. I am living more intensely than I ever have. I wouldn't have missed the last several years for anything in the world."

Had Bob requested assisted suicide during his years of depression, death fundamentalists would have considered the request "rational." They would have labeled his illness "hopeless." They would have believed, on the basis of their own fears and prejudices, that the quality of his life was not, and would never again be, good enough for his life to be worth living. They would have readily granted his request for a hastened death, thinking they were being compassionate. (In fact, ALS has become something of the poster disease for the entire euthanasia movement.) What they would not have considered was that by acceding to his suicidal desire, they actually would have been robbing him of some of the best years of his life. And no one would have ever known because those years would have been lost to Bob forever.

Recent studies verify Bob's experience. One of the primary reasons that dying people seek euthanasia, according to a study published in *The Lancet* in August 2001, is a sense of "existential isolation."[25] Another study conducted by Bioethics Institute of New York Medical College in 2001, confirmed this conclusion. Dr. Daniel P. Sulmasy followed fifty-eight patients hospitalized for serious illness such as cancer and dementia, and AIDS. The patient's doorways were videotaped for twenty-four-hour periods. Sulmasy found that the patients spent "the vast majority of their time in solitude, with few visits from medical personnel or family members."[26]

The answer to the problems of isolation and abandonment clearly isn't validating the sense of worthlessness that loneliness and boredom engenders. Rather, it is to reintegrate the dying patient into the community, restoring a sense that the patient is one of "us" and not "them."

In this regard, the words of Dennis Brace of Youngstown, Ohio, should also be heeded. Brace, forty-two, was told more than four years ago that his inoperable colon cancer would kill him within a few months. Several doctors told him there was no point in fighting, since his cancer had spread to his muscle tissue.[27] He felt abandoned and alone.

According to Brace, one of the greatest emotional burdens he faced in combating his malady were attitudes like those expressed by Jack Kevorkian, Judge Stephen Reinhardt, Dr. Timothy Quill, and other euthanasia proponents, who in their different ways sent the message that his life was as good as over. "What am I supposed to think when the government or the courts or society says it is okay to snuff people like me out because we are sick?" Brace angrily asked. "If you wanted to push me into giving up, that is how to do it. Any kind of negativism from the outside is devastating to a person in my position. This euthanasia stuff is the opposite of compassion and support. It is saying to me that no one cares."

Like Bob, Dennis Brace lived fully to the last. He cared for his roses, appeared in a video, *Euthanasia: False Light*, and did volunteer work. He died a pain free and dignified death, thanks to the quality hospice and palliative care he received from his friend and doctor Eric M. Chevlen.

CREATING A CULTURE OF COMPASSION

Rejecting the death culture does not mean we should accept the status quo. Quite the contrary. Euthanasia, like a fever, is a symptom, not the disease. To eradicate the symptom, we will have to cure the underlying, unhealthy societal conditions that cause it and take needed steps.

Overcome our death phobia: "People routinely think that doctors know how to prognosticate, how to mitigate pain, and generally how to serve dying persons," Dr. Joanne Lynn told the Senate Finance Committee. "Nothing could be further from the truth. This culture has been so thoroughly death-denying that we have not even described our course to death nor developed professional skills in service of the dying, except for the development of hospice services. . . . We do not know how to see to it that most who die get excellent care, shaped to their needs, and responsive to their symptoms."[28]

"By any standard one chooses," it has been observed, "medical schools in the United States fail to provide even adequate education in the care of the dying."[29] Only five of 126 medical schools in the United States offer a separate required course in the care of the dying. According to the AMA, as of 1995 only 26 percent of residency programs offered, as a regular part of the curriculum, a course on the medical and legal aspects of end-of-life care. A national survey of accredited residency programs in family medicine and internal medicine/pediatrics, the specializations from which primary-care physicians come, revealed that 15 percent of these programs offer no formal training in terminal care and that residents in the majority of these programs coordinated the care of ten or fewer terminally ill patients during the course of their studies. Only 17 percent of these programs use hospice rotations, despite the widespread availability of hospice programs that could be served by the residents and that could teach them. The report summarized this and other data to state that the evidence reveals a "well-established pattern of neglect of medical education in the care of the dying."[30]

People who are dying, disabled, or seriously ill are often abandoned by friends and are isolated by a culture that celebrates youth and vitality and often places cosmetic values ahead of human values. We treat those among us with disabling conditions as unwelcome reminders of our ultimate lack of control over life and of the fact that someday we too will come face to face with our own mortality. This needs to change.

The good news is that calls for more humane treatment of dying people are finally being taken seriously. For example, the Ethics Committee of the American Geriatric Society has produced a nine-point plan to improve the care of the dying, including renewed focus on respecting patient values in treatment decisions; the creation of multidisciplinary teams to treat dying people; more attention to the relief of symptoms with emphasis on pain control; better reimbursement policies for providers of palliative care; and education of doctors and patients on the desirability of a peaceful and natural death when this is desired by the patient rather than a drive for curative care until shortly before death. Those are good suggestions, and hopefully the medical profession will listen and act upon them.

The current and future dying people of America also need to change our attitudes toward death. We should strive to ensure that no one is left to face death alone. Rather than shy away from dying people, as many of us do, we should embrace them, let them know we love and care for them, and that we will be with them to the end. We need to stop avoiding visiting those we know who are ill or dying and should volunteer with hospice or other beneficent organizations that succor the ill and assist the needy.

To give ourselves peace of mind about our own end-of-life care, every adult should create an advance directive stating our preferences about desired medical treatment should we become incapacitated. A caveat is in order here. Advance directives should not be taken lightly. As we have seen, once you fill one out, you may get what you ask for—like it or not. Too often people wait until a hospital admissions clerk gives an advance directive form to them before considering these important issues. Federal law requires that every new patient to a hospital or nursing home be provided an advance directive form to sign, if the patient so desires.

The time to consider your preferences is before incapacitating illness or injury strikes. This brings us back to the concept of informed consent. As we have discussed previously, in our healthcare delivery system patients make healthcare decisions, not doctors. Under the law of informed consent, the doctor is charged with fully advising the patient of the pros and cons of treatment or non-treatment, testing, and the like, and charged with giving opinions. The patient is then free to accept or refuse a doctor's recommendation or get a second opinion or even a different doctor, if that is what the patient desires. This provides a valuable check on the power of doctors, who sometimes make mistakes, and it allows patients to pursue treatment or non-treatment as best fits their personal values and ethical systems.

There are two primary kinds of advance directive, generally known as the "living will" and "durable power of attorney for healthcare" (sometimes called a healthcare proxy). Living wills negate informed consent. Since no one knows the future, by definition their care or non-care instructions must generally be written. Thus, when an incapacitation occurs, the patient's feelings and desires about this specific circumstance may not be known. The living will puts tremendous power into the hands of doctors, who are empowered to decide whether, and when, the living will takes effect, when treatment should be withdrawn or withheld. Moreover, the decision regarding the type, and extent, of medical intervention to be withheld is the doctor's. And this power isn't restricted to "extraordinary care" such as ventilators to assist with breathing, but to any medical intervention—from not treating a curable bacterial infection to withdrawing food and fluids so that the patient starves and dehydrates to death. Thus, with a living will, the check of informed consent is surrendered to medicalized decision making—especially dangerous in HMO settings where doctors may have potent financial incentives to withhold care.

In contrast, with a durable power of attorney for healthcare (DPAHC) the right to informed consent is substantially retained. Why? Rather than appoint a doctor as decider, the DPAHC appoints an "attorney in fact" to be the patient's healthcare decision maker should he or she become incapacitated. The attorney in fact, also known as an agent or a proxy, for all intents and purposes steps into the shoes of the patient and decides issues of treatment or non-treatment as the patient would were he or she able to do so. Like the patient, the proxy can ask questions, request second opinions, or disagree with the doctor's recommendation. The DPAHC also permits people to choose life-prolonging care, an option often unavailable in the language of living wills.

Living wills are analogous to the used car advertised as a cream puff that is really a lemon. In a world of assembly-line medicine where many patients have little interaction with their doctors, isn't it better to eschew a doctor-empowering living will in favor of a patient-empowering durable power of attorney? It's not as catchy a name, but it is a much better document, one that may make the difference between suffering a premature death and receiving personal healthcare decision making, which everyone deserves.

If people are to become confident in the use of advance directives, laws need to be drafted to avoid the problem of denying people requested care if they become technically incompetent, when they have previously written an advance directive in which they refuse care. Michigan already has just such a law. "Under Michigan statutory law, the benefit of the doubt is given to providing lifesaving treatment if there is any expressed desire to receive it," says attorney John Hess, who represented Michael Martin's mother and sister and saved the disabled man's life (described in chapter two). "Even if you are incompetent and, secondly, even if you are unable to participate in general with your own healthcare decisions, as long as you have the ability to communicate a desire to live, it must be honored under the law, regardless of what a previously executed writing says."[31] The Michigan statute is a good model for the rest of the country.

Those who view advance directives as a vehicle for ending the lives of seriously ill or disabled people sooner might squawk that such a law interferes with the purpose for which these legal documents were created. But the purpose of advance directives is not to get sick people to check out, but rather to give them a tool to control their own destinies. People are far more likely to prepare advance directives that request non-treatment (assuming that is their desire) if they know that, in the event that they change their minds, there won't be a futilitarian or HMO executive opposing their newly expressed desire to fight to live.

One last point about advance directives. Most advocacy about signing these important documents stresses refusing care. That doesn't mean you have to go along with the non-treatment agenda. When preparing your advance directive, it is important to remember that you can opt for continued treatment.

Exert better control over HMO*s.* Health care isn't just another industry, like manufacturing computers. While the "invisible hand" of the marketplace might be the best way to assure the manufacture of quality goods at fair prices, it is not necessarily the best way to assure access to quality healthcare, and it can be extremely dangerous for patients—especially if euthanasia and futilitarianism ever become legal.

This book has only touched upon the dangers facing patients in the emerging profit-driven HMO healthcare financing system. In the long run, a system that is open and accessible to everyone, whether through government involvement or the private sector, is a moral and ethical imperative. However that is to be done—I suspect it will be a hybrid private-public approach—the system must be founded on the equality-of-life ethic that protects the lives, and upholds the moral worth, of patients who are expensive to care for properly.

At best, these necessary reforms are years away. For now we are stuck with the managed-care system where profits are made from cutting costs rather than providing care. In such a milieu, we must not permit the weakest and most vulnerable among us to be sacrificed to the bottom line of corporate medicine, whether through assisted suicide or quasi-healthcare rationing promoted by advocates of futile care theory. Here are some ideas I believe can help:

- Prevent insurers and HMOs from giving bonuses and other financial incentives to doctors and nurses for withholding care, improperly limiting hospitalization, refusing referrals to specialists, not writing needed prescriptions, and the like. It is especially imperative that capitation contracts requiring doctors to pay for patient-specialized care out of their own pockets be banned.

- Require safe staffing levels at all healthcare facilities.

- Provide whistle-blower protection for doctors, nurses, and other HMO employees, contract service providers, and other HMO-affiliated caregivers, so that they can report abuses without fear of job sanction.

- Prohibit mandatory arbitration clauses that bar wronged HMO members from taking their cause to the courts.

- If a physician commits malpractice as a result of pressure from HMO policies, allow the HMO to be a defendant in the case.

- Guarantee patients full access to information about their medical care by prohibiting gag rules that prevent doctors from telling the truth about their financial arrangements with the patient's HMO, from criticizing the HMO, or from discussing care that the HMO might not wish to pay for.

- Create nonprofit, HMO member-controlled consumer advocacy groups to serve as HMO watchdogs.

- Set a standard of care such that ninety cents out of every healthcare dollar be spent on patient care rather than on HMO bureaucracies, marketing, profits, or bonuses.

The civil justice system should also be used to deter improper HMO practices. The fear of loss of money can be a great deterrent to improper behavior. If HMOs could be sued for punitive damages (money beyond the actual damages caused) in cases of egregious and willful wrongdoing, the likelihood of their intentionally sacrificing patients to the bottom line would be greatly reduced. Federal legislation may be required to overcome a U.S. Supreme Court decision that prohibited beneficiaries from collecting punitive damages against wrongdoing by health insurance companies if the employee as an employment or union benefit received the insurance.

Consumers and business and union executives in charge of negotiating health insurance contracts for employees or members need to use the power of consumerism to punish "bad" HMOs—those that sacrifice quality of care for profits or put the desires of investors before the healthcare needs of patients—by withholding their business. On the other hand, "good" HMOs that put patient care first should be rewarded with patronage, even if the premiums cost a bit more.

Much is made in the media about the problems associated with HMOs—and properly so. But publicly funded healthcare is not necessarily a panacea—as demonstrated vividly by Oregon's Medicaid rationing scheme. The sad truth is that government funded healthcare systems that struggle with inadequate resources present many of the same dangers to the weak and vulnerable as do the HMO economic model. For example, because of a financial crunch, it was admitted by the Ontario Medical Association in April 2002 that 900,000 Ontario citizens do not have a primary-care physician despite having a legal right to a doctor and that, due to funding issues, Ontario loses 200 doctors a year.[32] Imagine if the people of Canada ever come to see assisted suicide as the answer to their health-funding dilemma. The "right to die" could easily become, under social pressures, a "duty to die."

Make pain control more accessible: If we want to create a truly humane healthcare system that cares for people rather than killing them, pain control must be made universally available. Toward that end, physicians who treat patients in the clinical setting should be required by medical associations and state law to educate themselves on pain-control techniques and other palliative protocols. For pain that average doctors cannot overcome, all HMOs must be required to make referrals to board-certified pain-control experts readily available to plan members without arbitrary restriction, on an as-needed basis. In that way, suffering people such as Rebecca Badger, Jack Kevorkian's thirty-third victim, who stated in a pre-suicide television interview that she would prefer to live if she could escape the pain, would be able to obtain relief without resorting to death peddlers.[33]

We also need to stop making pain sufferers the victims of the war on drugs. Too many states place burdens in the way of doctors in providing adequate pain treatment. For example, many states have rules that require triplicate prescription forms for the dispensation of certain medications, and some state authorities even harass physicians deemed to be too liberal in prescribing certain controlled substances.

One suggestion that requires reasoned consideration is the legalization of marijuana for medicinal purposes. (Several states have legalized "medical marijuana," but in 2001, the Supreme Court of the United States ruled that such laws do not prevent the United States government from enforcing federal laws prohibiting all use of cannabis.) Supporters of legalizing cannabis for medicinal purposes claim that the drug smoked in its natural state (instead of taken as a pill) can ease the suffering of patients with AIDS, cancer, glaucoma, MS, and other afflictions. Since morphine and other drugs are legalized for medicinal purposes, there is little reason to ban marijuana—assuming, of course, that it actually alleviates suffering. Controlled medical studies should be undertaken to determine marijuana's palliative effects on extreme pain associated with different illnesses. The government as soon as possible should authorize this research so that an appropriate public policy can be fashioned.

Improve hospital ethics committees: Hospital ethics committees have tremendous power in today's healthcare delivery system. Yet their membership is anonymous and their meetings are held in secret, leaving tremendous potential for abuse and decision making based on prejudice or incomplete information, as occurred in the Michael Martin and Robert Wendland cases.

"There are no unified standards and no regular performance reviews applied to ethics committees," says Lance K. Stell, MD, PH.D, a medical ethicist with the Department of Internal Medicine at the Carolinas Medical Center in Charlotte, North Carolina. Dr. Stell observes, "It is amazing how often ethics committees make judgments without even seeing the patient or discussing the patient with all concerned parties, including the nursing staff and other caregivers. More than once I have seen a decision made to stop treating a patient and then when I have gone to see the person, I have been appalled."[34]

Dr. Stell tells of one case he personally witnessed where a daughter requested that her mother be taken off a ventilator. Yet when Dr. Stell went to see the patient, the woman "vigorously nodded her head" when he explained her treatment and asked whether she wished to continue indefinitely with assisted breathing. "It turned out the daughter had financial problems and needed money and so she decided the time had come to get her mother out of the way," Dr. Stell told me. "If our ethics committee had been a rubber stamp, and if the surgeon hadn't vigorously opposed the idea, the patient's life might well have been ended. Some ethics committees are rubber stamps, and some doctors are very compliant in these cases."[35]

This concern is especially acute considering the power some futile care protocols are placing in hospital ethics committees. For example, in 2000 the Mercy Health Systems in Philadelphia published their futile care policy that empowers a hospital ethics committee, called an Institutional Interdisciplinary Review Board (IIRB), not only to say no to wanted medical treatment deemed "inappropriate" by a patient's doctor but also to prevent a different doctor from providing the treatment to the patient after a transfer of care.[36] Given that such policies literally give anonymous committees the power over life and death, serious consideration must now be given to preventing ethics committee deliberations from becoming star chambers.

With such potential for abuse against vulnerable (and expensive) patients, the time has come to give serious thought into the proper workings of these committees, their makeup, and the limits that should be placed on their power to impose a health institution's will upon patients and families. What kind of training should ethics committee members receive? (It should definitely be broader and better rounded than "right-to-die" seminars funded by healthcare foundations!) Should deliberations continue to be confidential? Should certifications be required? Should the proceedings of the committees be formalized, recorded, and subject to review? These are important questions for future consideration.

There is something that can be done now. Every ethics committee should take the advice of Diane Coleman, an expert on independent living and a disability-rights activist: Hospitals, HMOs, and other health-care organizations should make every effort to have substantial representation on their ethics committees of people who are disabled and who are knowledgeable about the independent-living movement and other care options for disabled people, which have such power to improve lives. In that way, fear, prejudice, and ignorance about life with disability will be far less likely to be the basis of ethics committees' decision making.

Commit to community. In the end, we will only have as compassionate a society as we, the people, decide individually and collectively to make it. The American people are a woefully undertapped resource in the care equation. There are so many ways to serve one another: as hospice or hospital volunteers, in a service organization that has outreach to marginalized people, through local churches, and individually and as neighbors as needs are identified. If each of us would commit to finding service opportunities and helping fill each other's needs, the feeling of abandonment, hopelessness, despair, and isolation that fuels the euthanasia movement would materially slacken, and with it the temptation to set foot on the slippery slope.

LOSING OUR UBUTU?

Once, when I was recounting some of the events I have written about in this book to my best friend, Arthur Cribbs, he shook his head and said to me, "Man, we are losing our *ubutu*." Art, an African-American, explained to me that *ubutu* is a Zulu word he picked up from a friend who has traveled extensively in Africa. The concept of *ubutu* has no exact English counterpart—the term "soul" is inadequate—but can be roughly translated as being all of the attributes that go into that exquisite spark that makes humankind unique in the known universe.

When we shrugged off the Kevorkian-facilitated deaths of desperate and depressed people, whose suffering could have been substantially alleviated with proper medical treatment and humane care, we were losing our *ubutu*. When the euthanasia policies of the Netherlands are perceived by many as "enlightened" and a model for our own healthcare system—even though they include infanticide and involuntary killing—we are losing our *ubutu*. When we stand by and watch desperately needed healthcare dollars transferred from healthcare delivery into the pockets of profiteers, threatening the well-being of patients, we are losing our *ubutu*. When "philosophers" such as Peter Singer explicitly equate the moral value of the life of a fish with the moral value of the life of a human infant and receive a prestigious appointment to a tenured chair at Princeton University, we are losing our *ubutu*. When courts convey through their rulings and decisions that death is preferable to disability and that the lives of dying, chronically ill, and disabled people are not as worthy of state protection as are the lives of those among us who are young, healthy, and vital, we are losing our *ubutu*. When the "right to die" has more resonance among much of the public than protecting the right to live, we are, without doubt, losing our *ubutu*.

And yet our *ubutu* may be vanishing, but it is not lost. We remain a caring and compassionate people. Indeed, death fundamentalists exploit those very attributes. And it will be these attributes—essential ingredients of *ubutu*—that will, in the end, restore us to a more humane and enlightened course.

A good step toward reclaiming *ubutu* is the Missoula Demonstration Project, the brainchild of Dr. Ira Byock, in Missoula, Montana. Under the direction of its executive director, the gerontologist Barbara K. Spring, PH.D, the project is restoring community to people approaching the end of their lives. "People who are dying tend to become isolated," Dr. Byock says. "We are changing that. We are committed to restoring a sense of belonging."[37]

The project is involving the whole city in a non-medical approach to these important issues. Under the direction of the project, workers are setting up intergenerational programs such as combining day care for children with care for the elderly. Discussions are held in schools, churches, among civic groups, and in healthcare facilities to teach people that dying is a natural part of living and that caring for terminally ill people is a life-enhancing experience.

Dying people also receive the message that they are important members of the community. Their life histories are recorded, and the tapes are available in the local library. They are helped to come to terms with their fears with support groups and innovative approaches such as art therapy.

"The intent behind the project," Dr. Byock says, "is to show what truly 'dying well' can mean and to demonstrate that one's life is not over because a terminal prognosis is given. Dying is a very scary, extraordinary time of life that requires adjustments and changes in expectations. But so do other times of change, such as marriage, having a child, or losing a spouse. What I have seen and know to be true is that people can exert a sense of mastery over this stage of life."[38]

Can dying really be a meaningful time in life, as Dr. Byock asserts? Dr. Maurice Victor certainly believes that such a time of life has tremendous potential. "Once pain and depression are treated," he says, "there is gratification to be obtained simply from living. I have talked with survivors of concentration camps who experienced as extreme suffering as can be imagined. One woman put it very well: Life matters. Just to have the opportunity to spend a boring evening at home is worth everything. There is so much pleasure to be gotten merely from the simple routines: getting coffee in the morning, reading the morning paper, planning the little errands of the day, so much pleasure to be derived from the most inconsequential type of things, from what some call a boring life. It comes from within."[39] That is exactly how life became for my friend Bob.

Dr. Victor sees euthanasia as antithetical to living a meaningful life in its end stage. "I am dreadfully offended by the whole notion," he says. "Euthanasia replaces the importance of life and replaces it with an impersonal, crass discarding of sick people on the ash heap. It is anathema to true compassion and care."[40]

Let us wish the Missoula Project and its blend of hospice, community education, and outreach well and hope that it serves as a guide in transforming dying from the too often lonely and isolated experience it is now into an event centered in the love and involvement of the entire community, the way it should be. If we care enough about each other to accomplish this task, we will have transformed isolation into inclusion, abandonment into an embrace, indifference into love—dying into an event steeped in *ubutu*. Do that, Dr. Byock firmly believes, and we will make assisted suicide and euthanasia superfluous, whether it becomes legal or not.

We don't have to be part of the hospice movement or engaged in the euthanasia debate to make a real difference in the lives of suffering and dying people. We have that opportunity even with virtual strangers. I recall my former law partner, Jack A. Rameson iii, of Woodland Hills, California, who many years ago taught me a lesson in compassion and dignity that I have never forgotten. Jack is an estate planner. We went out to a hospital to visit a woman who was dying of brain cancer, so she could sign her will.

As Rameson was explaining the will-signing process to her, she suddenly became ill. Now, there are those who would say throwing up in front of strangers is undignified. But dignity depends, does it not, on how others react to the afflicted person? In this case, Rameson transformed what could have been a disturbing and perhaps humiliating moment for our client into one overflowing with *ubutu*. He immediately ran to her side, gently held her head as she was in the act of being sick, so she would not soil her bedclothes. When she was finished he took a damp cloth, wiped her face and brow, gave her a cup of water, and, when she felt better, we went on with our business as if nothing had happened. That kind of outreaching love is the essence of community. It erases indignity. It welcomes those in need of assistance as vital parts of the community's life, as people of inherent value and worth.

Then there is the kind and loving care shown by my friend Tom Lorentzen as he intimately participated in his mother's death, not by mixing her a poison brew and hastening her end, but as a loving and caring son who valued and welcomed her in each moment of her natural life. And in that caring he found himself comforted and transformed:

> In July of 1990, my mother was diagnosed with early-stage kidney failure. I said, "Mom, I hope you will be okay." She responded by saying, "If I need you, I know you will know what to do." This statement was different from anything she bad ever said to me before. I sensed change and I shed a tear.

In November 1991 Mom's condition worsened, and she was placed in the hospital. I left Washington, D.C., my job, my girl-friend, and my dog behind, and rushed to her side. I sensed that my life had taken a dramatically different path, that I would not be soon in returning.

During the next seven months, I took care of my mother at home, cooking her meals, doing laundry, cleaning house, working at a job I was fortunate to obtain in San Francisco during the day. Leaving home at six in the morning, I would call her during the day to make sure she was all right.

She was in and out of the hospital until June of 1992, when the doctor told me she was dying. Together, we informed her, as I sat on the bed holding her hand. I watched her eyes change as the message was received. She looked at me with an expression that only Shakespeare could adequately describe. She then turned to the doctor, and with her New York. sense of humor, said, "Thanks a lot!"

We revisited the possibility of kidney dialysis with the doctor. She asked two questions: Would it hurt? The doctor said there would be some discomfort and explained why. She then asked, "Will it give me strength?" The doctor explained that it would for a day or so, and then she would have to undergo another treat-ment.

With that, she gently shook her head and said, "No." I saw tears form in the doctor's eyes.

For ten days I stayed in the hospital room with her, leaving only to shave, shower, and change clothes. At night, I would sleep on the bed with her, holding her in my arms. During that time I smelled the aroma of her hair and daydreamed about what her life had been like from the time she was born. A strange and comfort-ing sense of peace dominated my essence, as I held her like a child in my arms.

As my mother was traveling through the dying process, the intimacy of death became shared between us. She shared her love with others who visited the room.

As the end grew very near, gangrene began to set in, caused by her kidney failure. Mom required morphine to ease the pain, which she received during the last two to three days. At one point, I said to the doctor, "I can't believe I am saying this, but I hope she dies sooner rather than later." He and I agreed that we would do nothing to prolong her dying and that no treatment would be given to keep her going. We also agreed that she would receive sufficient pain medication to ensure that she felt no discomfort. I told him that I hoped she would die in my arms.

On the tenth day of her hospitalization, I awoke at four AM and noticed my mom fixing her hair. I moved to the reclining chair and awoke at six-thirty. Mom was lying quietly in bed. As I stirred, she asked, "Tom, are you still here?" I said, "Yes, Mom. Don't worry. Everything is all right." "Okay," she said—her last words.

A little while later, I looked down at her as the morning sun was beginning to illuminate the room. Her breathing was barely observable. I lay on the bed and took her in my arms. As I did, her breathing gently stopped.

Tears immediately covered my face. In addition, two feelings simultaneously dominated my being. The most powerful was a sense of loss. Immediately overriding it, however, was a sense of enrichment. We had done everything we could to save her life. I had done everything I could to take care of her and give her life value, and to make sure that she was cared for and loved during her dying, temporarily giving up on my life to take care of her when she needed me most. My wish had been granted that she die in my arms.

My reward was a deepening of our love and a tightening of our friendship. I knew that I had gained the greatest wealth that can be achieved in life. By participating in the natural dying process with a loved one in the most intimate, loving, and caring manner possible, I had become enriched beyond anything I ever expected in life. What I am now, what I will always be, will stem from this experience. I am a very fortunate and lucky person.[41]

A TIME TO CHOOSE

As we chart the early years of the new millennium, we are at a cross-roads that forces us to choose between two mutually exclusive value systems. Will we remain on the trail that leads ultimately to the full realization of the equality-of-human-life ethic and with it the tremendous potential for the creation of a true community, or do we take a hard turn down the slippery slope toward a coarsening of our views of the afflicted, the dying, the chronically ill, the disabled, and those in pain or depression, to the point where we feel they have a duty to die and get out of the way? To put it more bluntly: Will we choose the road of inclusion and caregiving for all, including the weakest and most vulnerable among us, or that of exclusion and ever-expanding killing opportunities? More simply yet: Will we choose to love each other or abandon each other? The bottom line: Will we keep or lose our *ubutu*?

The two paths that lie before us, the death culture or the struggle toward a truly caring community, lead to dramatically different futures. The choice is ours. So will be the society we create.

Resources

Sources of information about euthanasia from an opposition standpoint.

GENERAL

International Task Force on Euthanasia and Assisted Suicide
P.O. Box 760
Steubenville, OH 43952
740-282-3810
www.iaetf.org

800-958-5678 for ordering materials such as the PMDD, the video *Euthanasia: False Light,* and the book *Power Over Pain: How to Get The Pain Control You Need,* by Eric M. Chevlen, MD, and Wesley J. Smith.

The Task Force is the primary international source of information and background material on euthanasia, assisted suicide, and related health-care issues. Among its activities, the Task Force:

- Provides information for radio, television, and print journalists
- Maintains an extensive and up-to-date library devoted solely to the issues surrounding euthanasia
- Upon request, prepares analyses of pending legislation
- Analyzes the probable impact of policies considered and/or adopted by medical, legal, and social work organizations

- Provides speakers for local and national radio and television programs, and for major international bioethical conferences
- Files amicus curiae briefs in major "right to die" cases
- Publishes position papers and fact sheets on euthanasia and related issues
- Prepares and provides specialized materials for health-care professionals, attorneys, ethicists, and for students ranging from middle school through graduate school
- Conducts training in effective communication of issues related to euthanasia, assisted suicide, death, and dying
- Provides information and assistance to individuals and groups regarding resources for medically vulnerable individuals and caregivers
- Publishes the bimonthly *Update* and maintains an informative Website
- Networks with individuals and organizations on five continents

Individuals and groups who network with the Task Force have a common concern about the threat of euthanasia but hold differing views on other public policy issues.

Physicians for Compassionate Care
P.O. Box 6042
Portland, OR 97228-6042
(503) 533-8154
Fax: (503) 533-0429
www.pccef.org

Physicians for Compassionate Care is an association of physicians and other health professionals dedicated to preserving the traditional relation of the physician and patient as one in which the physician's primary task is to heal the patient and to minimize pain. The association promotes the health and well-being of patients by encouraging physicians to comfort patients and to assist those who are dying by support systems, minimizing pain, and treating depression. The association affirms the health-restoring role of the physician and works to educate the profession and the public to the dangers of euthanasia and physician-assisted suicide and the inherent value of human life.

Not Dead Yet
7521 Madison Street
Forest Park, IL 60130
(708) 209-1500
Fax: (708) 209-1735
www.notdeadyet.org

Not Dead Yet is a national disability-rights group in the U.S. that actively opposes legalization of assisted suicide and euthanasia. Although 10 other national disability-rights groups also oppose legalization, NDY is the acknowledged leader of this community's opposition. NDY has also been involved in fighting against the starvation deaths of people with cognitive disabilities. In addition to traditional forms of political advocacy work, NDY also uses nonviolent confrontation and civil disobedience when the organization considers it necessary.

Euthanasia Prevention Coalition (Canada)
Box 25033
London, ON N6C 6A8
Canada
(519) 439-3348
Toll Free: 877-439-3348
Fax: (519) 439-7053
www.epcc.ca

The Euthanasia Prevention Coalition was established to prepare a well-informed, broadly based, network of groups and individuals who support measures that will create an effective social barrier to euthanasia and assisted suicide.

The EPC provides research, information, and speakers, advocates on behalf of the vulnerable, and works to maintain the current legal prohibitions against euthanasia and assisted suicide.

Compassionate Healthcare Network (Canada)
11563 Baily Cres
Surrey, BC V3V 2V4
Canada
Tel: (604) 582 3844
Fax: (604) 582 3844
E-mail: chn@intergate.ca
www.chninternational.com

The Compassionate Healthcare Network (CHN) is a not-for-profit international anti-euthanasia network formed in 1992. CHN consists of both professional and lay people concerned with the crisis that medicine and healthcare are experiencing. CHN opposes euthanasia by actively defending the inherent value of all human life. CHN's work comprises a network of people who provide speakers and workshops, research data pertaining to euthanasia, assisted suicide, and palliative care to professionals, students, churches, the government, lay organizations, and individuals.

ALERT (Great Britain)
27 Walpole St.
London, SW3 4QS
Great Britain
Phone: 020-7730-2800
Fax: 020-7730-0710
E-mail: alert@donoharm.org.uk
www.donoharm.org.uk/alert

ALERT was founded in 1991 to provide well-documented information on euthanasia, assisted suicide, and related issues, and to defend the lives and rights of the medically vulnerable.

National Conference of Catholic Bishops
Attn: Richard Doerflinger,
Deputy Director of the Secretariat for Pro-Life Activities
3211 4th St., NE
Washington DC 20017
(202) 541-3000
www.nccbuscc.org/prolife/index.htm

New York State Task Force on Life and the Law
5 Penn Plaza
New York, NY 10001-1803
(212) 613-4303
www.health.state.ny.us

HOSPICE, PAIN CONTROL, AND PALLIATION

Agency for Health Care Policy and Research (AHCPR)
P.O. Box 8547
Silver Spring, MD 20907-8547
(800) 358-9295

This agency of the Department of Health and Human Services publishes many patient guides on topics of pain control and palliation that are available free of charge.

The National Hospice and Palliative Care Organization
1700 Diagonal Road, Suite 300

Alexandria, VA 22314
Phone (800) 658-8898
E-mail: info@nhpco.org
www.nhpco.org

Helpline phone number helps the general public locate a hospice anywhere in the country at no charge. Can also e-mail for general questions about hospice or location of a hospice.

American Academy of Hospice and Palliative Medicine
4700 W. Lake Ave.
Glenview, IL 60025-1485
(847)375-4712
Fax: (847)375-6312
E-mail: aahpm@aahpm.org
www.aahpm.org

Originally organized as the Academy of Hospice Physicians in 1988, the American Academy of Hospice and Palliative Medicine (AAHPM) is the only organization in the United States for physicians dedicated to the advancement of hospice/palliative medicine, its practice, research and education.

American Chronic Pain Association
P.O. Box 850
Rocklin, CA 95677
(916) 632-0922
www.theacpa.org

The ACPA offers support and information for people with chronic pain.

American Pain Foundation
201 N. Charles Street, Suite 710
Baltimore, Maryland 21201
www.painfoundation.com

A non-profit organization dedicated to providing information, advocacy, and education about the treatment of pain.

Amyotrophic Lateral Sclerosis (ALS) Association
21021 Ventura Blvd., Suite 321
Woodland Hills, CA 91364
(800) 782-4747
www.alsa.org

The ALS Association is the only national non-profit voluntary health organization dedicated solely to the fight against ALS. Its mission is to find a cure for amyotrophic lateral sclerosis and to improve living with ALS.

Independent Living Resource Utilization Training Center
2323 S. Shepherd St., Suite 1000
Houston, TX 77019
(713) 520-0232
www.ilru.org
The ILRU offers information about the independent-living movement, and provides the addresses and phone numbers of an independent-living center near you or one you love.

National Multiple Sclerosis Association
706 Haddonfield Rd
Cherry Hill, NJ 08002
(800) 532-7667
www.msaa.com
Offers information for patients and families about MS.

National Spinal Cord Injury Association
6701 Democracy Blvd., Suite 300
Bethesda, MD 20817
(800) 962-9629
www.spinalcord.org
The NSCIA offers information about spinal-cord injury and referral services and access to support groups.

United Cerebral Palsy Foundation
1660 L St. NW

Suite 700
Washington DC 20036
(800) 872-5827
www.ucp.org
The UCPF offers a referral service and information about interventions, patient and
family support, assisted technology, and employment.

BOOKS

These books are excellent sources for those who wish to learn more about the topics
discussed in this book.

Ira Byock, MD, *Dying Well: The Prospect for Growth at the End of Life*, (1997, Riverdale
Books, New York, NY). This moving and important book, written by the past president of the American Academy of Hospice and Palliative Medicine, illustrates the
beneficence of hospice and the quality of life available for dying people when they are
properly cared for and valued. If all dying persons were as well cared for as were the
patients whose stories are recounted in this book, the assisted suicide movement would
wither on the vine.

Kathleen Foley and Herbert Hendin (eds.) *The Case Against Assisted Suicide: For the
Right to End-of-Life Care*, (2002, Johns Hopkins University Press, Baltimore, MD).
This book of essays written by some of the world's most eminent secular opponents of
assisted suicide and experts in end-of-life and palliative care, makes a compelling case
against the euthanasia movement and in favor of hospice and palliative care. An excellent resource for persons involved in advocating about the issues addressed.

Herbert Hendin, MD, *Seduced by Death: Doctors, Patients and the Dutch Cure* (1997,
W.W. Norton, New York, NY). The noted psychiatrist may be the world's foremost
expert on Dutch euthanasia. Hendin provides a detailed and disturbing account about
what has gone wrong with Dutch medical ethics and the horrors that have resulted
from that nation's acceptance of euthanasia.

Eric Chevlen, MD and Wesley J. Smith, *Power over Pain: How to Get the Pain Control
You Need* (2002, International Task Force on Euthanasia and Assisted Suicide,
Steubenville, OH). Written by a noted pain-control specialist physician and the author
of *Forced Exit*, *Power Over Pain* is a consumer's guide to obtaining quality pain control
designed as a readable and understandable tool to help pain patients and their families
obtain optimal pain control.

Wesley J. Smith, *Culture of Death: The Assault on Medical Ethics in America* (2001,

Encounter Books, San Francisco, CA). The author of *Forced Exit* looks deeply into the bioethics movement and discovers that assisted suicide is just the tip of the iceberg. *Culture of Death* was named Best Health Book of the Year at the 2001 Independent Publisher's Book Awards.

Jack Kevorkian, MD, *Prescription Medicide: The Goodness of a Planned Death* (1991, Prometheus Books, Buffalo, NY). Jack Kevorkian is not and never was a "retired physician who helped terminally ill people commit suicide," as he is often described in the media. Learn the truth about his chilling and macabre agenda in his own words.

Robert Jay Lifton, *The Nazi Doctors: Medical Killing and the Psychology of Genocide* (1996, Basic Books, New York, NY). An excellent source for learning about the participation of German doctors in the Holocaust and how the values that led to the killing of hundreds of thousands of disabled persons between 1939-1945 are alive and well in the contemporary euthanasia movement.

Rita Marker, *Deadly Compassion: The Death of Ann Humphry and the Truth About Euthanasia*, (1993, William Morrow, New York, NY). This book, by the executive director of the International Task Force on Euthanasia and Assisted Suicide, had a tremendous influence on my decision to advocate against euthanasia and assisted suicide. Marker recounts the tragic story of the Hemlock Society's cofounder Ann Wicket: how she was abandoned by her husband Derek Humphry when she was diagnosed with breast cancer, and the reasons Wicket turned against the death culture before committing suicide.

Joseph P. Shapiro, *No Pity: People with Disabilities Forging a New Civil Rights Movement* (1993, Times Books, New York, NY). An excellent account of the prejudice faced by people with disabilities and the empowering potential of the independent-living movement.

Peter Singer, *Rethinking Life and Death: The Collapse of Our Traditional Ethics*, (1994, St. Martin's Press, New York, NY). Singer, an icon of the bioethics movement, is more candid than most euthanasia advocates about where the death culture would take us. He promotes the destruction of the "sanctity of life" ethic in favor of a "quality of life" approach in which euthanasia, assisted suicide, and infanticide would play vital parts.

Derek Humphry and Mary Clement, *Freedom to Die: People, Politics, and the Right-to-Die Movement* (1998, St. Martin's Press, New York, NY). Humphry and Clement give the euthanasia movement's perspective about the so-called right to die. The book isn't noteworthy except for its admission that in the end, euthanasia and assisted suicide will be about money.

ADVANCE MEDICAL DIRECTIVES

The American Medical Association, the American Bar Association, and the American Association of Retired Persons worked together to create a very detailed power of attorney that covers just about all circumstances, including whether you want food and fluids under specified conditions. To obtain the AMA/ABA/AARP Durable Power of Attorney for Health Care, contact:

AARP
601 E St., NW
Washington, DC 20049
(800) 424-3410
www.aarp.org

The International Task Force on Euthanasia and Assisted Suicide publishes a power of attorney for health care that is often state-specific, called the Protective Medical Decision Document (PMDD). The PMDD empowers a healthcare proxy to make treatment and non-treatment decisions while prohibiting the proxy from agreeing to medical actions that are directly intended to cause death. The proxy you name in your PMDD has the authority to make the same medical decisions you could make if you were able to do so. Your proxy may also approve a DNR (do not resuscitate) order or a "no aggressive treatment" order. He or she may determine that surgery, ventilator support, or other interventions should be provided, withheld, or withdrawn. However the PMDD specifically denies your proxy the authority to approve of any *direct and intentional* ending of your life. For more information on the PMDD, contact the International Task Force at the address and phone number provided earlier in this resource section.

Like a will or a trust, an advanced directive is a legal document and should be treated as such. The laws of each state differ regarding their preparation and contents. A few states require specific language not used in the forms mentioned here. It is a good idea to have your attorney review any advance directive you sign, or prepare yours on the basis of your instructions and desires. To find an attorney who knows the ins and outs of the laws concerning advance directives, contact your local bar association and ask for a lawyer who specializes in "elder law." Or contact:

National Academy of Elder Law Attorneys (NAELA)
1604 N. Country Club Rd.
Tucson, AZ 85716
(520) 881-4005
www.naela.com

Notes

Introduction

1 "A Peaceful Passing," *Hemlock Quarterly* 30 (January 1988).
2 Ibid., 7.
3 Ibid., 6.
4 Ibid., 4-5.
5 Derek Humphry, "Self-Deliverance with Certainty," *Hemlock Quarterly* 30 (January 1988).
6 Ibid., 4.
7 "Suicide Rate Among Elderly."
8 Wesley J. Smith, "The Whispers of Strangers," *Newsweek*, June 28, 1993.
9 Ibid.
10 Personal correspondence, June 24, 1993.
11 Personal correspondence, June 30, 1993.
12 Personal correspondence June 29, 1993.
13 Personal correspondence, June 24, 1993.
14 Personal correspondence, August 23, 1993.
15 Personal correspondence, June 29, 1993.
16 Personal correspondence, June 23, 1993.
17 Personal correspondence, July 7, 1993.
18 Ibid.
19 Personal correspondence, June 24, 1993.
20 Smith, "Whispers of Strangers."
21 Ann Landers, "One Eighty-Five-Year-Old's Old Age Solution," *St. Louis Post Dispatch*, October 3, 1993.

22   Margaret E. Hall, ed. *Selected Writings of Benjamin Nathan Cardozo*, (New York: Fallon Publications, 1947), 388.

1. Death Fundamentalism

1   Stephanie Gutmann, "Death and the Maiden," *New Republic*, January 24, 1996, 24.
2   "Kevorkian Patient Was on Halcyon," *Detroit News*, November 3, 1991.
3   At the time of the Wantz and Miller killings, Michigan did not prohibit assisted suicide by statute. On the basis of previous court rulings, the Michigan Supreme Court later ruled that assisted suicide was a crime.
4   Wes Allison, "Study: Kevorkian Patients Weren't Dying," *St. Petersberg Times*, December 8, 2000.
5   "Attitudes Toward Euthanasia Sharply Divided, Survey Finds," Reuters, June 29, 1996.
6   Andrew Coyne, "The Slippery Slope That Leads to Death," *Globe and Mail* (Toronto), November 21, 1994.
7   At this writing there are two exceptions to this general rule: Oregon, which legalized assisted suicide in 1994, and the Netherlands, which has permitted euthanasia since 1973, formally legalizing the practice in 2001.
8   Derek Humphry, Letters to the Editor, *New York Times Magazine*, August 11, 1996.
9   James L. Werth, "Using Rational Suicide as an Intervention to Prevent Irrational Suicide," *Crisis*, 19:4 (1998).
10   Elliot D. Cohen, Ph.D, "Permitted Suicide: Model Rules for Mental Health Counseling," *Journal of Mental Health Counseling*, 23:4 (October 2001), 279-294.
11   Arthur Caplan, "System Messed Up, Hands Down," *Oakland Tribune*, May 31, 1996.
12   Jack Lessenberry, "Physician Assisted Suicide Is a Constitutional Right," in Carol Wekesser, ed., *Euthanasia: Opposing Viewpoints* (San Diego: Greenhaven Press, 1995), 91.
13   Matthew Rothchild, interview with author, June 6, 1996.
14   Dr. I. van der Sluis, interview with author, October 14, 1995.
15   Michael Vitez, "Right-to-Die Activists Study New Methods," *Philadelphia Inquirer*, November 12, 1999.
16   Advertisement published by the Right to Die Network of Canada. Emphasis in original.
17   "Euthanasia Sets Sail," interview with Philip Nitschke, *National Review Online*, June 5, 2001.
18   "They Go to War, They Can Vote, So Why Can't Teenagers Read about Suicide Pill? Asks Nitschke," *Sydney Morning Herald*, August 11, 2001.

19   Mark Hosenball, "The Real Jack Kevorkian," *Newsweek*, December 6, 1993.

20   Jack Lessenberry, "Death Becomes Him," *Vanity Fair*, July 1994, 106.

21   Hosenball, "The Real Jack Kevorkian."

22   Jack Kevorkian, *Prescription Medicide: The Goodness of a Planned Death* (Buffalo: Prometheus Books, 1991), 211.

23   Ibid., 43. Emphasis in original.

24   Ibid., 214.

25   *Report of the University of Rochester Medical Center Task Force on Physician-Assisted Suicide* (Rochester, NY: University of Rochester, 1993), 5.

26   "Wait, An Alternative to Assisted Dying," *Patient Care*, May 30, 1994.

27   Derek Humphry and Mary Clement, *Freedom to Die: People, Politics and The Right to Die Movement* (New York. St. Martin's Press, 1998), 333.

28   Andrew Solomon, "A Death of One's Own," *New Yorker*, May 22, 1995.

29   Dr. Eric Chevlen, interview with author, September 6, 1996.

30   Lonny Shavelson, *A Chosen Death: The Dying Confront Assisted Suicide* (New York, Simon and Schuster, 1995).

31   Ibid., 75.

32   Ibid., 92.

33   Ibid., 93.

34   Ibid., 94.

35   Ibid, 93-94.

36   Lonny Shavelson, interview with author, June 19, 1996.

37   Lonny Shavelson, personal communication, at the studio of KQED-FM, San Francisco, March 14, 1996.

38   Shavelson, *A Chosen Death*, 94

39   Shavelson author interview.

40   Peter Singer, *Rethinking Life and Death: The Collapse of Our Traditional Ethics* (New York: St. Martin's Press, 1995).

41   Wesley J. Smith, *Culture of Death: The Assault on Medical Ethics in America* (San Francisco: Encounter Books, 2000).

42   Ibid., 213-214.

43   Daniel J. Kevles, "We All Must Die: Who Can Tell Us When?" *New York Times*, May 7, 1995.

44   Scott Judd, book review of *Rethinking Life and Death*, *Hemock Timelines*, May–June 1995, 10.

45   Ralph Mero, "Executive Director's Report," *Compassion in Dying Newsletter*, No. 4 (1995), 2. Emphasis in original.

46   Lisa Belkin, "There's No Such Thing as a Simple Suicide," *New York Times Magazine*, November 14, 1993, cited hereafter as "No Simple Suicide."

47   Ann Landers, "When Taking Your Own Life Makes Sense," *San Francisco Examiner*, February 6, 1994.

48 Ibid., 53.

49 Harvey Max Chochinov, et al., "Will to Live in the Terminally Ill," *The Lancet*, 354 (September 4, 1999): 816-19.

50 Herbert Hendin, "Selling Death and Dignity," *Hastings Center Report*, May-June 1995, 22.

51 Ibid.

52 Belkin, "No Simple Suicide," 74.

53 Ibid.

54 Ibid., 75.

55 Ibid., 63, 74.

56 Ibid., 50.

57 Hendin, "Selling Death and Dignity," 22.

58 On June 10, 1996, I telephoned the Washington State office of Compassion in Dying seeking comment from Ralph Mero. I was informed by Barbara Coombs Lee, now the executive director of the Compassion in Dying Federation, that Mero was no longer with the organization. She refused to tell me where I could reach Mero but promised to pass on the message to him along with my phone number. I never heard from Mero thereafter.

59 "Crick Forced to Die: Campaigner," *The Australian*, May 24, 2002.

60 Darren Gray, "Doctor Poses Doubts on Crick Suicide," *The Age*, May 27, 2002.

61 Australian Associated Press, "Nitschke: Right-to-Die Civil Disobedience Has Begun," as published in *The Age*, May 23, 2002.

62 "Diary Records Cancer Doubt," *Herald Sun*, May 27, 2002.

63 Reuters, "Australia Euthanasia Doctor Rejects Cancer Doubts," May 25, 2002.

64 Chris Griffith, Paula Doneman, and Hedley Thomas, "Crick Told She Wasn't Dying," *Herald Sun*, May 29, 2002.

65 "Crick Forced to Die: Campaigner."

2. *Disposable People*

1 I have changed Sally's name to protect her family's privacy.

2 Sharon S. Orr, interview with author, April 2, 1996.

3 Medical records of Robert Wendland, a nurse's note to the chart dated July 25, 1995.

4 *In re Conservatorship of Robert Wendland* (Case No. 65669 Superior Court of California, County of San Joaquin), testimony of Rose Wendland, September 5, 1995.

5 Jon Dann, Producer, "A Matter of Life and Death," KRON-TV (San Francisco) News, November 6, 1995.

6 *Wendland* (Superior Court), testimony of various witnesses.

7 *Wendland* (Superior Court), declaration of Florence Wendland, July 12, 2001.

8 Margaret Goodman, San Joaquin County Ombudsman assigned to Robert Wendland, interview with author, September 5, 1995.

9   *Wendland* (Superior Court), testimony of Margaret Goodman, September 5, 1995.
10   Janie Hickock Siess, interview with author, June 23, 1995.
11   *Wendland* (Superior Court), testimony of Dr. Ronald Kass, September 5, 1995.
12   Much was made of this aspect of the case by the California Supreme Court, where the case was ultimately decided. See *Conservatorship of Wendland*, 26 Cal. 4th 519 (2001).
13   Richard John Neuhaus, "The Return of Eugenics," *Commentary* (April 1988), 19.
14   For a more detailed description of the threat posed to the equality of life ethic by the bioethics movement, see Smith, *Culture of Death*.
15   At this point, it is important to make a crucial distinction between cognitively disabled patients receiving tube-supplied food and fluids and actively dying people. The cases I write about in this chapter concern the former, people who are profoundly cognitively disabled and whose tube-supplied food and fluids are removed for subjective, non-medical "quality of life" considerations. There are other patients, however, who as part of the dying process quit eating as their organs shut down. This is a natural process. It would be medically inappropriate—not to mention pointless and cruel—to force nutrition and hydration into these actively dying patients.
16   American Medical Association Council on Ethical and Judicial Affairs, "Opinion 2.15," 1986. Emphasis added.
17   See, for example, Geoffrey E. Pence, *Classic Cases in Medical Ethics*, 2nd ed. (New York: McGraw Hill, 1995), 17.
18   *Cruzan v. Harmon and Lampkins*, Case No. CV384-9, Circuit Court of Jasper County, Missouri, transcript for March 9, 1988.
19   *Nancy Beth Cruzan v. Robert Harmon* et al., 760 SW 2nd 408, Nov. 1988. Emphasis added.
20   *Cruzan v. Director, Missouri Department of Health*, 110 Supreme Court 2841, 1990.
21   Dianne Gianelli, "Major Figure in Right to Die Debate Dies," *American Medical News*, September 2, 1996.
22   Scott Canon, "New Right to Die Case Goes to Court," *Kansas City Star*, January 6, 1991.
23   Ibid.
24   Sharon Orr interview.
25   Theresa Tighe, "State Releases Videotape of Busalacchi, Patient Appears to Be Responsive," *St. Louis Post Dispatch*, February 5, 1991.
26   Dann, "A Matter of Life and Death."
27   Wesley J. Smith, "Creating a Disposable Caste," *San Francisco Chronicle*, December 8, 1995.
28   American Medical Association Council on Ethics and Judicial Affairs, "Opinion 2:20," 1994.
29   Dr. William Burke, interview with author, 1996.
30   *Wendland*, (Superior Court), trial testimony of Dr. Ronald Cranford.

31 *Wendland* (Superior Court), transcript of Cranford Deposition, May 7, 1996.

32 *Wendland* (Superior Court), Cranford trial testimony.

33 Dr. Vincent Fortanasce, interview with author, Jan. 9, 1995.

34 Fortanasce interview.

35 *In re Correan Salter*, Case No. CV-94-160, Circuit Court, Baldwin County, Alabama.

36 This depiction is based on Ronald Comeau's medical records, deposited with the court, which the author reviewed, and on interviews with most of the participants in the Ronald Comeau case.

37 Amy Swisher, interview with author, Jan. 11. 1994.

38 *In re Guardianship of Ronald Comeau*, Bennington Probate Court, 1993, Findings and Order of the Court, court transcript, Aug. 17, 1993.

39 Joseph Schaaf, interview with author, Jan. 11, 1994.

40 Comeau medical records.

41 Schaff interview.

42 Comeau medical records.

43 Dr. Peter Zorach, interview with author, Jan. 12, 1994.

44 Stephen L. Saltonstall, interview with author, Jan. 12, 1994.

45 *In re Guardianship of Ronald Comeau*, Findings and Order of Court, court transcript, November 9, 1993.

46 Rev. Mike McHugh, interview with author, January 10, 1994.

47 Ibid.

48 Saltonstall interview.

49 "To Live or Die," editorial, *Rutland Herald*, November 18, 1993.

50 Jack Hoffman, "Vermont Press Fails to Take a Stand," *Rutland Herald*, November 18, 1993.

51 John Howland Jr., "Wonderful or Ruthless: Some Question Motives That Guide Michael McHugh," *Burlington Free Press*, November 22, 1993.

52 Mike Donoghue, "Dad: Keep Comatose Son Alive," *Burlington Free Press*, November 19, 1993.

53 Renald Comeau, interview with author, January 14, 1993.

54 Patricia Comeau, interview with author, May 9, 1996.

55 Schaaf interview.

56 Renald Comeau interview.

57 Medical Records of Michael Martin, New Medico Neurological Center of Michigan, Speech-Language Pathology Daily Treatment Notes, December 7, 1992.

58 Ibid.

59 Medical Records of Michael Martin, New Medico Neurological Center of Michigan, Augmentation Evaluation Summary, April 19, 1992.

60 *In re Michael Martin*, Michigan Court of Appeals, Docket No. 161431, Judge Grieg's observations of Martin, attached to the appeal brief, court transcript, 12-16.

61 John H. Hess, J.D., "Looking for Traction on the Slippery Slope," *Issues of Law and Medicine*, 11:2, 105-22. Hess and his brother were the lawyers for Michael Martin's mother and sister.

62 Butterworth Hospital Ethics Committee, correspondence to Mary Martin, January 15,1992.

63 Hess, "Looking for Traction," 107-108.

64 *In re Michael Martin*, 504 NW 2d, 917 (Michigan Appellate, April 1993).

65 "Mary, Mary, Quite Contrary, How Was I to Know? Michael Martin, Absolute Prescience, and the Right to Die in Michigan," *University of Detroit Mercy Law Review* 27 (1996): 828, 832.

66 Ibid. Emphasis added.

67 *In re Conservatorship of Wendland*, 78 Cal. Ap 4th 517.

68 *Wendland* (Superior Court) trial testimony of Dr. Ronald Cranford.

69 *Wendland* (Superior Court) trial testimony of Dr, Ernest Bryant.

70 *In re the Conservatorship of Robert Wendland*, Court of Appeals, Third Appellate District, Case no Civil C-029439, "Appellant Robert Wendland's Opening Brief," 30.

71 *Conservatorship of Robert Wendland*, "Respondent's Opening Brief on the Merits," in the Supreme Court of California, Case No. S 087265, 29.

72 *In re Guardianship of Theresa Marie Schiavo*, Circuit Court for Pinellas County, Florida, Probate Division, File No. 90-2908GD-003.

3. *Everything Old Is New Again*

1 "A New Ethic for Medicine and Society," editorial, *California Medicine*, 113:3, (September 1970), 67-68.

2 See Peter Singer, *Rethinking Life and Death*. See also Smith, *Culture of Death*.

3 Robert Jay Lifton, *The Nazi Doctors: Medical Killing and the Psychology of Genocide* (New York: Basic Books, 1986), 14.

4 Michael Burleigh, *Death and Deliverance: Euthanasia in Germany, 1940-1945* (New York: Basic Books, 1986), 4.

5 Lifton, *Nazi Doctors*, 48.

6 Ibid., 46.

7 Quoted in Burleigh, *Death and Deliverance*, 13.

8 Ibid., 13-14.

9 Ibid., 14.

10 Ibid., 15.

11 Karl Binding and Alfred Hoche, *Permitting the Destruction of Life Not Worthy of Life: Its Extent and Form* (Leipzig, Germany: Felix Meiner Verlag, 1920), reprinted in *Issues in Law and Medicine*, 8:2 (1992), 231-65.

12 Lifton, *Nazi Doctors*, 46.

13   Binding and Hoche, *Permitting the Destruction*, 247.
14   Ibid., 260-261. Emphasis in original.
15   Ibid. 249.
16   Ibid. 252.
17   Burleigh, *Death and Deliverance*, 15.
18   For a thoroughly detailed account of the eugenics movement, see Daniel J. Kevles, *In the Name of* Eugenics (1985, Harvard University Press, Cambridge, MA).
19   Adolf Hitler, *Mein Kampf*, quoted in Lifton, *Nazi Doctors*, 257.
20   Lifton, Nazi Doctors, 27.
21   Burleigh, *Death and Deliverance*, p 22-23.
22   New York Times, October 8, 1933, as cited in, Hugh Gregory Gallagher, *By Trust Betrayed: Patients, Physicians, and the License to Kill in the Third Reich* (1995, Vandamere Press, Arlington, VA), xiv.
23   As described in Lifton, *Nazi Doctors*, 49, and Gallagher, By *Trust Betrayed*, 61.
24   Lifton, *Nazi Doctors*, 50.
25   Burleigh, *Death and Deliverance*, 95-96; Lifton, *Nazi Doctors*, 50-51; Gallagher, *By Trust Betrayed*, 95-96.
26   Quoted in Burleigh, *Death and Deliverance*, 100.
27   Ibid., 125.
28   Ibid.
29   Lifton, *Nazi Doctors*, 77.
30   Hugh Gregory Gallagher, interview with author, May 21, 1996.
31   Ibid.
32   Ibid.
33   Quoted in Gallagher, *By Trust Betrayed*, 200, and Burleigh, *Death and Deliverance*, 178.
34   Ibid.
35   Michael Franzblau, MD, "Investigate Nazi Ties of German Doctors," *San Francisco Chronicle*, December 29, 1993.
36   *Buck v. Bell* 274 U.S. 200.
37   Ibid.
38   "Three Generations of Imbiciles," editorial, *Detroit News*, December 16, 1992.
39   Rita L. Marker, et. al., "Euthanasia: A Historical Overview," *Maryland Journal of Contemporary Issues*, Summer 1991, 276.
40   Ibid.
41   Cited in Rita Marker, *Deadly Compassion* (1993, William Morrow, New York, NY), 39.
42   Arthur Caplan, "The Relevance of the Holocaust in Bioethics Today," in John J. Michalczyk, ed., *Medicine, Ethics, and the Third Reich: Historical and Contemporary Issues*, (1994, Sheed and Ward, London, UK), 10-11.
43   Lifton, *Nazi Doctors*, 17.
44   Burleigh, *Death and Deliverance*, 5-6.

45   Michael J. Franzblau, interview with author, February 27, 2002.

46   Binding and Hoche, *Permitting the Destruction*, 241.

47   *Compassion in Dying v. Washington*, 79 F. 3d. 790.

48   Binding and Hoche, *Permitting the Destruction*, 241.

49   *Compassion in Dying*

50   Binding and Hoche, *Permitting the Destruction*, 241.

51   *Compassion in Dying*

52   Binding and Hoche, *PPermitting the Destruction*, 241.

53   *Compassion in Dying*

54   Binding and Hoche, *Permitting the Destruction*, 242.

55   *Compassion in Dying*

56   Binding and Hoche, *Permitting the Destruction*, 265.

57   *Compassion in Dying*.

58   Binding and Hoche, *Permitting the Destruction*, 261.

59   *Compassion in Dying*.

60   Carol J. Gill, interview with author, December 4, 1995.

61   Diane Coleman, Interview with author, February 16, 1999.

62   Gill interview.

63   Leo Alexander, "Medical Science Under Dictatorship," *New England Journal of Medicine*, 241 (July 14, 1949), reprint, 8.

64   Ibid., 11.

4. Dutch Treat

1   Alexander, "Medical Science Under Dictatorship," 9.

2   Ibid.

3   Dr. I van der Sluis, interview with author, October 13, 1995.

4   Eugene Sutorius, interview with author, October 17, 1995.

5   "Euthanasia Case Leeuwarden—1973" (Excerpts from court's decision), trans. Walter Lagerway, *Issues in Law and Medicine* 3 (1988): 429, 439-42.

6   "Implications of Mercy," *Time*, March 5, 1973, 70.

7   Ibid.

8   Ibid.

9   "Dutch Parliament Approves Law Permitting Euthanasia," *New York Times*, February 10, 1993.

10   Carlos Gomez, *Regulating Death* (New York: Free Press, 1991), 32.

11   Timothy Quill, "Physician Assisted Death: Progress or Peril?", *Suicide and Life-Threatening Behavior*, 24:4, 315-25, 318.

12   K.F. Gunning, interview with author, October 18, 1995.

13   Ibid.

14   J. Remmelink, et al., *Medical Decisions about the End of Life*, 2 vols. (The Hague, 1991). Cited hereafter as Remmelink Report I and II.

15　Remmelink Report I, 14, n.2.

16　Richard Fenigsen, "The Report of the Dutch Government Committee on Euthanasia," *Issues in Law and Medicine* 7:3 (November 1991): 340.

17　Remmelink Report I, 13.

18　Ibid., 15.

19　Remmelink Report II, 49, Table 6.4.

20　Ibid., 50, Table 6.6.

21　Ibid., 58, Table 7.2.

22　This figure was arrived at by calculating 8.5 percent (the approximate percentage of all Dutch deaths that resulted from killing by physicians) of the total number of yearly U.S. deaths, which in 1985 was a little over 2 million (*New York Public Library Desk Reference*, 1989, 613).

23　"Dutch GPs Report Euthanasia as Death by Natural Causes," *British Medical Journal* 304 (February 1992).

24　J. van der Maas, "Euthanasia and Other Medical Decisions Concerning the End of Life," *Health Policy Monographs* 2 (1992): 49.

25　Fenigsen, "Euthanasia in the Netherlands," 239; and "Special Report from the Netherlands," *New England Journal of Medicine* (November 1996), 1699-1711.

26　Henk Jochemsen and John Keown, *Journal of Medical Ethics* 25 (1999): 16-21.

27　"Dutch Court Rejects Nurse's Defense in Euthanasia Case," Reuters, March 23, 1995.

28　Tony Shelton, "Dutch GP Found Guilty of Murder Faces No Penalty," *British Medical Journal*, March 3, 2001.

29　Dr. K.F. Gunning interview.

30　Herbert Hendin, "Assisted Suicide, Euthanasia, and Suicide Prevention: The Implications of the Dutch Experience," *Suicide and Life Threatening Behavior*, 25:1 (Spring 1995): 202.

31　Ibid., 200-02.

32　Herbert Hendin, "Seduced by Death: Doctors, Patients, and the Dutch Cure," *Issues in Law and Medicine* 10:2 (Fall 1994): 137.

33　Ibid., 139.

34　"Choosing Death," *The Healthcare Quarterly*, WGBH-Boston, March 23, 1993.

35　Ibid.

36　Ibid.

37　Hendin, "Assisted Suicide, Euthanasia, and Suicide Prevention," 197.

38　"Choosing Death."

39　Ibid.

40　Ibid.

41　Mark O'Keefe, "The Dutch Way of Doctoring," *The Oregonian*, January 9, 1995.

42　Herbert Hendin, "Dying of Resentment," *New York Times*, January 9, 1995.

43　Ibid.

44 Dr. K. F. Gunning interview.

45 Bert Keizer, *Dancing With Mr. D: Notes on Life and Death*, (New York: Doubleday, 1996), 37.

46 Ibid., 39.

47 Ibid., 94.

48 Ibid., 61.

49 "CQ Interview: Arlene Juditch Klotzko and Dr. Boudewijn Chabot Discuss Assisted Suicide in the Absence of Somatic Illness," *Cambridge Quarterly of Healthcare Ethics* 4:2 (Spring 1995): 243.

50 Gene Kaufman, "State v. Chabot: A Euthanasia Case Note," *Ohio Northern University Law Review*, 20:3 (1994): 816-17.

51 Ibid., 817.

52 Eugene Sutorius interview.

53 Ibid.

54 "Choosing Death."

55 "Dutch Court Says Baby's Euthanasia Justifiable," Reuters, April 26, 1995.

56 Agnes van der Heide, et. al., "Medical End-of-Life Decisions Made for Neonates and Infants in the Netherlands, *The Lancet*, 350, 251-55, July 26, 1997.

57 "Report of the Dutch Royal Society of Medicine: Life-Terminating Actions with Incompetent Patients," Part I, "Severely Handicapped Newborns," *Issues in Law and Medicine* 8:2 (1992).

58 Lifton, *Nazi Doctors*, 115.

59 "Choosing Death."

60 Fenigsen, "Euthanasia in the Netherlands," 240.

61 Ibid.

62 Ibid.

63 G. G. Humphrey, Letters to the Editor, *Journal of American Medicine*, 260 (1988) 788.

64 Royal Dutch Medical Association, *Vision of Euthanasia* (1986, Royal Dutch Medical Association, The Hague, Netherlands), 14. Emphasis added.

65 Tony Shelton, "Dutch GP Cleared After Helping to End Man's 'Hopeless Existence," *British Medical Journal*, 2000; 321:1174.

66 "Dutch Minister Favors Suicide Pill," cnn.com, May 1, 2001.

67 Dr. Pieter Admiraal, interview with author, September 14, 1995.

68 H. Jack Gleiger, MD, editorial, "Race and Healthcare—An American Dilemma," *New England Journal of Medicine*, 335, No. 11 (1996.)

69 W. C. M. Klijn, interview with author, September 14, 1995.

70 Dr. van der Sluis interview.

71 Pieter Admiraal interview.

72 Hendin, "Seduced by Death," 158-59.

73 Ibid.

74   Ibid.

75   Ibid.

76   "Helping a Man Kill Himself Shown on Dutch TV," *New York Times*, November 13, 1994.

77   Andrew Kelly (Reuters), "Audience Plays Solomon on Dutch TV," *Chicago Tribune*, October 28, 1993.

78   Sarah Lambert, "Dutch Stand Idly By as Child Drowns," *San Francisco Examiner*, August 28, 1993.

79   Ibid.

80   *Levenswens-Verklaring* (Declaration on the Value of Life), wallet card, distributed by Stichting Schuilplaats, Veenendaal, Netherlands.

81   Pieter Admiraal interview.

82   Eugene Sutorious interview.

83   Ploes Pijnenborg, *End of Life Decisions in Dutch Medical Practice* (The Hague: CIP Gegevens Koniglijke Bibliotheek, 1996), 146.

84   BBC News, "Doctors Help Kill One in Ten Belgians," November 24, 2000.

85   Andrew Osborn, "Belgian Outcry over First Mercy Killing under New Law," *Guardian*, October 8, 2002.

5. Inventing the Right to Die

1   Jack Kevorkian, MD, "Fail-Safe Model for Justifiable Medically Assisted Suicide ("Medicide"), *American Journal of Forensic Psychiatry*, 13:1 (1992): 11-12. Kevorkian used the term "medicide" for "being killed by a doctor." But it really means to kill a doctor. When the Oakland County medical examiner Dr. Ljubisa J. Dragovic pointed out the actual meaning of "medicide" to local reporters, Kevorkian took some ribbing among the press. Later, after Kevorkian helped kill Ali Khalili, a physician, Dragovic told me he received an anonymous phone call on his voice mail, saying, "Ha, ha, ha. The first medicide has been accomplished." (Dr. Ljubisa J. Dragovic, interview with author, August 21, 1996.)

2   Ibid., 22.

3   Derek Humphry, "Oregon's New Assisted Suicide Law Gives No Sure Comfort to Dying," Letters to the Editor, *New York Times*, December 3, 1994.

4   Ibid.

5   *Lee v. State of Oregon*, (Civil No. 94-6467-HO, U.S. District Court for the District of Oregon, 1994), Opinion (equal protection) of Judge Michael Hogan, court transcript, 5-6.

6   Transcript of "Yes on 16" advertisement aired on various stations, beginning October 24, 1994.

7   Transcript of "Yes on 16" advertisement aired on various stations, beginning October 12, 1994.

8   Interview with author (interviewee asks anonymity), October 10, 1995.

9   Oregon Death With Dignity Act, Section 2.01.

10   Ibid., Section 3.01.

11   Gary L. Lee, MD, interview with author, November 30, 1995.

12   Ira R. Byock, MD, interview with author, June 18, 1996.

13   Erin Hoover Barnett, "Man With ALS Makes Up His Mind to Die," *The Oregonian*, March 11, 1999.

14   Correspondence of David Schuman, Oregon Deputy Attorney General to State Senator Neil Bryant, March 15, 1999.

15   See, for example, New York State Task Force on Life and the Law, *When Death Is Sought: Assisted Suicide and Euthanasia in the Medical Context*, report, (New York: New York Task Force, 1994).

16   Oregon Death with Dignity Act, Section 1.01.

17   Ibid.

18   *Lee v. Harcleroad*, Case No. 94-6467:TC, U.S. District Court, District of Oregon, 1994, Complaint for Declaratory and Injunctive Relief.

19   *Lee v. State of Oregon*, 891 F. Sup, 1995, 1421, 1438.

20   Ibid., 1438-39.

21   Ibid., 1439.

22   "Federal Judge Refuses to Enforce Assisted Suicide Law," Associated Press, May 10, 1996.

23   Ibid.

24   *Lee v. Oregon*, 107 F. 3d 1382; 1997.

25   Interview with Gregory Hamilton, MD, March 8, 2002.

26   Timothy E. Quill, MD, *Death and Dignity: Making Choices and Taking Charge*, (New York: W.W. Norton & Co., 1994)

27   Ibid.

28   Kim Murphy, "Death Called 1st Under Oregon's New Suicide Law," *The Los Angeles Times*, March 26, 1998.

29   Herbert Hendin, et al., "Physician-Assisted Suicide: Reflections on Oregon's First Case," *Issues in Law & Medicine*, 14:3 (1998).

30   Erin Hoover Barnett, "Is Mom Capable of Choosing to Die?"*The Oregonian*, October 17, 1999.

31   Quill, *Death and Dignity,* 162.

32   Oregon Health Department, "Fourth Annual Report on Oregon's Death with Dignity Act," March 2002.

33   Robert Salamanca, "I Don't Want a Choice to Die," *San Francisco Chronicle*, Feburary 19, 1997.

34   Paul Longmore, Testimony before the California Assembly Judiciary Committee opposing AB 1592, April 20, 1999.

35   *Compassion in Dying v. Washington*, U.S. Court of Appeals for the Ninth Circuit, 79 F. 3d. 790 (1996).

36   Ira Byock, MD, interview.

37   Howard Mintz, "Dissenters Rip Right-to-Die Vote," *The Recorder,* June 13, 1996.
38   *Quill v. Dennis C. Vacco,* U.S. Court of Appeals for the Second Circuit, 80 F. 3d 716 (1996).
39   Ibid.
40   *In re Quinlan,* (Supreme Court of New Jersey), 70 NJ 10.
41   Diane Gianelli, "Karen Ann Quinlan's Family Remembers," *American Medical News,* December 15, 1989, 49-50.
42   *Washington v. Glucksberg,* 521 U. S. 702 (1997); *Vacco v. Quill,* 521 U. S. 793 (1997).
43   *Washington v. Glucksburg,* 728.
44   Ibid.
45   Ibid., 730-31.
46   Ibid., 731.
47   Ibid., 730-32.
48   Ibid., 732.
49   Ibid.
50   *Vacco v. Quill,* 801-802. Citations omitted.
51   *People of Michigan v. Jack Kevorkian,* 447 Mich. 436 (1994).
52   *Krischer v. McIver,* 697 So. 2d 97 (1997).
53   *Sampson v. State, Supreme Court,* 31 3d 88 (2001).
54   Rita Marker, "Dying for the Cause," *Philanthropy,* Jan/Feb 2001.
55   The *Chronicle of Philanthropy,* September 20, 2001, reported that OSI had given both CIDF and the Death with Dignity National Center $100,000, while granting $75,000 to Oregon Death with Dignity Legal Defense and Education Fund.
56   Rita Marker, interview with author, March 21, 2002.

6. *The Betrayal of Medicine*

1   Quill, "Phyisician Assisted Death, 317.
2   Dr. Quill doesn't really mean it when he writes that hospice care must fail before assisted suicide can be considered. Later in the same article (320), he writes that it should be considered if hospice is "unacceptable to the patient." Thus, in the world envisioned by Dr. Quill, a patient who could be effectively treated with comfort care but who wants to die immediately instead can still receive assisted suicide. So much for "last resorts."
3   Kevorkian, *Prescription Medicide,* 175.
4   Stephen Jamison, *Final Acts of Love: Families, Friends, and Assisted Suicide* (New York: Putnam Books, 1995), 258-60.
5   Shavelson, *A Chosen Death,* 224.
6   New York State Task Force on Life and the Law, *When Death is Sought: Assisted Suicide and Euthanasia in the Medical Context.*
7   Ibid., ix.

8 Ibid., xiii.

9 Ibid.

10 Ibid.

11 Ibid., xv.

12 Ibid.

13 Ibid.

14 *Report of the University of Rochester Medical Center Task Force on Physician-Assisted Suicide* (Rochester, New York: University of Rochester, 1993), 4.

15 "When Will Adequate Pain Treatment Be the Norm?" *Journal of the American Medical Association*, 274:23 (December 20, 1995).

16 "Painfully Clear," *American Medical News*, September 26, 1994.

17 Ada Jacob, et al., "Special Report: New Clinical-Practice Guideline for the Management of Pain in Patients with Cancer," *New England Journal of Medicine* 330:9 (March 3, 1994).

18 Eric M. Chevlen and Wesley J. Smith, *Power over Pain: How to Get the Pain Control You Need*, (Steubenville, OH: International Task Force on Euthanasia and Assisted Suicide, 2002).

19 Bruce Hilton, "Hospital Chains Are on a Buying Binge," *San Francisco Examiner*, August 23, 1996.

20 Jeff Wong, "Woman Says She Would Seek Kevorkian's Help Days before Death," Associated Press, July 10, 1996.

21 Richard Leiby, "Just How Sick Was Rebecca Badger?" *Washington Post*, July 29, 1996.

22 Dr. Ljubisa J. Dragovic interview.

23 Leiby, "Just How Sick?"

24 United States Department of Health and Human Services: Healthcare Financing Administration (HCFA).

25 Robert Pear, "Many Doctors Shun Patients with Medicare," *New York Times*, March 17, 2002.

26 Daniel Sulmasy, "Managed Care and Managed Death," *Archives of Internal Medicine*, January 23, 1995, 134.

27 "When Doctors Become Subcontractors of Medical Care," *USA Today*, January 22, 1996.

28 *In the Matter of the Accusation of the Commissioner of Corporations of the State of California v. TakeCare Health Plan, Inc.*, hearing before the Department of Corporations of the State of California, November 17, 1994, File No. 933-0290.

29 Ibid., 7.

30 Ibid., 4.

31 Ibid., 5.

32 Ibid., 6.

33 Ibid., 12.

34 Humphry and Clement, *Freedom to Die,* 333. Emphasis in the original.

35 Ibid., 334.

36 Harvey Rosenfield, *Silent Violence, Silent Death: The Hidden Epidemic of Medical Malpractice* (Washington, DC: Essential Books, 1994).

37 Charles B. Inlander, Lowell S. Levin, and Ed Weiner, *Medicine on Trial: The Appalling Story of Ineptitude, Malfeasance, Neglect, and Arrogance* (New York: Prentice Hall, 1994).

38 T/ a/ Bremmam. et al., *Patients, Doctors and Lawyers: Medical Injury, Malpractice Litigation, and Patient Compensation in New York*, Report of the Harvard Medical Practice Study to the State of New York (Cambridge, MA: Harvard University, 1990).

39 Inlander, Levin, and Weiner, *Medicine on Trial,* 178.

40 I interviewed several people in the spring and summer of 1996 who were close to the administrative and civil cases that resulted from this incident. Although several spoke freely about what happened and all were in substantial agreement about them, none would permit me to use their names, nor would they disclose the names of the principals.

41 "Review Process at UCSF Regarding Withdrawal of Life Support Case," *UCSF News*, March 29, 1995.

42 Sarah Henry, "The Battle over Assisted Suicide," *California Lawyer*, January 1996, 34.

43 O'Neill, "Suicide Aid Worries Oregon Doctors."

44 "Physicians 'Polarized' about Ethics of Helping Patients Die," *Physician's Management Newsline*, October 1994.

45 Diane E. Meier, "A Change of Heart on Assisted Suicide," *New York Times*, April 24, 1998.

46 "AMA Soundly Reaffirms Policy Opposing Physician-Assisted Suicide," American Medical Association Press Release, June 25, 1996.

47 British Medical Association, *Euthanasia: Report of the Working Party to Review the British Medical Association's Guidance on Euthanasia*, 1988.

48 World Medical Association, "Statement on Physician Assisted Suicide," adopted by the 44th World Medical Assembly, Marbella, Spain, September 1992.

49 Allen J. Bennett, MD, "When is Medical Treatment Futile?" *Issues in Law and Medicine* 9:1 (1993), 40,43.

50 Correspondence to California State Senator Ray Haynes, March 12, 2002, signed by Matt Moretti, Legislative Advocate, California Healthcare Association. Emphasis added.

51 Marcia Angell, MD, "After Quinlan: The Dilemma of the Vegetative State," *New England Journal of Medicine* 330:21 (May 1994): 1524.

52 See Smith, *Culture of Death.*

53 Charles B. Clayman, ed. *The American Medical Association Encyclopedia of Medicine*, (1989, Random House, New York, NY).

54 Thomas Marzen, Attorney at Law, interview with author, November 14, 1995.

55 "The Unconscious Experience," *American Journal of Critical Care*, 4:3 (May 1995).

56 Jeremy Laurance, "Vegetative State Diagnosis Wrong in Many Patients," *The Times* (London), July 5, 1996.

57 Daniel Callahan, *The Troubled Dream of Life* (New York: Simon and Schuster, 1993), 201-202.

58 Steven Miles, Interview with author, February 9, 1999.

59 State of Minnesota District Court, Probate Division, County of Hennepin, *In re Helga Wanglie*, Findings of Fact, Conclusions of Law, and Order, July 1, 1991.

60 *In re Terry Achtabowski, Jr.*, Docket No. 93-1247-AV, Michigan Court of Appeals, 1994, Appellee's Brief, 2. Emphasis added.

61 Washington Department of Child Protective Services, Intake Summary Report for Referral, dated November 23, 1994.

62 Miles interview.

63 *In re Ryan Nguyen*, Case No. 94-06074-5. State of Washington Superior Court, Sacred Heart Medical Center Brief.

64 Dominic Lawson, "The Death of Medicine," *Sunday London Telegraph*, April 25, 1999.

65 Policy Perspectives "A Multi-institution Collaborative Policy on Medical Futility," *Journal of the American Medical Association*, 571-74, August 21, 1996.

66 Lawrence J. Schneiderman and Alexander Morgan Capron, "How Can Hospital Futility Policies Contribute to Establishing Standards of Practice?" *Cambridge Quarterly of Healthcare Ethics* 9 (Fall 2000): 524-31.

67 Ibid., 529.

68 Draft Guidelines Supported by CCMD, CCMD press release, May 17, 1996.

69 Dr. Donald J. Murphy, interview with author, July 3, 1996.

70 Dr. Murphy quoted in Nat Hentoff, "Death: The Ultimate in Managed Care," *Washington Post*, July 16, 1994.

71 The tale of the demise of CCMD was first published in Wesley J. Smith, "Philanthropy's Brave New World," *Philanthropy*, January/February 2001, 20-24, from which this recounting is taken.

72 Ezekiel J. Emanuel, "Cost Savings at the End of Life: What Do the Data Show?" *Journal of the American Medical Association* 275:24 (June 1996): 1907-14.

73 Senate Finance Committee Hearings, "Advance Directives and Care at the End of Life," testimony of Joanne Lynn, MD, May 5, 1994.

74 Ezekiel J. Emanuel and Linda L. Emanuel, "The Economics of Dying," *New England Journal of Medicine* 330:8 (February 1994): 543.

75 Dr. Donald J. Murphy interview.

76   Ibid.

7. Euthanasia as a Form of Oppression

1   For example, see James M. Humber and Robert F. Almeder, eds., *Is There A Duty to Die?* (Atlanta, GA: Georgia State University Press, 2000).
2   Paul Longmore, interview with author, July 13, 1996.
3   Evan Kemp, speech before Capitol Hill Club, Washington D.C., October 10, 1995.
4   Diane Coleman, "Not Dead Yet," in Kathleen Foley and Herbert Hendin, eds., *The Case against Assisted Suicide: For the Right to End of Life Care* (Baltimore, MD: Johns Hopkins University Press, 2002), 221.
5   Kathi Wolfe, interview with author, May 21, 1996.
6   Paul Longmore interview.
7   "Disability Rights and Assisted Suicide," editorial, *One Step Ahead*, August 22, 1994.
8   "Advanced Directives and Disability," *One Step Ahead's Second Opinion*, 2:1 (Winter 1995).
9   William G. Strothers, "Death and Life—It's Time to Choose Up Sides," *Mainstream*, February 1996.
10 Diane Coleman, interview with author, July 9, 1996.
11 Ibid.
12 Denny Boyd, "Where Were the Doctors When Robert Latimer Needed Them?" *Vancouver Sun*, November 30, 1994.
13 Larry Johnson, personal correspondence, February 7, 1994.
14 Larry Johnson, interview with author, February 7, 1996.
15 This and other writings of Teague Johnson quoted herein are copyrighted by Larry Johnson and are reprinted with his permission.
16 Teague Johnson, "My Body Is Not My Enemy," *Vancouver Sun*, December 9, 1994.
17 Teague Johnson, Compuserve open letter, April 4, 1994.
18 Ibid, undated letter.
19 Paul Longmore interview.
20 Larry Johnson interview.
21 Canadian Broadcasting Company, "Petition Demands Clemency for Jailed Robert Latimer," December 14, 2001.
22 As set forth in Euthanasia Prevention Coalition newsletter, Winter 2001, and confirmed with Dick Sobsey by author, May 15, 2002.
23 Richard Sobsey, interview with author, April 17, 2002.
24 *Bouvia v. Superior Court* (California Court of Appeals, 1986) 179 California Appellate Report 30.

25 Mark O'Brien, interview with author, July 10, 1996.
26 Pence, *Classic Cases in Medical Ethics*.
27 Paul Longmore, "Urging the Handicapped to Die," *Los Angeles Times*, April 25, 1986.
28 Paul Longmore, interview.
29 Joseph Shapiro, *No Pity: People with Disabilities Forging a New Civil Rights Movement* (New York: Times Books, 1993), 259.
30 Ibid., 287.
31 K.A. Gerhart, et al., in *Annals of Emergency Medicine* 23 (1994): 807-812.
32 R. Stensman in *Scandinavian Journal of Rehabilitation Medicine* 17 (1985): 87-99.
33 J.R. Bach and M.C. Tilton in *Archives of Physical Medicine and Rehabilitation* 71 (1990): 191-96.
34 Betsy J. Miner, "Messenger Jury Selection to Begin," *Lansing State Journal*, January 10, 1995.
35 Valeri Basheda, "Verdict's Message: Parents Have Rights," *Detroit News*, February 3, 1995.
36 Singer, *Rethinking Life and Death*, 213-14.
37 Lucette Lagnado, "Mercy Living," *Wall Street Journal*, January 10, 1995.
38 Mary Voboril, "The Assisted Suicide of Myrna Lebov," *Newsday*, January 16,. 1996.
39 "Writer Wanted Relief," *Charleston Daily Mail*, July 8, 1995.
40 Lucette Lagnado, "How Lebov Bared Her Soul to Rabbis of Lincoln Square," *Forward*, November 3, 1996.
41 Lucette Lagnado, "DA Stepping Up Inquiry in Death of Myrna Lebov," *Forward*, July 21, 1996.
42 Beverly Sloane, interview with author, April 19, 1996.
43 George Delury Diary, "Countdown: A Daily Log of Myrna's Mental State and View toward Death," dates February 27-July 4, 1995.
44 *Dateline NBC*, aired September 27, 1996.
45 Delury Diary.
46 Ibid.
47 Ibid.
48 Ibid.
49 Ibid.
50 *Dateline NBC*, aired September 27, 1996.
51 George Delury, *But What If She Wants to Die?* (Buffalo, New York: Prometheus Books, 1997).
52 Susan Cheever, "An Act of Mercy?" *New York Times Book Review*, July 20, 1997.
53 Beverly Sloane, Interview with Author, August 3, 1999.
54 *Sloane v. Delury, et al.*, Supreme Court of the State of New York, County of New York, Index No. 111960/97, "Judgment," November 14, 2001.

55 *60 Minutes*, CBS, "Family Values," February 25, 1996.

56 *In the Matter of Gerald Klooster Sr.* ALI, Case Summary, File No. 95-01060 GD.

57 Sabin Russell and Henry K. Lee, "Custody Fight Father Hospitalized, *San Francisco Chronicle*, September 25, 1996.

58 Transcript of taped conversation between Susan Reynolds and John Bement, July 31, 1996.

59 Susan Randall, Interview with author, July 30, 1999.

60 Dr. Gerald (Chip) Klooster II, interview with author, April 12, 1996.

8. *Common Arguments for Euthanasia*

1 Pieter Admiraal interview.

2 Nat Hentoff, interview with author, July 21, 1996.

3 Rita Marker, interview with author, July 16, 1996.

4 Hentoff interview

5 Paul Wilkes, "The Next Pro-Lifers," *New York Times Magazine*, July 21, 1996.

6 Yale Kamisar, "Some Non-Religious Views against Proposed Mercy Killing Legislation," *Minnesota Law Review* 42:6 (May 1958).

7 Hentoff interview.

8 Keizer, *Dancing With Mister D*, 36-42.

9 Hendin, *Seduced by Death*, 116.

10 Hendin, "The Dutch Experience," in Foley and Hendin, *The Case against Assisted Suicide*, 120

11 American Medical Association Council on Ethics and Judicial Affairs, "Opinion 2.20," March 1986.

12 Ibid, 1992.

13 Gregory Hamilton, "Oregon's Culture of Silence," Foley and Hendin, 187.

14 Rita Marker, interview with author.

15 "Kids and Pets are Welcome at Dr. Cicely Saunders' Hospice for the Terminally Ill," *People*, December 22, 1975.

16 Dr. Ira Byock interview.

17 Dr. Linda Emanuel, quoted in Wilkes, "The Next Pro-Lifers."

18 See *Update*, International Task Force on Euthanasia and Assisted Suicide, 16, No. 1, 2002, citing several Australian newspaper sources, including *The Courier-Mail*, March 28, 2002, and *The Australian*, April 9, 2002.

19 Eric M. Chevlen, MD, interview with author, July 22, 1996.

20 Ibid.

21 Reuters, "AIDS Pain Similar to Cancer Pain," August 27,1996.

22 Singer, "Sanctity of Life or Quality of Life?" *Pediatrics* 72: 1 (July 1983.).

23 Singer, *Rethinking Life and Death*, 220.

24 Judd, review of *Rethinking Life and Death*.

25 I use the terms each side of the abortion debate uses for itself: "pro-choice" for

those who are in favor of abortion rights and "pro-life" for those who favor significant legal restrictions on abortion.

26   Yale Kamisar, "Abortion Right is No Support," *Legal Times*, March 2, 1996.
27   Ibid.
28   E. J. Dionne, interview with author, July 24, 1996.
29   National Hospice Organization, "New Findings Address Escalating End-of-Life Debate," press release October 3, 1996, describing NHO-sponsored poll conducted by the Gallup Organization of Princeton, NJ.
30   The telephone survey was conducted on March 13-17, 2002, among a random national sample of 1,021 adults. The poll has a three-point margin of error.
31   Rita Marker, interview.
32   Phyllis Robb, interview with author, August 12, 1996. See also Robb, "The Bitter Lesson of Living Wills," *AMA Medical News*, July 12, 1993.
33   Ibid.
34   David Wasson, "'No Code' Nightmare," *Yakima Herald Republic*, March 14, 1993.
35   William F. Stone, Attorney at Law, interview with author, August 27, 1996.
36   "Rose Kennedy Doing Well after Surgery," *Boston Globe*, July 29, 1984.
37   William F. Stone interview.
38   *In re the Interest of Marjorie E. Nighbert* (Case No. 95-4 PSA, Circuit Court of the First Judicial Circuit of Florida, 1995), Report of Guardian ad litem, March 23, 1995.
39   William F. Stone interview.
40   Ibid.
41   Ibid.
42   Ginny McKibben, "Patient Not Ready to Check Out," *Denver Post*, July 13, 1996.
43   Ibid.
44   Ibid.
45   E. J. Dionne, interview with author, July 22, 1996.
46   Dr. Eric Chevlen interview.
47   Gary Lee, MD, interview with author, November 30, 1995.
48   Dr. Eric Chevlen interview.
49   *Oregon v. Ashcroft*, United States District Court for the District of Oregon, Civil No. 01-1647-JO, "Opinion and Order."
50   European Court of Human Rights, *Pretty v. the United Kingdom*, Application No. 2346/02.
51   "Exit This Way," *The Economist*, December 6, 2001.

9. Hospice or Hemlock?

1   Robert M. Arnold and Stuart J. Youngner, "The Dead Donor Rule," *Kennedy Institute of Ethics Journals*, June 1993, 271.
2   Dr. Robin Bernhoft, interview with author, August 27, 1996.

3   Physicians For Compassionate Care, "Per Capita Morphine Use Figures Debunk Chilling Effect Myth," November 2001, based on DEA figures tracking morphine use state-by-state.

4   See Chevlen and Smith, *Power Over Pain,* 56-60.

5   Judith S. Blanchard and Debra D. Seale, "Lessons From the First Year of a State Cancer Pain Initiative," *Journal of Oncology Management* (November-December, 1993.)

6   Chevlen and Smith, *Power Over Pain,* 210.

7   For readers interested in learning more about pain control, see *Power Over Pain,* which I co-authored with Dr. Eric M. Chevlen, a brilliant pain-control specialist. The book is a consumers guide to obtaining quality medical care for pain. It is written in a highly readable and approachable format and is intended to help you and your doctor work together to ensure that you receive optimal pain-controlling care. For more information go to www.poweroverpain.com or contact the International Task Force on Euthanasia and Assisted Suicide at 800-786-3839.

8   "A Guide to Hospice Care," *Harvard Health Letter,* April 1993.

9   Dr. Ira Byock interview.

10   Shavelson, *A Chosen Death.*

11   Cicely Saunders, "A Hospice Perspective," in Foley and Hendin, *The Case Against Assisted Suicide,* 291.

12   House Subcommittee on the Constitution, testimony of Carlos M. Gomez, MD, April 29, 1996.

13   Ira Byock, "Consciously Walking the Fine Line: Thought on a Hospice Response to Assisted Suicide and Euthanasia," *Journal of Palliative Care,* 9:3 (September 1993): 25-28.

14   Dr. Gary Lee interview.

15   For more information on hospice, ask your physician, look in your local Yellow Pages under "Hospices," or contact one of the hospice resources listed on pages 320-21 of *Resources.*

16   *Charles Grodin Show,* CNBC, aired August 6, 1996.

17   Mark O'Brien, interview with author, August 5, 1996.

18   Ibid.

19   Beth Roney Drennan, interview with author, April 13, 1995.

20   Beth Roney Drennan, interview with author, May 27, 2002.

21   Beth Roney Drennan, 1995 interview.

22   *Charles Grodin Show*

23   Salamanca, "I Don't Want a Choice to Die."

24   My conversations with Bob were private and not undertaken for inclusion in this book. I placed them in the first edition not only with Bob's express permission but his enthusiastic encouragement. Although he has since died, I know he would want them included in this revised edition.

25 Ed Edelson, "Dying Cite Loss of Social Ties in Seeking Suicide," *HealthScout*, August 4, 2001.
26 Melissa Schorr, "Terminally Ill Patients Spend Too Much Time Alone," Reuters, November 12, 2001.
27 Dennis Brace, interview with author, April 13, 1995.
28 Senate Finance Committee Hearings, "Advance Directives and Care at the End of Life," testimony of Joanne Lynn, May 5, 1994.
29 Patrick T. Hill, "Treating the Dying Patient," *Archives of Internal Medicine* (June 1995), 23.
30 Ibid.
31 John Hess, interview with author, August 12, 1996.
32 Joseph Brean, "900,000 in Ontario Have No G.P: Report," *National Post*, April 11, 2002.
33 Wong, "Woman Said She Would Seek Kevorkian's Help Days Before Death."
34 Dr. Lance K. Stell, interview with author, September 28, 1995.
35 Ibid.
36 Rev. Peter A. Clark, si, ph.d, and Catherine M. Mikus, "Time for Policy," *Health Progress*, July-August 2000.
37 Dr. Ira Byock interview.
38 Ibid.
39 Maurice Victor, interview with author, August 7, 1996.
40 Ibid.
41 Thomas Lorentzen, interviews with author, June 6 and August 8, 1996.

Index

abortion, 260–62

A Chosen Death
  (Shavelson), 21, 175

Achtabowski, Terry, 202–3

ACLU. *See* American
  Civil Liberties Union

Adkins, Janet, 3, 4

Admiraal, Pieter, 133, 135,
  138, 244

advance directives
  cases involving, 266–72
  confusion about, 266–67
  end-of-life care and,
    301–4
  refusal of unwanted
    treatment and, 265–
    66

African-Americans, 215

African Americans, 297

"aid in dying". *See*
  euthanasia

AIDS, 16, 104, 183, 250,
  257–58

Alabama, 62

Alaska, 171

alcoholism, 21

Alexander, Leo, 105–6,
  108

Algus, Michael, 64, 66

ALS. *See* Lou Gehrig's
  disease

Alzheimer's disease, 3, 237

*A Matter of Life and
  Death*, 137

American Academy of
  Hospice and Palliative
  Medicine, 149, 247, 256

American Civil Liberties
  Union (ACLU), 226, 228

American Foundation for
  Suicide Prevention, 34,
  247

American Geriatric
  Society, 301

*American Journal of
  Forensic Psychiatry*, 140

American Medical
  Association, 53, 58, 97,
  194, 254, 300

American Medical
  Association Council
  on Ethical and Judicial
  Affairs, 53, 54, 56, 58,
  64, 254

American Medical News,
  179–80

American Nurses
  Association, 194

American Psychiatric
  Association, 233

Americans with Disabili-
  ties Act, 82, 150

Amish, 294–95

Angell, Marcia, futile care
  theory and, 197–200

animal life, human vs.,
  310–11

animal rights movement,
  27

ABOUT THE AUTHOR

WESLEY J. SMITH, a senior fellow at the Discovery Institute, is an attorney and consultant for the International Task Force on Euthanasia and Assisted Suicide.

He is the author or co-author of nine books and has written for *Newsweek*, the *New York Times*, the *Weekly Standard*, *National Review*, the *Wall Street Journal*, *USA Today*, the *New York Post*, *First Things*, the *San Francisco Chronicle*, and the *Detroit News*. He lectures frequently at political, university, medical, legal, and bioethics gatherings in the United States, Canada, Great Britain, and Australia.

This book was designed and set into type
by Mitchell S. Muncy,
with cover art by Lee Whitmarsh,
and printed and bound
by Edwards Brothers, Inc.,
Ann Arbor, Michigan.

The text face is Adobe Caslon,
designed by Carol Twombly,
based on faces cut by William Caslon, London, in the 1730s,
and issued in digital form by Adobe Systems,
Mountain View, California, in 1989.

The index is by IndExpert,
Fort Worth, Texas.

The paper is acid-free and is of archival quality.

34